Fashion in the Age of the Black Prince

A study of the years 1340 – 1365

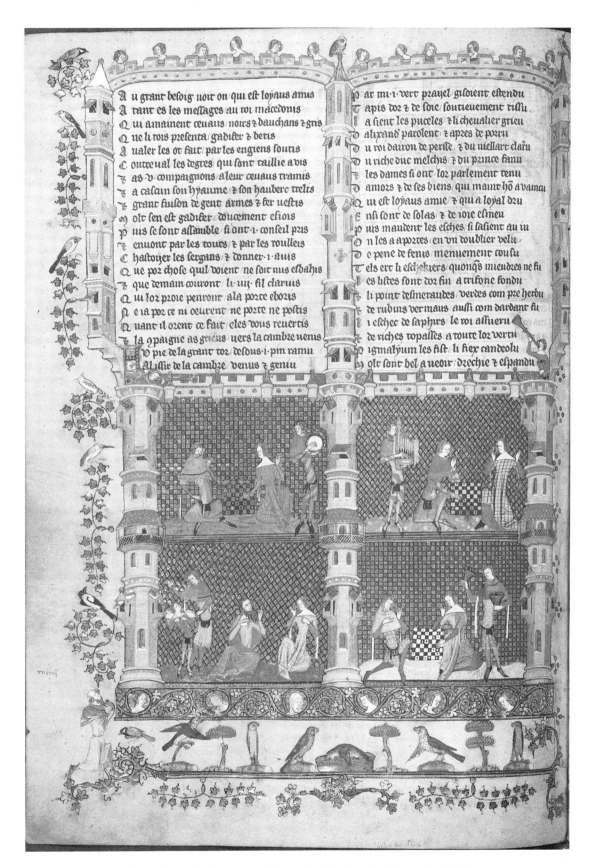

Scene from the *Romance of Alexander* showing fashions of c. 1340
(*Bodleian Library MS Douce 264 f.127v*)

Fashion in the Age of the Black Prince

A study of the years 1340 – 1365

Stella Mary Newton

THE BOYDELL PRESS

First published 1980
The Boydell Press/Rowman & Littlefield

Reprinted in paperback 1999
The Boydell Press

ISBN 0 85115 125 6 hardback
ISBN 0 85115 767 X paperback

The Boydell Press is an imprint of Boydell & Brewer Ltd
PO Box 9, Woodbridge, Suffolk IP12 3DF, UK
and of Boydell & Brewer Inc.
PO Box 41026, Rochester, NY 14604–4126, USA
website: http://www.boydell.co.uk

To Professor Lord Robbins
in gratitude for his encouragement in the furtherance of the study of the history of dress

A catalogue record for this title is available
from the British Library

Library of Congress Cataloging in Publication Data
applied for

This publication is printed on acid-free paper

Printed in Great Britain by
St Edmundsbury Press Ltd, Bury St Edmunds, Suffolk

Contents

List of Illustrations

Acknowledgements

To Elizabeth Danbury, for introducing me to the fascinations of paleography; to Jane Bridgeman, Jacqueline Herald, Elizabeth O'Kelly, Dr David Oppenheimer, Dr Barbara Reynolds, John Braun, Dr Michael Evans; Dr Maria Kresz, Professor Makkai and Dr György Rozsa of Budapest; Dr Sigrid Müller-Christensen of Munich; Dr Anna Masarykova and Dr Vera Olivova of Prague; and especially to Agathe Lewin and Catherine Gordon, grateful thanks.

September 1979

Note on spelling

Because of the difficulties of arriving at a standard form, the original spelling has been retained for proper names and technical details. The abbreviated Latin, quoted from unpublished documents, has not been extended because in the past this has sometimes led to misreadings. So far as has been possible with the use of modern type, the original abbreviations have been retained; translations of these passages are the author's own.

Abbreviations

BL	British Library
BN	Bibliothèque Nationale
CMH	*Cambridge Medieval History*
EETS	Early English Text Society
Latham	*Revised Medieval Latin word-list*, ed. R. E. Latham, London 1965
Mem	Membrane
PRO	Public Record Office
RIS	*Rerum Italicarum Scriptores*, ed. L. A. Muratori, Milan 1723–38, 1751
RS	Rolls Series, London
SHF	Société de l'Histoire de France

Foreword

The subject of this book is the universal phenomenon known in England (rather curiously) as 'fashion', as it applied to clothing during one quarter of the fourteenth century.

It would probably be generally agreed that changes in fashion are ignoble, whereas changes in style are not. That the majestic progression of architectural styles is approved can be judged by the widely held idea that in their late versions each becomes decadent – a quality that is only very occasionally acclaimed, and then by a very small minority.

In a minuscule way, the same applies to dress, for although those who show too eager an interest in the new appear light-minded, those who allow themselves to remain for too long clothed in a fashion that has passed reach a point where they cease to be appealingly indifferent or quaint and begin to look suspiciously mad.

There have been occasional attempts to eliminate fashionable clothing altogether: Maoist China, for instance, tried to impose a uniform dress on the community, but it did not last. Uniforms, it seems, must be adopted voluntarily and by minority groups in the population – too many black shirts lead to unease amongst those who resist them. It may not, all the same, be altogether an accident that, throughout the Middle Ages, those who disapproved most strongly of changes in fashion did themselves wear the uniform of one or other of the religious orders. The strength of the feelings aroused in the breasts of some of them by current changes in fashion have been useful; without them they would have been recorded only by tailors, too professionally involved to see fashions other than in lengths of stuff or hours of workmanship, and by poets, novelists and artists, all of whom were primarily pursuing other ends; which does not, of course, mean that they did not record the fashions which they saw.

The chroniclers were, naturally, pursuing other ends too, nor were they, as were the poets and the painters, obliged to infuse their works with descriptions calculated to call up visual images. Nevertheless, they did.

In attempting the present study of fashionable dress worn over a comparatively short space of time at a comparatively remote period, the object has been to explore the relationship between the mundane accounts of tailors, the perhaps mainly unconscious records by painters and the severe judgements of chroniclers of the day. That the chroniclers were not infrequently writing some time after the event need not invalidate their views, except in minor details. In writing of the outcome of a battle or the death of a bishop, they were no less dependent on the records left behind by their predecessors than they were in writing of a fashion recently past.

To study in isolation the dress of those most likely to have worn the newest fashions would have been to ignore the fact that the pioneers inevitably dragged the whole of society that was not in uniform after them, at varying distances in time. But, important as it is to the study of society, a detailed investigation of the part played by dress in the social hierarchy as a whole has been very much a secondary aim.

Although a comparatively large number of books has been written on the history of dress, not many authors have spent much time in the contemplation of the curious part played by changing fashions in dress in the world's history, or even in modern society, which is perhaps not as strange as might at first appear. Those, for instance, who would be happy to have their libraries or their gardens admired would seldom be pleased to have the dress they are wearing examined with an equal interest – for fear, perhaps, that something might be 'wrong'. Wrong, but what, in the context, could be wrong? The wrong *persona*, the wrong disguise? The subject is surrounded by an unexpressed embarrassment, but why?

Since the moment when the selling of clothes became a matter of high commerce it has been possible to shift the blame for changing fashions on to the shoulders of those who make money out of them, which means, surely, that it is less shameful to be gullible than awkward. The nearest equivalents to today's traders in the fourteenth century were the silk merchants of Italy and the cloth weavers of Flanders; at the moment at which this study begins, the newest fashions probably involved buying slightly more stuff, which would have helped to keep the looms clicking in Lucca and Brussels; but workmanship was paid for out of the household purse, so that the profit motive did not come in. Italian merchants bankrupted themselves in lending money to the English king, but his patronage of their products can hardly be held as an act of charity responsible for the changes in dress he was obviously willing to accept.

The brief and far from exhaustive notes and appendices aim rather to avoid misrepresentation than to cover the field, and also to help those who may be interested in following up a particular topic or aspect of the subject.

I

1340: A New Fashion

When Edward III came to the throne in 1327, and for at least twenty succeeding years, England was experiencing one of her recurring periods of poverty from which, at the time, there can have seemed little prospect of relief, especially under the government of an ambitious young king. In 1340, Edward was twenty-eight. The son of a father whose disastrous life was terminated by a loathsome murder following a forced abdication, and of a mother, a French king's strong-minded daughter, openly unfaithful both to her husband and to his memory, Edward should have provided successive generations of students of psychiatry with a model case; he has not.

In the earliest years of the 1340s, Edward and his wife, Philippa of Hainault, were dressing themselves, their family and members of their household well though not extravagantly, while Edward himself was, in effect, seeking an empire, as his almost equally impoverished descendant, Elizabeth I, was later to do with rather more fruitful results. Elizabeth I had a new world to look to; Edward's best chance seemed to lie in France, where he already had a decent foothold in Aquitaine. Moreover, he could just maintain a case for a right to the French throne.

Had, therefore, England been richer, the earlier members of the second Valois dynasty might have lived more tranquilly in France. Philippe VI de Valois' own claim to the French throne was shaky, but no better one was to hand on his side of the Channel or, in reality, on Edward's. Edward launched what was an immediately victorious naval attack on the French fleet anchored off Sluys in 1340, which showed Philippe to have been a deplorably inept organizer of his own forces, but one who appears to have been well cushioned by a comfortable and nicely equipped existence for himself, his family and a large number of relations.

Philippe was certainly supported by friends in powerful positions. In 1340, the popes and their courts had been settled in Avignon for thirty-two years and were by that time housed, if not as magnificently as their history may have demanded, at least in respectable comfort in their new custom-built palace on the Rhône. It is true that the city of Avignon did not at that time actually belong to the papacy but to the throne of Naples, occupied in 1340 by Robert d'Anjou, count of Provence; but Anjou itself was joined to France as a part of the dowry of Robert d'Anjou's sister Margaret, Philippe de Valois' mother.

Nor were these the only French connections in Europe, for Robert d'Anjou's nephew, Charles Robert – Caroberto – had ascended the throne of Hungary in 1308 and still occupied it. Caroberto's second son Andrew was dispatched at an early age (though perhaps not one to be accurately described as 'tender') to the Neapolitan court, where his marriage to king Robert's granddaughter, Joanna countess of Provence, took place exactly according to plan in 1333, when Andrew was six and Joanna a year, or perhaps two years, older.

The French court in Paris had furthermore attracted to itself as a frequent visitor a ruling monarch, John, king of Bohemia, whose capital, Prague, had no reason to feel any affection for its absentee king. John's son Charles was eventually to make amends, both by struggling his way to the imperial throne and by founding the respected University of Prague – but that was later. Kings and their cousins, step-mothers and aunts also occasionally provided not merely a sympathetic environment but something more substantial to some of those more gifted but less well placed than their own peers and relations – poets and demagogues, for instance. Among the former, Petrarch moved from his native Arezzo between Rome, Avignon, the Angevin court at Naples, Prague, Milan, Venice and Paris. Boccaccio, half French, besides his *novelle* and poems, contributed to history when, like Petrarch, he too was drawn to what, from this distance in time, seems to have been a most unattractive social scene: the court of Naples.

Bereft of the papal court, Rome gave a temporary welcome in 1347 to the sartorially sophisticated self-styled 'Tribune of the People', Cola di Rienzo, and he also made his way about Europe, first to Avignon, later to Prague. Meanwhile in Florence, Giovanni Villani was covering in his chronicle not merely current events in his own city-state and the other

1

sovereign states of Italy, but also to a surprising extent happenings in the whole of Europe. Perhaps it is therefore not strange that, in 1342, Florence should have invited a Frenchman to occupy the position of head of state rather than the traditional 'foreigner' from another part of Italy. The result was disappointing, but the international point of view which led to it seems typical of that historical moment when Catalans inhabited Sicily and fought as mercenaries north of Rome, when the French were supported at the battle of Crécy by the Genoese under a Doria and when Venice quarrelled with Hungary over the occupation of the Dalmatian coast.

So it need cause no surprise that, although members of these closely linked nations often abused each other as foreigners, there was comparative unanimity in the acceptance of changes of fashions in dress as they appeared – simultaneously, it seems – in Europe's capital cities. In spite of the violent protests with which contemporary chroniclers greeted each successive change of fashion – protests which they thought fit to record in their histories (and no doubt ordinary members of the older generation everywhere gave way to equally violent vocal protests which they did not record) – a comparison between the altarpieces, manuscript paintings and sculpture produced all over Europe in the 1340s shows that changes of fashion followed the same sequence wherever men and women wore 'fashionable' dress. This *lingua franca* did not mean, however, that no local accents existed, for indeed they did. There were differences as great in their own field as the differences in modern speech of, say, a Yorkshireman and a Texan. Women in Paris did not adopt and almost certainly would have been sorry to have been seen dead in the hairstyles so generally fancied at the moment in Barcelona, for instance; and this in spite of the assistance given on occasion by Catalan troops to the armies of the king of France.

From surviving accounts we learn, furthermore, that the very finest linens used at the English court came from Rheims; the second-best quality from Paris. That their most expensive silks came from 'outremer' – the Holy Land – and from Lucca; their best cloth from Brussels. By the beginning of the 1360s, a coarser linen from Prussia was to be in common use in England, and so was leather from Hungary; while, in Hungary itself, cloth from Tournai had been imported at least as early as the thirteenth century and was, according to a record of 1344, by that time statutory wear for Hungarian judges.[1] Local accents in dress must therefore have been considerably modified by such cross-currents in the textile trade.

A span of twenty-five years may not seem very long in the history of fashion, and, of course, changes of fashion in dress do not as a rule coincide with the change from one decade to another as registered by the calendar. Nevertheless, a close look reveals that a distinct change was noticed round about 1340, even by those who could hardly have been expected to interest themselves in matters of such kind. Towards the end of that decade, the mode in which men and women of fashion presented

themselves to the world took another turn. So it seems wise to proceed cautiously, considering no more than five or six years at a time.

Soon after 1340, then, a change occurred in the fashion of European dress, a change which did not seem to those who noticed and recorded it to be a development or a mutation of the fashion which had previously been worn (though, of course, it was), but something quite new. It would be foolish to ascribe this change – which transformed human beings from soft rounded creatures with a mobile surface into harsh, spare, attenuated insect-like things – to a development or a series of developments in the political or the cultural situation, though both may have played their parts. The Italians ascribed the change to Spanish or French influence; the English to Flemish prototypes; the French themselves were no less distressed by the new fashion, but apparently they did not seek for a culprit.

Issues of sumptuary laws in both England and various parts of Italy in the later 1330s may conceivably have accelerated the change. Sumptuary laws usually have the effect of stimulating fashion to outwit them, but this too, by itself, would be too simple an explanation. It is prudent, at least for the moment, simply to record the fact that the new fashion was not only noted by chroniclers and clerks of great wardrobes in the first years of the 1340s, but that all over Europe panel and fresco painters, sculptors and illuminators of manuscripts portrayed its physical appearance with a minuteness which cannot be ascribed to an artistic prototype because they almost invariably include local though minor differences in the dress itself. The design of dress did not, of course, congeal as a result of what to some

1 *Adoration of the Shepherds*, fresco cycle completed 1338, by Taddeo Gaddi. Detail: St Joseph. One of the methods of cutting an over-tunic before the arrival of the new close-fitting fashion of 1340. The careful representation of seams is typical of Italian painters' interest in the construction of clothing.

observers seemed a violent revolution, but since modifications and developments naturally continued for some time to exaggerate further the turn which fashion appears to have taken, they gradually ceased to be remarkable.

At the beginning of the 1340s, the clothes of men and women closely resembled each other, except in three respects: the treatment of the head, the shape of the neckline and the length of the skirt; but, because of the great importance of these particular aspects in the design of dress, men and women would not, at the time, save to an exceptionally sensitive observer, have looked at all alike. Commentators did, however, record the fact that it was the clothing of both men and women that had changed in style. The dress of the two sexes continued for another thirty years at least to follow the same pattern.

Physically, the changed character of the new fashion was probably brought about by the technique of setting the sleeves into small rounded armholes at the point where the arms spring from the shoulder. Previously, and for a considerable time, sleeves had been cut together with the upper part of the garment, so that, united, they formed the shape of a T, usually elongated, where the sleeves were concerned, by the device of joining a rectangular piece of stuff sewn into a cylinder to each of the short arms of the T at about or somewhat above the elbow. As a covering for the torso and arms, this method of cutting precludes a tight fit above the waist, but once the sleeves have been set high, to coincide with the articulation of the whole arm, both they and the body-covering can be fitted as tightly as desired without unduly restraining the movements of the wearer.

In the early years of the fourteenth century (and for some time before that), sleeves had been wrapped round the lower arm and sewn up for some distance above the wrist each time that the garment was put on,[2] which meant that, above this closely fitted area, sleeves drooped loosely over the upper arm and seemed to form a single unit with the rather loose covering of the torso itself. In contrast, the tightly fitted torso and sleeves of the new fashion of the early 1340s isolated, it might be said, the arms from the body to form three distinct units – a change in composition which not only produced a new aesthetic effect but also marked a change to a less sympathetic appearance than that characterized by the shawl-like 'cosy' look of the previous fashion. The new fashion meant, moreover, that tunics and dresses could no longer be pulled on easily over the head, and, indeed, before long the new close-fit of the upper part of the dress necessitated a long opening down the front, down the back or under the arm. In condemning the new style, more than one eye-witness asserted that it was no longer possible to dress without assistance.

But another feature of the new fashion was that, while it was less bulky than its predecessor, it was, in relation to its size, more extravagant in its use of material. Instead of consisting entirely, like its predecessor, of rectangular elements of stuff which could be cut from the whole piece without leaving

2 *Romance of Alexander*, completed in 1344. The new fashions of the early 1340s; marked similarity between the dress of the two sexes particularly in the general fit, the hanging sleeves and even the line of the men's hoods, which echo the feminine decolletage. Early appearance of 'cornettes'.

awkwardly shaped and probably unusable fragments unused, the new sleeves were not rectangular. At the top they were necessarily rounded to fit into the cut-out armhole of the body-piece (further waste), while the hanging pieces with which the sleeves of most over-tunics now terminated demanded more extravagant use of stuff. The new cut was, in fact, a modest demonstration of what a very much later philosopher with a puritanical attitude towards fashionable dress condemned as 'conspicuous waste'.[3] It was not the first time in the history of European fashion that cloth, as it came off the loom in a natural rectangle, had been cut into pieces of exotic shape which had involved some waste. The appearance of the new fashion of the early 1340s marked, however, the definitive end of the totally rectangular cut so far as western fashion was concerned. Although it lurked until the early twentieth century in peasant communities all over Europe, it has never returned to high fashion.

Laboriously built up thread by thread on the loom, the natural rectangle was retained, too, for some ceremonial dress – the Christian church's alb and dalmatic, for instance – and it also seems to have continued to be worn by princes and nobles in a few European countries less closely in touch with the main stream of fashion for some time after it had been abandoned elsewhere.[4] It could well be argued that the destruction of the basic woven rectangle marked a social change more significant than any mutation that could take place in the aesthetic composition of dress; but it will not be pursued here.

Before attempting to describe in general outline the developments which led to the new European fashion of the 1340s, it should be pointed out that the normal suit of clothes for a lady or a gentleman of the fourteenth century consisted of from four to six garments. Beneath the tunic (*tunica*) was worn a shirt (*camisia*), while an over-tunic (*supertunica*) was worn on top. Other garments, such as a hood, a cloak of some kind and perhaps an extra over-tunic, might be added to these three; together they made up the suit (*roba*).[5] The situation is complicated by the fact that, in the inventories of the period, shirts are almost invariably listed separately among the linens, so that although they were worn as a part of the suit, they were not usually reckoned in with it in the accounts of the wardrobes. In France, the royal wardrobe accounts of the fourteenth century were already written in French, but in most other countries they continued to be written in Latin.

Unless the subject demanded some special type of dress – archaic, official or sporting – most pictures of the period show people of the middle and upper classes wearing over-tunics beneath the less than full-length sleeves of which the tight lower sleeves of the tunic itself can be seen. The change to sleeves set snugly into small armholes appeared simultaneously in both over-tunics and tunics. Sleeveless over-tunics (perhaps usually called something else) existed, but they need not be discussed at the moment. The practice of sewing up the lower part of the sleeve every time the tunic was put on had been abandoned in fashionable circles by the beginning of the second quarter of the fourteenth century. It was replaced by a row of buttons with corresponding buttonholes – a considerable advance.

By about 1335, sleeves of over-tunics had been shortened until they barely covered the elbow, and, at the same time, widened at the elbow to form the shape of a bell or the mouth of a trumpet. At this stage therefore, when the arm was bent, the wide mouth of the sleeve lay flat over the crook of the arm, but naturally, with the force of gravity, it hung down below the elbow at the back forming a shape, which, seized on by fashion, was gradually lengthened into a hanging hollow oval until, by 1340, all semblance of a bell had disappeared. During the following decade, this hanging oval was further lengthened and, at the same time, narrowed and flattened into a long strip, no longer able to function in any respect as a sleeve.[6]

So the new fashion of the early 1340s was composed of an upper part, rectangular in aspect, terminated by a horizontal break on a level with the navel, to which line a skirt was attached which ended, in the dress of men, at about the knee or just above it. In women's dress, this skirt touched the ground and often lay upon it in folds. Sleeves, straight and tight, were usually accented by the falling pieces described above at about the elbow. Skirts were joined to the upper part of the dress with a little fulness, sometimes only at the back, to allow freedom of movement. The skirts of men's tunics were sometimes slit up as far as the waist in front.[7] The hairdressing of both men and women, rather bulky and rounded in outline in the 1330s, had become more compact.

During the course of the following few years, the line of what it is convenient to call the 'waist' was further lowered to a level with the crutch; the upper

3 Detail of sinopia from the *Triumph of Death* from the Campo Santo. Probably before 1340. An Italian version of the sleeve extensions of the end of the 1330s.

4 *Luttrell Psalter*. A typical upper-class man of the early 1340s. His over-tunic, not yet fastened down the front, has a skirt open to the waist. See also p. 104.

part of the tunic was further tightened, and buttons, already becoming necessary in 1340, were set closer together. This was the first time in western dress that buttons had appeared set in a line down the front of a garment; in the East they could be found much earlier.[8] These buttons were not merely functional; they also added a decoration to the formerly plain front of the dress.

As the 1340s advanced, sleeves of over-tunics were shortened as a rule to reach only half-way down the upper part of the arm while, at the same time, their attachments grew longer, flatter and narrower. Hair was dressed ever closer to the head, and, seen together with the close fit of the clothing and the elongation of the torso, made the whole person look taller – an effect which might, perhaps, be regarded in architectural terms as 'gothic', coinciding, strictly speaking, with the 'decorated' style. But since the fashion by no means settled permanently on this composition, it would be foolish to equate what was an extremely fugitive design in dress with the slow-moving dignity of an architectural style.

Concurrent with the lowering of the waistline and a further shortening of the masculine tunic, a new elaboration became increasingly noticeable and was indeed noticed in due course by contemporary commentators. This consisted in the cutting of the edges of garments into fanciful patterns – especially the edges of short shoulder capes to which hoods were attached, the edges of hanging pieces attached to sleeves and sometimes to the edges of over-tunics. It was not a new device, but it was one which grew in popularity towards 1350. For purely practical reasons, it did not lend itself conveniently as a decoration to the hems of the dresses of women.[9]

The common characteristic of all historical periods is that each is unique, but then, of course, every minute, every slice of every second is unique. In most respects there is nothing so special about the years 1340 to 1365, but the inventories of clothing which survive from those years present a manageable quantity of details which, glanced over in general and then looked at closely, produce a convincing account of the fantastical coverings in which human beings of the time either wrapped themselves or were wrapped in by others. The respective prices per ell of *camocas*, or of mixed cloth in grain, or of Welsh russet governed the class of person to whom each could economically be given, as well as the kind of occasion on which each could be worn. If – even when they were at war with each other – Brussels longcloth was still the favoured stuff for everyday wear in the royal houses of both France and England, it can reasonably be assumed that its quality was unbeatable; and this is borne out by its position in the great wardrobe accounts of England and the *argenterie* accounts of France. This may be accounted for by the fact that Brussels seems to have felt it necessary to keep up with the times by introducing, or perhaps reviving, complex weaves to replace plain ones, which ensured that not only the cut and the colour of each suit but also its surface moved along with the dynamism that fashion demands.

But if those who paid for the clothes they wore or provided for their supporters used them to proclaim their personal tastes, their consciousness of prevailing opinion and the precise position they inhabited in society, these very same clothes were, to contemporary poets and novelists, the metaphors essential to the realization of the fictional characters who acted out their plots. The silent language of dress, signalled by the princes, the tradesmen and the paupers of the real world, was shared by the virtuous and the vicious of the worlds of poetry and romance. The furred hood of the serjeant-at-law – *servientis ad legem* – which represented to the king's tailor forty skins of miniver, symbolized for Piers the Plowman the corruption of the state. Meanwhile the miniver itself, culled in Russia and carried through 'Almain' to London, had been trimmed down to a degree suitable for a serjeant but not fine enough for a prince. That kind of practice was already long established by 1340; but some others, not affecting serjeants but important to princes, were not.

Of all man's artifacts, clothing is, of course, physically closest to him; so close, indeed, that when it ceases to enfold him and is taken off it loses its character completely. Worn on the body, on the other hand, it becomes a potent means of communication, more stable than a glance or a grimace, much less permanent than a painting or a piece of sculpture. Carefully chosen, its design may be a gauge of the wearer's taste, his assessment of the situation or the company in which he finds himself; or, alternatively, a deliberate concealment of his views on life or society. It is not therefore surprising that when, by a mysterious unspoken agreement, the 'fashion' of clothing is changed, its whole use as personal communication must in consequence be readjusted: those whose business it is to watch their times find the change both uncomfortable and puzzling.

5 *Luttrell Psalter.* A lady's hair is dressed in cornettes by her maid. The difference in class is exemplified by the dress of the two women.

II

What They Said About it

There survived in the minds of scholars what was almost a tribal memory of an ancient and honourable dress: a vague recollection of the toga, the chlamys and the pallium of classical Rome. The toga had been given a long entry in the *Catholicon* which, in spite of the modern view that it had been 'clean swept aside in the new curriculum' of the middle of the fourteenth century,[1] was still used as a dictionary or, rather, encyclopedia, a fact demonstrated by the survival in the university library at Liège of an expensively illustrated and well-thumbed copy made in 1348 by Guillaume de Dycka to the order of Jean de Mierle, provost of the Benedictine monastery of St Trond. The *Catholicon*, originally compiled in 1286 by John Balbi, is also especially interesting on the subject of the *antichimissimo abito* – the *tunica* – as well as on the *socculus* worn by Roman comedians.[2] The toga had been long and ample, the chlamys and the pallium long and flowing; the fashions of the early 1340s included none of these qualities.

The first precisely dated comment on the new fashion was made by Galvano della Flamma; what was probably the second, by Giovanni Villani. Both were disturbed by the introduction of foreign fashions into what they saw as the decent stability of the Italian attitude to clothes. Della Flamma's account refers to the year 1340, Villani's to 1342, but because the events which led to Villani's strictures were the more spectacular, they should, perhaps, be discussed first.

Giovanni Villani's acid comments are to be found in book twelve of his *Cronica* where, in recording the arrival in Florence of Walter de Brienne II, titular duke of Athens, to take up the position of *capitano* and *conservatore del popolo* in the commune at the beginning of June 1342, Villani designated de Brienne as *conte de Brenna di Francia*, as well as *duca d'Atene*, thus identifying him as a Frenchman. De Brienne, whose family had risen to prominence during the Fifth and the subsequent Crusade, had, by 1342, long lost his tenuous hold on Athens and, until he was invited to Florence to occupy the highest office in the state, had been fighting in France for Philippe de Valois, the French king.

De Brienne was welcomed with considerable enthusiasm by some sections of the population of Florence as a probable solution to the dissension which had tormented the state throughout more or less the whole of the first half of the century. Indeed, Villani tells us that, in the September of the same year, the *grandi* as well as the *popolazzo minuto* (an uncouth community within the general populace in Villani's view) were shouting for the appointment of de Brienne as permanent *Signore* of Florence. On 8 September his banner was run up the tower of the scarcely completed Palazzo Vecchio[3] and the bells were rung in praise of God. Accompanied by exuberant celebrations, his appointment was confirmed the same evening – a move soon to be regretted.

Villani proceeds to transcribe a letter to de Brienne from his uncle by marriage, Robert, king of Naples, on hearing the news, and then follows this immediately by remarking that it should not be forgotten that the duke, when he first arrived in Florence, had introduced that disfiguring change in dress lately accepted by the French, to replace the traditional Florentine attire, nobler, handsomer and more dignified than that of any other nation and directly descended from the ancient clothing of those entitled to wear the Roman toga. Now the young had taken to tunics so short and tight that they found it impossible to dress without help, strapped round them like the girths of horses and ornamented with showy buckles and points, while elaborate pouches in the German style hung down over their fronts and their hoods hung like cowls, reaching the waist or even below so that they were both hoods and mantles, both hoods and mantles moreover being cut into patterns round the edge and the liripipes of their hoods reaching to the ground or being wrapped round their heads for warmth. They wore long beards to make themselves look fiercer, and their knights were dressed in tight belted over-tunics with hanging sleeve-pieces lined with miniver or some kind of ermine, long enough to touch the ground. This outlandish dress, neither beautiful nor decent, was from that very moment taken up by the youths of Florence, and the young women too adopted the most ridiculous sleeve-pieces.[4]

All this, Villani believed, was a sign of the change for the worse which the state itself had undergone, for the citizens of Florence were not by nature frivolous nor temperamentally disposed to welcome changes of fashion, nor to copy the fashions of foreigners who were constantly led into impropriety. Then, after a brief discursus into changes in architecture introduced by de Brienne, Villani returned to the subject of dress, for de Brienne, he explained, out of his weakness for women, repealed the sumptuary laws which had been imposed on their manner of clothing and allowed them to dress up as much as they liked, thus pandering to their worldly tastes and leading them into spending a lot of money.[5]

De Brienne need not as a matter of fact be held responsible for introducing Italy to the new fashions, for two years before Villani expressed distaste for what was going on in Florence, Galvano della Flamma, biographer of Florence's prime enemies, the Visconti family, had recorded a similar state of affairs in Milan. Della Flamma described the young men of the city as having adopted the tight (*stricta*) and meagre clothing of the Spanish style, while, at the same time, they were cutting their hair in the French fashion. They were, moreover, growing beards in very imitation of barbarians, tramping about ferociously like Germans and using the language as though they were Tartars. Women, too, had changed for the worse, their dresses being tight enough to strangle them and cut too low at the neck. They wandered around wearing gold brooches, silks and sometimes even gold brocades. Their hair was crimped in the foreign style, their heads had been turned by foreign ideas, and going about with their gold girdles and their shoes with long beaks, they looked positively like amazons. What was worse, they were as tough and hard-hearted as men-at-arms.[6]

Galvano della Flamma does not sigh for the toga, but more surprisingly he follows his attack on the new fashion by a section, *De Moribus antiquorum*, which looks back nostalgically not to ancient Rome but to the time when the emperor Frederick II was in Lombardy. Then manners were rude and men wore mantles (*chlamydes*) either of leather with no covering of cloth, or else of coarse wool minus any fur or lining. Young unmarried girls wore the simplest woollens, with a cloak over the top of whitest linen and no ornaments at all in their hair.[7]

Galvano – Gualvaneus de la Fiamma – a Dominican monk of S. Eustogio in Milan, was not the first to look back to these particular fashions of an earlier medieval period (the middle of the thirteenth century) nor even, just possibly, the second. His passage, *De Moribus antiquorum*, was taken directly from a report by the chronicler, Ricobaldo of Ferrara, who ended his history with the coronation of the emperor Henry VII in Rome in 1312.[8] Under the heading *De rudibus moribus in Italia*, Ricobaldo was writing of the time of the emperor Frederick II, when, he says, men wore *chlamydes* made from hides without any further elaboration – *operimento* – or else made from wool

without any leather at all. Women wore tunics of coarse woollen cloth, and young girls also wore a similar tunic of rough wool called a *sotanum*, and a cloak of linen which was called a *xocca*. Whether they were married women or maidens, they were satisfied to wear no precious ornaments in their hair at all.

There is no mystery about the source of Galvano della Flamma's passage on the state of clothing a hundred or so years earlier, for, writing in 1340, he stated explicitly that things had got worse since the time when Ricobaldus Ferrariensis was writing his chronicle. It is the interest he displayed in making, in his own chronicle, so careful a repetition of Ricobaldo's report that is so striking, for it may, indeed, suggest that it was not uncommon for later chroniclers to treasure the comments of their forebears on current social manners.

Galvano's rendering of Ricobaldo's passage is almost but not totally identical. Both used the word *pignolato* for the rough homespun wool stuff; both say that a girl's tunic was called a *sotanum*; Galvano says that over them – *desuper* – they wore a cloak – *paludamentum* – of whitest linen. Ricobaldo says that they wore a tunic and a *paludamentum*, but does not state that it was worn over the tunic, nor does he refer to the whiteness of the linen. Galvano says that this is a *socca* – *idest soccam*; Ricobaldo says that they used the word *xocca* – *quod dicebant Xoccam*. The word socca (something worn on the head – *soccapolo, succaporo*)[9] were probably regional forms which may have been unfamiliar to Galvano. Ricobaldo suggested that customs and manners were rough in Italy in Frederick II's time; Galvano, writing in Milan, narrows his remarks to Frederick's visit to Lombardy.

But perhaps it may not be too daring to suggest that Dante, too, knew Ricobaldo's account of these fashions of the past when he wrote in the *Paradiso* of his ancestors and their contemporaries. Dante and Ricobaldo were themselves almost contemporaries.

> Fiorenza, dentro della cerchia antica
>   ond'ella toglie ancora e terza e nona
>   si stava in pace, sobria e pudica
>
> Non avea catenella, non corona,
>   non donna contigiate, non cintura
>   che fosse a veder piu che la persona . . .
>
> Bellincion Berti vid' io andar conto
>   di cuoio e d'osso, e venir dallo specchio
>   la donna sua senza il volto dipinto
>
> e vivi quel Nerlo e quel del Vecchio
>   esser contenti alla pelle scoperta
>   e le sue donne al fuso ed al pennecchio[10]

The concept of the sobriety and stability of the 'olden times' is and has always been popular, but the possibility of a connection between Dante's stanzas and Ricobaldo's account lies mainly in the idea that, in the past, people were *contenti* (Ricobaldo's word in reference to women) with clothing of leather that was 'uncovered', in other words, unlined.[11]

It is only because Dante refers to clothing comparatively seldom, and almost always in general terms,

7

that it is possible to suggest, even in the most tenta- tive way, that a connection might have existed be- tween the two texts. It is a putative connection that would not have been worth referring to but for the importance to the present argument that chroniclers, and even poets, may not have been unaware of references to current fashions in dress made by their predecessors and contemporaries.

The reflections of Villani and della Flamma in Florence and Milan were echoed by the fourteenth- century biographer of Cola di Rienzo, known as the *Anonimo Romano*. Immediately before his report of the death of Robert of Naples in 1343, he discussed the sudden change in dress in Rome. At this time, he wrote, clothing changed immeasurably. Men began to wear very long peaks to their hoods and very tight clothing in the Catalan style and to carry daggers in their belts. On their heads they wore little hats on top of their hoods, and on their chins huge tough beards, looking absolutely as though they were adherents of the Spanish army. Things used not to be like that at all; men used to shave their beards and wear decently long gowns. Indeed, if a man wore a beard, unless he were a Spaniard or a hermit, he was suspected of being a person of the worst type. Now look at the new fashion for wearing a knife like a pilgrim on the road and, what is more, those who do not go in for wearing hats on their heads, great beards and knives tucked into their belts are not regarded as being anything at all.[12]

It seems unlikely that Villani was unaware of what was going on in fashionable circles in other parts of Italy. In placing the blame on the duke of Athens and his followers, he was surely defending the youth of Florence against the frivolity of those cities which he regarded as less admirable. That he did not ascribe the new fashion to Spanish influence is interesting in view of the fact that cities as far apart, culturally as well as geographically, as Rome and Milan seemed to discover a Spanish flavour in the new fashions. The *Anonimo Romano* was actually writing more than a decade later than the events he described, which probably accounts for his reference to hats, for it seems certain that these did not appear as a part of high fashion in the early 1340s. In describing the new styles as being tight, however, he was probably recalling a change that had struck him forcibly at the time and that had remained in his memory; in his references to the wearing of beards, he is supported by della Flamma; and to knives by both della Flamma and Villani.

Young men and women in Florence had not, of course, dressed like descendants of ancient Romans before the arrival of de Brienne or the 'Spanish' fashion. In Villani's day, the interior walls of virtu- ally every church in Florence were covered with frescoes demonstrating the fact that fashions in Florence had changed as frequently as those in any other European state. Villani's sentimental argument was based on his comparison between de Brienne's young French bodyguards and the dignified middle- aged members of Florence's merchant class, who did, indeed, wear impressive, long semi-official gowns (very much like those in which Dante is depicted in near-contemporary portraits), cut in a style which had remained unchanged, or almost un- changed, over a comparatively long period.

The new clothing was tight; its edges were broken by decorative incisions; its surface punctuated by decorative accents produced by pointed daggers, the sharp metal points of laces and conspicuous buckles. It included, moreover, pendant sleeve-pieces which provided a further sharpness to the outline. Upper- class Italians adopted it, but as they did so softened it a little so that, after the dismissal of the duke of Athens, a travelling Frenchman would still have been identifiable as a foreigner in Florence and almost certainly in the much more frenchified society of Siena as well.

Villani, commenting on the fact that the new tunics were shorter than those worn previously, had felt able to relate the appearance of the change with pre- cision to Walter de Brienne's arrival in Florence in 1342. That the French had indeed already adopted the new fashion was claimed by the last of the *Con- tinuateurs* of the *Chronique Latine de Guillaume de Nangis*, who wrote of the years 1340 to 1368 and who seems to have been identified, with justification, as Jean de Venette.[13] This author, after describing Edward's III's victory at Sluys in 1340, his appoint- ment as Vicar of the Empire and his assumption of the arms of France conjointly with those of England as well as his siege of Cambrai (all of which the *Continuateur* places in the same year, though in fact they covered a period of more than two), reports a drastic change in the masculine fashion in dress.

Following closely the sequence of events which certainly did take place at almost the same time, his announcement of the arrival of the new fashion in dress in 1340 can probably be accepted. Neverthe- less, as compared with the lengthy, minute and lively detail in which he described the fashions in the later part of his chronicle, his account of the early 1340s is sparse, and it is reasonable to assume that it was written a good deal later than its apparent date.[14]

His actual description of the new fashion, how- ever, and his reference to it again when he looked back on the early 1340s from 1356,[15] certainly inspire confidence and demonstrate the way in which the shock of the change had lingered in the public mind. The passage runs as follows:

But at this time men, and particularly noblemen and especially high-born squires and their following, as well as some citizens and practically all servants, began to redesign their mode of dress. They started to wear short clothing, and that so short that both their buttocks and their private parts were pretty well visible, which was really very strange because previously things had been getting more decent. All men began to grow longer beards, a fashion which almost everybody who was not of royal blood took to, and one which provoked more than a little ridicule from the common people.[16]

It may be significant in considering the attitude to dress of the French as a nation that, even as early as the fourteenth century, this change in fashion was not ascribed to foreign influence either by the last de Nangis *Continuateur* or by the current author of the

Grandes Chroniques de France, whose outburst about the then not so very new fashion followed the French defeat at Crécy.

In the meantime, in the year 1340, the chronicler responsible for the current material in the *Chronicon Angliae*[17] – who very rarely mentioned clothing – recollected a miraculous happening connected with the death of the mean and avaricious but very powerful bishop of Lincoln, Henry Burghersh. He noticed that immediately after the prelate had expired, the bishop's ghost appeared to one of his men-at-arms with instructions that some of the common land he had enclosed as his park should be given back to the people. He carried, says the chronicler, a quiver, bow, arrows and horn, and wore a short green tunic (*brevi tunica viridi*).[18] Considering that it had been the custom from time immemorial for archers – for obvious reasons connected with their skill – to wear short tunics, the inclusion of the word 'short' in this context must, taken with other north European comment of the time, be seen as an extremely slight, but nevertheless significant, example of the persistence of memory.

The tunics of the first years of the 1340s were not, in fact, so very much shorter than those of the late 1330s, but because they were much tighter, they appeared at the same time to be shorter, and this close fit would tend to make the legs, like the arms, more conspicuous. The French chroniclers resembled the Italians in that they were mainly concerned that the new fashion was short and tight, whereas to the English it also looked outlandish. An English chronicler, John of Reading, depending on earlier writers for the years leading up to 1356,[19] includes a highly coloured entry for the year 1344, when he condemns the current fashion, saying that the English had been madly following the fashions of foreigners ever since the coming of the Hainaulters some eighteen years back, in which he was presumably referring to the entourage of Philippa of Hainault when she arrived in England soon after the coronation of Edward. The decent long and ample fashions of the good old days, says John of Reading, are deserted in favour of clothing that is short, narrow, hampering, cut all about, laced up in every part and altogether changed. With the buttoned sleeves and tippits – *typeitis* – to their over-tunics and hoods hanging down to excessive lengths, in their clothes as well as in their footwear, they are more like tormentors, or, to be truthful, demons, than men. And moreover, clerks and members of religious orders do the same so that they are judged irregulars rather than regulars. Women, too, have changed in a transient manner. Their bizarre clothing is so tight that they wear the tails of foxes hanging under their skirts at the back to hide their arses. The sin of pride exemplified in all this bodes no good for the future.[20] John of Reading, even if not an eye-witness, was writing of a stirring period in English history; what moved him to include so emotional an outburst on the fashions of the time?

His passage, or the original source which inspired it, must also have been the source for an attack on the current fashions in the entries that covered the years 1333 to 1377 in the chronicle of England known as the *Brut*, which, in this period, is in English and exists in two or three slightly varying versions, the first from the early fifteenth century.[21] In an entry which follows Edward of Woodstock's investiture as prince of Wales in 1344 and precedes an account of the battle of Crécy, fought in 1346, the author of the *Brut* complains:

> In this time Englishmen so much haunted and cleaved to the wodnes and folly of strangers that they change their clothing every year, especially since the coming of the Hainaulters years ago. Sometimes their clothes are long and wide, at others they are short, tight, dagged and cut about and boned all round. The sleeves of their surcoats like their hoods have tapets, long and wide which hang down too far. They look, to tell the truth, more like tormentors and devils in their clothing than like normal men. And the women surpass the men in their clothing which is so tight that they hang fox-tails under their dresses at the back to hide their arses, a kind of behaviour which may well have provoked many of the evils and misfortunes that have beset the kingdom of England.[22]

The difference between the accounts by John of Reading and in the *Brut* is as interesting as the similarity. The *Brut* speaks of clothing that is boned all round, but fails to note that sleeves are buttoned and shoes grotesque. It seems likely that the copyist read 'buttoned' as 'boned', though this would not fit well into the context. If the source of this continuation of the *Brut* really recorded that current clothing was boned all round, it would be fascinating, but there seems no other evidence at all to support the theory that bones were used at this time to stiffen the tight clothing. It will also be noticed that what John of Reading called *typeitis*, the *Brut* translated as 'tapets', a term which, in the middle of the fourteenth century, was used for carpets or tapestries of small size; it has to be remembered that the scribe responsible for that copy of the *Brut* was not familiar with the fashions he was describing and living at a time when the terminology must, where details of dress were concerned, have changed entirely.

John of Reading and the author of the *Brut* for that period seem to have been the only chroniclers to suggest that things had been bad for some time past. The last de Nangis *Continuateur* was apparently of the opinion that, until the violent change in 1340, things had been getting better. The suggestion in the *Brut* that the new fashions had provoked the Almighty to visit England with misfortunes seems to confirm the date of the entry about clothing; England could hardly have regarded herself as unfortunate after her victory at Crécy.

With the French, of course, things were different. Round about the middle of the 1340s tunics did become noticeably shorter, and it was specifically this development which aroused the author of the current section of the *Grandes Chroniques de France* to the same degree of indignation as that expressed by the de Nangis *Continuateur* three or four years earlier. Written between 1344 and 1350, the section of the

Grandes Chroniques echoes the strictures of the *Continuateur*, writing what is regarded as a contemporary report. Describing the defeat of the French army at Crécy on 26 August 1346, the author of the *Chroniques* considered that the destruction of the flower of French knighthood could only be seen as God's punishment for the sins of pride, greed and indecency in dress which infested the nobility of France – and other Frenchmen too. Some, he continued, wore their clothing so short that it scarcely covered their rumps, with the result that when they bent down to serve their lords they showed their breeches (*braies*) as well as what was inside them to those who stood behind. In addition to this, their clothes were so tight that they needed help both in dressing and in undressing; it seemed as though, when one was being undressed, he was literally being skinned (*escourchoit*). Others among them had their tunics gathered (*fronciées*) at the back over their loins (*rains*) like women's dresses. Moreover, their hoods were minutely cut about all round and, given the chance, made of one cloth on one side and another on the other. The liripipes (*cornetes*) of their hoods as well as their sleeves hung almost to the ground so that they looked more like minstrels than anything else. So, in view of this kind of thing, it was not surprising that, to correct these French excesses, God employed the king of England as his scourge.[23]

Although the current author of the *Grandes Chroniques* attacked the vices of the new fashion, he was, in fact, like Villani, writing specifically of the dress of the young, for he referred to them as 'stooping to serve their lords'. Those who wore the new fashion were not necessarily therefore 'the flower of French chivalry', but, as one would expect, the young squires who had not yet won their spurs. It seems likely that the chronicler, like the last *Continuateur*, was here seizing the opportunity to attack the French nobility, an opportunity the latter seldom missed.

While the author of the *Brut* evidently considered that it had been mainly the clothing of women that had aroused the anger of God, the author of the *Grandes Chroniques* was gallant enough to refrain from commenting directly on their dress. But it may perhaps have been an age of strong-minded women: king Edward's mother – Isabella of France, the 'she-wolf' – managed to make herself felt throughout the long years of enforced retirement, during which she was repeatedly referred to as having been given additional property as well as benefits for her attendants and friends.[24] Edward's wife, Philippa, is best remembered for her intervention on behalf of the citizens of Calais, but that was by no means the only time that she persuaded the king to follow her advice. The very same year and in Calais, for instance, an order by the king granted a pardon, urged by Philippa, to a citizen of Beverly who had been caught smuggling wool out of England without paying duty and smuggling in currency of Luxembourg.[25]

As for Philip of France, not only has his wife Jeanne of Burgundy been described as the 'masculine queen',[26] but his second wife, who outlived him, was extremely successful in making trouble for his grandson, Charles V.[27] In Brittany, when the death of the de Montfort duke left two pretenders with equal rights to succeed him, Jeanne de Montfort, the mother of the finally successful claimant, fought so valiantly for the family cause that she was described as a woman with the heart of a man and lion.[28]

But more convincing than the careers of a group of high-born ladies is an English manuscript known as the *Taymouth Hours*,[29] decorated in the late 1330s with illuminations in miniature which can hardly have been calculated to stimulate the religious devotion such books of hours were intended to promote; the little paintings that fill the borders consist almost entirely of upper-class young women, singly or in pairs, pursuing, with no masculine support, activities normally undertaken by men in the hunting field. Mainly unveiled – and therefore presumably unmarried – these young women ride or stride through the countryside, aiming at anything that moves, from stags to rabbits, accompanied by appropriate hounds. Nor is this the only manuscript to include paintings of such women, strong in mind as in body. If the *Taymouth* girls were not suitable ornaments to a book designed to encourage private devotion, their counterparts are even more inappropriate as decorations to a copy of the *Decretals of Gregory the Great*, its text produced as a guide for the Church herself – a copy made, or at least decorated, in about 1340.[30] Here, again, appear sporting young women on their own, gonging for wild duck, exercising their hawks, in compositions based, in some cases, on the *Taymouth Hours*, though their dress has been slightly adjusted to the later fashion. The *Decretals* do include some sporting little boys, fishing or whipping tops, but it is the young women who provide the novelty.

It may therefore be that the women who appear to have aroused displeasure at a Berwick tournament of 1347 were merely a part of a feminist movement which was already recognized, and certainly Henry Knighton, an Austin canon from the house at Leicester, tells us in his *Chronicon* that people had begun to make a fuss because, where tournaments were held almost anywhere in the country, they were attended by troups of ladies who formed, as it were, a side-show, dressed up in all sorts of extraordinary masculine attire. These women, numbering sometimes as many as forty or fifty, were certainly among the most attractive specimens of womanhood in the realm, though not the most virtuous. They disported themselves in mi-parti tunics – one half in one colour and one in another – with tight little hoods, their liripipes twisted round their heads and their girdles, set low across their bellies, below the navel, and lavishly decorated in gold and silver, while hanging down low in front they wear those little knives known as 'daggers'. They parade about the lists on carefully chosen chargers or equine beasts of some other well-groomed kind, ruining both their bodies and their fortunes by their wanton and scurrilous behaviour, or so everybody says. But they neither fear the anger of God nor blush at the comments of God-fearing citizens,[31] and so Henry Knighton continues until he has finished his attack,

10

which, if it had no parallel in a French chronicle, certainly echoed Galvano della Flamma's description of the amazons of Milan of half a decade earlier, with their golden girdles and their hard masculine hearts. Knighton, like many of his contemporaries, was writing a considerable time after the event, but his narrative, like theirs, not only reads like the account of an eyewitness but presents a detailed and accurate picture of the dress of the date at which, he claims, the Berwick tournament took place: a contemporary account must have existed as a source.

The particular tournament which provoked the anger of the monk of Leicester on behalf of the Almighty was held in 1347, soon after the English victory at Crécy and the submission of Calais when, it is related in the *Chronicon Angliae*, not an Englishman returned empty-handed; and, indeed, that woman was of no account who did not possess something from Caen or Calais, or one of the other cities across the sea. Clothes, furs, cushions and household goods; table-linen, necklaces, cups of maplewood and silver; bed linens and napery were to be found in private houses all over England, and it was a moment when English matrons began to flaunt themselves in the finery of the ladies of northern France, and as the latter mourned the loss of their possessions, so the former gloried in all the things listed above.[32] A new day in the history of fashion was dawning, one during which historians were to find a target in what they regarded as a new and unwarrantable luxury in dress. They were to fire their statutory attacks, but with considerably less vigour than they had displayed in attacking the new styles of the early 1340s.

The *Chronicon Angliae* and the chronicle of Henry Knighton are written in Latin of a lively if pious character which brings their writings close to the vernacular of Villani and Galvano della Flamma as well as of the authors of the *Grandes Chroniques* and the *Brut*, whose vocabulary seems likely to have been close to the speech of the man in the street. It is therefore worth examining the names they gave to specific garments, if only because it is very rare, in medieval documents of any kind, to come across named garments accompanied by descriptions of them. But Villani even took the trouble to correct himself. When he wrote of the tunics of the French supporters of de Brienne, he used the Italian word *cotta* but added that he meant, rather, *gonella*, which provides the modern reader with the information that, although the fourteenth-century *cotta* was not actually identical to the *gonella*, it was very much like it.

Villani did not complain that the clothing of the French knights, as distinct from de Brienne's other supporters, was unduly short, but he did say that it was tight, belted and extravagant where sleeve-pieces were concerned. He refers to what must have been an over-tunic (since it had hanging sleeves) as a *guarnacca*, which established the fact that it was different from a *cotta* and a *gonella* as well as that it was an outer garment. The sleeve-pieces themselves he called *manicottoli*, and he used the same term for women's sleeve-pieces – *lunghi infino al terra*. His

statement that their linings were not only of *varo* – miniver, the white belly of the Russian squirrel – but alternatively of *ermellini*, is also important. At this period ermine was rare and very expensive; it was usually controlled by sumptuary regulations so that none but those of royal blood or at least holders of the very highest offices in the state could wear it. Whatever *ermellini* was, it was not ermine, a fur that de Brienne's adventuring knights would have been neither able to afford nor, if they had been, permitted to wear.

The author of the *Grandes Chroniques*, writing of the French at the time of the battle of Crécy, was less precise. He used the general term *vesture* for dress and the word *robe* in the current sense, corresponding to the Latin word *roba* – a suit of clothes. But it is to him that we owe the clarification of the strange word *frounciata*, to be found in many entries in the English and French great wardrobe and argenterie accounts of the same date, for he clearly showed that he was using *froncée* in today's sense, meaning stuff gathered together.

In the *Brut*, the word 'sircotys' was used for those over-tunics to which hanging sleeves were attached —the hanging pieces that the author refers to as 'tapets'. These may well have been referred to in the 1340s and 1350s as 'lapets' and have been misread.

The chroniclers seem to have experienced the greatest difficulties in describing hoods. Villani, writing of the point at the back which had by his time grown into the long hanging tube called in English a 'liripipe', called it a *becchetto*, whereas Knighton, writing later of women at tournaments and using the Latin of his time, identified the long ends of their hoods which, like the followers of the duke of Athens, they had wrapped round their heads, as *liripipis ad modum chordarum*.[33] In the *Brut*, the word 'tapet' had been used for liripipes as well as sleeve-pieces, both of which, in their mid-fourteenth-century form had disappeared from the fashion together no doubt with the names by which they had been called; their earlier existence, however, had not been forgotten.

There is one more term which should be noticed before leaving the sartorial gossip of the chroniclers: *secta*, which appears in Knighton in the sense of motley or mi-parti. The tunics of the ladies at the joust were described as having 'una parte de una secta et altera de alia secta'. *Secta* had, in fact, become the normal word for an identifiable livery; archers, for example, were described as dressed in the *secta* of their employers. Villani demonstrated that a similar term – *assisa* – was current in Italy when he described the arrival of Carobert, king of Hungary, in Naples in 1333, and adds that an embassy was sent from Florence dressed *tutti d'una assisa*, 'to do honour to the king'.[34]

It would be absurd, of course, to leave the impression that comments on contemporary fashions, favourable or otherwise, were uttered for public consumption only by historians. Poets, novelists and, above all, professional preachers had always felt it their pleasure or their duty to praise or reprove the gentlemen and ladies of their day for the things they went about in. Such evidence as may reasonably be extracted from the works of poets and novelists will be discussed later; sermons are more difficult. The earliest examples of sermons concerned with contemporary fashion to have survived date from the fifteenth century, but there is no need to consider that they were then an innovation. The clergy had inherited (as had everybody else for that matter) rules which provided what their promulgators regarded as permanent guides to proper dressing. The successive authors, from those responsible for the Old Testament (especially Solomon) to St Paul and, later, St Thomas Aquinas, had all, however, failed to allow for the fact that the thoughts, expressions and actions of human beings are, and have always been, subject to prevailing fashions – sometimes flatteringly referred to as the 'spirit of the time'.

In 1340, the views of St Thomas Aquinas, who had examined the question of 'modesty in apparel' with his customary thoroughness, would certainly have been familiar, through his highly respected writings, to the chroniclers, almost all of whom were members of religious orders. St Thomas had conducted his inquisition into the clothing of men and of women separately. Where men were concerned, his opinion had been that, while there was nothing intrinsically wrong with fine clothing, deliberately to seek admiration through excessive attention to dress, to spend too much thought on it or to derive undue sensuous bodily pleasure from wearing it were grievous faults, but, at the same time, to court admiration by wearing affectedly coarse or humble clothing was equally reprehensible. In other words, it was not the dress but the attitude to it that was important.[35]

Women, on the other hand, had, he believed, to be much more guarded, because while they should make themselves as attractive as possible to their husbands to keep them from adultery, they really must not go out of their way to lead those to whom they were not married into temptation. After giving the most careful consideration to the opinions of his predecessors, among them the Evangelists, St Cyprian and St Augustine, St Thomas decided that he saw no harm at all in women who dressed themselves in styles suitable to their various stations in life, nor, in fact, in accordance with the general custom; at which point, surely, he loosened the latch on the gate to the approval of changes of fashion.[36]

Furthermore, while he would not regard it as permissible for women to use make-up as a means of falsification, he thought it perfectly reasonable to use it as a means to rectify unavoidable blemishes, especially those incurred by illness. In this he was supported by the regulations issued by the fourteenth-century Church on the use of false hair.[37] St Thomas would even allow women to wear masculine dress in order to escape from an enemy, or if they had absolutely nothing else to put on.[38] Moreover, he could see no real harm in those who made pretty things for women to wear, unless the ornaments they invented were really too fantastic; even here, though, he seems to have allowed a 'perhaps' to creep in. [39]

6 *Weltchronik*, Rudolf von Ems with later additions, *Golden Legend* section. The virgin of Antioch, here confused with St Theodora who, wanting to be a nun, escaped from a brothel, having changed clothes with a soldier. The saint, whose long blond plait shows beneath her mantle, wears the German style of the 1360s.

It would have been difficult for fourteenth-century historians or preachers to find a more recent and equally authoritative opinion than that of St Thomas Aquinas; their respective views as to the reactions of the Almighty to the fashions of their day must therefore be regarded as their own.

At no other time in the fourteenth century did fashionable dress receive a comparable consensus of adverse opinion, though later fashions were certainly criticized in their turn. This unique group of emotional outbursts against the clothing of the early 1340s is invaluable in that it completely supports the evidence as to the composition and ornamentation of

12

clothing portrayed in works of art of the period produced in Italy, France and England. What is even more remarkable, is that the change of fashion, once the chroniclers have called our attention to it, can be traced statistically through the accounts of clothing made for members of the royal households of France and England.

Several of the chroniclers, writing of the dress of the early 1340s, stated with assurance that the new fashions in dress had been introduced to a (presumably) hitherto innocent population by foreigners.

It is doubtful, however, that any of them expected the population, once corrupted, to revert to its former style of dress when the foreigners left. One contemporary historian, the unknown author of the *Chronicon Estense*, records that when the population of Florence turned against the duke of Athens in 1343, some of the noblemen who had followed him, hearing rumours of the uprising, quietly left the palace by night, disguised – *transfigurates vestibus*. The writer does not, alas, tell us what kind of clothing they changed into.[40]

III

The Great Wardrobe and the Round Table

By 1340, the English great wardrobe had been firmly established as the royal department responsible for supplying the court, not only with clothing but also with soft furnishings (very little 'hard' furnishing existed), napery, packing-cases, portable urinals, tents, wax and spices. Its accounts, of which several but by no means all have survived from the fourteenth century, are of two kinds: those concerned with the cost and the quantities of materials of which the clothing and the furnishings were made, and those which recorded the fees and wages paid to those who made them. Expenses involved in the carrying of the finished articles to the places where they would be needed were sometimes but not always included. The appearance of wax in the accounts is logical; not only were candles required to work by in winter, but sometimes cloth was itself waxed to make it waterproof, and candles 'of Paris' were occasionally costed in with the making of a garment.[1] The inclusion of spices may seem less rational; they probably came under the great wardrobe for the simple reason that the important foreign merchants who supplied expensive velvets, brocades and furs also imported spices.

The term 'great wardrobe' referred not only to the goods and labour involved, but also to the place where the things were made and stored. That it acted as a repository can be seen from the fact that lengths of stuff left over from the régime of an earlier keeper were sometimes issued for the use of a successor.[2] In the 1340s, the great wardrobe seems to have led what must have been a rather uncomfortable existence, for it moved constantly from one house to another in London, though it was always situated either in or near Lombard Street or the Tower.[3] From 1338 to 1340, it was actually established in Antwerp, but that was the last time it functioned overseas.[4] During the period to be considered here, therefore, apart from this one absence, the great wardrobe was situated in London, though not always under one roof.

Soon after the middle of the thirteenth century, the great wardrobe could be seen to be emerging as a sub-department of the more important umbrella organization – the wardrobe. The adjective 'great'

did not imply greater standing, for the great wardrobe remained for a long time a subordinate department which concerned itself with more limited aspects of the royal expenditure than did the wardrobe itself. Occasionally indeed, some items which seem appropriate to the great wardrobe still appeared in the accounts of the wardrobe, to which, for a long time after its first emergence, the great wardrobe continued to render its accounts. It was not until 1324 that the situation was tidied up and accounts of the great wardrobe were required to be submitted direct to the Exchequer, by which time its chief officer had been designated keeper (*custos*) or clerk (*clericus*), terms which in this case seem to have been used indiscriminately. Letters of appointment of keepers during the reign of Edward III were enrolled variously in the Fine Rolls and the Patent Rolls for reasons which need not be discussed here.[5] At the beginning of the reign, keepers received an annual fee of £20, which was increased in various ways, though not apparently officially, as the reign progressed. Annual accounts of the great wardrobe began at Michaelmas, but did not always run for a complete year; an account of 1343–4 which started at Michaelmas ended on 1 August, for example.[6]

Keepers or clerks of the great wardrobe were given a staff of assistant clerks which varied in number, presumably according to circumstances. The largest number at any one time was six, which was exceptional.[7] The keeper was also responsible, of course, for tailors and their assistants, armourers (who were employed on a slightly different basis), tent-makers and spicers, as well as for assistants who worked under these specialist heads of departments, sometimes on a permanent basis, sometimes by the day. John Marreys, who appears in the great wardrobe accounts of the early 1340s as the king's tailor (*cissor*), is referred to in the English translations of the Patent Rolls as the 'king's yeoman'.[8] It has been pointed out elsewhere that the nineteenth-century translators of the State Papers faced considerable problems in arriving at English equivalents for the shifting social groups assembled under Latin terms in the original rolls, where John Marreys was rated as a *vallettus*. It was probably normal for royal tailors to be given extra perquisites; in 1348, for instance, John Marreys was appointed to the office of alnager (inspector of measurements) of canvas, linen, napery and several other cloths, an office which, presumably because he was too busy, was actually carried out by a deputy; in 1349, he was given an opportunity of further increasing his income by a grant which had nothing at all to do with tailoring.[9]

The armourers, whose workrooms were permanently established at the Tower during this time, came under the management of the clerk of the great wardrobe, but they functioned as a completely separate body. Embroiderers seem always to have worked under the armourers rather than the tailors, and garments which, though not necessarily to be worn on military occasions, were required to be embroidered, seem always to have been sent to the Tower for the work to be carried out. This may have been partly because most embroidery involved the use of metal – gold or silver – thread, sometimes issued direct to the armourers, but it was certainly also because the greater part of royal embroidery at this period appeared on banners, pennants, horse-cloths and clothing actually made to be worn with armour. Some of the king's armourers, among them John of Cologne, already included *brodaria* among their duties as early as 1330.[10]

The embroiderers worked side by side with draughtsmen and painters, who not only provided them with designs and patterns for their work but themselves carried out painted decorations, especially on banners and housings which were never destined to be embroidered, as well as on wall-hangings and bed-curtains. Artisans working for tailors and armourers appear in the accounts as valets (*valetti*), a general term for servants employed in the royal household and one which clearly made no distinction between the tailor-in-chief, such as John Marreys, and those who worked under him.

By comparing a sequence of accounts of the great wardrobe, beginning with an unpublished group concerned with Edward's coronation early in the year 1327, Philippa's coronation in March 1330, an account of her extensive liveries of 1333, a fairly long though mutilated later account of 1338–9, two accounts of 1342–3 (all of these also unpublished), and the surviving fragment of an expense account of 1343–4, consisting of one mutilated membrane published by Sir Nicholas Harris Nicholas in 1846, in *Archaeologia*, xxxi, it is possible to observe both the development of fashion in the composition of some garments and the change of taste as expressed in combinations of colour and of the materials used during this seventeen-year period.[11]

In the earliest group, of 1327 to 1333, no reference is made to buttons or any other kind of fastening, nor does the word *frounciata* (which it is perhaps permissible to translate as 'frouncing') occur. On the other hand, suits (*robe*) already consisted of tunics and over-tunics, while cloaks and mantles appear under the Latin names still given to them in the 1340s; hoods were already the normal headwear, and the enigmatic corset (*corsettus*) was already being dis-

tributed to court ladies and worn by both the king and the queen. For the suits for the king, gentlemen of the court and servants down to, say, the ferreter's assistant, varying quantities as well as varying qualities of stuffs were supplied. It is evident from the amount of material issued to their tailors that the king and the nobility wore long and ample clothing, the knights clothing which was somewhat shorter and squires and valets at this time quite short suits.[12]

Five or so years later, the expense account of 1337–8 shows that a fundamental change had taken place since 1333.[13] The king himself had begun to order suits of two kinds: long and short. This was a drastic development and one which must have had social implications. That fashions more frequently rise from below than that they descend from above in the social scale can be demonstrated by numerous examples from the eighteenth century until today,[14] and there is no reason to suppose that it was a phenomenon which began in the eighteenth century. In wearing short suits – hitherto the dress of valets and artisans – Edward and his high-born European contemporaries were making a gesture. A similar gesture, more easily interpreted, was made by English aristocrats of the turn of the nineteenth and twentieth centuries when they began, on their country estates, to wear a coarse woollen material known as 'tweed'. That was a fashion which coincided with the acceptance, in England, of a third political party – the Labour Party – representing the interests of the workers but joined by a considerable number of members of the upper class. On the reasons behind the decision (unrecorded and almost certainly unconscious) taken by European aristocrats of the 1340s to adopt the short dress of the rank and file (military as well as civilian), it is not the business of this study to speculate.

Nor was the issue of short as well as long suits to the king of England in 1337–8 the only indication of a change towards the kind of clothing condemned by contemporary chroniclers and revealed in the great wardrobe accounts. In this fairly long but badly damaged account of the eleventh and twelfth years of the king's reign, buttons are, for the first time, mentioned in a surviving account in relation to the king's suits.[15] Although they are mentioned, however, the function they fulfilled is not. Some suits are described not as buttoned (*botonata*), but 'with' buttons, which may mean that buttons were used only for the sleeves, the usual way of doing them up by this time. Examples of one or two entries in this account can be translated as follows: '1 short suit of red mixed cloth for the King, a gift of the lord W. Northampton, made and lined with fur, with silver gilt buttons and jewels in the form of doublets worked on the courtpiece of the same';[16] '1 long suit of four garments and one short suit of two garments made and lined with fur for the King'. Only one or two padded tunics or over-tunics, made in John of Cologne's – the king's armourer's – department, and almost certainly designed to be worn with parade armour, are described as being open over the chest (*ante pectum*) with large buttons of silk and silver gilt. Of the suits supplied by the tailor, whose

15

name is illegible but who must, at this date, have been Nicholas Wight, perhaps half are referred to as 'with buttons'; no buttons are mentioned in connection with other suits.

In an expense account of 1342–3, submitted by Thomas Cross (or 'de Crosse'), clerk of the great wardrobe,[17] the picture has changed again. The account is for the king's clothing from Michaelmas and covers the year during which Lionel of Antwerp, a child of four years old, was betrothed to the lady Elizabeth de Burgh, of about the same age.[18] Special clothing for the king and members of the court circle to wear at two tournaments held during that year, one at Dunstable and one at Northampton, is included in the account.

By this time 'frouncing', which was not referred to in the expense account of four years earlier, had certainly come into fashion. It must have meant stuff that was gathered up in the manner referred to in the *Grandes Chroniques*[19] – presumably the stuff of the tunic below the waist. The actual term, if not the fashion, may have been picked up during the king's residence in Antwerp, where the great wardrobe had been temporarily situated between 1338 and 1340. At the time of the present account, after the return of the great wardrobe, normal tunics which buttoned down the front, as distinct from those to be worn with armour, must still have been a novelty, because most entries now mention the position of the buttons. Beginning with clothing for which John Marreys was responsible, the account opens by stating that it concerns his supervision and expenses involved in the making, cutting, lining with fur,[20] trimming and embroidering divers suits, tunics and super-tunics and other various things both for the king and for certain nobles and others. This is immediately followed by four long and four short suits lined and short over-tunics frounced – *frounciata* – and buttoned in front over the chest – *ante pectum* – for the king for the feasts of All Saints, the Purification and Easter. A short suit for Pentecost, a warmer time of year, follows: it is not fur lined but merely lined. Attached to it, presumably as one of the four garments, was a short, frounced over-tunic, buttoned in front. Another suit, this one long but also of four garments, which included a short frounced over-tunic, was given to the king at about the same time by his eldest son, Edward, duke of Cornwall.[21] Short over-tunics frounced and buttoned 'in front' abound in this account, either as a part of a suit or singly, and at one point, not an over-tunic but a frounced and buttoned tunic was given by the king to his tailor, John Marreys. It was made of Fries cloth, a simple inexpensive stuff, and lined with fur but although the suit had been made of a cheap cloth and the fur was no doubt humble, John Marreys had seen to it that with its frouncing and buttons it was up to date.

Immediately following this entry comes one for a tunic and a hood, and a large cloak – *cloka* – frounced and buttoned in front. It is just possible that the frouncing and buttoning belonged to the cloak but this is unlikely; they were probably used on the hooded tunic, made of the same stuff. Other aspects of this extremely important account will be discussed

in a later chapter; but what is important to emphasise here is that in comparing it with its 1337 – 8 counterpart it becomes apparent that not only had frouncing come into fashion during the very short interval that separated them but that tunics as well as over-tunics were now of necessity buttoned down the front. At this period the frounced skirt of the tunic was still full enough to enable it to be left open in front, but even tunics with closed skirts could be pulled off over the head because the waist line was set very low and the skirt itself was not tight. This was to change with tunic skirts tightened so that the process of undressing involved awkward contortions, testified by various chroniclers who insisted that it was almost impossible to undress without help.

Like his account of 1342–3, the surviving fragment of Thomas Cross's succeeding account (published in *Archaeologia xxxi*) is mainly concerned with clothes for the king's person, though it does include some furnishings. Whereas the account of a year earlier broke down some of the costs so that it is occasionally possible to discover payments to individual workers, the *Archaeologia* account records only the total cost of making each garment or suit of garments. It has already been pointed out that although expense accounts usually mentioned the materials of which the various clothes were made, inventories of the purchase of those materials were drawn up separately.

The heading of Thomas Cross's expense account of 1343–4, written in the usual abbreviated Latin, survives on one damaged membrane. It is published in its original form and translated reads:

> Various expenses of the great wardrobe of the Lord Edward third after the Conquest in the time of Thomas Cross clerk of the same wardrobe beginning at the feast of St Michael in the eighteenth year of the reign of the same Lord the King and the first day of August following on which day *dominus* (sic) John Charnels took over the said office.[22]

Above this heading, Nicholas Harris Nicholas, who wrote a foreword to the published account, added his own heading, in English, of course. His dates read: '. . . from the 29th of September 1344 to the 1st of August 1345'.[23] The earlier date, Michaelmas 1343 to 1 August 1344 is confirmed, however, not only by the date of the Round Table tournament which is referred to in the account itself, but also by entries in the Patent Rolls which show plainly that Thomas Cross retired on 1 August 1344, to be succeeded immediately by John Charnels and that Charnels himself retired from the office in 1345 to become Constable of Bordeaux.[24]

Like the previous account, the *Archaeologia* account shows that almost all the clothing was supplied specifically for one of the feasts in the calendar on which, traditionally, the royal family and important members of the court circle appeared in new clothes. It opens with John Marreys's expenditure on the making of clothing for the king during the relevant months, from the beginning of October to the end of July. The total sum, for fees and wages, amounted to

£1,762 3s. 9½d. but this obviously included the lists of things which must have appeared on those membranes which no longer survive but which must have followed the tailor's initial list of expenditure on clothing. As it survives, the tailor's account shows that nineteen suits consisting of from four to six garments were made for the king and, in addition, seventeen separate tunics were made for him, a cloak and a mantelette – *mantilletum* – as well as four summer over-tunics. Seven of the suits had been made for the feasts of All Saints and Christmas, four for Easter and six for Pentecost. As in the previous account, all the suits were specified as being either long or short.

Brief as the surviving part of the account is, it marks even more than its predecessors a chronological advance for it contains what can fairly be described as a new dimension in that, in relation to two distinct types of garment, it literally acknowledges the existence of two fashions: a new and an old. The first of these fashions appears in reference to what, it seems, would have been breeches or drawers of some kind which, as described here, must rather, perhaps, have resembled quite short 'divided skirts', designed to be worn under the new short tunics and to fit well under the skirts of the tunics themselves.

These garments are listed with the linens, a usual practice where under-clothing, shirts and breeches (*braccae*), for instance, were concerned. In this account they are, as was customary, described as being in pairs and are called *robae*, presumably in the Italian sense of 'things' and probably out of delicacy; this too was quite usual in English (though not in French) great wardrobe accounts. In this 1343–4 account the *robae* cost 14d. a pair to make and appear in the following entries: 'Six pairs of linen *robarum* for the king made frounced and lined in the new fashion [*de novo modo*], each pair xiiijd.vijs.' These are followed immediately by: 'twelve pairs of linen *robarum* made for the king in the old fashion [*de antiquo modo*] each at vijd a pair'. From the substantial difference in price and the fact that the 'old-fashioned' garments were neither frounced nor lined, it seems reasonable to conclude that those in the new fashion served a different purpose and one which had only recently made itself felt. Presumably the earlier pattern of unlined under-drawers would have been perfectly adequate for wear under long gowns.[25]

Whatever these particular things were, in this account they are followed by other linen objects for personal use, familiar from earlier accounts and these in turn are followed by a return to, among other items, short frounced and buttoned tunics and long tunics not described as being either frounced or buttoned. After these, and some hose of various cloths, the second of the two types of garment to belong to a new fashion appears. In most great wardrobe accounts the feast of Pentecost seems to have been the occasion for the introduction of summer clothing and it is among the garments made for Pentecost that a shirt (*camisia*), lined throughout, frounced and made in the new style (*de novo modo*)

occurs, followed by an entry for two shirts for the king, lined throughout, frounced and buttoned down the front as far as the knee (*ad genua*), with long lined sleeves reaching the hand (*ad manum*) and buttoned up the forearm (*ad cubitum*). Each of these shirts cost 2s. 4d. to make. Here, then, is another innovation: a garment buttoned down as far as the knee, not simply over the chest (*ad pectum*).

It seems probable, since shirts are not normally described as being lined, and would, indeed, as washable garments be very impractical if they were, that those referred to are not shirts in the ordinary sense at all, but are, in view of the careful description of the position of the buttons, designed to be worn as an outer garment, either for a special occasion such as the Round Table, or else in hot weather. They very likely corresponded to some *camicie* made at almost exactly the same date in France and recorded in a French account to be discussed later.

The frounced and buttoned shirts cost 2s. 4d. each to make, as compared to a tunic with a hood, frounced and buttoned and lined with fur, which cost 2s. 6d. The relatively high cost of the shirts may perhaps imply that work on the extra buttonholes, from the waist down, was expensive.[26] It is noticeable that long and short suits cost the same to make; those consisting of six garments and lined with fur were usually reckoned by John Marreys at 12s., and this may well be because the long suits, not described as frounced, in spite of their longer seams, involved no more work than the short suits with their additional frouncing. Suits consisting of four instead of six garments cost 10s. to make at this time – the prices of complete suits do not seem to have increased since the previous account was drawn up, but it must be remembered that the expense accounts cover labour only.

It would be unwise, however, to draw definite conclusions from simple comparisons where costs were concerned, because they obviously varied in the great wardrobe, not only according to the number of garments included in the suit and the presence or absence of fur lining, but also in regard to the precise standing of the wearer and perhaps to the occasion for which a suit or a single garment was intended; to, in fact, the quality of the workmanship and the degree of elaboration and therefore of workmanship demanded. When, for example, three fur-lined tunics, of green cloth of Brussels, frounced and buttoned, were made for the king and two of his knights to wear at the Dunstable tournament of 1343, the king's tunic cost 5s. 4d. to make, but those of the knights only 20d. each.[27]

It is worth summarizing the important differences in wording which appear in the great wardrobe accounts of 1337–8, 1342–3 and 1343–4 – a small but significant indication of the acceptance of the new fashion. In the earliest of the three, buttons are mentioned but their position is not specified; in 1342, when he entered a buttoned tunic or over-tunic, John Marreys felt it necessary to state that it was buttoned 'in front' and often to add 'over the chest'. Two years later, he was content to state simply 'buttoned'. The progression was therefore from 'with buttons', through 'buttoned in front over the chest' to 'buttoned', and, finally, to a single example of a tunic for the king 'buttoned in front down to the knee'. That the introduction of buttons down the front may not have occurred anywhere much before this time may be judged by a sumptuary law of Lucca, issued in 1336, which had included the direction that the *guarnacca* could be fastened across the chest so long as the fastening did not involve the use of pearls, and that the sleeves of the *gonella* could be closed with buttons of silver or silver gilt. The actual phrase, 'Tutte potevano affibbiare la guarnacca . . .', makes it absolutely clear that the front fastening would be some sort of pin or brooch.[28]

The dogged reiteration of the terms 'short', 'buttoned' and 'frounced' surely means that none could be taken for granted as a part of the traditional dress, but were an indication of a fashion still comparatively new. They are, in fact, the only features of the dress to be emphasized in this way at this period. Sleeves, for instance, were presumably long and close-fitting, but there was evidently no need to mention the fact; tunics and over-tunics were cut to fit closely round the back of the neck, but this, too, could apparently be taken for granted.

Together therefore with the appearance of frouncing, with the reference to a new and an old fashion and, most important of all, with the adoption of short tunics by the upper classes, the great wardrobe accounts of the period contain statistical confirmation of the arrival of the short tight clothes which so much shocked Villani and his peers. They were none of them, of course, concerned with the design of clothing of working people, which had always been comparatively short, but with the impropriety of its adoption by members of the upper class – courtiers and knights. In the great wardrobe accounts of Thomas Cross of the beginning of the 1340s, the English king's short suits are as numerous as his long ones.

The accounts and inventories of the great wardrobe were summarized annually and at considerable length in the Exchequer, where short rolls, consisting of two membranes and written on both sides, were issued annually and sewn into files covering a number of years; in some cases, a single year was covered by more than one of the short rolls.

A substantial file which includes rolls from the final years of the reign of Edward II and continues well into the time of John Cook's keepership of the great wardrobe, provides a rather alarming picture of the moment of Thomas Cross's retirement, when entries for a number of great wardrobe years jostle each other in what today seems a random sequence and clearly demonstrate that lengths of stuff from as much as five and six years earlier were being issued at the time when the clothing for the Round Table festivities was being made.[29] The annual rolls are now numbered as though they were single membranes (although, in fact, each contains two sewn together), and on the dorse of membrane 35, in the position where the name of the current clerk and the year of the account were customarily entered, the name of Thomas Cross appears, but the last digit of the

year – xviij – was washed out so that it reads 'xvii', though the elongated last 'i' can still be seen as a ghostly shadow. This is the year of the *Archaeologia* account.[30]

On the next membrane, 36, John Marreys first appears in succession to Nicholas of Wyght, the king's former tailor, and it is here that a suspicion is confirmed that the new fashion, although the new clothing was shorter, was being claimed to involve more work, for John Marreys states that, in respect of a super tunic and cloak for the king, the present fashion 'demandant plures custus circa opatōōs eardem rẹ f'tis', a circumstance that the king noted and agreed.[31]

On 1 August 1344, Thomas Cross relinquished the office of keeper of the great wardrobe, and in the following January arrangements were on foot to provide him with a visible and practical mark of the king's gratitude for his services. On 18 January 1345, the 'chancellor and keeper of the great seal' was 'instructed to present Thomas with the first prebend or living in the king's gift, notwithstanding any mandate of the king to the contrary of any grants or graces previously made to him'.[32] Thomas Cross, whose accounts are consistently orderly in their presentation, apart from the complication of his last year and who has been described as representing 'the sound subordinate official type',[33] was fairly soon after this given various benefits and, finally, the deanery of St Stephen's, Westminster, a modest reward as compared with the promotions of some of his predecessors.[34]

From August 1344, John Charnels took over the keepership of the great wardrobe. Less than a year later, on 8 July 1345, an entry in the Patent Rolls reads as follows:

Whereas John de Charneles, king's clerk, keeper of the great wardrobe, who has now gone to sea with the king on his service, has deputed John de Nesfeld, his clerk, to discharge his office in his absence during pleasure, the king commands all sheriffs, mayors, bailiffs and others to be attending, counselling and helping unto him whenever he requires them.[35]

John did not move the great wardrobe to Flanders as Thomas Cross had done at the end of the 1330s; he must have travelled with the king as a trusted official in his own right. In the event, the king returned to England almost immediately, but three months later John Charnels, in order to take up his new post as Constable of Bordeaux, was replaced as keeper of the great wardrobe by John Cook.[36]

Thomas Cross's two expense accounts are supported by concurrent inventories of the stuffs supplied to the great wardrobe during those four years, though one of them, like the *Archaeologia* account, is mutilated. Inventories of stuffs begin, as a rule, with a list of the most expensive imported woollen long cloths dyed 'in graine',[37] continue with those which are coloured but either dyed in half grain or not dyed in grain at all, these being followed by short cloths, which are in turn followed by striped cloths at this period. Cheaper cloths made in England usually conclude this section. Furs then follow, and then the section devoted to exotic imported silks and velvets. The name of the merchant who supplied the particular length of stuff or consignment of fur often, though not always, precedes the entry. Linens and cottons usually follow the silks, and then come the miscellaneous articles classified as mercery, which include sewing and embroidery threads, small ornaments and trimmings for clothing, buttons and pearls.

Although a careful comparison between the actual amounts of each kind of stuff supplied during each of the periods covered by the great wardrobe accounts might be rewarding, it is enough at the moment to point out that whereas in the 1342-3 inventory twenty-nine lengths of velvet, each containing eight ells, were bought by Thomas Cross, only seven lengths were bought during the years 1343-4. In the earlier account the colours of the velvets are not mentioned, though a few of them are specified as being striped or chequered.

The only reference in Thomas Cross's *Archaeologia* account to velvet clothing is interesting. Following an entry for thirty pairs of hose of various colours supplied for the king at various times, there appears an entry for making a long and a short suit of six garments of red velvet lined and trimmed for the king for the festival of the Round Table held at Windsor *hoc anno*. These two suits included a short frounced and buttoned super tunic lined with ermine. Together these two suits probably accounted for some of the very large amount of velvet bought during the previous year, while, in the same inventory, in the section devoted to furs, there appears an entry for one *cloka* of 369 skins of ermine and one *mantilletum* of 67 skins, in addition to 500 skins for unspecified use.[38] Both the cloak and the *mantilletum* must have formed a part of the two ceremonial suits ordered for the feast of the Round Table.

The prosaic and undramatic appearance in the middle of the *Archaeologia* account of the king's suits for the Round Table feast whets the appetite. A good deal of controversy has surrounded the institution of the Order of the Garter, and into this the Round Table feast has entered. It is probable that the festival at Windsor early in the year 1344 was the first of its kind to be held by Edward III. Arranged at a time when he was manifestly preparing for a major invasion of France to support what he apparently considered to be his right to the French throne, this new version of a famous and romantic custom which had exemplified courage allied to a just cause was a happy inspiration, but it was an occasion which must have involved considerable forethought and preparation. Indeed, this was the case, for, if Edward was to impersonate King Arthur – and a contemporary states categorically that this was his intention – *ibique ritum recolens Arthuri quondam regis Britonum*[39] – he could hardly do so adequately without his crown. His crown, however, had been pawned, together with the queen's and his own second crown, in 1339.

The transaction had been a complicated one,

doubtless made more so by the feeling that respectability as well as cash was involved. The archbishop of Treves, who by his office was an Imperial Elector, and the duke of Gueldres[40] could provide the former; a certain Vivelin Rufus, described as a Jew of Strasbourg, the latter. Sixty-one thousand florins of Florence were to be paid before Palm Sunday of that year, an additional 50,000 before midsummer. The court was at Antwerp at the time, where, presumably, the king would not have been required to appear in state. The pawning of Edward's 'second' crown, and of Philippa's crown as well as some of her other jewels, was a less august affair.

Perhaps with the Round Table in mind the redemption of the crown was, in fact, already being negotiated in May 1343, and in the July of that year Philip de Weston and Hugh de Ulsby were appointed as the 'king's proctors to procure the deliverance of the great crown and other jewels pledged beyond the seas'.[41] On 20 December 1344, an entry in the Patent Rolls consists of an acknowledgement that the king had received from 'Conrad Clippynge, Tidemann Lymbergh, John Clippyng and their fellows, merchants of 'Almain', his great crown which by his order they had lately had from Master Paul de Monte Fioram by indenture between him and the king's clerks, Philip de Weston and William de Northwell, of the one part and the said Conrad, Tirus de Wolde, Albert Clippynge and the said Tidemann of the other part for 45,000 gold crowns which amount to 8,062 £ 10s of sterlings . . .';[42] from which it is clear that the merchants of Almain (which signified the north Netherlands as well as Germany) had been persuaded to produce enough money out of their profits from English wool and Flemish cloth to satisfy both the archbishop of Treves and the Jew of Strasbourg.

The matter did not end there. On 16 January in the new year 1344, from Ditton on Thames near Windsor, an acknowledgement was issued over the privy seal which stated that 'the king received a crown of his of gold and precious stones, which was in the custody of Philip de Weston, king's clerk and which by letter the king commanded him to deliver to Henry de Ingleby, king's clerk, by indenture, from the said Henry who brought it by order of the king by word of mouth to Wyndesore Castle, in the same Castle with his own hands on the day of the making of these presents, and acquittance to them both in respect of that crown'.[43]

This must have been the king's second crown, redeemed just in time, for on 1 January 1344, Edward had caused to be proclaimed a great tournament to take place at Windsor, his birthplace, at which, as was customary, foreign knights were invited to appear. Fearing that they might attach themselves to Edward's cause, the French king, Philippe VI de Valois, forbade the attendance of French knights and is said to have arranged a Round Table of his own to keep them at home.[44] The tournament, again as was customary, was to last the best part of a week, starting, according to the chronicler Adam Murimuth, on Monday 19 January: the Monday before the Conversion of St Paul.[45] Rymer called it the Monday after St Hilary, whose feast is held on 14 January.[46]

In either case, the date would account for the sense of urgency which pervaded the official acknowledgement of the handing over of the crown on 16 January, on an order 'by word of mouth' and the delivery on the day of 'these presents'.[47]

Murimuth says that the company assembled on the Sunday of that week, on which day the king appears to have held an opening banquet attended by two queens – Philippa, Edward's wife, and Isabella of France, his mother – as well as by nine countesses, the wives of the military earls, *et uxores burgensium Londoniensium*, so presumably citizens' wives were there too. The prince of Wales, earls, barons and knights were seated in tents and elsewhere for this liberal feast, at which the food was both delicate and abundant.[48]

On the three days following, there was jousting at which the king and nineteen of his knights held the field against all comers, and then, on the Thursday, very early in the morning – *circa horam primam* – the king vested himself in royal and ceremonial robes covered by a mantle of costly velvet – *mantellum de felveto pretiosissimum* – with the royal crown on his head. The queen was already arrayed in noble state and, accompanied by the assembled company of men and women, they walked in solemn procession from the castle to the chapel, where they heard mass. Henry, earl of Derby, seneschal of England, and William, earl of Salisbury, marshal of England, carried their wands of office; the king, his sceptre. It was on this day that Edward held his first Round Table.

Roughly translated, this account has been put together from two variants of the *Continuatio Chronicorum* by Murimuth, who died in 1347 and who was therefore writing of an event he may well have heard of at first hand.[49] The variants extend but do not contradict each other except as regards the date, which varies between 19 January and 3 February as the Sunday on which the week of jousting began. The king was certainly at Windsor on 16 January, when he issued an order for ships to be searched for smuggled wool, but the court had spent Christmas at Woodstock, so Meaux is in error in saying 'round about Christmas'[50] for the Round Table festival. Thomas Cross's account for the carriage of clothes and bedding from London to Woodstock was 3s. 4d.; from London to Windsor for the tournaments, 3s.[51]

Edward's suits of red velvet for the Round Table had occupied seven furriers for three days and two others for one day each, working with the greatest speed – *cum summa festinacione* – cutting, sewing and trimming 102 tunics, all with hoods, for the king's squires and men-at-arms, together with 16 tunics with hoods for his minstrels (mentioned by Murimuth as playing trumpets and kettledrums), all made for the Round Table festivities. Each tunic, lined with fur and buttoned in front, cost 10d. to make. The only other garment stated in the account as having been made for the Windsor jousts in which he had taken an active part is an unlined black tunic for the king.[52]

Judging from the impression it made on contemporary chroniclers, the whole thing had been a success, but the end of the week of festivities did not see the end of the business connected with getting the crowns back from the Continent, nor of the people involved in the transaction. A belated entry in the Patent Rolls for 10 March 1344, issued from Westminster, records the appointment of the king's merchants, Thomas de Melcheburn and William his brother, to bring the great crown secretly and safely to him;[53] an entry in the Close Rolls a month earlier, on 1 February, from Westminster not Windsor (which suggests that the Windsor week was already over) records the appointment of Thomas de Melcheburn as mayor of the wool staple at Bruges, a lucrative job, and evidently a reward for his efforts.[54] In spite of this official position, however, Thomas Melchburn was still trading in his own right in Flanders – sixteen striped cloths from Louvain were bought from him for the great wardrobe in 1344.[55] On 25 April, 'in recompense of his great labour and diligence about the deliverance of the great crown', William, Thomas's brother, was granted an annuity for life of £20 out of the customs of the port of Boston.[56] In June of the same year, cash payments were made to merchants of Almain, among them Tidemanns de Revele (Reval, now Tallinn, was to become one of the most important Hanse towns on the Baltic).[57] Actual payments in cash by the king to anybody at this date were exceedingly rare, most of the innumerable merchants to whom he was in one way or another indebted were rewarded with permits to export wool from England to the Netherlands or to Italy, but the negotiations over the return of the great crown were evidently considered to have been of prime importance.

Edward was not unique in pawning his crown. The king of Norway, Magnus Smek, who was excommunicated by the pope in 1355 for failing to pay his debts, had already pawned his two crowns to the city of Lübeck for a modest loan.[58]

IV

English and French Royal Clothing in the Early 1340s

For reasons which are difficult to explain but easy to apprehend, embroidery has always been and continues to be valued more highly than weaving, except in peasant communities, where imported woven cloths were always luxuries. Both embroidery and woven textiles can be produced by a single craftsman; both can be composed of either the cheapest or the most expensive substances, ranging from jute to gold and silver threads and silks coloured with rare dyes. A rich, varied and even three-dimensional surface can result from either method, and, in exceptional circumstances, one may be mistaken for the other: the St Cuthbert orphries in Durham, for instance, were thought of at one time as being too fine in scale to have been worked with a needle and were regarded as having been woven. Nevertheless, the highest dignitaries in the Church and the state have always chosen to appear on the most important and ceremoniously solemn occasions in clothing that has depended for its magnificence on embroidery.

Embroidery is a slower but less laborious process than weaving. The needle brings the worker into closer contact with his material than does the loom, which, even when handled with the most creative freedom, produces a more mechanical final result than the technique which depends on a multiplicity of single stitches. At Napoleon's coronation, the velvet of which Josephine's mantle was made cost 800 francs, the embroidery on it 16,000.[1] In the English great wardrobe accounts of the fourteenth century, the actual number of days worked by embroiderers on a garment or a suit are almost always listed in detail, whereas the time spent by tailors and their assistants on their making is mentioned only rarely.

In the English accounts of the early 1340s, referred to in the previous chapter, some embroidered garments appear, and, perhaps to emphasize their importance, not only the time spent on the workmanship but the actual patterns which were worked are often carefully described. Apart from the frouncing and buttoning and the almost ubiquitous lining with fur or silk, embroidery is the other specific feature of fashionable dress to be recorded in detail in the accounts of these years. Most of the embroidered masculine garments were directly associated with jousts, and it is noticeable that the red velvet suits lined with ermine which Edward wore for the Round Table banquet were not, apparently, embroidered, which may imply that, although some were short, they were on the whole traditional in character and depended on their ermine trimming to establish them as appropriately royal. In fact although, as compared with the earlier years of his reign, the use of embroidery had definitely increased by this time, it was still being used sparingly. In July 1330, a suit of violet velvet embroidered with gold squirrels had been made for queen Philippa to wear for her churching after the delivery of her first-born child – Edward of Woodstock – but it was probably a mark of the economical habits of the impoverished English court at the time that, among five or six important suits made for her coronation and to celebrate the birth of her son, this purple velvet suit was the only one to have been embroidered.[2]

When Thomas Cross drew up his accounts for the year 1342–3, England was still poor, but the king's ambitions made a good show at court imperative and John of Cologne's department at the Tower, which had been responsible for the embroidery on the queen's squirrel suit more than a decade earlier, now included in its own departmental expenses the cost of embroidering a *guyt* for the queen and two *guyts* – *duas guytas* – for her two daughters to wear at the tournament at Dunstable, an event of considerably less importance than the birth of an heir to the throne.

The queen's *guyt*, which is more recognizable in its later spelling as 'ghita',[3] is described as having been made of scarlet cloth of red colour, a gift of the king, powdered with a design made up of squares of enamel, worked with gold thread and, in the middle of each enamel square, a quatrefoil of pearls with a ring in its centre.[4] Fifteen ounces of gold and silver in the form of plate and thread were used on this work. The charges for what seems to have been an excessively large number of embroiderers for several days' work on this garment are listed, but in so confused a way that it is safer simply to quote the total cost, which, including a furrier working for two days on its lining at 6*d*. a day, amounted to £3 0*s*. 3*d*. The daily wage of the embroiderers appears to have ranged between 10*d*. and 2½*d*., but 10*d*. sounds too high as payment to any embroiderer, however skilled, and more probably referred to the wage paid to the designer of the work; in 1330, painters employed in the armourers' department at the Tower were paid at that rate.[5]

The ghitas for the two princesses, made of black cloth, also a gift from the king, were, like the queen's, powdered with enamel squares and embroidered in gold, but there is no mention of pearls. The embroidery must in fact have been less elaborate because the wages of the embroiderers came to £3 4*s*. 9*d*. for the *two* ghitas. The squares of enamel, mounted with pearls for the queen and used without pearls for the princesses, must have been distributed over the whole surface of the ghitas, as the word powdered – *pudrata* – explains. The motifs were almost certainly regularly spaced to produce the type of strictly geometrical pattern which would have conformed to the taste for geometrical patterns in the woven silks of the time, most of them probably from Lucca.

The Dunstable tournaments, for which the ghitas seem to have been made, were held in honour of the betrothal of Lionel of Antwerp, the king's second son, to Elizabeth de Burgh, an event which was later to bring him the dukedom of Clarence.[6] The tournaments, opportunities for prolonged appearances by members of the royal family in front of a wide public, were, to judge from the elaborate clothing ordered by the king to wear on successive days, almost as important as the betrothal ceremony itself, but the king's suit for the actual day of the betrothal is specified as being long at a date when short suits were becoming more and more popular so that it seems probable that, for a traditional ceremony, a long suit would still be correct as royal dress. The suit was lined with silk (suitable for July) and involved some goldsmith's work in its fastenings.[7]

An inventory of materials bought during the same year – 1342–3, the year covered by this account of Thomas Cross's for the making of the royal clothing – has survived.[8] The two parallel accounts cannot be safely integrated, however, because the purchase of stuffs must necessarily have preceded the making of the clothing. Nevertheless, the existence of an inventory of the same date serves as an indication as to the general taste of the time, and from it it is possible to discover, for instance, that pearls were purchased as large, at 3*d*. each (165 were bought that year), as small, at ½*d*. each (more than 2,000 were bought), and as minute, at 13*s*. 5*d*. the ounce. Leaf gold and gold – *soudatum* – for casting as buttons or for pressing into moulds as small ornaments in low relief, were bought in fairly large quantities. *Soudatum* is transcribed throughout the *Archaeologia* account as 'sondatum', a meaningless word; *soudatum* is the normal term for gold used in ornamenting clothing in the great wardrobe. In the same section of the 1342–3

inventory, there also appear 400 small doublets – *doubletta* – and 164 pieces of enamel – *aymell* – on silver.

A more interesting comparison can be made between the clothing made for members of the English royal family and the corresponding clothing made at about the same time for the royal family of France, for which an account survives from the year 1342.[9] As it had happened in England, so in France it was in the early fourteenth century that a special department for the supply of royal clothing and household effects, headed by a professional officer responsible for its conduct, could first be said to have emerged. Judging from surviving records, the first man to hold the post of *Argentier* (which roughly corresponded to that of clerk of the great wardrobe) was Geoffroi de Fleury, nominated in 1317 to draw up the accounts of those aspects of the king's household (the *Hospitium regis* or *Hôtel du roi*) which concerned clothing, soft furnishings and, in addition, household silver, some cooking utensils and spices. De Fleury had, in fact, already rendered his first account of *Argenterie* a year earlier; it began with supplies for the journey to Paris of Philippe, count of Poitiers, on 22 July 1316, to prepare for his coronation at Rheims in the same year; he was to be known as Philippe le Long.[10] Until that time, the duties of *Argentier* had been performed by various officers holding other posts in the king's service.

The argenterie accounts, parallel to the great wardrobe accounts of England, were rendered to the royal treasurers, who were, in France, responsible for actually placing the orders for goods appearing on the lists drawn up by the argentier, who himself calculated the quantities required and their prices. Now and again, however, as also happened in England, orders were placed directly with merchants on mandates from the king.

A further parallel with the clerks of the great wardrobe can be seen in the promotions accorded to some of those who held the position of argentier. Geoffroi de Fleury, for instance, was ennobled in 1320; three years later, a successor, Guillaume de Mousterel, was appointed argentier; and in 1339, de Fleury was promoted to the office of a royal treasurer.[11]

The fourteenth-century inventories and other English accounts of the great wardrobe are, for the most part, enrolled on membranes of parchment sewn together and originally unnumbered, though fairly recently in most of them the membranes have been numbered for convenience by hand.[12] The French accounts too were enrolled, but, as sometimes happened in England as well, they were later cut up into folios and bound as volumes. The English and French accounts are also alike in that many of those which have survived are not complete but are fragments, some more substantial than others.

A short but apparently complete account, published in 1874 in his *Nouveau Recueil de comptes de l'Argenterie* by Louis Douët D'Arcq, is a *compte particulier* of 1342, for cloth of gold and silk, submitted by one of the mercers by royal appointment, a merchant of Lucca whose name (except in documents in Latin) almost always appears as Edouart

Tadelin. The *compte* comprises goods delivered on the order of Guillaume de Mousterel (whose name is very variously spelt), at that time argentier.[13] From the summary with which it ends, it is clear that this account refers to textiles and 'mercery' for which Tadelin had received payment in March 1341 by order of the treasury, based on de Mousterel's list. The total amounted to £2,413 9s. 4d. in the currency of Paris.[14]

Involved in this typical account were, therefore, three people: one of the king's treasurers – *tresoriers* (the number of them at any one time varied, but in the 1330s there were usually two or three) – a mercer by royal appointment and the official argentier. Apart from their salaries, which were good by the standards of the day, the treasurers received from the argenterie the robes and bedding appropriate to their station, the use of three horses when required and, presumably by ancient tradition, a woollen mitten, a deerskin glove, a spoon, two knives, one large and one small, a beaver hat for winter, a felt hat for summer and, in addition, an *écriture*.[15] Apart from the members of the royal family who received clothing and furnishings, other people appear by name in this and some other similar accounts. They are the heads of sub-departments responsible for certain branches of craftsmanship in connection with the various things that were being made.

Édouard Tadelin, the Lucchese merchant who, unlike some of the merchants who operated in England, does not seem to have received robes from the argentierie,[16] evidently had a high reputation in Paris, where his name could still be found repeatedly in accounts of the middle 1350s as a supplier of pearls, cloth of gold, silk and wax.[17] By that time, Guillaume de Mousterel had retired as argentier (he was succeeded in 1348 or 1349 by Étienne de la Fontaine), but his name continued to appear in accounts of the royal household as *nuper argentarius regis*,[18] so that it is plain that a good deal remained to be cleared up after his official retirement.

Tadelin's account rendered in 1342 not only lists the fabrics and mercery together with their quantities and prices and the garments for which each was supplied, but also invariably names the person for whom the garments were destined and the master craftsmen who were responsible for their making. It begins with a delivery to Nicholas du Gal, *coustepointier du Roy*, the head of the sub-department of the argenterie in which all quilted objects, whether garments or bedding, were made. In England, where the same term for this technician was used, his work was carried out at the Tower, probably because quilted garments were so often worn with armour – always made there at this period.

In 1342, Nicholas du Gal, who seems, like John of Cologne and John of Standerwyk, his English counterparts, also to have been responsible for embroidery, was engaged in making furnishings for the king, Philippe VI de Valois; for his eldest son Jean, duke of Normandy, the future Jean II; for the duchess Bonne of Luxemburg, Jean's first wife; for their son Charles, to become, in 1364, Charles V; and, of course, for the queen, Jeanne of Burgundy, as well as for other members of the royal family who are also named in this account.

The second recipient of fabrics is Lucas de Borgne, the king's tailor, whose first delivery consisted of wide *cendaulx de Vermeilz* in grain[19] to line pelicons of sable. The identification of textiles of the fourteenth century, either in the French or in the English accounts, is not at all easy; a few that can to some extent be explained are discussed in Appendix IV, but there is little difficulty in identifying *cendal* or *sendal*, which, it is safe to assume, was, at this particular date, a light-weight silk of plain weave used as a rule for linings and facings in both countries. A curious practice in France at this particular moment was to measure cendal, like sewing threads, by weight, which means that it is a complicated matter to draw any conclusions as to the size or nature of the garment for which the lining was ordered from the quantities given, which are always by the piece and by the ounce.[20] In this instance, the first delivery of *cendaulx* was a gift to the king from the Constable of France at the time, Raoul de Brienne.

Because cendal was a thin, light-weight silk, it seems reasonable to assume that *pelicons* were short capes, usually worn with the fur on the outside. They almost certainly corresponded to the *mantilleta* found in the English accounts, such as the *mantilletum* worn by Edward at the Round Table feast. It gave rise to the much later word, the Anglicized *pelisse* – a short cape.

Long cloaks with the fur on the outer side do not appear at all in representations of upper-class dress in European works of art of this time, but short fur capes do; moreover, when long cloaks are referred to in accounts, they are almost always described as being either lined with fur or else 'single'. But a further difficulty in the identification of the exact form of the *pelicon* occurs in the next entry in the French 1342 account, which is for green cendal not to line – *fourrer* – but to cover – *pour couvrir* – pelicons. This may seem to the English a curious phrase, but its use in Italian references to dress and in French accounts of this kind is relatively common. The cendal must have been used to 'cover' the leather back of the fur capes.[21]

The third entry for the first delivery to Lucas de Borgne of cendal silks is for vermilion cendal *not* in grain *pour estofer* robes for the king. Only seventeen ounces were delivered for this purpose, and again it is important to remember that the term *estofer* must not be thought of in the English sense 'to stuff', but rather to garnish or trim. In this particular case, it may have been used for bindings and facings on the suits. A delicately thin silk was used for facing the inside turnings of a surviving fragment of a sleeve found fairly recently in Puddle Dock, near the site of the great wardrobe when it moved to Baynard's Castle on the Thames.[22] This fragment manifestly belongs to the later fourteenth century; the same silk was used to bind its very small buttonholes and to cover the minute buttons which are set in a row up the lower sleeve. The workmanship throughout is extremely fine, and it would be very reasonable to regard the silk as cendal, which can be found constantly as lining material in English great wardrobe accounts of the time. Cendal, although modest as imported silk, would certainly not have been used for stuffing in the form of padding, for which purpose what is now called cotton-wool, and layers of cotton fabric were specifically ordered for *coustepointier* workers.

In the French account of 1342, wide cendal (*des larges*) appears over and over again. In green, it was supplied for lining the king's suits – *robes* – for those of the king of Bohemia (John, father of Bonne of Luxembourg, duchess of Normandy, who spent most of his time at this period at the French court) and for the king of Navarre – Philippe, comte d'Evreux. These suits, which obviously matched each other, were all made for the feast of Pentecost and, at the same time, wide vermilion cendal was supplied for lining a surcot for the king, for riding. Apart from their manifest interest to students of the history of dress, the French accounts are particularly important for the light they shed on the exact relationship in which members of the court circle stood to the king at the particular time.

No less difficult than the identification of named textiles is the identification of named garments, difficulties which have not, in the past, deterred scholars from offering well-supported, or in some cases ill-supported, theories on the subject. The most important contribution is still indisputably that of the incomparable Louis Douët D'Arcq. In the introduction to his first collection of *Comptes*, published in 1851 from original documents that had escaped destruction during the French Revolution, he drew up two tables which compare the number of skins of miniver used to line the most commonly occurring garments, the first from an account of 1316, the second from one of 1387.[23] By this means the relative sizes of many garments have been established and certain changes in fashion can be observed. What now remains is the task of comparing the quantities of fur and fabrics used for what appear to be similar garments, sometimes with similar and sometimes with dissimilar names, worn at any one moment in the various European centres of fashion.

Douët D'Arcq was astute in choosing to reckon quantities of fur-skins rather than lengths of stuffs; the skins could be relied on to be of more or less the same size, whereas in the early 1340s cendal, for instance, was supplied by the piece in both France and England but in France fractions of the piece were calculated in ounces and in England in ells. Careful scrutiny of the French accounts of 1342 reveals the number of ounces of cendal to the piece at that particular moment but the number of English ells to a piece of cendal has not yet been established. Lengths of stuff in terms of ells varied according to type and, furthermore, the ell itself could vary in length not only from country to country but also in some cases from city to city.[24]

The *super tunica* of the English accounts may well have corresponded to the *surcot* of the French *comptes* but there is no suggestion in the *comptes* of 1342 that a change in fashion had taken place. Not

only is there no reference to old and new fashions but neither are short as compared with long surcots referred to. The buttoning of surcots is not mentioned which probably means that by this time it was taken for granted in France.

Such slight but important differences between the accounts drawn up in the two countries means that they are more valuable when they are studied together than apart. In spite of the fact that they were written in French, problems of identifying individual garments are just as great in the French accounts as they are in the English accounts which are in Latin, for while the English clerks did not, apparently, find it necessary to use a vernacular term for the ubiquitous *tunica*, they showed no hesitation in interpolating English terms for any garments which could not be precisely identified by an existing Latin word. This practice sometimes provides a clue as to the nature of less commonplace pieces of clothing. It has to be remembered, of course, that not only were clerks, in contrast to chroniclers, very inconsistent in their spelling, but that neither did they appear to have felt any obligation to be consistent in the names they gave to the most familiar garments, matters which the treasurers to whom the accounts were rendered viewed, no doubt, with indifference.

The king's *surcot a chevaucher* in the French account of 1342 probably presents no difficulty; the next entry concerns two pieces of *tiercenal azuré* to make a *surcot ront* as a gift from the king to the queen. The adjective 'round' is not used in a similar context in English accounts and although it might seem that it was an indication that by this time in France most garments were buttoned up the front – the term *ront* being used for a garment which was slipped on over the head – *corsets ronts* can be found in the early accounts which belong to the time before front fastenings had appeared in fourteenth-century fashions, so that 'round' must have had some other significance as well. In an account of 1338 in Latin, which records the clothing in the wardrobe made for the young prince Andrew of Naples, there is an entry for a *rotundellus*[25], by which time front fastenings had begun to appear.

Two pieces of stuff were required to make the French queen's round blue surcot of *tiercenal* and since it was probably a silk imported from Italy (from the point of view of price *tiercenal* comes fairly far down in the list), it must have been measured at about eight ells to the piece.[26] It is safe therefore to assume that the queen's round surcot was long, that it reached the ground and that it had, perhaps, a short train. The king's riding surcot used only twenty-six ounces of cendal for its lining from which it would seem, though this is not certain, that it was a short and not a long garment.

Édouart Tadelin's account then moves on to an issue of samite for covering a cushion, to sewing silks in a variety of colours as well as to silks for making ties and laces – *lasnières* – for the king. At this point a subheading states that there follow other things ordered by Lucas de Borgne for the young princes and this begins where the previous section left off, with sewing silks, partly for work on their clothing in general but also, which comes as a surprise, for making ribbon for striping their suits – *ruban pour rayer leurs robes* – a sudden reminder of the current fashion. Striped cloth, a great deal of which was made in Ghent, was a commonplace and indeed, being cheap, was not as a rule used for the clothing of exalted people; stripes decoratively applied in ribbon, however (certainly in this instance made in the workroom by the process known as 'tablet-weaving'), suggests a degree of *haute couture* appropriate to princes of the royal blood.[27]

Throughout this short account are entries for cendal, mainly in red or green but occasionally in other colours, issued for lining suits for the queen and the princes and princesses of France for the important feasts of the year between Candlemass and St John the Baptist. The princes were given *pelicons* and corsets 'covered' with green cendal, and these are soon followed by an entry for two pieces of velvet, one *quenele*[28] and the other *eschiquete* – chequered – in gold and silver to make mi-parti corsets for the said lords, lined with miniver.[29] The chequered velvet cost £70 the piece of Paris currency and the *quenele* £60. Cyprus gold thread for making ribbons as ties for these corsets follows immediately.

A comparison between the queen's *tiercenal*, obviously for a fairly unimportant dress at £12 the piece, and the velvets ordered for the princes' corsets gives some idea of the relative value of the two kinds of stuff – the pieces were probably about the same length, though if anything the velvets would have been the shorter. It gives, however, no indication as to what that very controversial garment the fourteenth-century corset might have been[30] – nor can its size be estimated from the amount of stuff issued in this instance because we are not told how many of the royal princes were given these astonishingly magnificent mi-parti corsets. This section of the account ends with an entry for seven ells of black Irish *sarge* to make their hose.[31]

The corset was worn by members of both sexes in England and France throughout the fourteenth century. In de Fleury's account of 1316 it is referred to several times and more than once as a *corset ront*, which shows that, like the surcot, it might have been sometimes an open mantle or an open gown. The English queen, Philippa of Hainault, had corsets made in 1333 for all her ladies in waiting.[32] In 1338 a green silk *cursettus* was made for the youthful Joanna, heiress to the throne of Naples and, at the same time, another in the same silk for her younger sister Marie. It was usual at the Angevin court at Naples for Joanna, Marie and the eleven year old prince Andrew of Hungary (Joanna's husband who had his own household) to be dressed exactly alike. In this instance, however, Andrew's green silk garment was a *surcottus apertus*, not a corset.[33]

In the English account of 1343–44, published in *Archaeologia*, is an entry for two corsets, buttoned with silk laces and points – *botonata cum laqueis serici et punctibus*, which certainly must have belonged to exactly the same fashion as the splendid mi-parti silver and gold velvet corsets, lined with miniver and tied with ribbons woven of gold thread, made at

about the same time for the French princes. Lined, or 'covered' with cendal, sometimes appearing as a *corset ront*, often lined with miniver, corsets were made for the French king and his queen, for the duke of Normandy (whose two corsets were embroidered), for his duchess and for the king's other daughters-in-law. Corsets of *zetonnine azuré* were made and embroidered for the two daughters of the king of Navarre for the occasion of their mother's 'uprising' or churching, after the birth of the latest addition to the family.[34] *Zetonnine* was probably the French version of the term *zatanys*, which appears in an English Exchequer account of the following year, and which may well have been unfamiliar in England at the time, for it is entered in the account as 's'ici [serici] vocat' zatani' and, although it appears differently spelt, on more than one occasion it is qualified as *vocat'*.[35]

In France, the embroidery on the corsets for the princes was carried out under the supervision of Perrin de Paroy and worked mainly, it seems, in pearls *pour faire greine* – to enrich the surface? The brothers, the three sons of the house of Navarre, were given clothing which must have appeared quite distinctive at the French court for the same occasion of the arrival of the new baby: three embroidered *chemises*, 'faites a point de l'equile de Navarre', lined with vermilion cendal in grain, with orphreys (presumably rectangles of embroidery) worked in pearls. With the *chemises* were three belts, together embroidered with 1,000 round pearls as well as with emeralds and rubies.

The reference to a local type of embroidery, in this case needle-point of Navarre, if not unique at this period, is extremely rare. It has its own importance as the kind of source from which were to grow, over the centuries, those peasant embroideries of Europe whose designs became not merely national but characteristic of single villages. Nor is this the last item relating to the ceremonial clothes given by the French queen to the royal children of Navarre, one of whom, Charles the Bad, was in later years to bring so much distress to the royal house of France, for, among the information about corsets and chemises for their mother's churching scattered through the folios of this account, nearing the end appears *or de la touche*, thin plate of pure gold, to make *gaufres* of goldsmith's work for these several garments which the queen gave to the children of monseigneur de Navarre. These *gaufres*, or wafers, were small ornaments stamped into fanciful shapes from thin sheets of gold or silver-gilt, and either powdered at random, sometimes held by a couple of stitches through a small hole, so that they hung loose all over the garment and caught the light as the wearer moved, or else used to punctuate embroidery worked in a close pattern of silk, pearls or jewels. Sometimes referred to as bezants,[36] a great many of these charming ornaments have survived. They appear frequently in European accounts, bills and other documents of the time. The royal goldsmiths centred round the Hungarian court at Visegrad were particularly famous for their manufacture: an enormous quantity was captured at the battle of Visby, but those were probably made locally.[37] To add to their curious costume, the Navarre boys were also given darts – *dars* – ornamented with pearls.

In spite, however, of the considerable number of corsets mentioned in this account, it is still not possible to deduce either their character or their size from the materials of which they were made. As garments, they baffled Douët D'Arcq, who admitted that he was not able to identify them.[38] What is certain is that they were never considered to be part of a suit of clothes, but were always thought of as separate garments, occasionally accompanied by a hood or by a mantle of some kind.[39] So far as can be calculated from the number of ounces of cendal used to line it, one of the corsets of the queen of France required slightly less for its lining than did one of her *surcots longs*, but such evidence is too slight to be useful.

Following the entries for the clothing made for the occasion of the queen of Navarre's first appearance after the birth of her child, an occasion of the kind always signalled in all the courts of Europe by fine new clothing and the refurbishing of the royal apartments and the chapel, the French account of 1342 returns to listing some of the normal clothes supplied for the main feasts of the year. The previous section actually ends, however, with a note which states that the argentier owed Édouart Tadelin for Perrin de Paroy's bill up to June 1341, which he had paid on behalf of the argenterie, as well as for Perrin's bill up to the same day, the feast of St John the Baptist, in the current year, 1342. There is no evidence, however, to prove that under the departmental headings and sub-headings the entries are arranged chronologically, and although in some instances the occasion for which a certain garment was made is mentioned, in others it is not.

The account of Robert Selles, tailor to John, duke of Normandy, the king's eldest son, follows the first Perrin de Paroy account for embroidery. Once more a great deal of cendal was involved, and at this point it may be suspected that, at the French court, as in the royal courts of England and Naples, members of the royal family appeared at the great feasts of the year for which new clothing was obligatory, dressed in the same colour or colours. Grouped together near the beginning of the account, as we have seen, are entries for green cendal for linings for various suits or garments for the king and the other men of the royal family, both for Easter and for Pentecost. Much later in the account, these two feasts appear again, logically, because it covers a year and a half, but this time azure cendal is issued for lining a corresponding number of garments for the young princes both for Easter and for Pentecost, though in both years separate garments were made for each of the two feasts. Similarly, of the five hoods mentioned in this account, three are of fine violet velvet, two for the queen and one for her sister-in-law, called in this entry Madame de Beaumont but probably Isabella, duchess of Bourbon who, incidentally, like the young princes, wore an azure lining to her *surcot ront* for Easter.

This *compte particulier* is, of course, too restricted in scope to give more than a hint of the heraldic effect produced by this practice, but it proves that it was current at the court of France. In an account of payments made in 1338 to the royal tailors at the court of Naples already referred to, it is recorded that Joanna's tailor, Johannes, had made for her, among other things, a closed and an open surcoat and a hood in violet velvet and exactly similar garments in the same stuff and colour for both her sister Marie and her husband Andrew.[40]

As in all wardrobe accounts, several of Tadelin's entries are tantalizingly inexplicit. Fine green cloth and vermilion velvet to be embroidered as 'coverings' for swords for the king and the duke of Normandy present no problem, nor do pearls issued to Marguerite.de Léry, embroideress, for working eight embroidered buttons and a girdle in the style of a friar's – *seurceinte a Cordelier*; but a piece of wide tan-coloured cendal and the tan-coloured silks to sew it with were ordered for hausses and headdresses – *atours* – for the queen, and as to the nature of these we know nothing. The term *atour* was used in France throughout the fifteenth and sixteenth centuries to signify a headdress, but for the probable meaning of *hausse* it is necessary to look elsewhere.[41] In 1342, both Englishwomen and Frenchwomen were beginning to wear their hair set into stiff plaits placed vertically at each side of the face, and these probably needed some form of internal, if not external, support; references to such small things cannot be found in wardrobe accounts as they were probably contrived within the household itself. Married women also invariably wore veils, but not one is particularized in any of these accounts. Finally, there is only one reference to hats: three ells of green *tartaire* to line summer hats for our lords *des Comptes*, presumably officers of the Chambre des Comptes – the Exchequer – who certainly wore a special livery. It will be remembered that the *tresoriers* were, by custom, issued with both summer and winter hats, and hats for these officers appear in later argenterie accounts. In the early 1340s, most men were wearing hoods, unless they were especially exposed to the weather as, for instance, on the hunting field, so the inclusion of hats for officers of the Exchequer shows that they certainly wore a distinctive dress which did not change with the changing fashion.

Édouard Tadelin, as a Lucchese merchant, was responsible for supplying the silks with which the account is mainly concerned; he does, however, as we have seen, seem to have been to some extent a go-between, or even a private banker, who advanced money to pay bills for the argenterie among others. This appears at the very end of the account as payments on behalf of the argenterie for large orders of linens of Rheims (the finest quality linen in the fourteenth and fifteenth centuries came from there), bought from Berthelin Vassal and Quentin le Chenevacier (canvasman). This consignment of linens is rather vaguely referred to as for the queen's use, but it is important in that the entry for it states that it was costed according to the ell of Rheims. The passage may be translated as follows:

6 pieces containing, according to the ell of Rheims, 418 ells at 6s. the ell of Rheims, amounting to £132 18s. 0d.; 6 more pieces of Rheims [linen], at 8s. (Paris) the ell, amounting to £179 4s. 0d.; 10 pieces of another linen of Rheims containing, in ells of Rheims, 760½ ells, per ell 10s., amounting to £390 10s. 0d. Cost of the whole of the said linens, £692 12s. 0d. ['vj^c iiij^{xx} xij^s parisis'].

Édouard Tadelin's *compte* of 1342 seems to be the only French account to have survived from this period. The types of garment it includes are few: suits – *robes*; surcoats, surcoats for riding, round surcoats and a long surcoat for the queen; corsets and round corsets; *pelicons*; chemises; hose – *chausses*; hoods – *chaperons*; hats – *chapeaux*; *atours* and *hausses*. Except where it is particularly specified that the clothes were made of an expensive silk (the queen and the duchess of Normandy had suits of *tiercemal* and the duchess a suit of fine *camoquoys d'Outremer*), it can safely be assumed that the suits and surcoats for which so much cendal was supplied for linings, and some of the corsets too were either made of fine woollen cloth imported from those markets in the Low Countries which the French court favoured at the time,[42] or else bought at the fairs of Champagne.[43]

The accounts of Thomas Cross and of Edouard Tadelin belong to different categories. The former lists the cost of workmanship and mentions textiles only in order to identify the garments referred to; the latter lists the silks and mercery and their costs in relation to what emerge as corresponding garments. *Robes*, under the same (or almost the same) name, occur frequently in both accounts. *Surcots* and *supertunice* are almost certainly the French and English way of referring to the same, or a very similar type of garment. Both accounts include a *surcot/supertunica* for riding, which suggests a modification of the normal design.[44] Both include corsets, hoods and hose. The *courtpec'* and the *clocha* of the English account have no recognizable counterparts in the French *compte*. Both accounts include elaborate fully lined chemises, referred to in the French account under that name, and as *camicie* in the English account. Both are described in detail, which certainly seems to indicate that they were not altogether familiar as garments, and, indeed, nothing that corresponds to them has so far come to light in earlier or later accounts of either country.

Things worn on the head, at this stage unidentifiable, occur in both accounts. The feminine *hausses* and *atours* in France, in England long and short *couvrechiefs* for the king, the short ones ornamented with stripes sewn on in white silk as well as five *volupior' per capite*, worked in pearls and tied with black ribbons, also for the king.

The French and the English accounts are both exclusively concerned either with clothing worn at a royal court or by a member of a royal family, and the fact that the *courtpec'* and the *clocha* can be found only in the English account is probably simply because no silk was involved in their making, and there would therefore have been no reason for their appearance in the French account. This royal clothing must, of course, have been very different from the rough dress of peasants or artisans. The degree to which it differed from the dress of prosperous middle-class people can be judged by comparing some of the royal garments with those which appear in an inventory drawn up in 1345 for Ponce Clair, lawyer – *jurisconsulte* – and citizen of Valence-sur-Rhône, of the clothing of his late wife.[45] The difference between her clothing and that of the queen and the princesses of France of a year or two earlier (when she would probably have been wearing the clothes) is surprisingly small.

The inventory, which is in Latin, begins with an entry for a sanguine *supertunicale* of scarlet cloth, lined with miniver, evidently part of a suit which also included a tunic and a hood of the same cloth, embellished with six pearl ornaments – *opera perliarum* – and seven silver buttons. There follows a woman's hood – *capucium mulieris* – with embroidery in beaten gold[46] and twenty-one large white pearls and eight silver buttons. Two more hoods appear in the inventory, one of camelin[47] lined with green *sandeli* (which is certainly cendal), the other lined with black cloth.

Madame Clair's wardrobe had also included four corsets. One was short and described as a *corsetum mulieris* and made of camelin of Malines, lined with *gross vair* – grey squirrel; with it was a tunic of the same cloth. The second corset was of two camelins, mi-parti, lined with 'old' miniver (presumably transferred from another garment), and it too had a matching hood. The third corset, also lined with old miniver, was made of green camelin of Bernay, its matching hood trimmed with eleven silver *carcanelli* called, in Tadelin's account, *gaufres* – the small stamped-out metal ornaments of *orfèvrerie*. The fourth corset was of green camelin of Malines lined with cendal.

Thus a little more light is shed on the nature of the corset. In the first place, one is described as a feminine version of the garment, which points to differences between those of the two sexes; in the second place, a short corset was provided with a tunic to match, which must have been worn beneath it to make a complete dress but not a suit of clothing. Two others had matching hoods.

Following the corsets in the inventory are three *gardecorsa*, one of them made of camelin and lined with green cendal; another, of camelin of Montevelier, was lined with *gros vair* and was accompanied by a tunic and a hood to match; and a third *gardecorsum* was of blue – *de persico*[48] – lined with popellus.[49]

That a *gardecorsum* too was a garment which could be worn by either sex is demonstrated by the fact that these accounts of Ponce Clair include an inventory of his own possessions, drawn up in 1348, in which four *gardecorsa* lined with fur appear in a brief list of his clothing. The nature of this garment is not easy to deduce from the extensive documentary evidence for the normal repertory of garments worn in the early 1340s both by royalty and by members of the middle classes when, in English, French and Italian documents respectively, a suit seems to have been made up of: (a) *tunica, cote* or *gonella*; (b) *supertunica, surcot,* or *guarnacca*; (c) hood and mantle, variously named. Single additional garments were the *corsetum, mantilletum* and *pelicon*, as well as a variety of shorter garments: in France and the Netherlands the *cote-hardie*, in Italy the *cotaditta*. *Aketons*, the *court pec'* (or *courtpie*) and the doublet appear frequently in English accounts and, though more rarely, on the Continent too. The *gardecorsum* of Valence-sur-Rhône may simply have been a local version of one of these, a special kind of undertunic; it is unlikely, in view of the fact that it could be worn by a woman, that it was a short waist-length garment.

But the most remarkable feature of the clothing of the wife of the lawyer of Valence is not the fact that it included garments which, apart from the *gardecorsum*, bore the same names as those in the wardrobe of the queen of France but that they seem to have been similar to hers in other respects. Although, except in the case of one or two silks, the Tadelin account of 1342 does not specify the type of cloth that was used for the royal garments, by the beginning of the 1350s *camelin*, of which most of Madame Clair's clothes were made, was the cloth most generally worn by members of the French royal family. Furthermore, those garments which had belonged to Madame Clair were, like those of the queen, lined either with fur or with cendal, which like the queen's,

was often green. Even more interesting is the fact that, again like the queen, she owned a hood with silver buttons embroidered in gold and large white pearls and another powdered with silver ornaments and goldsmith's work.

Nevertheless, similar as members of the French royal family and of the French prosperous middle classes seem to have been in their dress, it is very doubtful whether the queen's tailor would ever have admitted to using 'old' miniver. To Madame Clair, who also wore gros vair, which was much cheaper, miniver would have been precious: to the queen, obligatory. Less than a decade later, Gilles li Muisis, abbot of the monastery of St Martin at Tournai, whose interest in fashionable clothing was intense and charged with emotion, wrote; '. . . today maidservants are ladies and valets are lords. They used often to wear old clothes; valets dressed like servants and wore simple clothing; often they remade their furs . . .'[50] Certainly, both in the fourteenth century and earlier, great emphasis was placed on new fur, for Chrétien de Troyes, writing *Ywain, the Knight of the Lion* at the end of the twelfth century, refers to the gift of a robe of fine red stuff lined with fur with the chalk still on it – the chalk, that is to say, with which the skin had initially been dressed. He writes later of a lady who wears an imperial dress, new ermine and a diadem, all of which suggests that there had long been a traffic in second-hand furs.[51]

V

Court Dress after Crécy

The displeasure of those chroniclers who noticed the change in fashion at the beginning of the 1340s had been mainly aroused by the new tightness of masculine clothing, disapproval which culminated in the disgust expressed by the French author of the *Grandes Chroniques* at the clothes worn by his young contemporaries at the time of the Crécy defeat.

It was certainly Galvano della Flamma's opinion that in Milan as early as 1340 young women had begun to look distressingly masculine, but it was after Crécy that two chroniclers mustered their best invective to describe the clothing of women. Henry Knighton had cited the 1347 tournament at Berwick as just one occasion on which bands of women wearing something resembling masculine attire appeared on the scene, instancing, among other things, their mi-parti tunics. Knighton's voice, raised some time after the event, had been forestalled by another's, the complaint of Gilles li Muisis, abbot of St Martin's at Tournai.[1]

Li Muisis' *Annales* begin in the year 1349; after, that is to say, the Black Death and the appalling massacres of the Jews in the Low Countries. And what can I say, he asks rhetorically, of clothes and their decoration? The men's so tight, so short that their private parts could often be seen beneath them, which was shocking. And what can I say of the dress of the women? Their dress and their ornaments were made in the likeness of men's, so tight that their nude bodies could be seen through their clothing. And they went to church, through the streets, and, by turns, to weddings and funerals with their heads decorated with false hair, wearing horns like beasts. People of all stations of life and of all ages went about in public dressed in clothes and jewels that cost more than their total wealth.

As one reads on, however, it soon becomes clear that on this particular occasion the abbot had, for once, introduced the subject of dress not to stress the errors of the day but to demonstrate the profound mood of repentance which flowed through the country in that same year, 1349, and occasioned the abandonment of such frivolous attire. In city after city of the Low Countries the citizens collected themselves into bands of penitents, distinctive in their dress[2] and uniform in their practice of scourging themselves as they proceeded painfully through the streets. Infected by their example, the abbot continues, men and women everywhere reformed their manner of dressing. The women, he says, laid aside their horns and their *haucettas* and, with this information, provided by an abbot of Tournai, it becomes possible to identify the *hausses* which the queen of France had worn on her head in 1342[3] with his *haucettas* of 1349. There was never of course any necessity for clerks of the wardrobes to define the terms – perfectly comprehensible to themselves – in which their inventories were expressed. When, however, the same terms can be discovered in the writings of chroniclers their universality if not their precise meaning can be assumed.

Our own familiarity with works of art of the middle of the fifteenth century in which appear the immense horned head-dresses at that time in fashion in the north of Europe makes it difficult for us to understand li Muisis' loathing of the tight little plaits of the middle of the fourteenth century, which he saw as horns. It is a subject he returned to again and again elsewhere in his writings.[4] The particular style of dressing the hair of which he complained had actually appeared at the beginning of the 1340s and had merely grown rather stiffer and more aggressive by the end of the decade. If, however, it seems surprising that li Muisis should have continued to be so offended by the brevity and tightness of masculine clothing and by the rigid plaits of hair that framed the cheeks of women so long after both should have become familiar enough to have been acceptable, it must be remembered that by 1346 his sight was already growing so weak that he needed help in casting up his accounts and that by 1349 he was practically blind and dictated everything he composed. By that time he therefore spoke not of what he saw but of memories of his last impressions, when his sight had been good. That at the age of eighty what must have been cataracts on both his eyes were far advanced is not surprising; what, however, must be surprising to most people, is the fact

7 *Luttrell Psalter*. A seemingly English example of cornettes, first fashionable in the early 1340s. See also p. 103.

that in 1351 both cataracts were successfully removed by a local surgeon and he was able to see again. He even recorded that the operation was not particularly painful.[5] He lived a year or two longer, but wrote little more.

Chroniclers whose sight was not impaired did find a new character in the dress of the late 1340s, by which time the constriction and the brevity of the fashion of the beginning of the decade had been accepted by most of them. In fact a very strange modification in the fashion had taken place by the end of the decade, but it was one which was too subtle to be covered by the phraseology in which most of the chroniclers wrote their histories. The change may have been inspired in the first place by a new physical stance that seems to have been assumed in response, perhaps, to the long slim shape of the fashionable torso. At the very end of the 1340s and in the early 1350s, young men began to be portrayed in works of art with their legs placed elegantly and the upper parts of their bodies curved into a serpentine line – the small of the back hollowed and the hip-bones thrust forward – and, before 1355, the style of clothing itself appeared to assist this effect, not only by lowering the waistline further still, though in front only, but also by slightly padding the belly so that it seemed to droop a little over the belt, a characteristic often bestowed by nature on mature men but not on the young. The padding thus enhanced the curve formerly achieved by the stance and lowered waistline alone.

The actual existence of such a practice in high fashion would seem extremely unlikely but for the fact that a similar shape, though more aggressive and set higher on the body, was produced by the 'peascod' padding of the torso in the later sixteenth century. If this was a change which historians would have found difficult to express in words, neither was it a change which would have been revealed either by the quantities and qualities of stuffs with which royal inventories were concerned, nor by any marked variation in the salaries and wages paid to

tailors and their assistants recorded in the great wardrobe or argenterie accounts. It appears clearly, however, in works of art.[6] What, on the other hand, struck the chroniclers as new and reprehensible was not the recondite composition of the new fashion but an increase in elaborate decoration and richness of detail; and this is certainly reflected in inventories and accounts of the moment. Gilles li Muisis himself, writing in 1349, spoke not only of the masculinity of the feminine dress he remembered, but also of the beginnings of an excessive costliness in the stuffs of which women's dresses were made as well as in the jewels they wore.

Records of the bizarre career of Cola di Rienzo in Rome during the year 1347 included detailed and convincing accounts of the clothing which he had been remembered as wearing at some of his public appearances. A gown of mi-parti of green and yellow velvet lined with *vario*[7] is an echo of the magnificent mi-parti suits of velvet that were among the most

8 *Bible Historiale*. The new composition in masculine dress which appeared in the early 1350s, incorporating a low-set belt, producing a 'serpentine' stance and leading to the introduction of padding over the belly. See also p. 108.

expensive garments supplied to kings and princes at the courts of France and England at the beginning of the 1340s, but Cola di Rienzo went further, and he not only attended a gathering of the first nobility of Rome in St John Lateran wearing a gown and a 'German' mantle,[8] with a hood of the finest white cloth, and, on his head, an extraordinary white hat, but also, on another occasion, visited a palace near St Peter's dressed in what his anonymous biographer described as an imperial dalmatic over his armour, of a pattern worn by emperors of Rome at their coronations, but entirely embroidered with small pearls.[9]

Nor are these the only decorated suits worn by this Tribune of the People and recorded by his biographer. He appeared in *gonella*, *guarnaccia* and *cappa* of the expensive *scarlatto* cloth embroidered in gold thread; he appeared in white silk woven with a gold weft;[10] he appeared seated on a charger, when, again, he wore white embroidered in gold; and when, at last, on 14 September, his season of triumph drawing to a close, he once more showed himself to the people, Messer Stefano, of the ancient family of the Colonna, picked up a corner of the long train of his robe, saying, 'For your part, Tribune, it would be more suitable if you were to dress yourself decently in rough cloth than in all this pomp'; with which words he held up the Tribune's train for all to see.[11] Cola, in the words of a later historian, was a 'tragic actor in the tattered purple of antiquity'.[12] That he chose to dress his part in that particular way is an indication of the response he expected and, for a considerable time, received, from the populace of his day. In each instance it is not the tightness or the brevity of the clothing that is commented on but the richness of the stuff and, in many cases, the presence of gold embroidery if not pearls.

Writing in the year 1356 the *Continuateur* of de Nangis' chronicle reported that extravagance in dress had greatly increased among nobles and knights. They decorated their hoods and belts with pearls and precious stones to such a degree that the price of pearls rose steeply.[13] There is, indeed, evidence that in France as early as 1351 pearls were already becoming scarce; it can be found in an inventory of that year, when Jean, newly succeeded to the throne and lately married to a new wife, was arranging for the marriage of his eight year old daughter, Jeanne, to Charles, king of Navarre, known with reason as the Bad. Suitable clothing was naturally required for all the members of the royal family for the wedding celebrations; the list of jewels and stuffs recorded in one of the surviving inventories[14] includes an entry for ten and three-quarter pieces of sanguine velvet (a very considerable quantity) for the little queen-to-be of Navarre to make a suit embroidered in work of many and various kinds, carried out in large and small pearls – 'brodee a pluss et divers ouvrages de perles grosses et menues.' This is immediately followed by ten pieces of *vermilion* velvet for *une autre robe* for the queen of France (the bride's stepmother) on which, by the king's orders, pearl embroidery was begun but could not be completed, partly through shortage of time but also because it had not been possible to find enough pearls.[15]

That unpublished inventory, which suddenly turned from the regulation list of pieces of stuff and wages paid to tailors to an unexpectedly human explanation that the king's orders could not be carried out because both time and pearls were in short supply, is not complete. Its heading is missing and thus so is any immediate information as to its date and the name of the argentier who compiled it. It is mainly concerned with clothing for members of the Order of the Star,[16] established by Jean II the previous year as well as with clothing for the marriage of the little Jeanne, but it also includes some other very interesting material. It was followed, in the next year, 1352, by a long account drawn up by the argentier, Étienne de la Fontaine, and published by Douët D'Arcq in 1851.[17] Taken together, these two inventories reveal the fact that it was the practice in France to include some items omitted in one year in the next, for Étienne's published inventory also includes clothes provided for the wedding of Jeanne de France.

A third account, also from the year 1352, has survived and is included in Douët D'Arcq's 1851 publication. This is concerned with clothing in the trousseau of Blanche de Bourbon. Blanche, sixteen-year-old daughter of Peter, first duke of Bourbon, married Peter, king of Castille, called, again with reason, the Cruel, in July 1352. This account completes an entry included in the *compte* of Étienne de la Fontaine for that year, which, in its final subdivision of section three, recorded some particulars of furnishings provided as a part of Blanche's trousseau.[18] Jean's interest in this marriage was natural; Blanche was not only the sister of his daughter-in-law, the wife of his eldest son Charles, but the Bourbons were themselves connected with the French royal house,[19] which must have been the reason for the royal argentier's intervention in the trousseau.

All three French inventories should be considered in relation to the English accounts, covering the years 1347 to 1349, published in *Archaeologia*, as a continuation of the accounts of Thomas Cross for the years 1343–4.[20] The later accounts were drawn up by John Cook, the successor as keeper of the great wardrobe to John Charnels, who had held the office for only a few months.[21] The heading of this long account for royal clothing and liveries records the handing over of the office of keeper of the great wardrobe by John Cook himself to William Retford, who was appointed to the keepership on 3 January 1349.[22]

In 1347, Edward returned to England with the heady victories of Crécy and Calais to his credit. Although the editor of the *Archaeologia* accounts did not mention the fact (perhaps because he was chiefly interested in the establishment of the Order of the Garter), Calais actually appears by name in the accounts for the year 1347 in relation to some very expensive silks and velvets, provided, no doubt, for Edward's triumphal entry and his light-hearted distribution of more or less all that Calais possessed to his supporters.[23] It is not at all surprising that the couple of years following Edward's return to England should have been marked by what must have been an unprecedented sequence of joustings and masquerades, a fact recorded by, among others, Matteo Villani in Florence; nor that the junketings should not only have made demands on the talents of costume designers and tailors, but that they must inevitably have influenced fashionable taste and the design of fashionable dress. It is generally agreed that some time between the years 1347 and 1349, the Order of the Garter must have been founded;[24] both this and some of the theatrical and fanciful clothes made at the time will be discussed later, but there are some suits of clothing mentioned in these accounts which are not of a deliberately exotic kind and which are clear examples of the increased elaboration and richness noticed by the chroniclers.

Like the English accounts, those of the French court too must be considered against what, to the French, could only have appeared to be an improvement in the social and political situation. Philippe de Valois, who, with justification, must have been held responsible for the defeats at Sluys, Crécy and Calais, died in 1350. His eldest son Jean, aged a little over thirty, in spite of what had been his own blunders in his father's campaigns, was seen at the time of his accession, and distinctly erroneously, as a dashing, generous-spirited and chivalrous young man, likely to lead France into a better future; the epithet attached to his name – le Bon – should, it has been pointed out, be read rather as 'the Genial' than 'the Good'. It was not very long before Matteo Villani would be calling him Jean the Unfortunate – Giovanni lo Sventurato.[25]

In 1351 and certainly in imitation of Edward's Order, Jean II founded what was soon to be known as the Ordre de l'Etoile, and this too will be discussed in a later chapter. Quite apart from the clothing for this, and for the wedding of the king's little daughter, Jeanne de France, the three French accounts which survive also record features of fashionable dress which indicate that the new royal fashions were not only more complicated than those of the first half of the 1340s but also more 'theatrical'.

The French account discussed in the previous chapter is too fragmentary to provide a representative list of the garments that made up the princely wardrobe of 1342 but, as we have seen, those that do appear correspond well to their English counterparts. At the turn of the fourth and fifth decades the same basic garments were evidently still worn in the two countries. Robes still consisted of from four to six garments where royal clothing was concerned, though the official number was three.[26] There were surcotes, open and closed, and the term surcot (or seurcote) could still mean, when two were worn at the same time, that one was in fact a cote and worn underneath the other. Cotes hardies in these later French accounts were often, if not usually, made together with the houce, in the same stuff, as a set but this was not really an innovation, it had simply become, it seems, a more common practice.[27] A houce, spelt variously was, as Douët D'Arcq has satisfactorily explained, an over-garment, often with sleeves, often worn when riding. This combination of long hose, a short, padded, sleeved garment

reaching the waist, at which point the hose were tied to it, and a long thick loose overcoat was, in contrast to the tunic and over-tunic which constituted the formal dress of the upper classes, the sports wear of the day, shared with country people and wealthy peasants. The houce appeared in an inventory of 1316 and its absence from the partially destroyed inventory of 1342 has probably no significance. As at the beginning of the century, so in the early 1350s, a houce (or hausse) could have ailes, as their name implies, hanging cape-like sleeves, but both in the unpublished inventory of 1351 and in Étienne de la Fontaine's of 1352, the ailes of the houce had begun to be associated with languetes, which must have been small things because only six bellies of miniver were needed to line them, and it can be presumed that they occurred in pairs.[28]

Boccaccio, writing the Decameron round about 1350, provides very similar information in relation to the Italian wardrobe. His gonella is still an under-tunic; his guarnacca, but on one occasion his guarnello, is worn over it. A farsetto, like a farsettino, is a short and almost certainly padded garment;[29] Boccaccio's giubba is a short garment too, and could correspond to the cote hardie in that, in the Decameron it is always referred to as covered with thin silk – zendado, or cendal – as a cote hardie could be. Although for a complete suit of clothes Boccaccio's word was roba, for clothing in general he used the loose term panni.

Boccaccio established quite clearly that the normal use of the word camisia referred to the last garment to be discarded: Rinaldo d'Esti is reduced to nothing but a camisia;[30] the archbishop of Naples is robbed and left with only his camisia.[31] Such a shirt would inevitably have been thin and have afforded no protection to the body, its true purpose was to provide a washable layer next to the skin, so Boccaccio is using it, in both cases, emotively. This further illuminates the famous incident in which the burgesses of Calais came out of the gates carrying the keys and imploring Edward to give up the siege. In almost all the accounts, they are described as wearing shirts, the scantiest clothing consistent with decency; but the poet Laurence Minot speaks of them as knights who came out weeping – in kirtell one –[32] which was certainly intended to imply that he was unarmed and in undress, if not actually, like the citizens, undressed. All of which makes the use of the word camisia for the handsome garments for Edward and for the princes of Navarre at the beginning of the 1340s more curious.[33]

Kirtell is not a word that appears in the wardrobe accounts, which may suggest that it had already become suitably archaic to be used romantically by contemporary poets, who, of course, were not concerned with terms which were appearing for the first time in the great wardrobe and argenterie accounts of their contemporaries, the clerks and argentiers of the beginning of the 1350s, when, for instance, poignets begin to be associated with sleeves, especially of surcotes and corsets. Two surcotes, each lined with 386 bellies of miniver, required 60 bellies to line the manches and poignets of each,[34] while corsets appearing in the inventory of Blanche de Bourbon of

1352 are each assigned 300 bellies for lining, and here one learns that by this time corsets too were provided with *manches* and *poignets*, for which 40 bellies were provided. The corsets at this time were still often, though not always, described as 'round'.

Each of Blanche's corsets was accompanied by a *mantel allemant*, which takes us straight back to the magnificent suit worn with a *cappa alamanna* by Cola de Rienzo when he appeared in Rome in 1347,[35] and is a further reminder of the international nature of fourteenth-century fashions. What a German mantle may have been is a matter for speculation; it was certainly not new to fashion, for at least one *mantel allemant* was made for the queen of France in 1316. The two *manteaux alemens* made for Blanche de Bourbon took 1,200 bellies between them to line: a very large quantity compared to linings for other garments.

The addition of *languetes* and *poignets* to the fashionable wardrobe may not seem to mark a radical change in fashion, but, taken together with other innovations, they appear more interesting. The English great wardrobe accounts for the years 1347 to 1349, published in *Archaeologia*, are long and not at all easy to disentangle, though in all but a few minor respects they are faithful transcriptions of the original manuscript.[36] The problem for the reader is that, not only is the material arranged in the main by departments and not chronologically, but also that confusions arise between clothing designed for the normal life of the court and clothing for the numerous jousts ordered by the king during the three years covered by the accounts. Nevertheless the entries can with care be rearranged in sequences which make the changes of fashion at the end of the 1340s more comprehensible.

These accounts include some expenses involved in providing a trousseau for princess Joan, the second of Edward's little daughters, who was about to set off to marry Pedro the Cruel of Castile. In fact, because Joan died on her way to Spain, Pedro eventually married not a daughter of the English king but the unfortunate Blanche, sister of a daughter-in law of the French king, whose trousseau has just been discussed.

Joan did, however, set out for Spain, taking with her not only her dresses but also beds and bed curtains as well as vestments and hangings to be used in her private chapel.[37] These, together with most of her suits and ceremonial garments, appear in the great wardrobe account for the year 1347, although she did not leave until 1348. Joan was, of course, as a king's daughter, a member of the court circle, and appeared at the English court at Christmas 1347, wearing clothes that matched those of her sisters. In February 1348, entries for liveries for some of those attached to her train on her journey towards Castile appear on membrane 21 of the *Archaeologia* account.

On membrane 19 can be found some details of the robes designed to be worn by the princess at the actual wedding ceremony: a *tunica* and a *mantilletum* of heavy quality *rakematiz*,[38] which was a thick imported silk woven with gold. But she also had a whole suit made of the same stuff, with the result that, for all the garments together, eighteen whole pieces of the silk, probably amounting to nearly 150 metres, were used. Even allowing for the fact that the material was certainly narrow, this was an immense quantity. On wedding days, as at coronations, the chief participants were expected to appear in at least three changes of clothing, and, indeed, three are listed in Joan's account, in which there appear, too, a mantle, an open super–tunic and a tunic of heavy *diaspinus*,[39] while in the same sub-section of the account is a suit of red velvet for which ten pieces were used. In addition, of course, Joan was provided with cloth suits for general wear and special garments for riding,[40] specified rather surprisingly as *cotes-hardies*, usually a masculine garment, as well as an extra mantle or two and five corsets, two of them of cloth of gold – 'pannus ad aurum cygastons'. Cigaston is one of the expensive imported silks which, it is a relief to find, can at least to some extent be identified from other entries covered by this account. It must have been woven with an all-over pattern, for suits of two garments of cigaston woven with a pattern of stars and crescents in gold were made for the King and four of his nobles,[41] and a suit of three garments, for the king alone, was made of cigaston with a dark blue ground and a woven pattern of lozenges and birds in gold.[42]

More interesting than these ceremonial suits of imported brocaded silks are references to other garments made for Joan, but easily overlooked because they appear on membrane 14, immediately following her furnishings for bedchambers and closets. Issued, like the rest of her trousseau, under the indenture of her treasurer, Thomas Baddeley, they include two ghitas, a term which, like the corset, was certainly given to a garment of a recognizable style which did not form a part of a suit. Of the two ghitas, one was made of green longcloth, the other of longcloth of a very dark shade – 'de panno longo brunetto nigro'. Embroidered ghitas had been made for the queen and the princesses to wear in 1342, and Joan's also were embroidered all over. The green ghita was embroidered in gold in a design which included rose arbours, among which appeared both wild animals and wild men; the dark ghita had a repeating pattern of circles, each enclosing a recumbent lion, while the whole ground was powdered with gold leaves. The embroidery, as can be discovered from the materials provided for the work, was carried out in coloured silks, metal thread and small ornaments cut or stamped out in thin plate gold. The fact that a pound in weight of this very thin light plate gold was supplied to make these ornaments shows that a very large number of them must have been used in the decoration of Joan's two ghitas, which, as compared with the patterns made up of squares of enamel worked on the royal ghitas of five years earlier, must not only have been much more elaborate but which revealed a change in taste.

Although only the embroidery of the two ghitas is described in such detail, one of her corsets of violet in grain was embroidered too, and so was a suit of green longcloth,[43] all of which is evidence of the taste for increased richness of surface in the period immediately following the looting in France.

The *Archaeologia* accounts for these years are worth investigating carefully; among the items of baggage made to carry princess Joan's trousseau, for instance, two sets of buttons unexpectedly appear. Each set, of different design, contained twenty-four buttons, all of them made of silver gilt and enamel. Buttons were not merely by this time established as a necessary ingredient in the current fashion, but they evidently provided further scope for embellishment. They appear frequently in royal inventories, where they are listed not among the mercery, as before, but among the jewels; and in 1352, among the regalia and jewellery used at the coronation of Joanna of Naples and Louis of Taranto, can be found thirty-nine buttons of mother-of-pearl and gold work set with precious stones.[44]

In the autumn of 1348, queen Philippa gave birth to a fifth son, William, who died so immediately that furnishings for his funeral appear in the account above those for the special clothing made for the queen's reappearance after his birth. For the vigil of this churching, a suit of dark blue – *ynde* – velvet of particular magnificence was made for her to wear. It consisted of a *mantilletum, capa*, open super tunic and tunic embroidered with gold birds, each bird surrounded by a circle of large pearls, the whole background powdered with a pattern worked in silks and small pearls and enlivened by 10,000 doublets.[45] Four hundred large pearls, thirty-eight ounces of small pearls, thirteen pounds of plate gold, eleven pounds of gold thread and seven pounds of embroidery silks were used in the decoration of this suit, as well as the $10,000 - \frac{ml}{x}$ – doublets, quantities which give some idea of the weight of the four garments, and to these must be added the nearly 2,000 bellies of miniver used for the linings and the 60 skins of ermine, probably for the *mantilletum*. And even this, moreover, takes no account of the velvet of which the suit was made: eight pieces and two ells, something like fifty metres, which can only mean that the *capa* had a long train, and perhaps the super tunic too.

That was for the vigil. For the actual day of the churching, the queen's suit was again made of velvet,[46] and again it was embroidered in gold, silk and pearls. This time the design consisted of oaks and other trees, beneath each of which was a lion, worked in large pearls, and again the whole ground was covered by a fine embroidery in silks and small pearls. For the day of the churching, too, another garment, a ghita, was made for the queen: it took just over two pieces of velvet, so it must have been fairly ample.

The preparation of the tomb for the baby prince was carried out, according to the account, on 5 September 1348, the twenty-second year of the king's reign. This means that it was after the first cases of death from the plague had been recorded in London in the August of that year, a month earlier. No hint of the effects of the Black Death appear in the great wardrobe accounts, from which it can be seen that all the usual items of clothing had been made both for the feasts of All Saints and of Christmas 1348, which the royal family spent at Otford that year.

Embroidered garments for the king are also included in these accounts, but most of them seem to have been either worn at tournaments or for festivals surrounding the institution of the Order of the Garter. The growing taste for embroidered decoration sometimes makes it difficult to distinguish what was theatrical, fanciful or exotic fashionable dress from what was made to wear at a joust. The stuffs of which some of these royal doublets and aketons were made, or, as the accounts put it, 'covered', include *camocas* (a heavy patterned oriental silk, and probably the most expensive of all) in murray, blue, cendre and pink; *camoca diaspř*;[47] samit and zatyn, all of them imported silks.

As compared with the early years of the reign, not only were far larger quantities of far more expensive silks used for royal clothing, but these accounts of the end of the 1340s show an enormous increase in the use in England of ermine, which had been used very sparingly indeed ten years earlier. During the years 1347 to 1349, about 3,000 skins of ermine were used for trimming the clothes of the royal family, in addition, of course to very much larger quantities of miniver.

If ermine, velvets, patterned silks, embroideries in pearls and bezants, as they appear in the English accounts for these years, were a reflection of the exuberance after the victories in France, French accounts for the years 1351 to 1352 betray by very similar means, though on a distinctly more modest scale, an optimistic view of the future. In spite of the ransom collected after Crécy, the English were still heavily in debt to foreign creditors, but it was the French who had parted with their personal luxuries to English looters, and who, in addition, had had to raise the enormous ransoms exacted for the release of nobles and knights captured at the battle.

A comparison between the two sets of accounts, both concerned with royal weddings and both with the institution of Orders of Chivalry, shows that whereas all the English royal children often wore suits trimmed with ermine, and that the queen, even on suits of a not particularly ceremonial kind, wore trimmings made from as many as sixty skins, in France, according to the accounts of Étienne de la Fontaine, for the year 1352, which included two important weddings, fewer than 600 skins of ermine were used altogether, and those were worn only by the Dauphin and by Blanche de Bourbon, Pedro the Cruel's bride. Both the English and the French accounts, on the other hand, show an immense increase in the use of embroidery.

Whether or not this new taste for embroidery implied a new social outlook, it was certainly a sign of a change in fashion. If pearls were not available for embroideries designed for the French queen to wear at the Navarre wedding, the intention to use them had been there. In France, there seems to have been a particular liking for embroidered hoods, made for members of both sexes. Three quarters of a whole cloth of fine *marbré*, and the same quantity of *escar-latte* of *paonasse* colour,[48] were supplied to the Dauphin's armourer and embroiderer, Thevenin Castel (whose first name appears later as Étienne) for a lined hood to be embroidered in pearls for the Dauphin. When the hood was thrown back on the shoulders (and at this period hoods were becoming almost too small to be worn on the head) both the outside and the lining would show, so there is no need to assume that this one was mi-parti and, in fact, no stuff is entered for its lining. Later in the account, Étienne Castel's own entry explains that the hood was striped horizontally – *tous fesse* – with a design of circles linked by curved lines worked in pearls, the whole background very intricately covered with a design of small leaves. For this hood Cyprus gold and silver thread were, together with the work, charged at £520 parisis, while Belhoumet Thruel, who supplied a great deal of mercery to the French court, charged a 'marc' of pearls at twenty crowns (*ecus*) the ounce, and, for a further marc two ounces of smaller pearls, at sixteen crowns the ounce. The bill he presented came to £256 parisis. But this was not all, for Édouard Thadelin too supplied pearls for this hood, 2,000 large ones.

Another hood in the same account, also for the Dauphin, this time of two cloths of *escarlatte*, one red and one pink, was embroidered by the same Étienne Castel in a design which included forty-four trees with large tufts of leaves, their branches worked in gold thread. A lapwing (*piment*) was perched on each branch. Round the edge of the hood was a band divided into sections of embroidery, each of the sections enclosing a wild man mounted on a beast. In the front, on the chest (presumably of the short cape to which the hood was attached), once again worked in pearls, was a castle from which emerged maidens also mounted on wild beasts, who jousted with the men – and we are back with the emancipated girls of the Taymouth Hours and the Berwick joust. The cloth, pearls, making and embroidery of this remarkable hood amounted to £589 16s. par. Two embroidered hoods of violet were made at the same time for the Dauphin, but no details of their decoration was recorded, so they were probably much less spectacular.

A dark blue *seurcot*, embroidered *bien et richement*, made for the Dauphin, may have been intended to wear with the pink and red hood, for it immediately precedes it in the account. If so, the effect must have been overwhelming, for the surcoat was embroidered with flowering trees, the flowers, of course, in pearls, while beasts known as panthers of various kinds, worked in pearls, formed a circle round each tree. The making of the surcoat and the material of which it was made cost £660 7s. 2d. par., but the embroidery, carried out by Étienne Castel, was extra; for the 131 trees and the panthers, including the thread with which they were sewn, he charged £104 16s. par. The surcoat was described as *à parer*, which meant, no doubt, that it was intended for some ceremonial occasion, perhaps a procession preceding the Navarre wedding. The term *à parer*[49] occurs fairly frequently in these accounts, often in

connection with mantles or other outer wraps, usually made for a marriage or a churching. The blue velvet for the Dauphin's surcoat was described as of the very finest quality. It was lined with cendal to match; the pearls used and their sizes are recorded in detail – there were a great many of them.

Four embroidered hoods were made for Jeanne de France, and hoods, described as hers were, as *chapperons pendens*, embroidered with pearls, were made for her sisters, Marie and Ysabel de France; the fact that these were classified as hanging hoods suggests that they were purely ornamental and not intended to be worn on the head. The suits of these younger princesses were not apparently embroidered, the decoration on them seeming to have been confined to twenty-five buttons, each one composed of four pearls with a diamond in the middle. An elaborately decorated belt, made in cloth of gold in sections, each section embroidered with fleurs-de-lys and birds, its buckle studded with sapphires and rubies, was made for the dauphin, and a considerable number of heavily jewelled coronets, most of the jewels from Genoa, were made for Jeanne de France, so that even though their suits may not have been embroidered, the princesses of France were magnificent in their jewels.

By far the most startling manifestation of a completely new fashion, however, was the appearance of extraordinary hats, described in both French and English accounts round about the end of the 1340s and the beginning of the 1350s. The white hat which had accompanied a white suit worn by Cola di Rienzo in 1347 must have belonged to this fashion. Cola had worn a German mantle, his hood thrown back to lie round his shoulders and on his head a small white hat, round which were golden coronets, one of them divided in the middle. From the upper part of the hat there descended a naked silver sword, its point penetrating the coronet which was, in this way, cut in half.[50] This bizarre and presumably symbolic hat was not the only one in Cola's wardrobe, for he is described at another time as wearing a hat entirely covered with pearls with, on its crown, a dove made in pearls.[51]

Although hats as fantastic as these cannot be found in the English accounts of the same period, two beaver hats, one lined with squirrel fur, the other unlined, were included in the trousseau of princess Joan. Under the date 1348 in her inventory they appear in a list of miscellaneous things, including baggage and furs. Besides these two hats for princess Joan, three felt hats trimmed with gilded buttons and silk ties were made at about the same time for the king her father. Writing of the same year, 1348, Froissart records that Edward, crossing the Channel, stood at the prow of his ship wearing a black velvet *jake* and a black beaver hat which suited him admirably – *qui moult bien le seoit*.[52]

It seems, therefore, that whereas extremely intricate and imaginatively designed embroidery for the decoration of ghitas and suits was carried out in England for the queen and her daughters, in France only the Dauphin's suits were embroidered, apart from the two embroidered suits made for the

Navarre wedding, of which the queen's was not completed. When it came to hats, however, the situation was reversed. For instance, Kathelot, the French king's hatter, embroidered and embellished a hat for the Dauphin, worked with a design of pearl lions, each holding (in a lozenge) his arms. Trees, resembling pines were also a part of the design and these too were, as usual, worked in pearls. Blanche de Bourbon, for her marriage in 1352, was, like princess Joan, given two beaver hats as a part of her trousseau. Blanche's, however, were a great deal more elaborate than Joan's and were made by Kathelot, the royal hatter.[53] The second and the simpler of the two hats was lined with *escarlatte* and trimmed above and beneath – *dessus et dessoubs* – with pearl buttons, bezants and small enamel ornaments surmounted by large rosettes worked in Cyprus gold thread. Its fine laces or ties, of silk and gold, were probably designed to enable it to be slung round the neck when it was not worn on the head, in which respect it would have corresponded to the already traditional cords and tassels attached to the hats of cardinals and bishops (which had already become their distinctive wear) as well as to the plain leather thongs which were a part of the functional hats of pilgrims and countrymen. The survival of such ties in hats of high fashion, certainly not intended, as were those of cardinals, bishops, pilgrims and peasants to protect them from the sun when travelling or working, may have been a sign that in introducing hats as decorative features of fashionable dress, those responsible for designing them had turned instinctively for inspiration to the only hats they knew.

Blanche's more splendid hat – à parer – seems to have been composed of strands of beaver fur worked over a fine *vermillion* velvet in grain on which, made of gold, were lifelike children (*pres du vif*) beating down acorns, made of large pearls, from oak-trees whose branches were worked in pearls and their leaves in gold. Beneath the trees, boars and sows, also modelled from life and also in gold, eat the acorns beaten down by the children, while among the branches above them were many strange birds, most beautifully made in gold. Nor was this all, for on a terrace, below the swine, were little embroidered flowers and tiny animals and the whole hat was powdered with pearls, leaves and enamel ornaments as well as pearl buttons. It had laces of silk and gold. A hat no less surprising, had been made for the king's fool, Jean, during the previous year.[54]

It should, by the way, be remembered that in the French accounts the word for a hat – *chappel* or *chapel* – is also used for a coronet but confusion between the two does not arise because in the accounts the basic material of the object is always stated first, so that just as a *chappel* of beaver or felt could certainly not be a coronet, a *chappel* of gold or silver was hardly likely to be a hat. The two are, moreover, listed in separate parts of the accounts, because they were made in different departments; Kathelot, *la chapeliere*, clearly did not make coronets; furthermore, every *chapel d'or* made or altered for Jeanne de France was approved directly by her treasurer and entered

among the jewels. In England, Edward's three hats were supplied by John Marreys, each at a cost of 12d.; the two beaver hats for princess Joan, by Nicholas Causton, at 6s. each.[55] Both types of hat appear among the merceries.

In the unpublished French account of 1351, Kathelot, the hatter, appears as having made seven hats of peacocks' feathers with wide silk ties and thirteen beaver hats, ten of them for the lords of the exchequer and three for the treasurers, as well as an extra one for a treasury clerk; all except one were lined with lambskin and embellished with buttons and goldsmiths' work, embroidered in gold thread and tied with silk laces.[56]

How far the world of high fantasy expressed in high fashion by means of golden nude children, grazing golden pigs, naked silver sword-blades and pearl-studded rose-bushes surrounded by golden panthers was familiar in the sight of the common man is difficult to ascertain, but he probably knew all about it. Round the fringes of the jousts, to which even girls of doubtful morality had access, jostled the everyday crowd, nor were these the only occasions on which royalty and the nobility appeared in public.

Before 1355, the demand for conspicuously expensive decorated clothing had become so great that, in France, a set of statutes was drawn up in the August of that year, regulating the practices of the goldsmiths of Paris.[57] These statutes leave no doubt as to what had been going on. The *Statuts des Orfèvres de la Ville de Paris* state clearly that, apart from exceptional circumstances such as the decoration of tombs in churches, goldsmiths were permitted to work in no other metals than pure gold and pure silver, and that pure gold must mean 19^1/$_5$ carats. There follows a prohibition on the placing of coloured foils beneath amethysts, garnets, rubies and emeralds to heighten their colour. Neither was any goldsmith permitted to use, in any work of gold or silver, Scottish pearls in place of pearls from the Orient, except in work for the Church; or together with stones designated as *etranges* (probably what would now be called semi-precious stones). There was to be no mixing in of glass ornaments with garnets or other precious stones, and no cutting of crystal to resemble diamonds. No 'doublets' (coloured foils sandwiched between two pieces of glass) were to be set in gold except for the king, the queen or their children. Buttons made by goldsmiths were not to be hollow at the back nor backed with steel, and in fact all buttons to be used on silk or the like were to be well finished at the back. No bezants or such ornaments to decorate silk stuffs were to be nailed – *clouées* – down on to the material, but all must be attached only by stitching with a needle so that their backs could be examined for base metals. No goldsmiths were to work in secret rooms to which masters of their craft could not gain access. The remaining statutes are concerned with hours of work, the employment of apprentices, conditions of sale and so on.

The fact that the king exempted himself and his family from the regulations governing the use of false jewels is surely an indication that he considered it more important to appear glorious in the eyes of those who viewed him from afar than wealthy to those who saw him close to. That the royal children did sometimes wear 'doublets' mixed in with other decorations can be seen from the accounts; the English queen certainly wore an immense quantity of them set into the embroidery on her suit for the vigil of her churching, as we have seen. Equally interesting is the order that the small ornaments cut or stamped out of thin gold plate, which appear under many names, including bezants and *gauffres*, must not be fastened down so closely to the fabric that a coating of thin gold foil on a base metal ground could be substituted for pure gold – *or de touche*.[58] A great many of these little things have survived;[59] most of those in the shape of disks have a hole through which a stitch or two could suspend them on the clothing. The fact that they could swing loose from the material to which they were attached would mean that the whole surface would provide an extra sparkle with each movement of the body.

To follow the exotic jewelled beaver hats with a description of any other article of clothing might seem an anticlimax and yet it is not inappropriate to mention an entry for a hundred and ten large pearls bought to sew onto a pair of slippers – *soulers* – for the Dauphin. They were made by Étienne Castel (referred to here as armourer and valet-de-chambre) and were embroidered in a gold fret, forming regular lozenges. On each side of each fret were five gold leaves, in the middle of each of which a large pearl and in each lozenge, a lion. The whole ground was covered in needlework – *faite a la broche* – in Cyprus gold thread.[60] In their design, therefore, the Dauphin's slippers exactly matched the beaver hat that had been made for him by Kathelot, surely a very sophisticated conceit? The slippers appear in the French account for the year 1353; they bring vividly to mind the shoes, cut into intricate open-work patterns, recorded in paintings from every part of Europe at about the same date.

It may have been noticed that in spite of the apparently unrestrained assemblage of wild men and wild beasts, oak-trees and naked children, lions and

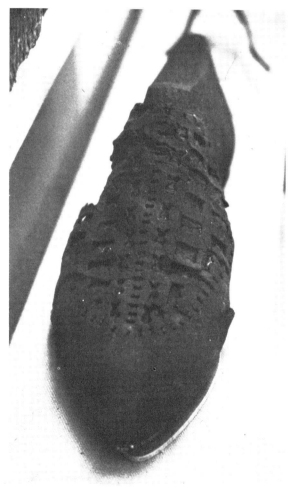

9 *Annunciation*, detail, the archangel Gabriel, before 1350, by the Master of the Vyssi Brod Altar. A unique example, in painting, of the use of bezants in a variety of shapes as a decoration for a mantle (here a cope). The archangel's shoes are cut into the fashionable fret.

10 A shoe cut into a decorative open pattern. A spoil from the Battle of Visby, 1360.

37

golden leaves, terraces sprinkled with flowers, a rigid order governed the actual patterns in which each fantastic feature played its part. The Dauphin's surcoat was embroidered with 131 apparently identical trees: his belt was divided into sections. Each golden bird on the queen of England's suit was enclosed in a circle of pearls. There was nothing baroque about these motifs, set as a repeating pattern on fields covered in minute embroidery to soften, a little, the outline of each separate feature. The richness, even down to the geometrical grid on the Dauphin's slippers, was strictly controlled. Nevertheless, looking back to the quatrefoils of the early 1340s, the increased complexity of the ornamentation of the end of the decade is very evident.

So the end of the 1340s, the half-way point between Crécy and Poitiers, saw the continuance of that sharpest of fashions, mi-parti, in upper-class dress, an immeasurable increase in decorated surfaces, the introduction of *languetes* and *poignets*. Above all, the arrival of the hat as a luxurious accessory. When in 1356, just before Poitiers, the *Continuateur* of de Nangis' chronicle recorded his impressions of the current fashions, he remarked that luxury and dissoluteness had increased among the knights and nobles. They decorate their hoods, he said, and their belts with pearls and precious stones, to such an extent that the price of pearls has gone up; he also noticed their practice of ornamenting their hats with feathers.[61]

And, finally, an *Ordonnance* issued in 1350 to *Tailleurs et Cousturiers* illuminates several dark corners in the current fashion. Directed to tailors, dressmakers, furriers and liners of suits, it refers to suits made in the normal and traditional fashion – 'de la commune & ancienne guise' – as consisting of three pieces, surcot, cotte and chaperon, for which no more than five *sols* could be charged for the making, unless the hood were double, in which case a charge of six *sols* could be made. This was to apply to suits for both men and women, but if the suit were made in any other style but the traditional one, that is to say, if the sleeves were too long – 'comme de trop longues manches' – or if the suit were trimmed with ermine, then the furrier could be at liberty to charge whatever he could get. In fact, those who wished to have suits not of the traditional cut but made according to their fancy – 'qui voudra avoir robbes deguisees autres que la commune & ancienne guise' (a clarification of the term *déguise* at the time), then they must pay for them. For lining a *housse* or a cloak (*cloche*) with a hood, the charge was not to exceed three *sols*, which underlines the similarity between a *housse* and a cloak. No more than eight *deniers* could be charged for making a woman's chemise, and for *robbes-linges*, which were presumably linen underpants, the price was to be the usual one for masculine underpants of the normal style – 'une robbe-linges homme d'oeuvre commune'; does this mean that women wore them too?[62]

The fact that it was found necessary to issue such explicit directions at this particular moment surely suggests that tailors and furriers, taking advantage of the extra details which the new fashion had introduced, had been charging more even for their run-of-the-mill suits. This *Ordonnance* is important, too, for the information that, unless the *robe* was definitely stated as including extra garments, it can be taken for granted that it consisted of three: surcoat, under tunic and hood.

In 1353, Étienne de la Fontaine left a list of jewels and precious stuffs remaining in the argenterie on his retirement. It includes a *chapiau de bievre* lined with ermine, powdered with pearls *d'Orient*, with one lace on which were four buttons of pearl. Eight pearl roses were apparently missing from this hat, each of them composed of twenty-one pearls, and there were fourteen other pearls missing too, to be returned by Étienne, who had removed them.[63] It was, of course, perfectly normal for jewels to be removed for use on later objects as the fashion changed, which is one of the reasons why so few elaborate pieces of old jewellery have remained intact. This ermine-lined hat is, by the way, one of the few pearl-trimmed items of dress in which the pearls are specifically stated to have been from the Orient.

In the midst of all this richness, the actual style of dress was changing too, but it is, as usual, more difficult to reconstruct it simply from the accounts of tailors, and, at this moment, not immediately easy to recognize it in works of art. Some clues are hidden in the poems and novels of the time, but not many, for, whereas several poets of the mid fourteenth century linger over descriptions of splendidly armoured and obviously handsome knights, only a few describe the appearance of the young civilians of the day, or even the young women, and then only in the most general terms.

The complexions of the young women are invariably seen to consist of a delightful combination of the lily and the rose; their hair is long and abundant, and very often they wear a garland either of real flowers or of jewelled and enamel counterfeits, and there, as a rule, the account stops. Boccaccio, so skilful in choosing a short pointed phrase to bring out the distinctive nature of one of his characters, contents himself by describing the beautiful Fiametta as having long golden curls falling on to her delicate white shoulders, a little round face in which the white of the lily and the vermilion of the rose were mingled;[64] while, in another story, he describes two young girls, aged, perhaps, fifteen, who appeared in messer Neri's garden wearing their ringlets as blonde as gold threads set with the lightest of little garlands, so delicate in their beauty that they looked more like angels than anything else.[65] Their gowns were of the finest – *sottilissima* – linen, white as snow; they fitted them as closely as could be above the belt, while below it they spread out as wide as tents, reaching their feet.[66] Those, according to Boccaccio, were the youthful Italian beauties round about 1350.

Nevertheless, in spite of what appear to be descriptions of stereotypes of the young and lovely in any country in Europe in the middle of the fourteenth century, something emerges. Those blonde curls fall on to white shoulders, so their necklines were cut low. Their linen dresses fit closely from the belt upwards, while skirts spread out like pavilions below the belt (*not* below the waist – the belt, therefore, probably being set low). These are not facts that can be gathered from great wardrobe accounts, but they fully support the images produced by contemporary sculptors and painters.

It is not surprising to find the French poet Guillaume Machaut weaving a rondeau round the lines:

> Blanche com lis, plus que rose vermeille
> Resplendissant com rubiz d'Orient

at about the same date, or not much later.[67] Or, again, declaring himself faithful to one who:

> Juene est, gente, gaie et jolie
> Et tout douce, blanche et vermeille[68]

Nor do these by any means exhaust his preference for white and vermilion in the female face. With the clothing of his lady, Machaut is not concerned: he contents himself with referring occasionally to her *atour*, used in the sense not of her head-dress but of her attractive looks in general.

On one occasion, however, Machaut includes a careful description of the physical appearance of his ideal girl, and the points he emphasizes are in some respects a surprise. As would be expected, her hair is like golden threads, neither too blonde nor too sombre in colour; her forehead is white and polished

without the trace of a wrinkle – 'ne fronce n'i avoit' – and below it her eyebrow seems like a black thread chosen from a thousand. Her eyes – well, Machaut is overwhelmed by those, as he is, too, by her little vermilion laughing mouth. Her nose is neither too small nor too big; her cheeks are a little plump and her chin is rounded, but it is her complexion that is *nompareille*. The surprise is the freedom with which he writes of her body: her long straight arms, her white hands and long fingers; her firm white breasts set high; her whole form long and straight, charming, with her well-shaped hips and thighs, her long legs and plump feet cunningly shod.[69]

Machaut was a clerk, a celibate, and writing at a royal court in a tone of high chivalry;[70] it is unlikely that he was describing his lady unclothed, which means that, at least in movement, the current fashion was supple enough to reveal through its folds a shapely thigh. This is borne out by a very similar description of the princess Olympias in the alliterative *Gestes of the Worthie King and Emperour, Alisaunder of Macedoine*, a surviving fragment by an unknown author. Good reasons have been put forward for identifying him with the author of the translation of *William of Palerne*, commissioned by Humphrey de Bohun in about 1350.[71] Here, again, were well-shaped arms, shapely hands and 'faire fyngers' are noted and so were her 'sides seemely sett', her hips being fair as were her thighs and her legs. She had the fairest feet that man ever saw, with well-formed toes.[72]

11 *Madonna and Child, c.* 1350. Czech Master. The Madonna is represented as the ideal Bohemian beauty of the day, with heavy golden curls and a metal head-band decorated with enamel flowers. This is the type of beauty that seems to have been admired by all the contemporary European poets.

Now it is noticeable that, at all periods, the physical features selected for praise by poets are those which are emphasized in the current fashion in dress. In a period, therefore, when bare arms were unknown, the fact that two poets mention long and shapely arms almost certainly means that the sleeves which covered them fitted closely. Feet, too, in soft and well-fitted shoes, could evidently be seen and freely admired. Hints such as these can support a proposed date for a poem or a novel even if they are not specific enough to establish one by themselves.

Among the English poets whose works can be dated within the limits of this study, several were almost entirely occupied with martial themes. Langland was not. His *Lady Meed* provided him with an opportunity to describe a really alluring woman of the time but his talents did not, of course, lie in that direction. She represents the attractions of worldly goods, but Langland's statement that she is 'wonderliche clothed' her dress being of red cloth of scarlet, trimmed with the richest furs on earth and tied with gold ribbons:

Purfylet with pelure . the ricchest uppon eorthe . . .
In Red Scarlet heo Rod . I'Rybaunt with gold;[73]

is not very imaginative. And there Langland's description of the dress of women of fashion ends.

But authors with less serious intentions also confined themselves to banal generalizations when it came to presenting the dress of the heroine. *Sir Launfal* in the English translation by Thomas Chestre, considered to have been made in about 1350:

1/943

The lady was clad yn purpue palle,
Wyth gentyll body and myddyll small,
That semely was of syght;
Her mantyll was furryth wyth whyt ermyn,
I reversyd jolyf & fyn
No rychere bene myght.[74]

disposes of the lady's appearance, but the translator describes her saddle with relish and in greater detail, as did other poets. In *Ipomadon*, for instance, again in an English translation of about the same date, the descriptions of the men's clothing is fairly specific, but of the lady's only that:

2384

In a riche araye
And as whyte as any mylke
The sadull couvvered in white sylke
Was never won better seene.[75]

On the other hand the youthful knight is described as follows:

367

His dobelett was of red velvet
Off bryght golde botuns ihett
That warthey was wraught
His mantell was of scarlett fyne
Fworyed with good armyne,
Ther myght no better been
The bordome all of red sendell
That araye became hym welle . . .[76]

It is worth noting that in Hue de Rotelande's twelfth century French version of *Ipomadon* there is no mention at all of buttons and indeed translators of the fourteenth century freely adapted the original descriptions of clothing to fit the fashions of their own day as can be judged especially well by a glance at the late fourteenth-century translation of the *Roman de la Rose*, which has been published with the original French text printed in parallel.[77]

In virtually ignoring the clothing worn by women of the beginning of the 1350s the poets were, perhaps, acute. Their dress was indeed less interesting than the men's, nor had it changed its style as conspicuously as had the men's in spite of John of Reading's opinion that it was far too tight and too revealing of the body (a characteristic which had occurred to both Machaut and the author of the translation of the *Gestes of Alisaunder*, as we have seen). The principal change in the fashion of women's dress between the early 1340s and the early 1350s was its increased richness of ornamentation in the form of embroidery and jewelled belts and—although this applied to the dress of men too—theirs had actually changed its outline far more noticeably.

40

VI

Tournaments and Orders of Chivalry

Into the environment of the end of the 1340s, of the ermine-covered pelisses, the vermilion in grain, the pearl and enamel powdered hats and the royal thrones painted by Gerard d'Orléans himself, at least four Orders of Chivalry were born, each in a European capital. Coincidence sits awkwardly in a study of fashion, but since, from a chronological point of view, the habits of these Orders should be discussed now, the coincidence of their highly decorative behaviour and outward appearance may legitimately perhaps be seen to have been timely.

The first of the four seems to have been the rather insubstantial Order of the Sword of Cyprus, founded by Peter of Lusignan before 1347, before, that is to say, his accession to the throne of Cyprus as Peter I in 1359. Peter's intention was to accumulate a body of dedicated and responsible supporters of high standing with a view to recovering the Holy Places of Palestine.[1] The Second Order to be founded was the Most Noble Order of the Garter, already in being in 1348 but certainly not in existence at the beginning of 1347.[2] The third was the Ordre des Chevaliers de Notre Dame de la Noble Maison et de Leur Prince, soon to be known as the Ordre de l'Étoile, founded in France in 1351 by Jean le Bon. And the fourth was the Neapolitan Ordre du Saint Esprit au Droit Désir, founded in 1353 by Louis of Taranto, titular king of Naples and husband of Joanna I, queen of Naples and countess of Provence, of the house of Anjou.

Although the four Orders varied considerably both in their avowed aims and in their composition, all four were certainly founded from motives which would today be called 'political': to strengthen, that is to say, the position of the founder, to forward his policies and to surround him with a band of loyal and active followers.

Today the earliest surviving statutes of the Order of the Garter date from the reign of Henry V, nor was a specimen of the original statutes in existence in the reign of Charles II when Elias Ashmole wrote his monumental work on the Order.[3] Edward himself had evidently regarded the Round Table festivities of 1344 as of outstanding importance, for he almost immediately embarked on the building of a round

tower at Windsor (called, at the time, a Round Table) so that similar occasions could be housed there – his birthplace from which he took his surname. He also set about enlarging the adjacent chapel of St Edmund, which he rededicated to St George, moves which led some early writers to assume that the Order had come into being three or four years before in fact it had. It all must have meant, nevertheless, that the king's mind was already turning in the direction of founding a confraternity of his closest supporters during those years. He may even have been vaguely influenced by the Order of the Sword with its crusading connotations.

The concept of an intimate fellowship between the king and some of those nobles who were his valued companions, and more or less his contemporaries, is illustrated by some of the jousts which had taken place before the founding of the Order, when he and his supporters often entered the lists either dressed alike or dressed as members of an integrated group. In a tournament at Smithfield, just outside the gate of St John's Hospital in London on 24 June 1343, for instance, the king, appearing as usual as a simple knight bachelor[4] formed, together with his companions, a group dressed as the pope and twelve cardinals.[5] The device was not as bizarre as might appear; it was certainly one which proves without question that political overtones were produced by these great public demonstrations of what pretended to be picturesque expositions of old-world chivalry. In 1343, Adam of Murimuth reported that Edward had sent a letter to the pope voicing both his and his people's displeasure at what he saw as his Holiness's contributions to the French cause at the expense of the English taxpayer.[6] The fact that the king and his companions chose to dress up not as themselves but as their adversaries must surely have meant that a good deal of buffoonery accompanied their appearance. If, as seems reasonable, this joust can be associated with a precise political move, it should encourage us to look more closely at some of the other devices assumed by Edward during the most active period of his reign.

In the previous year, 1342, three green tunics had

been made for the king and two of his knights to wear at a Dunstable tournament; these appear in a great wardrobe account, and probably merely indicate a small group united by the colour of their dress.[7] Other jousting clothes seem to have been more interesting. At the beginning of Edward's reign, in 1331, when the affairs of state were still conducted by the queen mother and Roger Mortimer, the young king and his companions appeared at a joust in Cheapside dressed alike as Tartars;[8] and in a later tournament, in 1359, again in London, the king and his four sons – Edward, Lionel, John and Edmund – were, with nineteen nobles, dressed as the mayor and twenty-four aldermen of the City.[9]

If representations of popes, cardinals, mayors and aldermen could be understood as communications of *ad hoc* propaganda – devices deliberately adopted by Edward to let the public into his confidence – then others, less overt, may have come to bear a recognizable significance. Some he wore repeatedly, and the idea of a permanent badge, which the Garter was to become, may not have been – indeed, almost certainly was not – a new one to him. In the year 1342–3, Edward attended jousts at Dunstable, at one of which he and his knights wore those green tunics which appear belatedly in an account of 1344, and he also attended a joust at Northampton, wearing a number of distinct devices: clouds, from which sometimes rays of the sun emerged, Saracens, compasses and Catherine wheels. Although the original concept which lay behind some devices at this period may have been a temporary one, soon forgotten or lost, they arouse curiosity because the choice of them at the time cannot have been purely arbitrary. Why, for instance, of all the peoples of the world, choose Tartars in 1331? Saracens, noble or otherwise, were naturally familiar from information disseminated by returning Crusaders, and the sun's rays penetrating clouds have been popular as variants of a great many badges and have simple connotations, but why, in 1342, St Catherine's wheel? An answer to this particular question may not be too difficult to discover.

One of Edward's mottoes, which appears in the great wardrobe account published in *Archaeologia*, has often been noticed. It runs, 'it.is.as.it.is.'; embroidered on a jousting doublet of white linen along the border, on the sleeves and hem was a design of golden clouds and vines together with the *dictamine regis* – 'It is as it is.' This entry follows immediately after one for a tunic, a mantle and hood ornamented with a hundred garters, which points to a date after 1347, and precedes an entry for a bed-cover of green camocas, embroidered with two figures carrying what might perhaps have been scrolls, inscribed with the same motto.

What seems, however, to have escaped notice is the occurrence in John of Cologne's section of the unpublished account for the year 1342–3[10] of twelve suits of green cloth with hoods and a white border (which reversed the king's white tunic with a green border of about 1347 just referred to) on which were embroidered Catherine wheels, with letters in jewels and pearls spelling the motto, 'It is as it is.' These

had been made and embroidered for the 1342 tournament in Dunstable. Catherine wheels with the same motto formed the centre-piece of the coverlet for the king's bed, made for the same event, its corners filled with the arms of England and France enclosed in circles. The arms of Lionel of Antwerp were, as was natural in view of the occasion, also included in the design. It was for this joust that the queen and her daughters wore red *ghitas* embroidered in enamel work; and, following immediately the entry for the *ghitas*, come the twelve hoods with their white borders which belonged to the tunics listed above. The hoods were embroidered with Catherine wheels and the same motto, which appeared again on a green velvet *jupon* for the king. For the Norwich joust,[11] a harness of green cloth was embroidered, as was the *jupon* with a powdering of *rotul*, bearing the motto once more. What are these things referred to as *rotul*? It is tempting and reasonable to interpret them as scrolls, but the word *rotulus* could equally signify a wheel, and it seems probable that both at Norwich and the later event referred to in the *Archaeologia* account of 1347–9, wheels and not scrolls were carried by the two figures embroidered on the king's coverlet, and that the figures themselves represented St Katharine of Alexandria.

At the conclusion of a legal battle fought between 1333 and 1334 over details concerning the patronage of the ancient hospital of St Katharine, founded near the Tower of London in the twelfth century by queen Matilda,[12] the young queen Philippa emerged as its patron in place of Isabella, the queen mother. By 1343, an ambitious project for the rebuilding of the church of St Katharine and a part of the hospital itself was on foot, following the queen's appointment of William de Kildesby (who had a special devotion to St Katharine) to the Mastership of the hospital.[13] In 1343, with permission from the pope, Kildesby, fulfilling an earlier vow, set out to visit the saint's shrine on Mount Sinai, having already begun to collect funds for the rebuilding of the hospital's church on its original ground-plan. It seems extremely probable, therefore, that the king's appearance at a series of jousts wearing the insignia of St Katharine was a part of a fund-raising effort, a benevolent gesture by a monarch who had little cash but plenty of good will where his wife's interests were concerned. William de Kildesby returned from the Holy Land in time to fight at the battle of Crécy, where he lost his life.[14]

After two brief appointments, Paul Montefiore, who had earlier been involved in the recovery of the royal crown in pawn to the archbishop of Treves, was appointed Master of St Katharine's, by which time the rebuilding, postponed by the French war and the Black Death, had been resumed. Was it, perhaps, encouraged by a further propaganda exercise when the king, in 1348 or 1349, appeared again at a joust wearing the motto, 'It is as it is', embroidered on the same combination of colours, green and white? A great wardrobe account of more than ten years later shows that Edward once more had a garment embroidered with *rotalibz* made; it was packed up and transported from Westminster to Windsor. Unfortunately its colour is not mentioned.[15]

42

The next motto which appears in the *Archaeologia* account, 'Haẏ haẏ the Wẏthe swan bẏ godes soule I am thẏ man', seems to have been of a temporary nature, but the third is, 'Honẏ soit q mal ẏ pense', the motto of the Order of the Garter. Most of the contemporary information on this Order at the time of its foundation depends, like the St Catherine devices, not on state papers but on the rolls which recorded the activities of the royal tailors. It was not, of course, his interest in clothes, but in the establishment of the Order of the Garter that induced Sir Nicholas Harris Nicholas to publish a great wardrobe account in 1846 together with his *Observations on the Institution of the Most Noble Order*, among which he points out that Froissart, a child at the time and therefore writing after the event, mistook the Windsor Round Table of 1344 for the actual date of the Order's foundation.

In reading through the entries in this *Archaeologia* account, the significance of the change to blue clothing becomes apparent. It has been suggested that the choice of blue, both for the Garter itself and for the habit of the Order, was related to the blue field of the French coat-of-arms.[16] Whether or not this is true, blue was certainly a relatively uncommon colour for either official or informal royal clothing at the time when it was chosen, and, indeed, a colour most generally associated with the dress of the clergy and of the poor;[17] which should not be taken to mean that it was never used as a colour for fashionable dress, for, on occasion, it was. Could its choice as the one colour apart from white to be associated with the Order of the Garter have been intended to symbolize not only loyalty but also humility – humility, of course, of the most dramatic kind? More than one poet declared that blue symbolized loyalty, but that was after the Order's foundation, not before.[18]

As for the badge itself, it is well known that at least three explanations for its adoption have been put forward: the first, that it was connected in a sentimental way with the countess of Salisbury, said by some to have been greatly admired by the king; the second, that it was derived from a lace to be worn round the leg, given by Richard I to some of his chosen knights attacking Cyprus and Acre;[19] the third, and in many ways the most convincing, the recent theory that the device which looks like a garter actually represented the knightly belt in miniature.[20] That it was called a 'garter' from the time of its first appearance can be seen from the same great wardrobe account published in *Archaeologia*, in which it is made clear that, although powdered all over the king's mantle and hood, it was a three-dimensional object in that it was equipped with a silver buckle, silver pendants and silver bars.[21]

The order was founded, as we have seen, at a time when clothing was becoming more decorative where its surface was concerned, and this is emphasized not only by the elaborate embroideries worked on garments for the queens of France and England and for the Dauphin, but also from the fact that Edward's own clothes, even when they seem not to have been associated with a tournament, were often embroidered. In one instance, a tunic is mentioned as

having been embroidered with *colfacches*, and these were certainly variants of the bezants that could appear in so many forms. In view of their curious name, *colfacches* were perhaps small objects of metal actually stuck on to the fabric.[22] A suit of two garments made of cloth of gold powdered with stars and crescents may have been intended for wear at a joust; another, on the other hand, *woven* of gold on an indigo ground in a pattern of lozenges, although powdered with birds, may have been made for wear in the normal course of life at court.[23]

At the Lichfield joust of 1347, blue and white were the colours worn by the king, the queen and the royal children, as well as by the lords and their ladies, the knights and the squires. Was this a foretaste of the Garter habit, or had it already come into

12 An embossing block for making bezants of various patterns.

43

being? In reference to all these liveries, the colour blue is named in French – *bleu* – and, together with a comparatively small quantity of gold camocas, everybody who was given clothing (most of them mentioned by name) wore *bleu* and white – the colours to be almost immediately associated with the Order of the Garter.

The following entry in the same *Archaeologia* account is for furnishings and clothes definitely connected with the Garter; it includes pavilions and a state bed, and here the blue is referred to as *bluet/um* and *blu*, which suggests that this had become the term for a definite tint associated with the Order and used both for the garters themselves and for other furnishings made specifically for the Order. *Bluetum* is not at all a common term in great wardrobe accounts of the time; in entries in the *Archaeologia* account which are manifestly *not* associated with the Order – princess Joan's trousseau, for example – blue clothing is referred to either as *azure* or as *ynde*.

References to *blu* in association with white seem, in short, to indicate things made for the Order of the Garter. In an unpublished and earlier inventory of materials supplied for the years 1344 and 1345,[24] three pieces of heavy *blu* sindon of Tripoli and twelve pieces of heavy (*afforc*) *blu* sindon as well as six pieces of white sindon of Tripoli appear – too early for the Order of the Garter, of course, and yet . . .? As compared with sindon in other colours (*glaucos*, red, black, green, azure and *tull*), these quantities are not large, but they have made their appearance. An inventory of the following year, 1345–6,[25] survives, but it is in bad condition and difficult to read in the earlier parts concerned with the expensive woollen stuffs, of which the Garter habits could have been expected to have been made. An inventory for the years 1348–9 is legible, but mentions the actual colours of cloths only irregularly, though their quantities are always recorded; it is the inventory in which the painted clothes for the masquers published in the *Archaeologia* account are mentioned, and it is probably too late to have included stuff for the Garter suits themselves.[26] Nevertheless, the reference to *blu* and white sindon of Tripoli in the account of 1344–5 should be taken seriously; too cheap a stuff to be used for ceremonial clothing but suitable for wearing at a joust, it suggests that, at that time, the Order of the Garter, although not a *fait accompli*, was probably already envisaged.

The entries which refer directly to the provision of furnishings for the Order of the Garter in the *Archaeologia* account begin on membrane 8 with a bed of *Taffeta bluet* for the king, powdered with garters enclosing 'that' motto, 'Hony soit q̄ mal ẏ pense'. This is followed by an entry for making a *chlamidis*, super tunic, tunic and hood for the king's person, of *bluet* longcloth powdered with garters equipped with silver-gilt buckles and pendants. This is the only reference contemporary with the founding of the Order to the four ceremonial items of clothing which must have made up its original official livery. The Greek word *chlamys*, denoting the military cloak adopted by the Romans, is used very sparingly in English accounts and other documents, and then only to denote mantles of an exceptionally dignified kind.

Then, on membrane 9, appears an entry for the making of a *jupon* of *taffeta blu* for the king's person, powdered with garters with silver-gilt buckles and pendants, a second *jupon* of *zatẏ blu*, similarly powdered with garters, follows. It seems, therefore, that at least at that moment, ceremonies associated with the Order demanded a change of dress but not a change in its colour or its device. Membrane 9 includes entries for the clothing for the 1347 tournament at Bury, for which fourteen tunics and hoods of *bluet* short cloth were made. When, however, it came to describing clothing bearing the royal arms at this time, the clerks of the great wardrobe seem to have been uncertain as to whether to call the blue *ynde* or *blu*.[27]

The years 1347 and 1348 were notable for the number of tournaments which took place. For the Lichfield joust, held on 9 April 1348, the *Archaeologia* account provides the information that, for the clothing for the king's person and for those of his noble attendants of both sexes, 124¼ ells of *bleu* cloth and 56 ells of white were used, which gives some idea of the proportions of blue to white in the design of the habits; the length of cloth varied with the rank of the recipient, but more than thirty gentlemen and more than a dozen ladies were given these blue and white liveries. For the gentlemen, there was a cote and a hood *de secta regis*; princess Isabella and her ladies were also given cotes and hoods of the king's pattern, but, as well, ghitas and hoods in camocas of gold and *bleu*, as were other ladies in the court circle. Although the Order is not mentioned by name in this connection, the reference to *de secta regis* evidently made this unnecessary.

An unpublished great wardrobe account of 1360 includes an extremely interesting reference to *blu* when a whole longcloth of *blu* was issued for clothing to be presented by Edward to Jean II, king of France, in captivity in England but preparing for his return to France in the summer of that year. This particular suit included 700 bellies of trimmed miniver for a 'tabard', a cloak-lining of 500 bellies, a hood-lining of 100 bellies and a shoulder-cape – *mantilletum* – lined with, or made from, 80 bellies. This is a very large quantity of fur, far more than would have been needed to line a normal fashionable suit; the fact that a whole cloth was used to make it also suggests that it was of a peculiarly formal or regal kind. Where and when the captive king of France could have worn this *blu* suit, and another almost exactly like it, is a matter for speculation.

Apart from this ceremonial clothing, very little blue cloth seems to have been used during this year at all. In fact, *blu* is mentioned only four times in this account of 1360–61. On membrane 10 it appears among some oddments, such as breeches for the king and a coverlet embroidered with red griffins; on membrane 4 and an unnumbered membrane that follows it as a part of the humble clothing for four of the king's henchmen, who were given cotes and cloaks for a livery of russet, *blu* and white to wear at Christmas.

Three ells of blue and nine ells of motteley cloth appear in a very damaged account for the following year, 1362–3, but more may have been listed among the high-quality imported cloths with which the inventory probably began, but these are missing.[28] Far more important is a complete and very long great wardrobe account for the year extending from 29 June 1363 to 19 June 1364 (E III 37–38).[29] This is indeed one of the most outstanding great wardrobe accounts to have survived from the second half of the fourteenth century. The first membrane includes an entry for *gounes*[30] for the king and for some of his knights of the chamber, for which russet longcloth, blanket (white) and 12¾ ells of *blu* longcloth were issued. This was evidently a survival of the court livery which had been worn by the henchmen three years earlier, but it would have been unusual for henchmen to have been given longcloth, which was expensive, so the livery was probably, or had been, worn in varying qualities throughout the court. The only other entry in this account for *blu* cloth concerns a gift from the king for another suit of *blu* for the king of France, this time trimmed with ermine, delivered to Jean (presumably in England) by the hand of 'Hervey'.[31] Both these ceremonial suits are discussed in a later chapter. Although they were made of *blu* cloth no word in either account associates them with the Order of the Garter.

A miniver-lined coverlet of *blu* was made during this year for Edward's bed at Sheen and a suit was made for him, of unspecified colour, of the *sect* – pattern – of the knights of the Garter; it was trimmed with ermine and tied with narrow ribbons of gold. At about the same time 250 garters of *tartèryn ynde* were made for the king and other named knights (*aliis milit*); they were embroidered with the Order's motto in letters of silk and gold. From the number of knights named in this instance it can be calculated that about fifty garters were used to decorate each suit.

In the year of the reign 'xxxviii' – 1364 – fifteenth knights, again referred to by name as members of the Order, were given suits for the feast of St George, each made from five ells of sanguine longcloth in grain and one ell of black, perhaps for a hood. The feast of St George must have been the most important day in the Order's calendar so it seems probable that either the original *blu* habit was kept and worn from year to year, while suits of other colours were worn for other ceremonies on that day or, alternatively, that by this time only the mantles of the Order were blue and were not issued annually but were retained for wear over suits of colours that differed from one year to the next.

Three years earlier, suits specifically mentioned as having been issued to Knights of the Garter also present a difficulty for whereas some of the knights, including some of the royal princes, were each given five ells of 'coloured' longcloth together with an appropriate amount of miniver, others, including the earls of Stafford, Warwick and Suffolk, were each given six ells of black longcloth and similar qualities of fur. Because, however, the actual quantities of cloth issued varied only from five to six ells, it seems

likely that the word 'coloured' merely meant in this case 'dyed' and that, in reality, all the Knights wore black but some of them were physically bigger than others. If this is correct then all the suits may have been made to wear at one of the royal funerals which took place that year.[32]

Among the knights who were named as having received suits for St George's day in the year 1364 is that of Nigel Loring, whose name had already appeared in a great wardrobe account of three years previously. Loring is the one original member of the Order whose portrait has survived in a contemporary manuscript from St Albans abbey. In it he wears the Garter habit and, to the modern eye, its form is unexpected. Sir Nigel wears no mantle but is portrayed in a tunic of white cloth, probably *blanket*, long to the ankle, hooded and of strictly monkish cut. It is powdered with surprisingly large garters. On his head he wears a red cap of the type that was eventually to develop into the ecclesiastical biretta. The design of his dress suggests that it was intended to look, if not deliberately archaic, certainly romantically picturesque in a period when fashionable tunics were tight and short.

It may be that in discussing the earliest habits issued to Knights of the Garter too much emphasis has been laid on the use of the term *blu*. Referring to a distinctive shade, *blu* may have been no more than

13 Sir Nigel Loring as a knight of the Order of the Garter. Illumination from *Liber Vite* of St Alban's Abbey.

a useful means of identifying the statutory cloth for the convenience of the royal tailors. But as a colour blue certainly had symbolic connotations and both Froissart and Machaut described it as representing loyalty. Froissart, in his *Cour de May*, written in about 1360 in honour of Philippa of Hainault, presents himself, in approaching his lady, who is dressed *d'un drap d'or sur vert*, wearing a blue coronet:

> Je porte la couronne bleue
> La couronne de loyauté,[33]

by that time, although there is no proof of it, he had probably already written his *Dit dou bleu Chevalier*:

> Au loing percoi . i . chevalier venir
> Tour bleu vesti, sans differensce vir,[34]

which, whatever its date, was certainly written after the foundation of the Order of the Garter. Machaut, writing in France, was not necessarily concerned with the Order at all when he discussed the significance of certain colours, among which he set blue above all others:

> . . . a droit jugier
> Et dire la droite signefiance
> On deveroit le fin asur prisier
> Dessus toutes . . .[35]

From the point of view of the Order of the Garter itself, however, one of the most exuberant references to it in its early years can be found in the alliterative poem *Winner and Waster*, written in 1354. In this a 'caban' high on the crest of a hill (Windsor Castle stands high) is described as decorated with English bezants of bright beaten gold and bound round 'with garters of inde'; and, later, the king's robes are seen to be embroidered with golden falcons, each carrying a 'grete gartere of ynde', while that great lord is girdled round the middle with an embroidered belt of blue:
At the crest of a clyffe a caban was rerede,
Alle raylede with rede the rofe and the sydes,
With Ynglysse besantes full brighte, betyn of golde,
And ichone gayly umby-gone with garters of inde,

Fawkons of fyne golde, flakerande with wynges,
and ichone bare in ble, blewe als me thoghte,
A grete gartare of ynde . . .

Full gayly was that grete lorde girde in the myddis,
A brighte belte of ble, broudirde with fowles . . .[36]

'Ynde', yes, but blue too; earlier in the poem, garters are named as 'Payntted of plunket', yet another term for a blue colour. But all this is not, of course, the language of the great wardrobe.

Although it appears to have been the second Order of Chivalry to have been established in Europe between 1340 and 1365, the Order of the Garter has been discussed first because the date of the foundation of the Order of the Sword of Cyprus is based on slender evidence which not everybody can accept: a poem, that is, written, it is generally agreed, more than thirty years after it claims that the Order was established.

La Prise d'Alexandrie, by the French poet Guillaume Machaut, is the chief, if not the only, literary source of information on the Ordre de l'Epée, which does not mean that the Order existed in fiction rather than fact. Machaut had been secretary to John, king of Bohemia, after whose death at Crécy he became secretary to John's daughter, Bonne of Luxemburg, and finally, after her death, to her widower, Jean II, king of France. A prolific poet as well as a musician, after the death of Jean, Guillaume embarked, perhaps in 1367, on his long poem on the capture of Alexandria by Peter I of Cyprus.[37] The capture of the city was a very temporary triumph – it was almost immediately recaptured – but it was nevertheless the main fruit of Peter's determination to attempt a crusade.[38]

Although picturesque, Guillaume Machault's description of the sword as the insignia of the Order is correct; he followed it by the Order's motto: 'C'est pour loiauté maintenir'. Line 358 of the poem begins:

> Une espee de fin argent
> Qui avoit le pommel desseuré
> En signe de crois qu'on aeure
> Assisé en un champ asureé
> De toutes coulours espuré
> Et s'avoit lettres d'or entour
> Qui estoient faites à tour
> Disans, bien m'en doit souvenir
> 'C'est pour loiauté maintenit'[39]

In calling blue the purest of all colours, Machaut's view would have been accepted in the fourteenth century, when, apart from being one of the colours regarded as suitable to the clergy and members of monastic orders, it was usually chosen as the colour of clothing distributed to the poor.[40] In his poem on the Order of the Sword, Machaut explains that the 'white' sword signifies a pure heart and a clean life; and it signifies justice. Its sharp point reproves idleness and indulgence in the fountain of delights, which is surrounded by all the vices.[41] In its form, the sword represents the cross, most noble of all signs. It is drawn in battle, but also in the defence of righteousness and justice, orphans, widows and the Church itself.[42]

Apart from the poem, there are one or two other traces of the Order of the Sword. With its floating banderole which bears its motto, the sword of the Order is carved within a shield on the façade of the Cornaro Palace (now the Municipal Hall) in Venice in recognition of Federico Cornaro's membership of the Order. Peter of Cyprus had stayed in the palace during his tour of Europe in 1364.[43]

An even more tangible piece of evidence of the existence of the Order is a silver buckle, now in the Musée Cinquantenaire in Brussels, which has a sword as its prong and the motto of the Order engraved round its frame. On his silver grote, Peter of Cyprus, enthroned and dressed in a tunic which, though archaistic, can be recognized as belonging to the fashion current at the time of his accession in

1359, holds in his hands not a sceptre but a sword.[44] No statutes of the Order nor any descriptions of any habits worn by members of the Ordre de l'Épée seem to have survived.

In 1351, a year after his accession to the throne of France, Jean II established the Ordre de l'Étoile, ou des Chevaliers de la Noble Maison. As in the case of the original statutes of the Order of the Garter, no contemporary copies of the original of the Order of the Star have survived, but just as the English Order enjoyed a great revival of attention in the seventeeth century, soon after the restoration of the monarchy, so, in France, one of the founder-members of the Académie Royale des Inscriptions et Belles Lettres invited lovers of French antiquities to undertake research into the origins and character of Jean le Bon's Ordre de l'Étoile. The Order itself, unlike the Order of the Garter, had been short-lived.

14 Buckle from the insignia of the Order of the Sword. Actual length about 8.50 cms (3.25").

The result of the researches undertaken in response to the invitation are contained in a collection of letters in the Bibliothèque Nationale in Paris known as the Foncemagne papers,[45] and, almost certainly as a further result, in an address delivered by M. Dacier to the Académie on 17 March 1772, published in 1777.[46] The similarity between the form in which the findings are expressed in these two sources leads one to believe that they were almost certainly carried out by the same person. M. Dacier was not, however, the first of the later historians to take an interest in the Ordre; what he described in

his address as an Ordonnance, but what was, in fact, a circular letter, had found its way into the Grandes Chroniques de France. This letter contained instructions concerning the habit, ornaments and conduct of the Ordre as drawn up by Jean II; it had been published in Paris in 1729 in the second volume of the Ordonnances des rois de France by Dom Luc d'Archery.[47] André Favin, greatly to the disapproval of M. Dacier, had also investigated the Ordre de l'Étoile in his Theatre of Honour of 1625.[48] He claimed that it had been founded originally, not by Jean II but by king Robert, son of Hugh Capet, in 1022, an error which, according to Dacier, arose from the fact that Robert had named the Blessed Virgin Mary Étoile de sa Royaume.[49]

The chronicler Jean le Bel, who was followed by Froissart, stated explicitly that le roi Jean set up a large, handsome and noble company on the plan of King Arthur's Round Table of ancient times.[50] Jean's father, Philippe de Valois, had apparently held, it should be remembered, a Round Table himself in 1344, as a rival event to Edward's festival at Windsor that year. Jean le Bel's chronicle includes the remarkable statement that the number of members of the Order envisaged by Jean le Bon was 500, who were required to meet annually at a banquet at St Ouen, the king's palace, on the day of the Assumption in the presence of the three princes: that is to say, the king, his brother and his eldest son Charles, as well as the three Barones and the three knights who had most distinguished themselves during the past year.[51] Froissart, most of whose earlier entries were based on Jean le Bel, provides some further details, and at the same time says that the number of members of the Ordre was to be 300, not 500.[52] The Garter Knights were limited to twenty-six.[53] Froissart adds the information that the members were to repair to the Noble Maison of St Ouen for all the great festivals of the year – an expensive undertaking for those who lived at a distance. There were also, again according to Froissart, to be two or three clerks to keep a written record of the deeds and adventures performed or undergone by the Knights of the Order, so that they should never be forgotten. Provision was to be made, too, for knights in their old age, when they were to be attended by two servants at the king's expense.[54]

Jean le Bon's letter, issued on 6 November 1351 and published in the Ordonnances des rois de France, begins, Biau Cousin, which suggests, M. Dacier pointed out, that it was addressed to a member of his immediate family; it is absolutely explicit in its directions as to the habits of the Ordre and the occasions on which they were to be worn. Translated, the relevant passages are:

. . . we have ordered a Company of Knights to be formed, which will be called the Knights of Our Lady of the Noble House, each of whom shall wear a suit described as follows: That is to be understood as a white Cote, a vermilion Sercot and a Hood, when he appears without a mantle. And when he wears a mantle, which shall be made like that of a newly created knight,[55] when he

47

enters, or is present in the Church of the Noble House, it shall be vermilion lined with miniver, not with *Ermine*, or with *Cendal* or *Samite*; and beneath this mantle shall be worn a white *Sercote* or a white *Cote hardie*, black hose and gilded shoes; and he shall always wear a ring round the edge – *verge* – of which shall be written his name and surname; on this ring shall be a flat enamel plate, on it a white star and in the centre of the star a blue roundel, in the middle of the roundel a tiny gold Sun, and on the mantle, over the shoulder, in front of the hood, a clasp on which shall be a Star of exactly the same pattern as that on the ring.

And every Saturday, wherever he shall be, he shall wear vermilion and white for his *Cote* and *Sercot* and *Chaperon*, and if he wishes to wear the clasp, he can wear it on any suit that he pleases, and on mail or other armour, or where it pleases him.

And he shall fast every Saturday, if he can conveniently do so, if not he shall give fifteen deniers for God's charity, in honour of the fifteen Joys of Our Lady . . . and every year he shall be at the Noble House situated between Paris and St Denis, on the Eve of the Festival of Our Lady in mid August[56] at Prime and shall stay there all day and the whole of the following day until Vespers, so long as he can conveniently do so. And in every place where five or more [members] find themselves together on the Eve of the said August festival, if they cannot come to the Noble House, they shall put on their habits and go together to Vespers and Mass.

And on the day of his death, shall be sent to the Noble House the ring and the clasp, and a Mass shall be said as soon as possible for the repose of his soul.

And it is ordered that the arms and devices of all the lords and knights shall be painted in the hall.. [and there follow instructions as to the suspension of those who might disgrace the Order].

And it is further ordered that in the Noble House, shall be a Table called the Table of Honour, at which shall be seated at the Vigil and the feast, the three greatest of the Princes, the three greatest of the bannerets and the three knights bachelor who have most distinguished themselves in arms during the year . . . [no knights were to leave the country without permission].

No pictorial representation of the habit of the *Ordre* contemporary with the issue of this letter has survived, but in a manuscript of the *Grandes Chroniques de France*, whose miniatures were certainly executed within ten years of the coronation of Jean's son, Charles, in 1364, is a painting of the High Table on the occasion of a festival of the *Ordre*, and from this it is possible to see that the habits of the Order followed the pattern laid down, though it is doubtful whether by this time liveries were ever issued or that the Order ever met. Fashions in dress had changed by the time the miniature was painted: waists had become narrower, the toes of shoes drawn into longer points; trumpet-shaped cuffs covered the hand to the knuckles, chests were greatly inflated and hair was curled.[57]

The making of the first habits of the Order occupies considerable space in the unpublished inventory KK8[58] of 1351, and so does the jewellery of the Order. The habits appear in the first of the surviving folios in the manuscript, among the issues of clothing to Philippe, king of Navarre, Louis of Navarre and Charles d'Artois. These three lords were recipients of the order of knighthood at this time, and their suits of blue – *pers azure* – and inky green – *vert encre* – which had, of course, nothing to do with the Ordre de l'Étoile, are included. At the same time, they received a *cote* and a mantle of vermilion *samit*, and for lining the *cote* a sheet of 140 bellies of miniver, for its sleeves 45 bellies and for the mantle 282 bellies. Certainly for the ceremonies of the Étoile, however, are the surcotes, hoods and mantles which appear on folio iv, described as being made of scarlet cloth of vermilion; and the habit of Charles d'Artois is stated in detail as consisting of one *cote* of white camocas, *l surcot, mantel* and *chaperon* of vermilion camocas, which he had as one of the said company for the *feste de l'estoille*. Camocas, sometimes specified in the same account as *camocas de domasque* (Damascus), was an extremely expensive imported silk, the use of which for a livery of this kind is somewhat surprising.[59]

On the verso of folio vii in KK8, the section devoted to the dauphin's *Orfevrerie*, is an entry for forging a plain gold star without precious stones and a gold ring with the star, both given to him by the king; on the ring his name was inscribed in enamel-work. It was subsequently given by the Dauphin as an offering to 'monsieur' Saint Maurice on the vigil of All Saints. Together, the ring and the star weighed four ounces, and cost, according to the inventory, '10/-c sterling' for the gold and, for their making, £18. A silver star, a gold star, as well as a ring were also given to each of the king's younger sons – the duc D'Orleans and the comte d'Anjou; these were also offered to St Maurice, a warrior saint and, according to legend, a member of the Theban legion.[60] At the same time, stars, each decorated with four rubies and four clusters each of three large pearls, were made. Stars and rings were also made for the Constable of France and the five chamberlains as well as for the four masters of the king's household; the Dauphin's chamberlains and the masters of his household too were given rings and silver-gilt stars.[61]

The king's five chamberlains, as members of the Order, were issued with habits, the cotes of which were made not of camocas but of fine white longcloth of Brussels.[62] The surcoats must have been white too, and their mantles were almost certainly of vermilion longcloth lined with miniver.[63] They are described as open at one side – *fendus a un coste*. The Dauphin's three chamberlains (sometimes listed as four but that must include his treasurer) are named as Adam de Melem, Jehan des Essars and Pierre Dormont. Each was given a surcoat and not one but two mantles of scarlet cloth of vermilion colour, one *a parer* and the other open at one side. Two hundred and forty bellies of miniver are allowed for the lining of the surcoat, 100 for the hood, 360 for the *mantel a parer* and 300 for the *mantel fendu a un coste*, which probably means that the mantle *a parer* was longer than the other but not very much. These quantities correspond fairly closely to the amounts of fur issued to the princes who were members of the Order[64] which shows that although the material of which the habits were made differed, they were all of the same cut. Gloves were given to all members. The day of the Assumption falls on 15 August so that three layers of longcloth, two of them lined with fur or, for that matter, of camocas, a substantial silk, must have imposed some strain on the wearers. The directions in the open letter state clearly that mantles were to be lined with miniver and not with cendal or samite and there is no suggestion in KK8 that members of the Order were given summer as well as winter habits.

The mantle open at one side – on, that is to say, the right shoulder – was the traditional mantle of the knight; it left the right arm free to draw the sword, suspended from its scabbard on the left hip. This had been the pattern of the chlamys as worn by the Romans and the name had survived, as we have seen, for the mantle of the Order of the Garter; by this time, as an extremely honourable and ancient garment, it was not confined to knights but had been adopted by some other dignitaries too. That today's mantle of the Order of the Garter does not follow this cut is interesting and so is the fact that today the insignia of the Order are worn on the right shoulder, marking, perhaps, the spot where the knightly chlamys should properly be open. Equally interesting is the fact that the habit of the Order of the *Etoile* included in some, if not in all cases, two mantles both, judging from the quantities of fur needed to line them, of roughly the same size but only one open at one side. While a wholly unencumbered right arm is necessary for the quick withdrawal of the sword from its scabbard, a mantle open only on the right side virtually immobilises the left arm – an inconvenience, to say the least, in many of the activities of social life. In early warfare, the front of a bulky mantle could, if wrapped round the left arm, serve as a thick temporary shield for the body (a device still used in some connections – bull-fighting, for instance) but in the courtly circumstances of a meeting of an Order of Chivalry, this could be no advantage and, no doubt, the chamberlains changed their mantles at some point during the formal proceedings.

If the picture of the members of the Ordre de l'Étoile in the *Grandes Chroniques* is correct, the official white *sercot* reached the ankles and was, in this respect, therefore, archaic. Unlike the Garter habit in which Nigel Loring was portrayed, however, its cut seems to have been entirely fashionable, which means that the waist was set low, the upper part fitted the body with a rounded swelling over the chest. The skirt appears to have been gathered – *froncée* – onto the low waistline. The style of both this surcoat and of the fashionable clothing portrayed elsewhere in the *Grandes Chroniques* points to a date soon after the accession of Charles V for the execution

15 Illumination from the *Statuts de l'Ordre du Saint Esprit au droit désir*, 1353. Left, king Louis wearing the knightly chlamys; right, Louis and some of his knights wearing the black hoods, obligatory on every Friday throughout the year.

of its miniatures, not later than the end of the 1360s, perhaps, and earlier than most art historians have considered it to be.[65] The enormous size of the stars which the Knights of the Order are shown as wearing on their chests must certainly have been an exaggeration.

Soon after the founding of the Order of the Star, the king had ordered new coins to be struck to replace the 'gros blancs a la couronne et aux fleurs de lys'; they were known as the 'gros blancs a l'Etoile', some specimens of which, in two sizes, have survived. On the obverse is a Greek cross in the centre of which is a star; on the reverse, a temple with four stars, one at each of its corners. In the middle of each star is a small roundel, following the design of the stars on the rings and the clasps of the Order.

In 1352, canons and clerks were appointed to the Order which was, as we have seen, committed by its statutes to certain religious observances as well as to the performance of acts of charity towards the sick and the poor. It is unlikely that the number of knights reached anything approaching 500; the names of only about twenty-five of the original members have survived.[66]

Whereas no specimens of the original statutes of the Orders of the Sword, the Garter or the Star have been preserved, a set of the original statutes of the Ordre du Saint Esprit au Droit Désir ou du Noeud, with handsome painted miniatures, has. It is to be found in the Bibliothèque Nationale in Paris.[67] The truth of the engaging story that they were given by

16 *Statuts de l'Ordre du Saint Esprit*, detail from the full-page illumination of Louis and Joanna adoring the Trinity. Beneath his right arm Louis wears the insignia of the Order, a dove descending through rays of light. See also p. 106.

the Serenissima of Venice to Henri II has been questioned,[68] but their authenticity has not, and no other theory as to their arrival in Paris has been generally accepted. They were published with what were then regarded as facsimiles of the illustrations in chromolithograph by the comte Horace de Salviac de Viel-Castel in 1853; that is to say, 500 years after the meeting of their first chapter. The founder of the Order, Louis of Taranto, claimed that it was, in fact, established on the occasion of his coronation as consort of his wife, Joanna I of Naples, who was crowned at the same time, on the day of Pentecost, in 1352. In view of the unsavoury reputations of both Joanna and Louis before their coronation (he was her

second husband, her first having been strangled, almost certainly with her connivance, seven years earlier), there can be little doubt that the institution of the Order was designed to assure the people of the kingdom of Naples, the fraternity of European rulers and the pope at Avignon that the Neapolitan monarchy was, or would be, based on the highest ideals of morality, chivalry and charity.

In its form the Order of the Saint Esprit followed very closely the Ordre de l'Étoile, which was itself not unlike the Order of the Garter in many respects. The statutes of the Order of the Saint Esprit are precise and clear, and may, it has been suggested, have been drawn up by the Florentine, Nicola Acciaiuoli, Louis' *grand sénéchal*. The Holy Ghost of the title of the Order referred to the day of the coronation at Pentecost, to celebrate which Joanna founded a church dedicated to the Virgin Mary, a participator at the first Pentecost. The church, Sta Maria di Piedigrotta, was built in 1353.

The subsidiary name given to the Order, *du Noeud*, referred to one of its two badges; it became a pretty instrument in the game of chivalry. Members of the *Ordre*, of which there were to be 300, committed to render loyal counsel and to aid their sovereign to the utmost of their strength, were to wear the badge of the Knot at all times on whatever garment it pleased them to wear it, so that it was clearly visible. They must also wear on either an outer or an under garment and presumably embroidered, the words 'se dieu plaist'. On Fridays, in memory of Christ's Passion, the knights must wear on the chest a black hood with a plain knot of white silk attached to it, and the rest of their dress – the suits and hose – must be simple in colour, by which, presumably, was meant that on Fridays they must wear one single colour rather than patterned stuff or clothing made up of several colours.

Until a knight had visited the Holy Sepulchre in Jerusalem he must wear his knot untied and leave it there as an offering, putting on a new knot which was tied and bore his name and the motto 'il a pleeu a dieu'. Below the Knot, once tied, there was to be embroidered the symbol of the Holy Ghost (a dove descending through rays of light), but this must be worn only on white garments. The house of Anjou traced its ancestry to the kings of Jerusalem, hence the emphasis on the importance of visiting the Holy Sepulchre. Louis of Taranto called himself king of Jerusalem and Sicily.

Each year at Pentecost the knights were to assemble at 'that Castle' near the sea, between Naples and 'Nostre Dame', at the foot of the dark grotto, magically associated with Virgil, the Chateau d'Oeuf,[69] and on that day they must be dressed entirely in white, that is to say, in surcoat, hood and shoes, with the badge symbolic of the Holy Ghost set over their hearts. Notre Dame was the church built by Joanna on the site, one may presume, of one that had already existed.[70]

Writing in Florence about the Order, Matteo Villani said that the knights were to wear *cotardite*; all must be of the same colour and cut,[71] but except for the white ceremonial habits, this is not borne out by

50

17 *Statuts de l'Ordre du Saint Esprit.* Annual feast of the Order, held at Pentecost. A knight who has disgraced the Order sits alone at a small table, dressed in black.

the illustrations to the statutes, which show variations in both cut and decoration – some wear tunics which are buttoned down the front and some do not, for instance, and their colours likewise seem to have depended on personal taste. Villani goes on to say that they must wear the knot of *Salomone* on their chests, and that those who had a mind for it could have their *cotes hardies* and their knots embroidered in silver, gold and precious stones and could present a very grand appearance at very great cost. In this, if it was true, the knights of the Order would, of course, have been associating themselves with the current fashion for rich embroidery, whereas members of the other contemporary Orders were not. Villani then goes on to relate the story of the occasion on which the king had a 'royal' *cote hardie*, with a knot embroidered in large and costly pearls, made and sent to his brother, Robert of Taranto, who had not joined the Order; but Robert replied that the knot of fraternal love was worn in the heart and not on the exterior, and handed the tunic on to one of his own knights, to the king's annoyance.

The statutes set out one or two other occasions when the knot was to be first untied and, after performing some feat, tied up, and they also direct that there should at the Pentecostal gatherings be a table named 'la table desirée', at which should sit all the knights who had that year untied their knots as well as those who had performed outstanding feats of arms and wore the knot tied and the Holy Ghost badge; these were to wear on their heads wreaths of laurel. In contrast to the table of honour, a second table, placed directly in front of the king's, should be the place where should be seated any knight who

had disgraced himself and the Order during the preceding year. He was to be dressed entirely in black, whereas on that day the other knights must wear white, and on the spot where they wore their honourable badges, he must wear in words legible to all: 'iay esperance ou saint esperit de ma grante honte amender'.

Unlike the knights of the Order of the Garter and the Étoile, the knights of the Saint Esprit were not directed to wear knightly mantles, nor were their surcoats long, which accounts, no doubt, for Matteo Villani's description of them as *cotardite*. It was, in fact, only their white colour (and that worn only on the day of Pentecost) and their badges which distinguished them from fashionable men all over Europe, with the result that the illustrations to the statutes serve as an excellent record of the fashions current in 1353.[72] In the absence of the chlamys, only the laurel crown was a reminder of the victor's attributes, and by 1353 laurel crowns had become associated not with victorious generals but with poets – Petrarch had been crowned with one on the Capitol in Rome in April 1341.

If laurel crowns shared by contemporary poets and the heroes of the Ordre du Saint Esprit au Droit Désir could be connected nostalgically with Apollo as well as with triumphant caesars, the Neapolitan Order's nostalgic meeting-place between the Church of Our Lady and the dark grotto where the poet Virgil in his medieval role of magician floated an egg on the waves and gave the Château d'Oeuf its enchanted foundation, emphasizes its fairy-tale unreality.[73] The meticulously drawn and delicately coloured paintings which illustrate the statutes of the

51

Order must have been approved by its founder. Opinions have differed as to which of its numerous members this particular copy was actually designed for, and it may have been, indeed probably was, executed a year or perhaps two after the Order's foundation, but not more. Although, as records of masculine fashions in Naples at their moment, the miniatures are valuable, in their various scenes women appear only twice: on the 'frontispiece', where Louis and Joanna kneel before a representation of the Trinity, and at the Pentecostal banquet. There are one or two marginal vignettes, half-length and mainly of Joanna, and these seem to confirm the fact that a prayer book in Vienna which includes a portrait of Joanna and an attendant kneeling in adoration must have been done at almost if not exactly the same time; in a sequence of later prayers, each begins with a little painting of a dove descending, which surely means that the book had some connection with the Order itself.[74]

But the contrast between Louis of Taranto's attitude to his knights as we see him in these little pictures, and the impression conveyed, or at least intended, by contemporary references to the Order of the Garter, is remarkable. Louis does not appear as a knight among knights, but always as a sovereign ruler revered by an élite selection of his people. The impression is heightened by the absence of uniformity in the dress, both of Louis and of members of his Order, except on the day of Pentecost. Edward's frequent appearance at jousts dressed as one of a group of knights, on the other hand, strengthens the impression that, even if the high-sounding ideals of the Order of the Garter did not penetrate the surface very deeply, other motives besides pure political expediency were present at its foundation. The Orders of the Étoile and the Saint Esprit au Droit Désir scarcely survived the deaths of their founders; today's little annual procession, on foot, of the monarch and those Knights of the Order of the Garter who are still physically able to undertake the exercise from the Order's apartments in Windsor Castle to St George's Chapel (the others are driven at walking pace by car), besides being a sentimentally moving event, is an indication that such ideals of equality between the sovereign and the knights as may have contributed to the Order's original establishment have by no means diminished.[75]

A seventeenth century copy, unpublished, of an inventory of 1363 of the treasury of Charles the Dauphin, has survived.[76] It includes gifts of the king of Cyprus; a golden image of St Thomas of Canterbury; a larger one of St Louis of France; and some cloth of gold and various jewels. Item 1 is the 'coronne que le Roy fit faire pour la feste de l'estelle', and item 569 'l'anil de l'estoille'. It has never been suggested that, in spite of Edward's gifts to Jean II of robes of *blu*, he had ever been admitted to membership of the Order of the Garter. In July 1359, before the signing of the peace of Bretigny and before Jean's release, two rings decorated with stars were made for him in England. For whom had they been destined?[77]

At the end of January 1360, Charles V issued a mandate ordering the striking of *gros Deniers blancs* with the Étoile in the mint at Tournai; and, in February, in the mints of Paris and Rouen. This was the first time since Jean's capture at Poitiers that this coin had been issued; it must have been struck to celebrate his return to France.[78]

VII

Fashions after Poitiers

The battle of Poitiers was lost by the French on 19 September 1356; their king was captured and, together with other prisoners of great standing accredited to the Prince of Wales, taken to Bordeaux. On 15 October there gathered in Paris an assembly of high-ranking clergy, nobles and representatives of the important cities north of the Loire – the *Langue d'oil* – among them the archbishop of Rheims, Philippe duke of Orléans and, as spokesman for the *bonnes villes*, Étienne Marcel, citizen of Paris and prevost of her merchants, who had been supplying cloth to the royal family since the early 1340s.[1] A prolonged inquest was held on the reasons for the defeat of the army and the capture of the king. The meetings lasted for about two weeks and were followed, before the end of October, by a second assembly at Toulouse in the *Langue d'oc*, at which it was decided that, during the current year, should the king not be released (which meant should his ransom not be paid), no man or woman was to wear gold, or silver, or pearls, or miniver, or gris. Neither must they wear garments or hoods that were decoratively cut about – *découppez* – nor any other extravagant fashion whatever in their dress. Furthermore, no minstrels nor jugglers were to pursue their professions.[2]

To ensure obedience to these orders, representatives of the Three Estates which had been responsible for drawing them up were to be sent to Charles the Dauphin, duke of Normandy (the king's eldest son) in Paris, as well as to his lieutenant. The Estates were determined, in fact, that they and not the late counsellors of Jean II should take charge of the running of the country.[3] In December, Charles, to whom these decisions, arrived at without consulting him, were unwelcome, went to Metz to meet Charles of Luxemburg, king of Bohemia and emperor of the West.

On 23 May 1357, the Black Prince returned to England, bringing with him his royal captive. London turned out in its best clothes and its smartest liveries to celebrate a supreme moment of triumph. The king of France was conducted to a worthy prison, the *moult bel hostel* in the Strand, backing on to the Thames, called the Savoy, which belonged to

the duke of Lancaster. This was no moment for sumptuary laws to be imposed on the English; they were to come later.

Jean was naturally permitted to maintain a fairly large household in England, which included, among others, as well as knights and squires, his doctor, his tailor and his fool.[4] Rymer reports that a safe-conduct was granted to his secretary Johannes Peteri, who travelled between France and England bringing his suits – *robes* – and other clothes, books, money and other necessary things.[5] The clothes were probably some of those already in his French wardrobe, for money was certainly very scarce in France and a journal of the expenditure of Jean's household during a part of his stay in England, drawn up by his chaplain, Denys de Collors, shows that until he was actually preparing to return to France in 1360, when it was obviously important to make a suitably brave display, he lived economically.[6] Charles, his son, who was appointed regent of France in 1357, probably lived more parsimoniously still, but, as would naturally be expected, no accounts of his household, which moved to and from Paris, have survived, and indeed it seems unlikely that any were systematically kept during this unhappy period.

The same was not however true of England, where substantial ransoms had been paid for the release of socially important prisoners captured by the Prince of Wales, and these, together with payments of instalments on account of the king's huge ransom of over £165,000,[7] must have provided at least a sensation of relief if not of affluence to Edward, who had been short of money ever since his accession.

This comparative absence of financial strain in England was accompanied by or perhaps responsible for another outburst of indignation at extravagances in new fashions in dress. John of Reading, whose *Chronica* is regarded as having been written between 1366 and 1369,[8] described what he saw as innovations in 1365, and thought that it was not surprising that, in view of such insane frivolity, the Plague, which the English called the *Pokkes*, had returned. Hoods, he declared, were so minute and buttoned so tightly round the neck that they could hardly be pulled on to the head. Their liripipes were as thin as string, hanging down over their paltoks and other such extremely short closed woollen garments, sewn all over.[9] Their very long hose, tied up to them so tightly, are called 'harlots' or 'gradlings' or 'lorels' because their wearers showed the lunacy of those characters.[10] In fact they were tied so tightly to their hose that they could not kneel to God. Their shoes have long beaks and they wear long knives hanging from their belts between their legs.

John of Reading was perhaps a little belated in his criticism, because the author of the chronicle known as *Eulogium* had had almost the same things to say in writing of the year 1362. In a paragraph which begins *Eodem anno et in anno praecedenti . . .*, he accuses the whole community in England as having gone in for such a mad riot of corporeal ornamentation that a judgement of God was to be feared.[11] In the first place, there were super tunics which were very wide and at the same time short to the hips, though others were long to the heels; they were not open down the front in the proper masculine style, but, like women's dresses, extended at the sides up to the arms so that, from the back their wearers looked like women. This garment, he continues, is aptly named in the vernacular a *goun*, but this *gounyg* ought to be pronounced *wounyg*,[12] for it is indeed crazy. And, again like women, they wear tiny little hoods buttoned tightly round their necks and decorated all about with embroidery of gold and silver and precious stones, with liripipes down to their heels like professional fools. Then they wear a silk garment commonly called a paltok; their hose are parti-coloured or striped and tied up to these paltoks of theirs, which have been nicknamed 'harlots' because they barely cover their loins. Their belts of gold and silver cost a fortune, and they wear shoes with beaks in front as long as your finger, called *cracowes*,[13] more suitable as claws of devils than as the apparel of men. They look more like minstrels and jesters than barons, more like actors than knights, and more like comics than men-at-arms. We learn from reading the Book of Kings that Solomon had never worn that sort of thing during the whole of his life.[14]

John of Reading's comments were echoed in the same year by a contemporary chronicler in France, who continued the *Chronique Latine* of Guillaume de Nangis.[15] There is, he says, no honesty in the new fashions worn by the nobles, or, indeed, by most other people. It is not like the old times at all: they wear shoes with points in front as long as a horn and fit mainly for the feet of griffons – they are called *Poulenas Gallice* and are an abuse of nature.[16]

In England it had been a monk who had taken up his pen in 1361 to condemn the new gounes and paltoks; he had been right in regarding them as new at the moment of writing for they certainly were the latest thing. In the middle 1360s in France both Charles V and the Pope Urban V issued laws forbidding short suits and dissolute clothing.

As far as the fashion itself was concerned, the padding over the belly, a characteristic of the early 1350s, had not remained in favour for long and before 1360 a new design for the human body had emerged. This left the belt low, on a level with the crutch – where, that is to say, it had been in the 1340s – but gave the torso a completely new emphasis by abandoning the appearance of a rectangle and, instead, by moulding the tunic to the natural waist, which was induced to look narrower still by the addition of padding not over the belly but round the chest. This padding, at first moderate, was increased during the 1360s until the torso looked almost spherical round the chest.

In the middle of that decade skirts began to widen until, at varying moments according to the centre of fashion in which the change occurred, they achieved a stiff bell shape. Until this happened, however, they had remained tight and very short so that the chroniclers could be excused for attacking them. As the skirts began to extend in the middle of the 1360s, sleeves, still very tight over the forearm, were extended a little at the wrist to form small bells which covered the knuckles. But the most arresting change was in the shape of the upper sleeves, which began to be expanded above the elbow, with the result that, at a superficial glance, some resemblance might be discovered between the tunics of the later 1360s and those of the middle 1330s, tunics of a fashion, that is to say, before the great attacks of the early 1340s were launched. The similarity was not in reality great; but the return to a looser upper-sleeve marked the inevitable reference to a fashion of the past, after what was almost a statutory interval of time – an ingredient of all changes of fashion.

It was pointed out in an earlier chapter that at the beginning of the 1340s, the king of England was wearing suits which included a closed or an open super-tunic and perhaps both; an under tunic and, for certain circumstances, an aketon, a doublet or an occasional courtpie', usually for hunting; sometimes a corset but neither a goune nor a paltok. Both John of Reading and the author of the *Eulogium* found these two garments new and objectionable in the middle 1360s; not long before, an account had been drawn up by John Newbury, at that time clerk of the great wardrobe, which recorded the making of a paltok and a hood of russet longcloth for the king to wear at Christmas and, almost immediately afterwards, a long goune, garments which were delivered to him by the hand of William Hervey (as were two more paltoks, one of them of black cloth, the gift of the king's chamberlain, John Chandos).[17] The paltoks are described as being padded and, from the materials issued for their making, it seems that they must have been made of cloth stuffed with cotton-wool and lined with linen of Rheims. It can also be estimated from the quantity of silk thread that was used in making them that they were either quilted or closely sewn in some other way and this again confirms John of Reading's statement that paltoks and other very short garments were sewn all over. He also said that they had no front opening. In the *Eulogium* paltoks are described as being made of silk.[18]

Following these earlier entries in John Newbury's account of 1361 are six gounes of sanguine-coloured cloth in grain for the king, the queen, the duke of

Lancaster and the earls of Arundel, Duff and War-wick, as gifts from the king. The king's younger sister Joan, queen of Scotland[19] was given a goune too; four ells of murrey mixed cloth in grain were used to make it, its lining consisted of six hundred and forty skins of gros vair, each skin being, of course, very much larger than a belly of miniver so that the goune must have been very long and prob-ably ample. Slipped in, as it were, after this entry, is a note of eight ells of 'canabis' to make a pattern for a long goune for the king, which may mean either that it was still an unfamiliar garment to some workers in the great wardrobe or that the king himself was still a little nervous of the new fashion and wished to approve the pattern before the goune was made up.

This particular account[20] is very long and it soon becomes apparent that in the year it covers – 1361 to 1362 – members of the court circle were wearing as many gounes and paltoks as suits, though neither was yet being issued to valets or other servants. While gounes were worn by members of either sex paltoks were naturally worn only by men for, as the chroniclers explained, they were fitted with laces by which the long masculine hose were attached to them.[21] Corsets still appear in this account, issued to noblemen and their ladies as well as to the king and the queen.

A great wardrobe account of 1363 to 1364[22] ex-plains the amazing success of the two new garments, introduced for the first time less than two years pre-viously for, by this time, gounes and paltoks were no longer reserved for the royal family and members of the nobility but paltoks were already being issued to squires and gounes to falconers, the latter for wear-ing in winter time. Knights of the king's chamber were given gounes and two – a long and a short one – were made for the guardian of his chamber, an indication that gounes, like tunics, could be long or short. The king himself had a long goune of violet long-cloth furred with gris for the feast of All Saints and, an innovation that year, a long goune was *frounced* – a term which must have been almost forgotten for it had been out of use for the past fifteen years.[23] In-deed it may have seemed unsuitably out of date for on the subsequent membrane (15) it was dropped, and there appears instead a long goune for the queen entirely pleated – *plicat' totum* – and, what is more, this goune evidently had a long train, since canabis was provided to extend it along the ground – 'infra terra extendit'.[24] Only what the clerk entered as trimmings for this goune were listed at this point in the account – that is to say, ten ells of Flanders linen, three of canabis and half a pound of sewing silk – but another goune of Philippa's, made from blue and gold *baldekyn*[25] of Lucca, must also have been very long and full because four whole cloths – at least twenty-four ells – of this high-quality cloth of gold were used to make it, with a great deal of trimmed miniver to line it and thirty skins of ermine to trim it. At just about the same time that goune of *blu* long-cloth trimmed with ermine had been given by Edward to the king of France and delivered to him by the hand of Hervey.[26]

It is clear from all this that there had indeed been a major change in the fashion. The appearance of the term *goune* meant perhaps that the new fashion was English and not French, but this may not have been the case, for it is quite possible that a similar garment had appeared in France under a different name. That the goune almost certainly first made its appearance after the battle of Poitiers and not before it is borne out by the fact that the French de Nangis chronicle in-cluded a specific condemnation of the changes of fashion in France in 1365, whereas in 1356, in com-menting on the current fashion *before* the French defeat of that year, the author of the chronicle made little reference to styles of dress and confined himself to censorious remarks about the growth of extrava-gance in the use of sumptuous embroidery, especi-ally on hoods and belts, where gold, pearls and precious stones had been used so lavishly that their price had gone up. It was in 1356, too, continued the chronicler, that men began to wear feathers in their hats, all of which surely means that, in displaying this interest in contemporary clothing, he would cer-tainly have remarked on a dramatic change in its composition had such a change appeared in France at the time of writing.[27]

If, then, the fashion did start after Poitiers, and perhaps in England, it included other innovations besides the appearance of the goune and the paltok. In 1364, for instance, two *Jaks* were made for the king,[28] and here may well have been an example of a fashion which rose from below, for in France the *Jacque* was associated with peasants and artisans; some historians have thought it responsible for the term *Jacquerie*, the bands of peasants who harassed the French upper classes after Poitiers.[29] Froissart, presumably thinking as well as writing in French, had described Edward as wearing a *Jake* in 1348.[30]

The jacque or jak was probably a skimpy over-garment never designed to support the hose, and therefore one which could be worn over an aketon or paltok. From the rather large amount of linen used (of two qualities, the finer of Rheims, the less fine of Paris), it was probably long enough to reach the knee, and when made by the royal wardrobe was padded with cotton-wool, which would have been quite beyond the reach of peasants who probably padded their jaks with layers of old cloth. In 1364, the king's *jak* was made of linen with sindon of tripoli and interlined, almost certainly, with several layers of linen.

As for the paltok, though different in detail, it must have been related to both the aketon and the pourpoint, or it may, indeed, have been identical to the pourpoint, which, as its name suggests, was also equipped with eyelet holes and laces with metal points to thread through them in order not only to keep the hose up but to keep itself down. Froissart refers in 1358 to the *bourgois* of Tournai and other cities equipped with handsome saddles, swords, jakes and jupons, the last two of which appear in another manuscript of the same passage as 'gippons' and 'pourpoins'.[31] As for the frouncing and pleating of the goune, it may have been some such effect as this that the author of *Eulogium* was struggling to describe when he wrote of gounes that were dis-

18 *Herod's Feast*, dated 1364, Giovanni del Biondo or Orcagna. Italian version of the new fashion of the early 1360s, with tightened waist, padded chest and sleeves extended to the knuckles.

19 *Burgundian book of hours*. The executioner, although purporting to wear lower-class dress is shown, in fact, with the contemporary padded chest.

tended at the sides up to the arms, making men look like women when seen from the back. It had clearly been felt necessary to give this garment a new name, which surely means that its actual structure must have appeared new at the time; and, since it was stated categorically that it was not fastened down the front and that no other opening was mentioned, it may have been pulled on over the head. This might confirm the suggestion that it was wide and ample.

Chroniclers who chose to comment on current fashions had evidently forgotten their earlier distaste for tight clothing and long narrow hanging sleeves, which, by the way, had disappeared in the early 1360s. Besides the effeminate and apparently over-wide gounes and short paltoks, their chosen targets were shoes with long pointed toes (a fashion they were going to have to live with for a long time) and the new headwear called *cappes*. The account of 1363–4 refers to three cappes of cloth lined with the backs of gris. Fifty-four backs were supplied for these three linings, which seems a large quantity and one which might suggest capes and not caps, but for capes the quantity would be too small, and it is possible that some form of hat was intended. John of Reading has a curious passage, when he was writing of about the same date; he speaks of people wearing *capellis panneis retortis*, which could mean hoods, hats or caps of cloth turned back so that they take the shape of hose or sleeves – 'ad formam caligarum seu manicarum'.[32]

In both the great wardrobe accounts of the early years of the 1360s, clothing for members of the Order of the Garter was, as we have seen, included, and the making of the garters themselves, both for sewing on to the habits and presumably for fastening round the leg, must have occupied a good many workers at the Tower over a long period of time; but, as one would expect, embroidery continued to be used to decorate other things as well. In the later of the two accounts, two corsets trimmed with ermine are recorded as having been embroidered for the queen, and, at the same time, she had two more corsets embroidered with two of her mottoes. One of them, in sanguine cloth, was embroidered with the device *p'nitibus et billis*, the meaning of which can be guessed at in both Latin and English with very different results; whatever these things were, they were surrounded by the motto, 'Myn biddenye'. The other corset, which was like the first a gift from the king, was of black cloth embroidered with a wide ribbon of plate gold on which, in letters of coloured silks, gold and pearls, was the motto, 'Ich wyndemuth'; both had been made for the feast of the Circumcision. For Epiphany in the same year, an embroidered hood in sanguine cloth in grain was made for the king, and another, recorded in the same account, was embroidered with eagles and the letter E knotted together. References still occur, too, to garments for the king embroidered with a device of wheels,[33] and a rather touching entry is concerned with letting out one of his belts, made of velvet and gold.[34]

56

If 'Ich wyndemuth' is taken to mean 'I twine myself around', it might be a sentiment which could, surely, have been related to a motto of Edward's which appears in the previous account of a year earlier: 'syker as ye wodebynd', which, together with a spray of *wodebine*, was embroidered in letters of gold and silk on a cote and hood of black *satyn*. The fact that the queen's motto, 'Ich wyndemuth', was embroidered on a corset which was also black seems to underline the suggestion that there might indeed have been a connection between the two and that, although they appear in different accounts, either one was left over from the previous account or, alternatively, that the king was continuing to wear the same motto over a period of time, which, as we have seen, he had done before.

Embroidery is mentioned again in 1361 as the decoration on two long cloaks, one of green cloth embroidered in gold and silks in a design of leaves and branches, made for the king to wear on the feast of the Purification.[35] For both cloaks, large quantities of plate gold were entered in the account – two pounds in weight for the first cloak, one pound for the second. Probably cut or stamped out into little leaves all over the cloak, and probably suspended by a stitch through a single hole, the effect would have been a sparkling restlessness as the wearer moved.

There is no suggestion in the 1361 great wardrobe account that any embroidery was worked on clothes for the king of France during the previous year, much of which he spent in captivity, though preparing, in the later months, for a return to freedom in France.[36] Clothing which seems to have corresponded to the habits of the Garter knights, given to him as we have seen by Edward, had been entered in the great wardrobe account for the year 1360 by its clerk John Newbury. For details of what must have been most of the clothing worn by Jean in England, however, it is essential to study the journal of household expenses of his various places of residence in England covering the period from July 1359 to June 1360.

The second paragraph of this *Journal de la dépense du roi Jean* opens with the statement that 'Jehan de Royer, secretaire du Roy' had brought various sums of money both from France and from Avignon, part of which was allocated to the king for his personal use while the rest, noted in detail, was spent on charges of various kinds connected with the maintenance of his household and attendants - hay for the horses, benches and tables, wine for the barber and clothing for his relatives, for instance. But details of the king's clothing, its making and repair, appear in the *Journal* too.

The first entry is for the making by Jean Perigon and his valet, cousturiers, of a suit of four garments of tan-coloured cloth for the king, a *hopelande double*

20 *Catholicon*, copy illuminated in the 1360s, *bas de page* hunting scene. A Netherlandish version of the new over-tunics with padded chests and sleeves lengthened to cover part of the hand.

and another houpeland, tan coloured and lined with miniver, as well as three pairs of hose. This order involved some extra expense in that Jean Perigon and his assistant had been obliged to hire two horses for the journey from London to Hertford, where the king was imprisoned at that particular time. The king's tailor was actually Tassin du Bruil, whereas Jean Perigon was apparently only a couturier, an operative of a much lower standing.

As for the houpelands, these, like gouns, seem to have been over-garments recently created by fashion;[37] Froissart carefully described the clothing of a freelance knight who, in 1357, put a houpeland over his armour and then over them both a mantle, in order to appear to be in civilian dress when he tricked his way into the castle of Evreux, which he ended by capturing.[38]

It is indeed not impossible that the goun and the houpeland were two names for identical or almost identical garments: like the goun, the houpeland does not seem to have appeared until after the English victory at Poitiers. The colour tan, too, ordered by Jean for both his suit and his houpeland, may not have been a matter of chance, for the 'official' colour of the liveries at the English court for Pentecost is entered in the great wardrobe account of 1360–61 as tan and, like the gift of *blu* clothing to Jean, it may well have been an indication that, prisoner or not, the captive king of France was not merely invited to take part in occasional hunting expeditions and other pleasures but that he may have been actually accepted as a member of the court circle. A little earlier in his *Journal* is an entry for eight ells of *tanné* in grain, bought for the king of France, and it must have been from this fine cloth that his suit and houpeland were made.

In picking one's way through items which include an *establie* bought in, or not far from, Jean's lodging at Somerton, near Lincoln, for his tailor to use as a workshop, and the cost of a cover for the king's missal, one meets on the way the cost of making a *housse* for the king and for lining its 'wings' – *éles* – with miniver. A housse appears in the wardrobe of the Black Prince but in England it never seems to have been particularly popular whereas in France, as we have seen, it was an old-fashioned outer garment that was evidently too useful to be allowed to disappear.[39]

On 13 December Jean's *Journal* records that thirteen ells of *drap nayf* were bought which his tailor, Tassin, cut into a cote hardie, a cote *simple* (that is to say unlined), a mantle and two hoods for the king and, at the same time, a suit – *robe* – of three garments consisting of a cote, surcote, housse and hood of *drap azuré* was made for him. This shows that a housse could, on occasion, actually form a part of a suit and that the hood, at least in this case, cannot have counted as a separate garment, it may have been attached to one of the others. Later in December violet cloth in grain and marbré cloth in grain were bought from a certain Thomelin, a Lincoln draper, to make three garments and a *grant mantel* for the king of France. Marbré was the cloth of which the English liveries for Christmas appear in the great wardrobe

account for 1360–61; had they actually been worn during the previous year? The fact that Jean's marbré cloth was bought in December 1359 might suggest this, unless his choice of both marbré and tan clothing was purely a coincidence, which seems unlikely.

The *Journal* of Jean II's household expenses is in many ways not only more interesting than the straightforward great wardrobe and argenterie accounts of England and France but also more revealing in some of its details which relate to clothing. Payments were made, for instance, to Thomelin, the Lincolnshire draper, for dyeing six ells of cloth in grain in two colours (probably those later used for his hose), which proves absolutely that 'grain' did not refer to a specific colour but to the quality of the dye. After it was dyed it was shaved – *tondu* – at a cost of 12d.

Aymonnet the barber used an ell of linen to make four coifs and an *enveloppe* for the king's son Philippe, in captivity with his father.[40] In February 1360, eight pairs of russet-coloured hose were made for Philippe, and these at a moment when, like tan, russet was greatly favoured at the English court.[41] On the last day of the same month there appeared a long entry for clothing for the king of France which must have been made in preparation for his return to London where he had arrived before Easter Day, 5 April 1360. The clothes consisted of a suit of three garments: cote, surcote, *housse* and hood, with two pairs of sleeves for the cote, all in violet cloth in grain; a dressing-gown – *mantel à lever de nuit* – with a hood and two neck-pieces (*ammucas*); six pairs of hose in two colours in grain, a cote hardi, mantle, 'simple' cote (not padded or lined), a hood and two pairs of sleeves in blue (*pers*) cloth left over from the suit he had had made at All Saints in the previous year. On all these, Tassin and his assistants worked for twenty days and six *custuriers* valets for eighteen. At the same time, the king was supplied with twelve pairs of shoes. Eleven pounds of candles were bought for the tailoring department to enable the work to be carried out.

Once in London again, Jean and his household were accommodated in the Tower where additional comfort was provided by the building of four windows fitted with oiled linen and the sowing of seeds in the garden. In the second half of May, tailoring for the king started once more. Among the cloths bought for the purpose was some fine tan brown, some marbré for hose, a fine merlé in grain.[42] Already at Easter fur had been bought to line a housse and its wings, as well as a surcot, a cote, two or three hoods and *aumuces*, a cloak and a great mantle, presumably the mantle for which so much violet cloth was bought and for which 1,300 backs of gris were used for a lining.

But there are also revealing payments to Perrin for refurbishing and cleaning a great deal of fur that had been used on earlier garments, and for washing, for instance, and relining a hood, all of it a reminder that every penny the king of France spent in England had to be raised by taxes or levies on the French.

In June the whole French establishment was leaving London and settling up with two London drapers who had supplied cloth for new liveries for members of the household – new clothes which seem to have been made at the very last minute, and to produce an impression of grandeur both for the farewell to England and the arrival in France. Throughout June and the first few days of July before the actual crossing, the accounts of the departing king seem to be infused with a frantic sense of urgency. Fourpence paid to a poor woman in London whose milk was spilt by one of the king's greyhounds is followed by a tip to the guardian of the king of England's lions, visited by Jean during his short stay in the capital. Large sums were spent on sugar and spices, alms to a considerable number of hermits and other deserving people as well as to the prisoners in Newgate; money is paid out for cloth for last-minute liveries for chaplains and for vermilion cloth of scarlet for Jean de Dainville, his *maitre d'otel* whom the king proposed to knight. Money is given to a valet of the queen of England for bringing Jean venison she had sent him, more last-minute bills are paid by Tassin to London drapers. A cloth of gold is bought to cover a chair for the king, and as late as 22 June Perrin the furrier is lining suits for the king with fur. Perrin, whose name appears several times in Jean's *Journal*, is never referred to otherwise than as Perrin *le pelletier*, but he is almost certainly the same furrier

who is mentioned in the Patent Rolls of 26 April 1360 as having been given a safe-conduct in the city of London and 'elsewhere where the king's adversary of France shall happen to stay' until Michaelmas. The safe-conduct was issued to William Pellipari yeoman – *valetto* – of the said adversary, to serve him in the office of pelterer – *pellipar'*.[43] Only Perrin is mentioned in Jean's *Journal* as a furrier; it is reasonable to assume that William's safe-conduct had been issued sometime earlier and that it was, as necessary, extended. The order must refer to the previous year, for in April 1360, as we have seen, Jean had already moved to London in preparation for his return to France.

Among all the last-minute preparations, a saddle for Jean's charger was repaired and regilded;[44] his painter, Gerard d'Orléans, with the help of other artists mended, and repainted a throne. Jean had three more hoods made and a surcote; he bought a clasp of gold set with pearls, diamonds, rubies and sapphires.

On the last day of June, Jean dined at Eltham with queen Philippa and on 1 July, on his way to Calais, he set off for the coast by way of Rochester – where a donation was given to the church; through Canterbury – where nuns and monks were given money and where he heard Mass; to Winchelsea, where he

21 *Life of S Silvestro*, detail. Maso di Banco. A canon, seen from the back, wearing an aumuce.

gave more alms; and to Dover, where he lodged with the monks of the *Maison Dieu* – the local hospital, otherwise known as the hospital of St Mary, which was evidently flexible enough to be able to provide lodging for three nights for the king of France and his entourage. He arrived there from Canterbury on Sunday, 5 July, and sailed for Calais on Wednesday, 8 July. The following year, Simon, master of the hospital, was required by Edward to give permanent hospitality to James le Palmore, a clerk of London, who was to eat at the master's table, to receive a pension of 20s. annually, a suit of clothes of the master's pattern (or two marks in lieu if he preferred it) and the room newly built over the larder.[45] These rather exceptional privileges suggest that James le Palmore may have had some connection with the royal visit of the previous year.

During Jean's stay in Dover, and presumably for his entertainment, a man known as the Creeper crawled up the face of the cliffs, in front of the hermitage, watched by the king. He was given five nobles valued at 33s. 4d., so his performance must have been regarded as sensational.[46]

And still Tassin was making *certainnes robes* for the king, that is to say, a suit of pale grey – *cler plomée* – of three garments, a suit of tan, another suit of marbré, a suit of rose-coloured scarlet cloth, a surcote of violet and a suit of two garments of the livery of the knights – 'qu'il a faite a chevaliers' – was that the livery of the Ordre of the Étoile?

There are final payments to two valet couturiers for twenty-four days at 8d. each a day (a much higher rate than was usually paid in the English great wardrobe), plus a halfpenny a day each for their drinks. More ells of linen, of silk and of ribbon and, as the very last item in the *Journal*, 25 *escuz* paid to a certain Lalement for carrying letters to the pope and the cardinals on the subject of the advance of the subsidy for the king's release.[47]

Jean's departure from London had been preceded by a round of dinners;[48] he himself gave one for Edward on 14 June at the Tower, when great demonstrations of mutual love and esteem were apparent, but these were outdone by a banquet given by the Black Prince in Jean's honour on 6 July at Dover Castle, because on that occasion a ceremonious exchange of valuable drinking cups took place, Jean's gift being indubitably the more precious of the two. It was, in fact, the famous gold goblet which had belonged to St Louis of France and which had been noted in Étienne de la Fontaine's argenterie account of 1352 as having been fitted with a new pipe.[49] Mentioned in an inventory of the treasury of Louis le Hutin after his death, it was described then as the 'coupe d'or S Loys ou l'on ne bois point',[50] but at Dover Jean did drink from the cup 'qui fu monseigneur St Louis'[51] before it was presented to Edward in exchange for a less distinguished cup from which he himself had drunk. Edward had, however, recently relinquished his right to the arms, the battle-cry and the title of King of France,[52] so Jean may have felt that his generosity was not misplaced.

Jean's arrival in Calais was an anti-climax; once more a prisoner, this time on the English soil of

Calais, until the outstanding instalment of his ransom had been paid, he was not actually free to travel on until 25 October. At the beginning of November, together with a great crowd of English spectators, Frenchmen from all over the country and less desirable freelancers from the notorious *Grande Compagnie*, he witnessed *moult beles jousts* at St Omer and, arrived in Paris on 13 December, riding beneath a canopy of cloth of gold supported on four lances, he passed by a fountain running wine as though it had been water (some chroniclers say several such fountains) and, accompanied by a procession of clergy and cheered by citizens wearing their appropriate liveries, through richly draped streets to Notre Dame.[53]

In John Newbury's great wardrobe account for All Saints 1360 to 25 June (the feast of John the Baptist) 1361, it is necessary to distinguish between two kings, both of them issued with clothing. John Marreys – *cissor dm̄ Regis* (of England, of course) – made Edward a suit of four garments of marbryn longcloth lined with miniver and trimmed with twenty-five skins of ermine, and, as well, as suit of wide mixed cloth of Brussels lined with over 1,000 trimmed skins of miniver; both were ostensibly a present from Jean to Edward, but Edward himself paid for the gold ribbon and the twenty-five skins of ermine which were probably beyond Jean's means.[54]

In return, Edward sent Jean Boyer, Jean of France's secretary, with a gift to the king of France of a suit of the 'king's livery' for Christmas. It was made of red cloth of scarlet lined with 1,780 bellies of trimmed miniver. The colour worn by the English court for Christmas 1360 was marbryn (almost certainly a special weave incorporating more than one colour), and it is therefore not quite clear what this reference to the king's livery implies. What is particularly distinctive about the suit is that the number of its garments is not actually stated, but there cannot have been more than two plus a hood and a mantilletum. One of the garments is called a 'tabard'; the other is certainly a long cloak, as can be gathered from the fur provided to line it. This entry is followed immediately by another for a suit, this time carried to Jean by Guy Brian, who became a royal chamberlain in 1377.[55] Brian is recorded later in this account as being given clothing *ad modum ban'ett*. This second suit for the French king, described as having been made for Easter, is that suit of *blu* which has already been discussed in connection with the Order of the Garter,[56] and it, too, included a tabard. Exactly the same amount of stuff (one cloth) and of fur was used to make each of these two suits of the 'King of England's livery'. Both included eighty bellies of trimmed miniver, specified as for the *mannt*, which must mean the mantilletum, the short shoulder cape worn with the fur on the outside, which seems to have had royal connotations; it is noticeable that no ermine was provided for these two suits for Jean. It should also perhaps be noticed that, when new suits for the Knights of the Garter were issued in 1364, they were entered as having been made of red cloth.

The entry which follows is a suit *p eidm̄ dn̄e Rē*, but it is unlikely, in fact, to have been made for the

French king. It must have been for Edward, and was to be worn at the feast of St George.[57] More suits, paltoks and other things certainly for Edward follow, and for the first time his clothes are stated as having been delivered by the hand of William Hervey, confirming the new practice, for no such entrepreneur had appeared in earlier surviving accounts. Two long cloaks were made for Edward to wear at the parliament held that year at Westminster.[58]

This account for the year 1360–61 also included expenses for the wedding dress for Edward's daughter Mary, who married John de Montfort, brought up at the English court and, after a long struggle, to be accepted as duke of Brittany – to be known as the fifth duke.[59] Mary's tailor, William de Meetok, had by this time been succeeded by John Averay; for Christmas she was given a suit of marbryn as would have been expected, but her wedding suit, specified as being a gift of the king, consisted of a mantle and a tunic of cloth of gold *racamatiz* of Lucca and of cloth of gold *baldekyn d'outremer*; altogether seven pieces of these cloths were used, and, as this would amount to about forty-five ells, the mantle must have had an exceptionally long train. The usual immense number of bellies of trimmed miniver was used to line the two garments, 600 of them entered as a gift from the king of France; in addition, it was trimmed with forty skins of ermine. Apart from three standards with her arms, these are the only entries for the royal bride; far down the list of Edward's daughters, Mary was given a modest send-off that could not be compared with the stately departure of her unfortunate elder sister Joan; but then Mary's husband's title had not yet been accepted by the French, so that her position as duchess of Brittany would not become a reality until 1364.[60]

John de Montfort himself received generous donations of clothing from the great wardrobe, and so, to a lesser extent, did his sister, who is referred to as the damsel of Brittany – *domicella*. John's tailor was Roger Burleton, who made him the statutory suit of the king's livery in marbryn for Christmas 1360 (it included a miniver mantilletum as well as fifty-four skins of ermine, so that he outshone the captive king of France), but a good deal more besides. Two cotes and two long cloaks of sanguine in grain, cloth of scarlet and blanket for All Saints; a riding cloak as a gift from the king of sanguine and black with gold ribbons, both wide and narrow; 'divers garments', gloves and slippers; a suit for Pentecost of mixed tan-coloured cloth. These are followed, after an interval, by a long cloak of scarlet cloth in red and another of murray, made to wear at St Omer and embroidered by his tailor, Rogō Burleton. For the embroidery, three pounds of plate gold and three pounds of coloured silks were used. These cloaks are followed by a cotta with a hood of sanguine in grain embroidered with flowers and lions in gold and another hood, *broudat' barre* – with horizontal bands – of flowers and compasses, again delivered by Roger Burleton for the same occasion.

The tailor of the young lady of Brittany was Matheo Caleys, who made her a suit of the king's livery of marbryn for Christmas and trimmed it with forty skins of ermine. It was a gift from the king. Her suit for Pentecost, tan coloured, of course, is interesting in that it includes a 'begyn' of heavy red sindon and was lined with red taffetas. The beguin, made of a cheap material, may have been an interlining, or, alternatively, some kind of masquerade dress. It was customary to give the cloak lining, whether of fur or not, the name – or a name – of the garment itself: a *penne* or a *penula*, for instance, was the fur lining, evidently made up and ready to stitch staight into the cloak; and the same applies to the hood – *caputium* – which appears in that form among the furs, but which is, in reality, a lining that must have been made up by the furriers. Since the beguin was evidently the Whitsun equivalent of the winter fur lining, the furriers' practice may have infected the tailoring department.

For the feast of St John the Baptist, the king gave the *domicella* of Brittany two tunics and two corsets, issued probably as a set of two matching garments; the material supplied was longcloth and murray-coloured cloth. She was also given eighteen pairs of leather gloves and eighteen pairs of slippers; some odd ells of coloured cloth appear too as trimmings.[61]

This account of 1360–61 and the subsequent account are the two most interesting and comprehensive documents to have survived from the great wardrobe between 1340 and 1365. They present more vividly than any other official papers a picture of the normal life at the royal court which was never, of course, normal. They also show for the first time the use of gifts of clothing in the field of diplomacy, even of international diplomacy.

If these accounts were drawn up systematically year by year, then one is missing between the account which covers the period between All Saints 1360 and June 1361 and what appears to be the next surviving account for June 1363 to June 1364 – the thirty-seventh and thirty-eighth years of the reign of Edward III. By that time John Newbury had been succeeded as clerk of the great wardrobe by Henry Snayth, who must have had his own views as to how his accounts should be set out, for this later one is arranged in two and sometimes three columns whereas the previous accounts were not. The result is that the colour of the stuff of which any particular garment was made does not as a rule appear together with the specifications of the suit or garment itself, and it is therefore not easy to discover which colours were issued for the major feasts of the year. In the previous account, as we have seen, it had been marbryn for Christmas, tan for Pentecost.

The earlier of the two accounts of the 1360s included some clothing made particularly for meetings of the Order of the Garter; so does the later account – both have been discussed in an earlier chapter. The liveries made for attendants and servants at the court in their various degrees are also included in both these big accounts, and they will be examined in a later chapter. Distinguished members of the court circle had died during the earlier year – William de Bohun and John Beauchamp, for instance – and their deaths were marked in the great wardrobe accounts by records of 'oblations' of cloth of gold of Lucca from the king and the earl and countess of Ulster. The later account records the funeral of the countess of Ormond at Deptford;[62] the king and the queen sent oblations of cloth of gold. The earlier account signalled the arrival of the goune and the paltok; the later the wide dissemination of these two garments.

The account of 1360–61 is supported by a badly damaged inventory of stuff used in the great wardrobe.[63] It begins with a list of the tailors and the members of the royal family to whom each was accredited. The king of France's 'tabards' appear in this inventory, and there seem, in fact, to have been four of them in the account of the furrier, John Bruggeford. John Marreys is named as the king of England's former tailor, and his successor as Richard Carswell. The good-class cloths with which the inventory must actually have started are missing, but the expensive silks and the mercery are listed on the surviving membranes. Included in the section headed mercery are twenty-two *coifells* – coifs – of Paris linen, 4,000 brass pins and five pieces of *cou'chiefs crispes*.

The word 'couvrechief' could be applied to either an object or a stuff of which that object could be made, a practice not confined to couvrechiefs, for, as we have seen, a *capucia* could apply to the lining of a hood. The couvrechiefs *crispes* mentioned here may be of particular importance because they may well refer to the linen head-dresses which seem to have been composed of straight pieces of stuff surrounded by layers of crimped edges which frame the face. This particular type of elaborate veil can be found in English paintings and tomb effigies from about the middle of the century, and although they do not appear to have been worn in Italy or France, they were certainly worn in the Netherlands, Bohemia and Hungary at the time for they can be found in a considerable number of paintings and sculpture. These heavy linen scarf-like head-dresses were not, of course, at all the sort of thing to have appealed to Italian taste.

The mercery in this inventory is continued with a pouch and a belt of leather which Haukino Pouchmaker had made of leather he bought in London; Rogo Cordwainer supplied thirty-seven pairs of boots at 4s. the pair, 140 pairs of slippers and five pairs of 'pyncons'.[64] The inventory here informs us that leather from Hungary was being imported at this time,[65] and so was linen from Westphalia, which appears as the coarsest of the linens in use. Linens are still listed in order of their fineness and therefore of their price: Rheims still heads the list at 4s. an ell (very expensive indeed for linen), then Paris linen at 15d. the ell, Hainault at 12d., then Flanders at 12d. and finally Westphalian linen at 10d.

Some of the entries in the great wardrobe account for 1363–4 have already been noticed: gounes were frounced or pleated, for instance, and a jak was supplied for the king. On 6 November, Peter of Lusignan, king of Cyprus, who had been encircling the states of Europe in the hope of stirring their timid if not hypocritical rulers who had promised to undertake a new Crusade into action, arrived in London.[66] He was in time for a joust at Smithfield on Martin-

mass, 11 November, which may or may not have been staged in his honour. Several chroniclers have tried to establish the fact that this was the scene of a meeting between four crowned heads, but, in the view of most historians, Jean II had not been there, although David Bruce was; the question of Jean's possible participation is intriguing.[67]

For the visit of Peter of Cyprus, both Edward and Philippa had special clothes made which appear in different parts of the great wardrobe account. Edward's suit, made by his tailor referred to here as William Carswell,[68] *padventm̄R⁻ⁱˢCipre*, consisted, as a robe of state, of only two garments both of which were made of cloth of gold baldekyn of Lucca, partly lined with blanket, tied with narrow gold ribbons and trimmed with twenty-nine skins of ermine.[69] Its main lining was, as usual, trimmed miniver. Although the queen's goune, which appears later in the account, is not specified as having been made for the visit of the king of Cyprus, it is of exactly the same stuff as the king's suit and must have been designed to wear at the same time – the normal court practice. Of gold baldekyn of Lucca lined with 640 bellies of miniver and trimmed with 36 skins of ermine, it is described as having sleeves trimmed with ermine – 'manic' d̄ci goune pᵘfilianz cū Ermyns' – the first time that this particular fashion had been mentioned in the great wardrobe accounts.

At a date not precisely agreed but generally considered to have been either towards the end of 1363 or very early in 1364, Jean II is reported as having voluntarily returned to captivity in England following the defection of one of his sons left as a hostage against the payment of the remainder of his ransom. Jean's surrender was seen by most contemporaries as a fine gesture worthy of a king with a reputation for a noble and chivalrous nature, though at least one cynic suggested that he had, in fact, prisoner or not, found life pleasanter in England than in France and was far from sorry to return.

If, rather than the chroniclers, the great wardrobe account is to be trusted, then Jean may already have come to London before Peter of Cyprus arrived, because a suit was made for him for All Saints (1 November) 1363, and this time the suit, presumably not only because of his high-minded surrender but because after the signing of the Peace of Bretigny he was accepted by Edward as a reigning monarch, was trimmed with ermine – a very interesting and subtle differentiation between this and his earlier suits. It comprised five garments made of longcloth in grain, over 1,000 bellies of trimmed miniver were used to line it with, in addition, 190 bellies for the mantilletum and 75 to line the hood. Thirty-six skins of ermine were used as trimming, and the entry specifies that round the hood and the sleeves was narrow gold ribbon, three and threequarter ells of it altogether. The clerk of the great wardrobe may, of course, have been mistaken in stating that the suit was actually made for the feast of All Saints, nevertheless the entry is followed by two more for suits for the same feast, both of which begin: 'Eidem . . . p Rᵉ'; but these were almost certainly for the king of England and not of France. The situation is not made clearer, however, by three more suits definitely stated to have been made for Jean, one of mixed longcloth of Brussels (for an unspecified occasion) which seems to have been made on the same pattern as the suit described in his previous entry just above; this is almost but not quite immediately followed by two suits to be sent – *ad mittendz* – to the king of France on behalf of the king of England for the feasts of All Saints and Christmas. For these two suits (which share one entry), one whole cloth of scarlet and one whole cloth of *blu* were issued; two tabards are mentioned as having been a part of the two suits.

It is possible that all these things were sent to the king in France, but this is surely unlikely because they seem to form a comprehensive wardrobe and to lack the dignity of a ceremonial gift. Soon after these details, an entry in the same account mentions a blue goun trimmed with six skins of ermine as having been delivered by Hervey to Jean; it appears to have matched the blue gown made for Philippa as a gift from Edward at more or less the same time. For the following Easter – 1364 – a suit of murray longcloth (with a tabard) was made for Jean, and for the same feast Edward himself had two suits made, also of murray, and that was the last suit to be made for Jean; he had been taken ill in March and died on 8 April that year.[70] In the event, therefore, the entry for the making of Jean's murray suit is followed almost at once in Henry Snayth's account by an order to *eidem* (William Carswell) for a cote and a cloak with a hood of black longcloth in grain lined with trimmed miniver for Edward to wear at the funeral of the king of France.[71]

Although Jean had fairly recently taken the 'vermilion cross', Peter of Cyprus was unsuccessful in persuading him or, for that matter, Edward, to do anything about a Crusade. Froissart charitably suggests that Edward felt himself too old and frail to go, but that he hinted that he would not prevent any of his sons from taking the Cross should they feel so inclined, and that, in taking a tender leave of Peter, he loaded him with splendid gifts including jewels and a ship – the Katharine – to carry them away in.[72]

Soon, it seems, after Peter's arrival in England, Edward had ordered a complete suit of armour, described as *de guerr*, but more probably of the pattern used for parade. It was made, or rather covered, in gold baldekyn of sylk; a whole piece of each was issued which would have amounted to about thirteen ells altogether. It can hardly have been an accident that this padded armour – *hnes* – was, like Edward's suit ordered especially for Peter's visit, made of gold baldekyn of Lucca. A contemporary Exchequer account notes that the king's tailor was paid for covering a pair of plate armours, given by the king to the king of Cyprus, to wear at a joust at Smithfield for the feast of All Saints, which would have been almost a week before Peter is said to have arrived in London. The joust, however, was probably not the one held at Smithfield but the one already referred to which took place on Martinmass. Before leaving the problem of the All Saints day of 1363 it should, nevertheless, be noted that a marginal

entry on membrane 14 in the great wardrobe account states that two embroidered corsets and two gounes, gifts of the king, were made for the queen to wear on that very day – *primo die Novr A^n xxxvii*. Four hundred and ninety six ermine skins, an absolutely unprecedented number, were used to trim the two corsets.

John de Montfort and the princess Mary his wife do not appear in this account but for John's sister Joanna of Brittany, a suit was made by her tailor Richard of St Osyth; with a lining of miniver and trimmed with ermine, it was made of cloth of scarlet. Clothing for the royal princes and princesses is also included in this very extensive list, all of it entered under the names of their respective tailors. Edmund of Langley is specifically mentioned as having been given a black mourning suit of two garments, like the king's, for the funeral of Jean II. Collars for the royal leopards were also made in the great wardrobe during this year.

After a solemn service in St Paul's Cathedral the body of Jean II, apparelled in the habitual dress[73] and surrounded by a contingent of torchbearers (whose mantles had been made in the great wardrobe) was conveyed to Paris and taken to Notre Dame accompanied by three of his sons, by processions from all the Parisian churches, by representatives of the parliament (who carried the bier) and Peter, king of Cyprus.[74] The Valenciennes chronicler described the body of Jean in Paris as laid under cloth of gold, as though asleep, crowned with the crown *fleurdelysée* of France.[75] Froissart speaks of 1,000 torches.[76] On 7 May, Jean was buried in St Denys, traditional burying place of the kings of France, at the foot of the High Altar on the left. On 11 May, Charles, duke of Normandy, the dauphin, now Charles V, to be called the Wise, was crowned at Rheims: the king of Cyprus was present.

The great wardrobe account for 1363–4 includes, as we have seen, some clothing made for the obsequies of Jean II.[77] It also records details of a very unexpected gift, a suit of livery of our lord the king of England to be sent to the lord the king Charles of France for Pentecost and delivered by the hand of Simon Bochell. The suit was of cloth of scarlet and required for its lining more than 2,000 bellies of trimmed miniver, excluding the tabard, for which a further 700 bellies were used. Suits of scarlet, the colour never specified, had indeed been one of the king's liveries during that year; every member of the royal family had one, and so did the maiden Joanna of Brittany – but for Christmas, not for Pentecost. The liveries for the English royal family to wear at Pentecost are not included in this account; they are unlikely to have been made of the same stuff as those for Christmas. Only garments for the kings of France, Jean II and Charles V, are ever mentioned during the whole twenty-five years as having included tabards. Vaillant's and ffanton's (the king's heralds) suits did not.

Until the signing of the peace of Bretigny, Edward maintained his claim as rightful king of France; Jean, during most of the time of his imprisonment in England, was not therefore allowed the royal fur ermine, and, as a consequence, the first of his two *blu* suits had no ermine trimming; the second, given him after the Peace, had. As to the tabards which formed a part of the ceremonial clothing presented to the respective kings of France, they did not, apparently, form a part of English royal dress nor of the liveries distributed at court, even to the royal heralds, but the term was not unknown in England. Tabards with and without fur linings could be included in the statutory dress of academics,[78] though it was not the most important part of it; they were also worn by working men, as the poem *Piers Plowman* bears witness: 'Bitel-brouwed' Avarice wears a torn tabard.[79] Whether the magnificent robes of two garments presented by Edward to Jean and Charles were designed to meet a special need, or whether they had, perhaps, a French flavour, is impossible to determine. If they were somewhat French in style, French tailors could, no doubt, have produced the correct term for them, which may even have been *tabard*, used in France, as in England later, for a part of the livery of heralds. There is no reason, however, to think that there was ever any communication between the tailors attached to Jean's household and to Edward's.

It is tempting but dangerous to try to equate the changed taste for combinations of colour with changes in the historical situation. By 1360, the bright heraldic colours of the 1340s – dominated by the complementary pair, red and green – had been superseded by marbryn and the mixed cloths whose surfaces, broken by the complexity of their weaves, could not produce the brilliancy of plain dyed cloths. Nor, where they are cited in the accounts, do the colours of the 1360s themselves suggest the clear brightness of the earlier schemes. The colours chosen for the dress of the royal family and for the liveries of the English court were, for the most part, tan and violet (as had been the suits ordered by Jean while he was in England). In terms of cloths with sophisticated weaves, these colours must have looked subdued. The starkness of the earlier composition of individual garments had been changed from an outline consisting of sharp angles to one contrived to look padded and rounded, and, concurrently, sharp colours were replaced by those which were soberer and more subtle.

This is no place to enter into an investigation as to a probable date for the famous *Sir Gawain and the Green Knight*, but it is worth pointing out that, among the poets and novelists of the second half of the fourteenth century, apart from Chaucer, it is the Gawain poet alone who appreciated the dramatic

22 *Weltchronik*, copy made *c.* 1362. Rudolf von Ems and followers. German dress in the 1360s; tunics with padded chests. Compare the hood with its dagged edge with the hood worn by the saint in fig 6, above. This group of dancers provides an interesting back view of the German version of a layered veil with frilled edges.

possibilities of clothing, and when, very near the beginning of the poem, the mysterious Green Knight appears at the end of a New Year's day banquet in King Arthur's hall, both his physique and his dress are described. Immensely tall and broad, his loins and back were sturdy and strong, but his belly flat and his waist small; entirely clothed in green, he wore a straight *cote* so tight that it 'stek on his sides', and this is followed by a vivid description of his hood, the length of his hair and his mantle lined with the whitest ermine. The emphasis on the tightness of the clothing – a tunic so tight that it clung to his sides and revealed the flatness of his belly and his slim waist – is a very fair comment on the fashion of the middle of the 1360s, as exemplified, for instance, in the pourpoint of Charles de Blois; it is an appearance which would hardly have been remarked on as late as 1370, for by that time it was a composition which would not only have become commonplace but was, indeed, going out of fashion; by 1380, such tight tunics had disappeared altogether from the masculine fashion. The poem is infused with constant significant references to items of dress, but because no date can be attached to it, it would be inappropriate to discuss them here.

VIII

Livery and the Dress of the Poor

Within the royal courts of Europe – the *hospitia regum* – differences in social status from the highest to the lowest were outwardly marked by very subtle variations in the clothing that was distributed to those entitled to livery. At the same time, throughout that society, a strict though temporary aesthetic pattern was observed.

The position of each courtier and each servant in the English hierarchy does not seem to have altered during the reign of Edward III, but while English and French accounts usually followed more or less the same plan, the turbulent conditions in France between 1340 and 1365 make it difficult to generalize in the same way about the situation there. It looks as though at some periods the liveries distributed in the French court may have covered only a limited and socially high range of recipients, but this may be due to the fact that sometimes accounts concerned with the clothing of the lower servants were drawn up separately, and that these, along with so much else, may have disappeared. A French account of the year 1351 is very much like a typical English great wardrobe account, both in its layout and in the standing of the people who were given clothing, but whether this was the plan invariably followed in France is difficult to judge.[1]

The two long and comprehensive English great wardrobe accounts of the beginning of the 1360s provide an almost complete picture of the clothing of the English royal household – only one or two details as to the colours of the liveries are lacking, which is a pity, because this detracts from the near perfection of the pictorial image they evoke. These accounts include suits for the king's and the queen's own use for special or unique occasions, gifts to the kings of France and Cyprus already discussed, clothing connected with the Order of the Garter; but, these apart, there remains a list of clothing provided for everybody from the princes to the bearers of falcons for Christmas for the years 1360 to 1363, as well as for Pentecost for those of sufficient importance to be given suits twice a year – a considerable number.

The slight differences between the quality and quantity of stuff given to the most exalted persons are as interesting as the differences between the clothing of the most humble. The royal fashion for Christmas in the year 1360 was longcloth of 'marbryn' – an adjective denoting 'marble-like' and thence 'variegated', which must refer to a special weave incorporating, almost certainly, more than one colour. In French accounts the corresponding word *marbre* is to be found, but often qualified by colour as, for instance, *un marbre vermeillet*, which proves that, used alone, the word marbre refers to the composition of the weave and not to a colour.[2]

For that Christmas, John Marreys made Edward a marbryn suit of four garments: tunic, closed super tunic, open super tunic, long cloak and two hoods, for which eleven ells of cloth were required. Eleven ells is not very much, so that apart from the cloak, which is specified as long, the rest of the suit must have consisted of garments that were both short and tight – as the fashion of the moment demanded. The suit was trimmed with narrow gold ribbon – four ells of it – probably used for ties, and entirely lined with miniver with, in addition, twenty-six skins of ermine. It included a miniver mantilette so that the ermine may have been used for trimming the sleeves of one or two of the tunics.[3] Twenty years earlier, Edward's Christmas suit would almost certainly have included a long over-tunic.

Queen Philippa's Christmas suit was also of marbryn longcloth. It, too, was lined with trimmed miniver, and enriched with 106 ermine skins. But Philippa's dress included five ells of sanguine-coloured cloth, perhaps not too big a quantity to be accounted for by the four hoods lined with miniver which formed a part of her suit; a corset, too, was made for her of the same marbryn cloth, all of which means that, with interchangeable garments, both she and the king would have continued to wear clothes of this Christmas colour for some time. Joan, queen of Scotland, Edward's sister, was issued with what would appear to have been a suit and a corset identical to Philippa's, until one notices that, whereas Joan's tailor had been given almost exactly the same length of cloth, he received 322 fewer bellies of miniver, six fewer ermine skins and no sanguine longcloth.

The suit made for 'the Prince', that is to say, the prince of Wales, corresponded to the king's, except that, while he was given five ells more of marbryn cloth and a little more miniver (perhaps he was taller than his father), he received no ermine and no gold ribbon.[4] Roger Covedale, tailor to Lionel, earl of Ulster, on the other hand, provided a suit almost exactly like the king's, for it included similar quantities of cloth, miniver and ermine but no gold ribbon. John, earl of Richmond's[5] tailor, Richard of Walton, made him a suit of marbryn exactly like Lionel's, and Edmund of Langley's was the same too. It seems probable therefore that the Black Prince's wardrobe already included some spare ermine and gold ribbon which was used on his Christmas suit, which would mean that the four male members of the royal family wore what was to all intents and purposes uniform.

As for the princesses – Isabel, Mary and Margaret – their tailors made them for Christmas suits of marbryn longcloth which varied according to seniority. Isabel's must have been very much like her mother's, the queen's, trimmed with the same quantity of ermine, but instead of five ells of sanguine cloth, she was given seven of brown. Mary, on the other hand, in spite of the fact that she was about to be married to John de Montfort, was allowed only forty ermine skins, in contrast to over a hundred for the queen and for Isabel, and no contrasting cloth to use with the marbryn. Margaret was given quantities of cloth and fur which corresponded exactly to Mary's, and into almost the same category came Lionel's wife, Elizabeth de Burgh, countess of Ulster, and John of Gaunt's wife, the countess of Richmond.

John de Montfort, claimant to the dukedom of Brittany and a guest at the English court, was included as a member of this English royal group at Christmas 1360. His suit consisted of four garments of marbryn and a mantillette which must have been like the king's, but although he was given four ells of gold ribbon, he was allowed much less ermine. His sister's Christmas suit seems to have been exactly like those of the two younger princesses, Mary and Margaret. By scrutinizing membrane 9 very carefully, however, it seems that she had, in addition, a little garnet-coloured cloth.[6]

Here the suits of marbryn longcloth end. Entering the Abbey in procession, and perhaps grouped together after mass on a rostrum in Westminster Hall, the effect of this royal clothing must have been impressive. United yet subtly divided by their liveries, the twelve members of the party must have been not only dressed but assembled according to the exact position of each in the royal and ducal hierarchy. Had the marbryn cloth been bright in colour, this certainly would have been mentioned, so that the group can be envisaged as forming a rather dark composition accented by the brilliance of the ermine and the sparse touches of red, brown and garnet, with a flash or two of gold ribbon to echo their gold crowns, their coronets and their jewellery. The contrast between the long gowns of the women and the long cloaks of perhaps only some of the men

and the short tunics of the others must have produced an intricate linear pattern.

As well as the suits issued for Christmas and Pentecost, the 1360 account proceeds to enumerate a large number of single suits and some bedding, all of these occupying several membranes. It is much later that the rest of the liveries issued specially for this particular Christmas appear. These begin with academic gowns for the warden in charge of the students of King's College, Cambridge,[7] for six bachelors and for the twenty-five students of the college. All were of tan-coloured shortcloth, the doctor being given half a piece of cloth (ten to twelve ells probably), two fur sheets of bishe, each of seven rows of skins, a fur sheet of popellus[8] and two hoods lined with trimmed miniver. The bachelors each received nine ells of shortcloth together with one sheet of budge and a hood lining of budge. Each student's gown was reckoned at seven and a half ells of shortcloth – the gown itself was required to be long, but was evidently rather skimpy – together with a fur sheet of lamb for lining.

No hoods were given to students, which accounts for the importance attached to academic hoods in later years. This set of academic gowns was obviously specially designed for wear at Christmas, because not only is that stated in the great wardrobe account, but entries in the Patent Rolls show that gowns were normally issued in October. In 1361, for instance, an entry for 26 October reads: 'grant during pleasure to the king's clerk Master John de Shropham warden of the scholars supported by the king's alms in the university of Cambridge of 4*d.* a day for his wages and 8 marks a year for two robes, to wit one with fur and the other with lining,[9] out of the issues of the county of Cambridge'. Not, that is to say, from the great wardrobe.

At this point the relative status of the various furs can be estimated: ermine, trimmed miniver, bishe, popellus, budge and lamb. Ermine was very strictly confined to the use of the royal family; trimmed miniver, also worn by royalty, was not widely allowed, though miniver, untrimmed, was permitted in varying quantities down to linings of hoods to lesser but dignified people. Bishe, the autumn, and therefore not very thick fur of the squirrel came next, and after it popellus, the summer and therefore thin fur of the squirrel.[10] Budge (*bugetum*) followed, high-grade lambskin originally from Bougie in Algeria and still called *bougie* in French accounts. At the bottom of the scale came lambskin from the north European countries. Gros vair, the back of the grey squirrel, called also *gris*, was rated lower than miniver and probably on a par with bishe or popellus. Semi-trimmed miniver, when rather more of the grey surrounding the white belly-patch was left showing, also appears occasionally. French accounts include as well black lamb – *agneau noire* – both lamb and squirrel of Calabria, lamb from Aragon and black or white lamb from Sardinia. Their accounts also speak of *gros popres* and *menu' popres*, which probably corresponded to bishe and popellus in the English accounts.[11]

The liveries provided at Christmas in 1360 were

calculated as exactly as those of the members of the royal family. Almost all the indoor servants were given three ells of coloured shortcloth, together with three ells of striped cloth for their suits, which must have been, therefore, mi-parti. Even here, though, there was room for class differentiation, because whereas valets, squires of the king's chamber, valets of the stable and of the chase, minstrels, archers and night-watchmen as well as some rent-paying tenants[12] were given a sheet of white lamb to line their suits, the pages and other boys as well as the sailors and the bargemen were given no fur at all. A few chosen servants were allowed the more select budge instead of lamb; among those who were distinguished in this way were all the masons (*cementiers*), as well as Thomas Thornton, the king's pavilioner, and William Glendale, his armourer, both of whom were given budge for a hood lining as well as a budge fur sheet.

The Cambridge academic staff and their students did not, presumably, attend the Christmas festivities at the court, so that their gowns of tan did not form a part of the collective picture, but the household servants certainly did, and although the exact number of these is difficult to calculate, nearly 200 men about the court were dressed in the particular mi-parti combination of colours chosen as the livery of Christmas 1360, though not all of them would have been likely to have been assembled at any one place at any one time. To the casual observer, who would have been unlikely to notice the small differences in the quality of the fur, they would have appeared to be uniformly dressed.

These two groups – the royal party and the household servants – did not quite complete the picture. Some bishops and other clergy would certainly have been present at any of the large gatherings, including, in all likelihood, Brother John Wodegrove, the king's confessor, and his associate (*socius*), both of whom were given black cloth for habits and a little white cloth, blanket, presumably for their hoods or scapulas, as well as extra riding-mantles; their four valets received the same mi-parti liveries lined with lamb as the rest of the servants of the same rank; so did the valets attached to the duke of Brittany and his sister.

Between, as it were, the royalty and the servants were two newly created knights, John Mowbray and William Skipworth, the latter being a judge of the common bench.[13] Besides special clothing for the vigil of their knighting, these two were given mi-parti suits of marbryn and green longcloth; the marbryn was in grain, so it is extremely probable that the marbryn worn by royalty this particular Christmas was in grain too. The knights' green cloth was of Brussels. Suitable furs were provided with the cloth.

In any large assembly, then, these knights would, no doubt, because of their position in the society of the court, have been placed physically between the marbryn-clad royalty and the servants, and so would two more named knights not newly elevated to the Order, but simply knights of the chamber, whose Christmas liveries were less ample than those of the new knights and were made of tan mi-parti – long-cloth and striped cloth – and whose furs were gris and bishe. This may very well suggest that all the plain cloth used in the season's mi-parti was tan in colour.[14]

Looking down, therefore, from a putative gallery on the company assembled in Westminster Hall on Christmas Day 1360, a visitor would have seen a picture heraldic in its precision and clarity. The sombre effect of the clothing of the royal family and their important guests of Brittany would be gradually lightened as the eye passed across the border-line of knights and clergy before reaching the great band of motley, an agitated broken pattern combining only a very few colours, which decorated the far end of the hall.

Those in the know, who might have mixed with the crowd, would, however, have distinguished minor differences in the dress within each of the groups, certainly important at the time to their wearers and significant today. It is worth noting that the stone-masons and the tailors, both highly-skilled artisans (the stone-masons would probably today have been called sculptors and perhaps architects), were given budge, whereas the minstrels were given only lamb. The side-long scrutiny of an informed observer would have noticed this distinction, and he would, no doubt, have adjusted his behaviour accordingly.

For Pentecost, the king's suit of four garments included a mantilletum tied with ribbon of silk and gold, four ells of it, but there was no fur. The suit itself was made from eleven ells of *mixt* tan-coloured longcloth and twenty-four and three quarter ells of *demy satyn* of unspecified colour. Mixed cloth suggests cloth dyed in half grain, according to an entry in the Patent Rolls of 1347,[15] but this may not have been so in this case. The queen's suit and corset for Pentecost were also of tan, but apparently not mixed tan, though her tailor, John Salyno, was also issued with five ells of 'mixt cloth in grain' as well as 106 ells of taffetas. The taffetas was probably red because tan mixed cloth and red taffetas were issued for liveries to the Scottish queen, to the royal princes and to princess Margaret, but not, it seems, to Isabel or to Mary (who by Pentecost had almost certainly married John de Montfort). By this time, too, princess Isabel had been appointed Dame of the Isle of Wight,[16] and, in any case, in 1358 she had been given a grant of 1,000 marks a year (over £650) from the income of the priory of Okebourne, 'for the apparel of her body and of her chamber'.[17] As for princess Margaret, she appears in the account as having been given the usual livery of marbryn for Christmas, when she is referred to as the daughter of the lord the king, but the entry immediately below states that, for Pentecost, the same lady countess was given one cloth of mixed tan and seventy-two ells of red taffetas; this surely means that, in the interval between Christmas and Pentecost, she had married John Hastings, earl of Pembroke. The countess of Ulster was given a livery in the same two stuffs, and so was John of Brittany and his sister Joanna.

And there the liveries for Pentecost cease, but certain people about the court were given clothing described as being for the summer season, which was probably thought of as beginning at this time; and so, indeed, they had been for the winter season too. These may well have been the 'outdoor' servants, for Hugh Steynton, a falconer, had a cote and a hood of russet and blanket for winter, and so did two characters whose surnames must have been unknown to the clerk of the great wardrobe and who were therefore named from their occupations – Rico ffoxtarier[18] and John Othunt. Some of the king's retainers were apparently so anonymous that they were given nicknames: 'Mustard and Garlick', for instance, were two henchmen issued with their winter liveries of blue, russet and blanket. 'Clays, ffige and Vynegar', also henchmen, were among those who received the standard Christmas livery. Minstrels were almost always named after their instruments in these accounts: Lambkyn Taborer, Petro Clarion, Nicholas ffidler, John Sitoler, for example. The rather depressing fact that the minstrels were given almost the humblest of the court liveries was probably offset not only by unrecorded tips but also by grants for life, as in the instance of Lambkyn Taborer and Arnold Pyper, each given annuities of 100s. and, in addition, 7½d. a day for their wages. Both these payments are strikingly high in comparison with those of most of the wearers of the 'lamb' category liveries, so that perquisites attached to the job must have been consoling.

John Newbury, clerk of the great wardrobe, received a summer and a winter suit of longcloth and rather good furs – gros vair for lining and trimmed miniver for a hood. Henry Snayth, clerk of the king's privy wardrobe at the Tower, on the other hand, was given only budge, but he also received a suit of blu lined with budge for the summer season. Part of his duties as clerk of the privy wardrobe was 'to select in London and elsewhere in the realm the necessary armourers, fleechers, smiths and other artificers and labourers for the work of armour . . . and to put them to the said works in the Tower of London'.[19] Two years later, Snayth was promoted to keepership of the great wardrobe, but even so he did not immediately rate as grand a livery as his predecessor's. He drew up the next long account to have survived; it covers the year 1363–4, and is laid out rather differently from John Newbury's, and according to Snayth's own ideas no doubt. This was the year of the visit of the king of Cyprus, and the account appropriately begins with royal gifts as well as suitable clothing for the English court on exceptional occasions.

By this time a paltok had become the normal garment as a part of the suit of a squire of the chamber, while falconers were being issued with gounes, a fashion which, as we have seen, had caught on with extraordinary rapidity. These gounes were made of russet and blanket, so that whereas the style of the falconers' clothing had changed over the past two years, the stuff of which it was made had not. It is unlikely that the colour had remained the same, because it must have been important that new clothing should be conspicuously new. One goun for a falconer is described as short; both long and short

gouns were made for the king during this year. Gouns were issued to the knights, squires and valets of the king's chamber, made of blu and russet, both longcloths.

The colour of the Christmas suits for the king and the queen is not mentioned; the princes were given suits of scarlet cloth (which at this date may or may not have denoted its colour as well as its quality), together with black longcloth in grain, though the black may have been used for mantles, cotes and hoods for the funeral of the king of France. Princess Isabel, the duchess of Lancaster,[20] and Joanna of Brittany were all given scarlet cloth, but no black is mentioned. For Isabel's *roba*, more cloth and more fur were given than for the duchess's; she, in turn, received more than Joanna de Montfort of Brittany. For Christmas, too, fifteen knights of the king's chamber were each given four ells of plain and four ells of striped cloth, a fur of gros vair, a fur of bishe and some trimmed miniver for hood linings. It is noticeable that the knights received not only better fur but an ell more of each cloth than was issued to the household servants.

Once more this motley livery was modified, therefore, for those of lower rank than knights, by the issue of short instead of longcloth, by less cloth and by the substitution of budge for choicer furs. When the liveries were issued to, for instance, the keeper (*contrarotulatorus*) of the king's household, and for at least some of the masons, among whom we find the name of Henry Yevele, later to become famous as the architect in charge of the rebuilding of Westminster Hall, both can be discovered to have been thought of as in the same category. Yevele's name appears side by side with that of another 'cementarius', John Sponley, in this account. Once more a very large number of servants of various grades received those motley liveries: certainly more than 200 of them for the festival of Christmas alone with, in addition, twenty or so minstrels, who were, as before, given lamb but budge. Their liveries once more were on a par with those of the royal gardeners and carpenters. Once more the royal bargemen were given no fur at all; there were thirty-nine of these.

The king's confessor, John Wodegrove, and his companion again received Christmas habits, and the warden and students of Cambridge were given their gowns. One or two extra members of the household appear in this very long list, which includes some mourning not only for the king of France but also for the duchess of Clarence, Elizabeth de Burgh, who had died. Those two newcomers, the king's heralds, Valliant and ffanton, who must have been dressed exactly like the servants in other departments, wore motley and budge. This means that while they were usually thought of as being in the same category as the minstrels, the heralds received budge instead of the minstrels' lamb. Another new name is Randulf Chamberlain, keeper of the king's leopards, whose livery was similar and whose fur was lamb. Among the more exalted people to be mentioned in this account is William Manton, treasurer of the royal household, who was given ten ells of coloured longcloth with bishe and popellus and a miniver hood lining. William of Wykeham, keeper of the privy seal, and several other 'clerks' were also given long-cloth with fur, which evidently varied precisely according to their exact standing.

Not all those who received clothing by the king's order were members of his household. In the Patent Rolls and the Close Rolls appear the names of numbers of men and a few women who had served him in other ways and in other places, and the majority of these people, too, seem to have been given liveries which corresponded in design and according to degree with those who were actually employed in the household itself. A pension of 2d. a day for life and a robe, or 10s. to buy one, as well, quite often, as an additional 4s. 8d. for shoe leather, was granted to a variety of people: John de Helmeswell, maalman, 'maimed in the king's service so that he can no longer labour for him'; William Marre, one of his carters, also maimed; and John de Pasterheye, whose pension in October 1349 was in arrears and who had been maimed too, were among those who received liveries.[21] So was Margery Ingelby, who had given good service to the king's daughter, Isabel, but who was now too 'old to labour as she used to do',[22] and Nicholas Godefelawe, who had given long labour and service but who was now 'so broken by age' that he could no longer obtain his wages from the Exchequer.[23] Several of these old-age pensioners, such as William Daniel, who was pensioned in 1352, had given good service to the late as well as to the present king; like a number of other pensioners, William Daniel was to receive a grant and a livery to be paid out of local funds, in his case from the issues of the county of Nottingham.[24] It is extremely exceptional to find a record of a cash annuity unaccompanied by a grant of at least a robe a year – that is to say, a suit, though not everybody was given money for shoes.

This was the lowest category of royal pensioners: the wounded foot-soldiers and archers and the aged servants no longer officially on the pay-roll of the household; but there were some who were not paid directly by any central fund, but who were sent by the king to some monastery, convent or church which was in some way obliged to him, with the order that they should be housed, fed and clothed and, in some cases, paid a daily or a yearly fee at the expense of the house or the deanery. Again clothing was as much a part of the arrangement as the food or shelter. The hospital of St Nicholas at Carlisle had been given lands in perpetual support of alms to maintain the master and two, three or four lepers, and received the order that, 'the lepers should always be clad in clothes of russet, and enjoy the aforesaid rules forever'.[25] Russet was probably the cheapest local woollen cloth available, but the stipulation that lepers should wear it safeguarded them from being given something cheaper still and less protective – hemp, for instance. Lepers were accommodated in other places, too, of course.

Naturally there were those whose pensions were much higher. Some valets received 7½d. a day and robes for life. Robert of Mildenhall, king's clerk, keeper of the king's wardrobe at the Tower, 'on his appointment during pleasure' was paid 12d. a day

from the treasury and received two robes each of two garments yearly, 'such as were issued to clerks of the household'.[26] Some clerks were paid yearly in marks, one of these, W. de Calynton, receiving twenty marks annually and robes yearly, 'to wit half a cloth with fur for the winter and half a cloth with sendal for the summer'.[27] In these higher categories, too, wherever it was possible, the king arranged for somebody else to be responsible for providing the pensions and the liveries; master Michael de Northburgh, his secretary and keeper of the privy seal, was, for instance, to have £50 a year and 'two robes, winter and summer, out of the benefices of the cardinal Palestrina, whose proctor he is'.[28] The king's physician usually received 12d. a day and robes to the value of 8 marks, one learns from the Patent Rolls, but he may also appear in the great wardrobe accounts, in which case not the monetary value of his suits but his position in the hierarchy can be judged. The physician, incidentally, received the same wage as the king's surgeon.[29]

Undertakings were not always honoured on time. In May 1340, for instance, 'dilectae nobis Mariae comitessae de Fyff' was granted 40s. a week, a handsome sum, from the Exchequer, 'and two robes a year by the hands of the clerk of the great wardrobe'; but the countess of Fife did not, apparently, receive her suits, for on 24 May in the following year, Thomas Cross, then keeper of the great wardrobe, was ordered 'to deliver to Mary, countess of Fyff, the robes which are in arrear to her from 3 May in the 14th year of the reign and to pay her two robes yearly henceforth . . . befitting her estate, one for the summer and one for the winter'.[30] Nor was it only the royal department which was in fault, for about the same time the sheriffs of Cambridge were behindhand with the academic gowns they should have provided for the faculty at King's.[31]

The price of imported textiles had risen by 1352 when the king made an extra payment of £6 beyond the customary fee to the chancellor, the bishop of Worcester at that time, to cover the cost of robes and sendal (for lining) for the livery of the clerks of chancery, 'on account of the dearness of cloth and sendal'.[32] This happened again in 1355, when the then chancellor, the archbishop of York, was paid an extra £10 'on account of the unusual dearness of cloth and sendal', while in 1358 the extra payment to yet another chancellor was increased to £22 6s., 'because of the exceptional dearness of cloth.'[33]

Both Patent and Close Rolls are repositories, in fact, for miscellaneous pieces of information about liveries which could not be accommodated elsewhere. Sometimes the liveries were not of the king's own pattern. John de Burstall, citizen and vintner, and his wife, for example, were to receive a pension for life from the prior of the house of St Bartholomew, and John was also to receive a furred robe of the suit of their (the priory's) squires. In 1353, John Beane was to receive a robe of the suit of the bishop of Salisbury's officers.[34] In 1348, Robert Wyard received, among other benefits, the bailiwick of the manor of Jerdele, 3d. a day and a robe of the suit of the earl of Warwick's squires.[35]

Some suits were issued direct from the wardrobes of the households of the Black Prince, in Cornwall, or at Chester or some other castle of his. Lady Elizabeth de St Omer, his nurse and governess, and William, her husband, his steward, were on his payroll and received his liveries,[36] and, like the leading English noblemen, the prince was responsible for equipping and dressing his archers for the battlefield. On 26 June 1355, his Register included an entry for 6d. a day for the archers of Chester and 3d. a day for the archers of Flynt as well as for the delivery to them of white and green cloth. Earlier, on 14 September 1346, the prince's clerk, Master John De Brunham the younger, was ordered to buy suitable green and white cloth for the Welshman of Flynt and to deliver to each of them a *courtpie* and a *chaperon* of both colours, the green on the right. This instruction that the green is to be on the right is repeated frequently throughout the Register.[37]

What is certain is that everything was calculated with the greatest precision and care, with the result that not only within the precincts of the royal and noble courts but in the streets and byways all over England information as to each man's place in the society of his time was openly communicated to every one of his fellows and could be assessed at a glance. That excellent encyclopedia of canon law known as *Omne Bonum*, which, alas, reaches only the letter G, illustrates both the diversity and the uniformity of current dress by its text and its little illuminations, which must have been painted towards the end of the 1340s.[38] Small groups of archers, of knights, of judges, of sergeants-at-law, for instance, are each bound together by the uniformity of their dress. Tonsured clerks in minor orders are reprimanded by a senior cleric in long gown of dark blue, for carrying arms and appearing in lay dress – tight abbreviated tunics of identical cut. 'Adolescence' is represented by a tender young couple who gaze at each other, the girl in a long-sleeved underdress and over it a discreetly cut and not too close-fitting overdress. 'Adultery', on the other hand, is also represented by a pair of lovers, but here the woman is wearing only her underdress and is therefore improperly clothed.

To dress in a fashion outside the hierarchy was as reprehensible in the great as in the lowly. The poet Machaut, commenting on masculine dress deplored the current practice among lords of dressing too simply and too meagerly so that they too closely resembled their servitors. It was a criticism which Matteo Villani confirmed in writing of the various appearances of the emperor Charles IV in Pisa and in Rome, and he noticed with disapproval that he dressed like a hermit, in *bruno* with no ornaments at all.[39] Machaut's poem, *Le Confort d'Ami*, is addressed to another Charles, Charles the Bad of Navarre in prison; it was written in 1357.[40] The king, the count, the prince and the duke, says Machaut, are not ashamed:

De vestir un povre pourpoint,

whereas they should be separated in their dress from the others. Their men themselves should be dressed alike (in other words in livery), whereas at the moment one wears blue, another green; others again cover their bodies in camelin or fustian or in linen of

23 Miniature paintings from *Omne Bonum*, an encyclopaedia of Canon Law (unfinished), probably late 1340s.

(a) Archers in battle; both sides wear mi-parti uniform (f. 183ᵛ)
(b) Lawyers and knights. The knights wear white coifs and the knight in the centre wears the knightly chlamys. The clothes of the clerks are long to the ground (f. 52)

(c) A clerk reprimanding young tonsured clerks for wearing lay dress and carrying arms (f. 137)
(d) A pair of fashionably dressed young people representing adolescence in the article in devoted to that subject (f. 58ᵛ).

(a)

(b)

70

some kind. One is all in black, another in white, a third looks redder than blood. There is one who wears a yellow baldrick:

> Qui de jaune porte une bende,

another wears a houpelande,[41] another a pourpoint, another a *lodier*.[42] But all wear shoes with long points which have come to be called *poulaines*.[43] Now their lord, resumes Machaut, ought to order their dress:

> Et encore chose plus honnourable
> Que tu voies devant la table
> Tes chevaliers, tes escuiers,
> Tes clercs, tes servans, tes mestiers
> Vestis ensemble en ordenance
> A la bonne guise de France
> Que ce qu'il soient en tel guise
> Que chascuns einsi se desguise? . . .[44]

In the first five lines, Machaut is virtually reciting an argenterie account!

Machaut's poem was written in a spirit of friendship and even of admiration for Charles the Bad, who was presumably in need of such admonition; no such advice was necessary in the case of Edward III nor of Jean II. It is significant that Charles is advised to dress his men in the *bonne guise de France*; he had been far from consistently loyal to the French cause in spite of his connections with the French royal house.

If no French account which survives includes as wide a range of liveries as can be found in the two exemplary accounts of the English early 1360s, the big argenterie account for 1351 nevertheless does – apart from including clothing for newly created knights, for members of the Order of the Star, for the court fools – list a number of liveries issued to both the king's and the dauphin's servants. One finds here four garments and a mantle for Michiel de Brosse, the king's almoner, and of *violet*

acolez[45] for the king's doctors; the same combination of stuff and colour was issued to the king's secretary, who was also controller of the *deniers* (privy purse?), to his chaplains and to his under-almoners. Two longcloths of Brussels of fine *marbre* for the four secretaries of the dauphin and similar marbre longcloth for his doctor, almoner and chaplain appear here too. Marbre shortcloth of Brussels together with striped cloth of Ghent were both bought from the notorious Étienne Marcel and provided for the valets of the king's chamber, while similar stuffs, also supplied by Étienne Marcel, were bought for the valets of the dauphin's chamber. These valets, like their English counterparts, were each given three ells of plain and three ells of striped cloth. The plain cloths were marbre.

It is evident that valets occupying at least some of the posts at the French court were distinguished from others by the colours of their liveries because entries for cloth bought from Étienne do sometimes specify the colour of the cloth as well as the category of the servants for whom it was bought. Two of the king's personal butlers – *somellers du corps du roy* – were issued with *un autre* striped cloth of Ghent in vermilion, whereas three *somellers* of the Dauphin were given striped cloth of Ghent on a blue ground – *sur le pers*. It is likely, indeed, that the mi-parti liveries for that year consisted of a marbre cloth, relatively plain in colour, together with a striped cloth which varied from office to office. Camelin of the Château Landon was issued in October on the king's orders for cotes hardies and unlined houces[46] for the huntsmen and archers.

Agnes la Poullaine, whose duty it was to wash the king's head, was apparently the only female servant to be given livery; Kathelot the royal hatter does not seem to have received any. Agnes, like the male servants, was given marbre shortcloth, six and a half ells of it; her furs were *grosses popres* and a miniver hood-lining, so her services must have been rated higher than one would have expected, for the valets

(c)

(d)

were given lamb linings for their hoods as well as for their suits; the secretaries had miniver.

This 1351 account includes clothing for the marriage of the king's eldest daughter , Jeanne, to the king of Navarre, Charles the Bad.[47] For St Andrew's Day, a suit was made for him of a fine acolé longcloth of Brussels to match the king's – *sembl et de la couleur a celle le Roy ot le jour de la chandelleur* – which the king seems to have worn on St Andrew's Day as well. There also seems to have been some correspondence between clothing for the actual wedding made for the bride (who was eight years old), the queen, the dauphin and, perhaps, the duchess of Orléans.

Whereas in England further details relating to royal wages and liveries can be found in the Patent and the Close Rolls, in France similar details are recorded in the *Journaux du Tresor* and the *Ordonnances* of the French kings. The wages and gowns of the official councillors, magistrates and royal lawyers, for instance, appear in these *Journaux* as *pallii*, though usually no further information is attached because the *pallio* was the statutory gown which belonged to these high offices and more or less unchanging in style; the wearers were sometimes, however, given suits as well.

The *Ordonnances* of the French kings were severe on beggars and 'all manner of such lazy people, dice-players, street singers, both men and women who, if they were healthy in both mind and body, were to be given no more than a single night's lodging in a hospital [*opital ou Maison Dieu*]'.[48] Workers in the dress trade, on the other hand, were forbidden to work on the four annual feasts of the Virgin, on Sundays and on the feast days of the Apostles unless on some dress urgently required for mourning, for priests or for members of religious orders.[49] Overtime, forbidden in Flanders, was probably forbidden in France as well, two measures which were designed, no doubt, to help to keep down unemployment. Nevertheless a considerable number of people in Europe were regarded as deserving poor and given clothing.

The French *Journaux* are also similar to the English Patent and Close Rolls in that they, too, contain occasional references to this clothing of paupers. In December 1349, for instance, Pierre de Berne, master of the privy purse (*maitre de la chambre aux deniers du Roy*) provided the king's almoner with £100 *parisis* to cover the cost of *burellos*[50] and shoes for the poor; but the poor in France, as in England, were by no means dependent only on the monarch for maintenance. Extensive entries in surviving municipal and family papers in such cities as Lyon and Rheims provide a considerable amount of information as to how the clothing of the poor was achieved.

In Lyon in the fourteenth century, the wills of numerous well-placed citizens (many of them drapers) included directions that not only should a stated number of poor men be given clothing on the occasion of their funeral, at which they would serve as bier-carriers, but often insisted that their descendants should continue their own charitable works by providing clothing at regular recognized intervals.

Thomas III of the le Blanc family stipulated that twenty *livres* should be distributed to paupers who assisted at his funeral, and that they should be given forty ells of cloth, forty shirts and forty pairs of shoes between them.[51] Jean de Vaux, a draper of Lyon, ordered his executors to give to eleven *pauvres de Christ*, of whom seven were to carry his bier, black tunics and hoods.

In Rheims in 1346, the dean of the chapter was responsible for seeing that the will of one of the canons was properly carried out, so that, as the testator wished, tunics and shoes should be distributed each year by the dean himself.[52]

Italian records are even more explicit. Nicolai Acciaiuoli, notorious for the extravagance of his lifestyle, spent the last years of his life in his native Florence.[53] In his will he directed that two poor men should be fed in his house in aid of the repose of his soul; that each of his sons should feed a poor man and, in addition, clothe twelve paupers on each of four named feast days. He added later, in 1359, that furthermore, in memory of his father, a hundred paupers were to be given every year enough *pannus romanolo* for a cote hardie and a hood, and that this was to be continued by his heirs.[54]

In Milan, attached to the confraternity of the Misericordia, was a group of twelve knights who were required to distribute bread, wine, vegetables and clothing every day of their lives to the poor. In Naples the practice was to give blue clothing (*panni bleueti*), linen underclothing and shoes each Holy Thursday to a specified number of poor people, and, on the same day, like her forebears, Joanna of Naples washed the feet of thirteen paupers – an international custom performed by, among others, Edward III.

In England, the distribution of clothing was widespread. The archbishop of York, on petition of Thomas de Thweng, rector and patron of the church at Lythom, agreed that the rector should give annually to thirteen poor men of the parish a tunic worth at least 30*d.* and also, to each, 6*d.* for the good estate of the living and the repose of the souls of the dead, as well as peas and wheat at Christmas, mid-Lent and midsummer. In the same year, 1359, five poor men were given 2*d.* a day each and 10*s.* for a robe to pray for the soul of Isabella, the queen mother who had died in the previous year.[55]

Whether they were clothed in russet or bleuet, it is unlikely that these poor recipients made much of a show as they shambled away from the doors of the rich and the religious. The most spectacular liveries worn outside the royal and noble courts would certainly have been those in which the businessmen of the great cities appeared on ceremonial occasions. The splendour of the prosperous citizens of London gathered to greet the Black Prince as he arrived with the captive king of France was not only reported in the *Grandes Chroniques de France*[56] but must have reached the ears of Matteo Villani in Florence, who thought the fact worth recording.[57] His nephew was evidently equally impressed by the London liveries when Jean returned voluntarily to captivity in 1363, for he also mentioned them.[58]

Nor had liveries been absent when Jean himself returned to Paris after his coronation in Rheims. Men of all manner of occupations were dressed according to their trades, the *Grandes Chroniques* noted, making a special mention of the Lombard merchant bankers in very splendid clothing.[59] In Ghent, the citizens were already recognizable by the white hoods which, a century later, were to annoy Philippe le Bon; in Rouen, for the coronation of Charles V in 1364, the burghers all wore a livery of blue and tan.[60]

Examples of the liveries worn by such wealthy citizens could be multiplied, but none was so famous as the mi-parti of the hoods worn by the merchants and tradesmen of Paris under the provost, the draper Étienne Marcel, when, in 1357, followed by an assembly of liveried citizens, he forced his way into the palace of the unfortunate dauphin who, as regent, was attempting to hold France together during the imprisonment of Jean in England. After killing various royal officials who tried to block his passage, Étienne and his band battered their way into the dauphin's own chamber, where he and a handful of his knights were gathered. The demand by Étienne and his followers for a democratic share in the government may not have been entirely pure in its motive, for their invasion of the palace had the tacit support of both Charles the Bad of Navarre (who coveted the throne) and of his sister, Blanche, queen mother of France. Étienne's first act on entering the dauphin's chamber was to convince him that he was completely powerless by snatching the black hood off his head and replacing it by his own mi-parti hood of *rouge et pers* (in other versions *rouge et azure*), the livery of the burghers of Paris, assuring the dauphin at the same time that so long as he and his courtiers wore it they would come to no harm. The bodies of the members of the household who had been killed were left exposed on the pavement and the provost, on departing, declared that he and the citizens of Paris were the dauphin's good friends. Later he caused two lengths of cloth, one red and one blue, to be sent to the palace for the purpose of making bourgeois hoods for the members of the dauphin's entourage.[61] The red and blue livery of the Paris tradesmen became, for a brief moment, so famous that it served as a rallying-point for revolutionary movements elsewhere and was temporarily adopted by some among the citizens of Bruges.[62]

The liveries of merchants and well-placed citizens were not, of course, normally distributed by the monarch, though Edward did, on occasion, bestow clothing on some municipal officers who were natives of exceptionally friendly cities in Flanders. In 1340, for instance, master John Berengier, clerk and councillor of Ypres, received two robes, of the pattern of the king's valets, to continue as a yearly gift for life. Baldwin Vandenwall, *échevin* and burgess and William de Bourne, clerk and councillor, both of Ghent, were given robes and William £20 in addition, while Baldwin was retained as a member of the king's household.[63] This was unusual; Edward and his great wardrobe were in any case in Antwerp at the time and the exhilarating victory at Sluys was to be won within a month with, no doubt, their con-

nivance. There is no evidence that Edward ever provided robes for the councillors of the City of London.

The prosperous cities of Flanders were well able to clothe their own officers, and did so. The mayor and aldermen of Bruges had *Droits de Robes* and on 1 October the city granted to each *magistrat* a suit *van den sayzoene van bamesse* and on 1 May a suit *van den sayzoene van meye*.[64] That they equipped them with gowns of particular splendour for special occasions can be judged from the story proudly preserved in the chronicle of Flanders[65] concerning the mayors and the aldermen of the cities of Ghent, Bruges and Ypres, who accompanied Louis de Mâle, count of Flanders, when he went to Paris in 1351 to take his oath of fidelity to Jean, newly crowned king of an impoverished France. Louis and the Flemish *magistrats* were warmly welcomed by the king to a banquet in their honour. Noticing when they arrived that there were no cushions on the benches, the *magistrats* removed and folded up their superbly embroidered over-gowns of fine Flanders cloth lined with expensive fur, and sat on them. The banquet over, the mayor of Bruges, Simon van Eertrycke, signalled to his colleagues that the gowns should be left where they were when they approached the king to take their leave. As they finally retired, the French attendants ran after them to draw their attention to the fact that they had forgotten their gowns. 'We of Flanders', returned the burghermaster of Bruges, 'when we have been invited to dine, have never been in the habit of taking the cushions away with us when we leave.' Grandiloquent words, which evidently made a deep impression on Jean, for three years later he gave his second son, Philippe of Burgundy, in marriage to Louis de Mâle's five-year-old daughter, Margaret of Flanders.[66]

In October 1363, regulations governing the distinctive sign to be worn by all Jews in France were re-issued by the *Reformateurs generaux et particuliers & les Juges de Privilege*. These repeated an earlier rule that all Jews were to wear a red and white circle – *roüelle* – divided between the two colours – *partagé divisé* – on the outermost garments of their dress. The outer garments listed in the order, which must have taken cognisance of the fashion of the time, are: 'mantel, houce, cote, sercote ou autre vestement'.[67]

Apart from the *roüelle*, European Jews probably wore a dignified dress which differed little from that of well-placed merchants or tradesmen, with the exception of their hats, which may have been distinctive and governed by their own traditions, though at this particular period it is difficult to be sure; Jewish physicians at the royal courts were certainly given the livery appropriate to professional men of their standing.

Liveries of such professionals, as well as details of the liveries distributed to huntsmen, doorkeepers, smiths and laundrymaids employed at the royal courts, survive in the royal accounts, but the clothing of those prosperous peasants and artisans who must have provided for themselves is not, of course, described in official documents. It is this type of clothing which formed the ethnic dress that almost all over Europe emerged finally as the decorative and relatively static 'peasant costume' that can be found in works of art from the seventeenth century onwards. An immense number of specimens of this kind of clothing has survived; it was never the everyday dress of the communities to which it belonged, but was worn only on Sundays and at other special festivals.

In England, between 1340 and 1365, the dress of the prosperous independent farmers and artisans can be discovered only in descriptions in poems or novels and in works of art of the time. It is from Froissart that we learn definitely that a pourpoint is a protective garment that could withstand a blow.[68] That his lady:

> D'un bel corset estoit parée
> Lors dansoit . . .[69]

and with that we discover that the corset is not out of place on the dance floor, and, when it comes to the intermediate class which could wear a pourpoint but certainly not a corset, Froissart is the poet who composes a moving poem about a shepherd who confides to his mate that he longs for a houpeland; his mate rather brutally assures him that he will never be able to afford one. The poem is not dated, but with the author's knowledge of high society it can be assumed that once a houpeland had become a commonplace even a shepherd would not have sighed for one, even an arcadian, courtly shepherd, even in verse.[70]

It is, of course, from the more realistic Langland that a glimpse at least of the clothing of the farmers and the artisans can be caught here and there. His Pernel – Mrs John Citizen – is told to put away her fine trimmings – *Porfil* – which, indeed, she does to great effect, repenting of her proud heart and vowing to wear a hair shirt sewn into her smock.[71] Smocks and 'kertils' do not appear in great wardrobe accounts of the period but in popular poems they do. To judge not from literature but from works of art, the ordinary citizens and countrymen did not wear mi-parti, nor did their womenfolk wear the delicate veil that distinguished upper-class ladies. Indeed they were prohibited from doing so by at least one sumptuary regulation.[72] Nevertheless, in England at least, their thick veils and their aprons are not without style, they follow, as a rule, a fashion of twenty or so years earlier, which absolves the illustrators from the accusation of romanticizing their subjects to the extent that might have been suspected.

Occasionally the dress of the classes overlapped, as for instance in the case of the *houce* which was worn by the prince as well as by his archers, but as a rule the language was precise; it was not only the language of the church and the convent but also of the palace, the street, the farm and the ghetto – so normal as a means of communication that it could pass not only metaphorically but actually as a common tongue. Froissart reported that in 1346, when the rapid approach of the English armies was alarming the French, Philippe de Valois called together the prelates and the *fourés chaperons* in council. To to-

day's readers of the argenterie accounts it would seem that almost everybody wore a furred hood; Froissart's contemporaries, including William Langland, however, would have known exactly who qualified to be known not as himself but as his hood.[73]

Even so, fashion, as usual, out-smarted the dignitaries in their most official capacity, for at the very moment that Piers the Ploughman wagers both his ears that, if hungry enough:

> . . . Fisyk shal his Forred hod . for his [foode] sulle
> And eke his cloke of Calabre . with knappes of gold . . .[74]

and within a decade and a half of Philippe's calling together his *fourés chaperons*, fashionable hoods had become so small that to line them with fur of any kind would have been almost impossible. For a brief and characteristic period, therefore, before he could attain the equilibrium which tradition eventually provides, the wearer of the expensive turned-down, fur-lined hood becomes a pompous figure of fun. This was the exact moment in the history of fashion that Langland seized on to ridicule the silk hoods of the sergeants and the furred hoods of the doctors.[75]

The late Eileen Power held the view that, in the middle of the fourteenth century, the 'peasant himself began to be idealized and his figure to take on a kind of mystic significance . . . It was labourer and not priest who was the type of holiness, whose sweat quenched hellfire and washed the soul clean . . .';[76] but not, of course, if he stepped out of his appointed place in the scheme, which was maintained as regularly by the issuing of twice-yearly clothing at the papal court at Avignon as it was at the royal courts of France and England, at lodge gate of castle, grange or deanery. Peasants were not omitted from this general pattern, even though their clothing was usually the responsibility of one who was lower than a pope or a king.

The exact placing of each man and each woman in the appropriate position preoccupied not only royal civil servant and local landlord but poet and tailor too. Machaut was anxious that Charles the Bad's servants should do him honour by adhering strictly to the correct livery of the moment; Gilles li Muisis was concerned that servants were attempting to rise above their rank in their clothing. Now, he insists, maidservants and valets want nothing that is not new, and, indeed, these servant-maids and all these young things want to have their hair dressed and to wear *hauchettes* as though they were rich:

> Ches meskines si servans et toutes che garcettes
> Voellent lestre trechies et porter haucettes
> Ossi bien que les rikes . . .[77]

in fact:

> Meskines sont les dames; li varlet sont li sire[78]

a perennial complaint, of course, and Li Muisis was more confused than Machaut because he did not

74

approve of too much splendour among the upper classes either; he was severe (as was *Omne Bonum*) on secular clerks who presented themselves in over-fashionable dress:

> On rewarge comment chescuns se deffigure
> En habis cours, estrois, en toute se vesture
> Chescuns en controuver desgisance maitcure
> Tout chil nouviel habit sont moelte de luxure.

The short and the tight attacked once more, but in a line or two he has slipped into speaking not of special sections of society but (a common failing) of people – *les gens* – in general, though this does not prevent him from returning almost immediately to servants and peasants.

It is not, however, the luxury that really distresses him, it is the departure from the correct station in life:

> Les gens anchienement bien et biel se viestoient
> Et selonc leur estas lor viestures portoient . . .

> Pluseurs portoient bien jadis vièses viestures,
> Et en faisoient bien varlet siervant parures
> Et se passoit-on bien de ches simples coustures,
> Se faisoit-on moult bien rapparillier fourures.

They remade, that is to say, their old furs.

> Or voelt iestre chescuns aujourduy poestis;
> Nuls ne vault riens, qui n'est de nouviaus dras viestis …

> On voit ches davaldiaus, bierquiers et kiéruyers
> L'estre voellent viestis ensi k'uns esquyers …[79]

and here he attacked not only people of low degree (*davaldiaus*), but shepherds and carters too. Li Muisis was not the first nor the last to hold such views.

IX

Actors, Minstrels and Fools

To what extent professional actors existed in the mid fourteenth century is difficult to determine – professional, that is to say, in the modern sense, full-time actors whose livelihood depended on being able to find work on the stage. The most reliable evidence that they existed in England is almost certainly the report of their bad behaviour in the municipal theatre in Exeter, and the fact that such a theatre existed is as remarkable as the fact that actors who were apparently independent performers appeared in it.

In 1352, it is noted in the Register of the bishop of Exeter, John Grandisson, that he had called the archdeacon's attention to the disturbances of the peace which were arousing public indignation on account of the lascivious and riotous goings on in the theatre of 'our city of Exeter' – 'quodam Ludum noxium . . . in Theatre nostre Civitatis'.[1] Both actors – auctores – and comics – fautores – were to blame and unless their conduct improved, excommunication in the most serious degree would follow.[2] Naturally, bishop Grandisson did not go into details, but his language is exceptionally strong and it is clear that these actors cannot have been members either of a private company which formed part of the household of a local nobleman or of a trade guild. If they had been, the nobleman or the guild would have been held responsible for their behaviour.

Freelance minstrels and jugglers, if not actors, certainly existed in the second half of the fourteenth century; they were usually referred to, in company with beggars, as undesirable, which probably means that they performed as buskers in the streets and begged for money. At a meeting of the Three Estates in Toulouse in October 1356, just after the French defeat at Poitiers, sumptuary regulations were issued which prohibited the wearing of luxurious or over-fashionable clothing and also forbade minstrels and jugglers to exhibit their skills, and this must have referred to those who were self-employed.[3] Any who had been servants of princes or nobles would hardly have been reached by such a ban.

Those who were members of a confraternity, which could be almost equated with today's 'union', would also have been provided with some protection, unless their organization had acquired a bad name. It was, indeed, a period when few individuals were completely unattached. Those who were warmly enclosed within a royal or a noble court, or within a successful trading company, were probably in the strongest postion but there is widespread evidence that the system of banding together people of like interests in what the Italians usually called a badia – literally an abbey – under a recognized leader, included the majority of the rest of the males in the population who were not accommodated in some other organization. And even women sometimes received similar protection for, when Joanna of Naples was in Avignon, she gave permission for the prostitutes there to be given their own Badia, which was run according to well-regulated statutes. They included the direction that each woman should wear 'Une aiguilette rouge' on her left shoulder.[4] The fact that a brothel could be called a badia did not exclude the use of the same term for groups of monks or minstrels. It was the individual beggar and the self-employed minstrel who was unacceptable in such a highly organized society.

But in spite of what seems to have been a general disapproval of wandering minstrels, in preparing to return to France in 1360, Jean II took a stroll in the woods where he gave a crown to a minstrel who had entertained him with the help of a dog and a monkey.[5] Jean had himself brought with him at least one minstrel from France as a member of his household; he appears in the Journal as le roy des menestraux, but this may have referred to his rank and not to the fact that other minstrels served under him: he seems to have performed various duties for the king which had little or no connection with his professional work.[6] His title of 'roy' was perfectly normal; heads of the widely differing professional confraternities were variously named as 'roy', 'prince', 'abbot' or, in the case of a feminine organization such as a brothel, 'abbess' – bardessa. From 1338 until after 1539 there existed in the isolated valley of Soana in Piedmont a Badia of Fools, under its head, the Abate de'Folli.[7]

Minstrels employed in royal and noble households were not, as we have seen, rated very high in the order of degree, but their place in the hierarchy was precise. There was certainly a link between minstrels and heralds, who, in the twelfth century, could be referred to as 'herald-minstrels'.[8] In the English great wardrobe account of 1363, two heralds are mentioned by their titles as Vaillant and ffanford. They are sandwiched between two groups of minstrels and appear to have received the same liveries[9] and heralds, like minstrels, could be referred to as 'kings' when they held the highest office in their respective (or sometimes combined) professions; the title, of course, continues today. Jean II's *Journal* includes an entry for payment to *le roy des heraux d'Artois*.[10] There is no indication that, in their day-to-day lives, either heralds or minstrels wore a distinctive dress, nor do they seem to have been issued with special clothes in which to perform their official functions.

It is uncertain whether, apart from being musicians, minstrels were also actors. On the other hand, Murimuth, in his account of the Round Table festivities, wrote of music made by actors – 'histrionibus summa fit melodia' – and this certainly sounds as though the royal minstrels and not actors in the modern sense were involved.[11] The innumerable *balades* and *rondeaux* that flowed like rivers from the pens of contemporary poets (some of them historians) must have been intended for live performance, but there seems to be no indication as to who, in the court circle, would have been the performers. That minstrels were appreciated for the music they performed can be judged from the fact that when Jean was about to depart from England, the minstrels attached to the households of the king, the prince of Wales and the duke of Lancaster all performed.[12]

Several great wardrobe accounts, include clothing as well as masks or head-pieces – *visers* – of a fantastic kind, intended, presumably, for members of the royal household, some of whom were courtiers, and even for members of the royal family themselves. The most spectacular descriptions of such things are those published in *Archaeologia* (xxxi), and probably in connection with the various tournaments held after the Calais triumph. For a joust in 1348 at Canterbury, for instance, forty-four visers were made for the king, his earls, barons, knights and squires, but apart from the list of materials required for their making – heavy sindon, linen of Rheims, five sheepskins and some worsted – no particulars are given. The entry is, all the same, important for the statement that these disguises were part of the equipment for a tournament and not designed for actors or minstrels.[13]

Minstrels could be called on to play, nevertheless, at almost any official occasion – after a joust, on board ship – and they could evidently be joined by members of the court circle; for instance, according to Froissart, before the battle off Winchelsea in 1350, Sir John Chandos sang and danced together with the royal minstrels and performed a song he had recently picked up in Germany. They continued until the trumpets of the approaching Spanish fleet were in earshot. So spontaneous an entertainment provides a pleasing insight into life and relationships at the English court on board ship.[14]

The court was at Guildford for Christmas 1347 and there, for the king's plays – *ludos* – not only visers but garments to go with them were made. Fourteen of the masks represented the faces of women, fourteen of them bearded men, fourteen were heads of angels in silver. There were also fourteen heads of dragons, fourteen heads of peacocks and fourteen heads of swans. All these seem to have been designed for the same occasion as that for which a suit of four garments of green longcloth embroidered with pheasants' feathers was made for the king.[15] No viser is mentioned as having actually been made for the king himself but we are informed that the sets of fourteen visers were accompanied by painted buckram garments, either tunics or mantles, fourteen of them decorated with the eyes of peacocks and, as well, there were wings to go with the peacocks and swans. Visers were also made for a joust at Reading during the same year.[16]

Nor are these the only masquerade costumes included in the account. For Christmas 1348, celebrated at Otford, a great variety of visers were made, some of them representing the heads of men mounted on the heads of lions or of elephants; there were men's heads with the wings of wasps; the heads of virgins and of wodewoses. All these could have been mounted as crests on helmets, but, for whatever purpose, the materials of which they were made – fifteen pieces of *bokeram*, English linen and four skins of roan leather – indicate that, even if they were intended for a joust, they were comparatively flimsy. Furthermore, many were accompanied by appropriate tunics so that the final effect must have been theatrical rather than military; it seems probable that effects to some degree similar must have been worn by actors.[17]

It is not surprising that visers, tunics and various other things – 'aliis diu'sis' – were supplied for the king's play at Windsor in the year 1361 when Peter, king of Cyprus, was at the English court, and perhaps Jean II as well. There is, unfortunately, no information as to the character of these things, except that two pieces of *carde* were used to make them.[18]

None of these courtly entertainments bore any relation to the religious dramas, based on the Gospels, at this period, which had certainly survived from the thirteenth century, when most of them seem to have been particularly noted, but which may have become too common to be remarked on in the fourteenth century. They were to experience a rich revival and to undergo much elaboration in the fifteenth century, but if they were not news in the fourteenth, they had not disappeared. Such information as survives on clothing these dramas in, for instance, the *Jeu d'Adam*, probably written in about 1262, shows that when banishing Adam and Eve from the Garden, the Almighty wore a dalmatic, Eve a woman's white dress and Adam a man's red tunic.[19] In other words, if there had been an attempt at archaic costume this was not recorded. Whether the paucity of information about either religious or secular drama in the fourteenth century is due to documentary sources or not, this absence has been noted elsewhere.[20]

In Italy, and perhaps also in England, there existed, among the numerous kinds of organization already referred to, those attached to local churches which could be called on to take part in processions and to perform dramatic scenes related to them. Galvano della Flamma described in detail a very successful procession in Milan with dramatic interludes on the theme of the journey of the Magi; it first took place in 1336, and was ordered to be repeated yearly thereafter.[21] In this case, della Flamma does actually state that three men were dressed as the Magi, which probably meant no more than that they were richly clothed and crowned, because there is very little pictorial material from round about that date which shows the Magi wearing Oriental costume – in most representations of the moment, they look like western princes. While there are several references to Italian companies who performed similar scenes, there are very few references to theatrical costume. The famous Compagnia del Gonfalone (which still to some extent exists)[22] organized a procession in the native city, Rome, in October 1341, in which the *Confalonieri* were dressed in zendado with hose of scarlet cloth,[23] but this merely means that they wore livery.

Already in 1262 it may have become traditional for God the Father to be dressed in a dalmatic in religious dramas, because an inventory of 1339 belonging to the Confraternity of St Dominic in Perugia includes a *tonacella*, the usual Italian term for a dalmatic (the saccos of the Orthodox Church), which is the appropriate vestment in which to preach and therefore to teach and to admonish. At the moment when religious dramas were beginning to be performed by members of the laity and outside the church building, it is natural that some features of their earlier form, when they had been performed only by clergy, should have remained.

That 1339 inventory of the confraternity Dei Disciplinati di Perugia includes a black gown – *veste* – for the Madonna; a beard and a linen cap, *capella de lino*, both of them with black hair – *con pelo nero* – so the white cap must have been the basis for a black wig; two pairs of wings for angels; a shirt for the Lord for Good Friday. In the later 1367 inventory were added three pairs of gloves for the Magi, as well as a star and then the *storpiccio* and the *cacioppa*, the veil and the face of the Devil; and the Dove.[24] All these and some 'properties', such as a column for the flagellation of Christ and a flesh-coloured leather garment to simulate nakedness, must have been a part of the confraternity's wardrobe, used year after year in connection, as the inventory states, with the Lauds, for which a book of *Laude come dialogo* is also mentioned together with the costumes which survived. Records show that, by the fourteenth century, some English guilds already incorporated a clause in their constitutions ordering their members to see that an entertainment of a religious nature was put on on a certain day of the year, usually either Corpus Christi or the day of their patron saint. No English texts have survived from this period, but there is plenty of evidence that dramas were performed. The illustrations to the Holkham Bible, which was decorated in the first half of

the fourteenth century with tinted drawings of a manifestly popular style,[25] include an evil-looking woman in the act of forging the nails with which Christ would be nailed to the Cross. She is not in any Gospel or pseudo-Gospel, but, under the name of 'la vieil Hedron', she came into the text of the early fifteenth-century *Passion of Arras*.[26] In the Holkham Bible, no effort was made to show her in 'biblical' dress – Hedron is depicted as a neat and well-turned-out working-class Englishwoman of the day. She was evidently a firmly established and recognizable stage character during the hundred or so years between the illustrating of the Holkham Bible and the *Passion of Arras*.

If texts are absent, however, there is a good deal of pictorial evidence of the clothing of actors and dancers in secular performances of the middle of the fourteenth century. The manuscript of the *Roman de Fauvel*,[27] illustrated most probably towards the end of the first quarter of the century, includes the score of a musical interlude, accompanied by paintings of a troop of dancers and dancing musicians in a large variety of comic costumes. All are men but some are dressed as women. An actor with the legs and head of a monkey wears an abbreviated tunic; there is a devil; and at least one lion and a number of heavily bearded men partly covered with fur. All are amusingly grotesque and are viewed with wonder by clerks and elegantly hooded ladies who watch the fun each from a separate window on the two sides of the page. The presence of so respectable an audience emphasizes the uncouthness of the costumes of the actors. This is, of course, before 1340, but the practice of impersonating animals and animal spirits continued, as the entries in the *Archaeologia* account show.

Actors disguised as animals were almost certainly a survival from pagan times. In 1347, at a state banquet in Rome during Cola di Rienzo's brief ascendancy, a crowd of buffoons entertained the diners; one of them dressed in the skin of a bull and, wearing horns on his head, careered and leapt about.[28] Far less lively than that are the liveried men who caper along the lower border of a page or two of the *Romance of Alexander*, which, unlike the Fauvel manuscript, was actually executed in the early 1340s and can therefore be taken as reasonable evidence that the wearing of animal heads in north Europe was not confined to the lists. A more interesting little troop of dancers emerges from the gateway of what purports to be Constantinople, but which looks more like Bury St Edmunds or Bruges, in an illustration to the *Luttrell Psalter*, also of the early 1340s. In this extremely important example of theatrical dress of the period, the boy dancers, arranged in single file, hold hands and are led by a piper. Like the steps they perform, their costumes are identical and are not fashionable in design, but archaistic and certainly theatrical. That is to say, at a moment when fashionable tunics were severely condemned for being too tight above the waist, theirs are puffed out and have full skirts. On their heads, the boys wear wreaths of flowers, and their shoulders are covered by little capes, each with a horizontal design of gold circles enclosed between horizontal lines of gold, a trim-

24 *Luttrell Psalter*, early 1340s. A formal dance performed by a company of young boys, probably professional entertainers, wearing theatrical costume deliberately designed to look archaic.

ming which does not accord particularly well with current fashionable taste. The piper, who wears no wreath and no shoulder-cape, wears a mauve tunic, yellow hose, and has a yellow hood tucked into his belt at the back; the dancers wear, alternately, orange tunics and mauve hose and mauve tunics with orange hose. The upper part of their capes was probably meant to represent a painted stage version of miniver. It is very rare that anything so manifestly designed as a stage ensemble can be found in a fourteenth-century work of art.[29]

While to the eyes of today this little group of dancers must seem to bear an astonishing resemblance to a modern ballet, both in the repeating pattern of its costumes and in the uniformity of its steps and poise, to a fourteenth-century audience the costumes would almost certainly have represented a period of the past, probably biblical, possibly Greek. As such, it is a rare and valuable record of historical costume as seen through the eyes of the past.

The *Luttrell Psalter* is an outstanding example of the recording of fashionable dress of its period, which makes these carefully drawn theatrical costumes all the more remarkable. They are probably typical of dress expressly designed for a special moresca to be danced by a courtly household group. It is worth pointing out that, in the early 1340s, mi-parti must have been considered unsuitable for theatrical use because it formed an important element in high fashion. The fact that the maskers in the

Romance of Alexander of almost the same date do wear mi-parti with their animal heads suggests that these young men were liveried valets and not actors wearing specially designed costumes. They have nothing in common with the *Fauvel* illuminations.

It would be absurd to pretend that theatrical costumes of this kind could not have been found in all the noble courts of Europe in the middle of the fourteenth century. The numerous organizations already set up for producing public entertainment must also have been concerned with dressing up for the shows, but only precise evidence as to the styles of costume acceptable between 1340 and 1365 are relevant here, and of this there is not very much.

The current attitude to various grades of performers was, again, very probably based on the thoughts of St Thomas Aquinas, who pointed out that 'comedians especially would seem to exceed in play since they direct their whole life to playing. Therefore if excess of play were a sin all actors would be in a state of sin; moreover all those who employ them as well as those who make any payment would sin as accomplices of their sin'; but 'play is necessary for the intercourse of human life', and 'whatever is useful to human intercourse may have a lawful employment ascribed to it'.[30] St Thomas, while he went on to warn against over-stepping the bounds of propriety in the theatre, gave as one reason for believing that there was no harm in actors who behaved properly the fact that 'it is related in the Lives of the Fathers that it was revealed to the Blessed Paphnutius that a certain jester would be with him in the life to come.'[31] Which introduces the character of the court fool in the fourteenth century, a person about whom far more is known than about the professional actor.

In the fourteenth century, the court fool bore no relationship to those fools who were already beginning to associate themselves into bands and societies; there is no ambiguity about the position of the fools at the court of France at the time. A story told in the *Chronicon Angliae* may be apocryphal, but the author evidently thought it plausible enough to relate. It concerns the part played by Philippe de Valois' fool in 1340, and precisely sets the role of the court fool in King Lear's sense, for, when none dared to break the news to Philippe of the French defeat at Sluys, the fool was persuaded by the courtiers to do so, and, having made his way into the king's presence, he began to attack the English for cowardice. Presumably the king failed to respond to what he must have regarded as a statement of the obvious, for the fool continued to pile it on in the same vein – *multiplicare verbe* – until the king finally asked him what was all this about English cowardice. 'Those ones,' said the fool, 'they are so timid that they dared not jump overboard into the sea like all our brave Normans and Frenchmen did'; and so the king received the message.[32]

This sort of relationship explains the fact that in 1359 Jean II brought with him into captivity in England, his fool Jean, whom he evidently treated with as much consideration as his own son, Philippe of Burgundy, who came with him too. The *Journal* of his expenses contains repeated entries for clothing for Jean le Fol, who had already been a favoured member of the royal household in 1352 when he was actually associated with the Order of the Étoile by being given a vermilion scarlet cloth coverlet on the occasion of the meeting of the Order,[33] though no special clothes appear to have been made for him at precisely that time. The *Compte* of Étienne de la Fontaine seems to show that Jean le Fol was given two suits, a corset, three pairs of marbre vermilion hose, seventeen pairs of slippers and some hoods – *aumuces* – during that year. One of the suits consisted of four garments of mi-parti brown striped cloth of Ghent and a pale blue cloth – *pers cler* – lined with white lamb. The other suit, also of four garments, was marbre ash-coloured shortcloth lined with vermilion cendal. Both cloth of Ghent and cendal belonged to the high categories of stuffs in France, of which royal clothing could be made. It has already been noticed that the French accounts did not divide the clothing of the court according to social standing: in this instance Jean le Fol's clothes follow immediately after those given to the king of Navarre. Although Jean's clothes do not seem to have matched, as a livery, those of any other members of the household, there is nothing to suggest that in their design they referred to his profession.

Clothes for another court fool, Micton, who belonged to the dauphin Charles, are entered in the same compte. Micton too was given two suits during that year, each of four garments with, in addition, not a corset but a cote hardie and a mantle, as well as twenty pairs of slippers. A remarkable proof of the esteem that the dauphin must have felt for his fool is the fact that for the Navarre wedding Micton was given a suit of violet velvet lined with miniver; the velvet was actually a gift of the king.[34] Both Jean le Fol and Micton were given boots and Jean's corset is specified as having been made of a stuff which was *oeuvré* with a pattern of chains.[35] Perhaps the most astonishing discovery is an entry in the unpublished account of 1351 for two gold rings, which were hung and attached – *pendus et attachiez* – to the ears of Micton, *fol de monseigneur le Dauphin*.[36] This is, so far as I know, the only reference to ear-rings at this period.

If the reference to ear-rings is surprising, almost equally startling is a present given by the dauphin to his father's fool, Jean, for the Christmas of that year, 1351. Described in great detail in the same account,[37] the gift was a hat. It is worth discussing. Kathelot the royal milliner was provided with the materials for making this hat which was of beaver but trimmed with ermine and decorated with a rose bush – *rosier* – its stems of Cyprus gold thread, its leaves of beaten gold set with pearls and garnets and its flowers mainly composed of pearls. Extra ornamentation took the form of bezants, gold buttons, enamel pieces and gold laces, while on the summit of the crown was a silver tube supporting a dolphin, modelled from life – *pres du vif*. This fantasy might have appeared to have been an extremly expensive joke, designed to make Jean le Fol look absurd, but the dolphin provides a clue to what had been, perhaps, a perfectly serious intention. In 1349 the king's eldest son Charles inherited the Dauphiné after the retreat of its former heir to a Dominican monastery. The pun was therefore a topical and yet familiar one, because the canting arms of the dauphins of the Viennois had included a dolphin as early as 1199.[38] Although the hat with a silver dolphin on its crown appears in the argenterie account of 1351, the gift to the king's fool may actually have been made a year earlier as a celebration of Charles's acquisition of the Dauphiné – it would in that case have been the year of the king's coronation. Once a connection of this nature has been suspected, further study of other decorative articles of clothing might be rewarding. There is no indication in any of these accounts as to who might have been responsible for designing the beaten-gold extravagances for these royal hats. Presumably they were actually made by the royal jewellers or, rather, goldsmiths. Kathelot the milliner had made other hats at about the same time, a set apparently composed of peacocks' feathers for the royal treasurers, whether traditional in design or especially festive we do not know.[39]

In the year and four months covered by the two *comptes* – February 1351 to July 1352 – each fool was issued with two suits, one for Easter and one for Pentecost; the extra corset or cote hardie may have been made for winter or some intermediate season. Such accounts overlap, however, and the actual number of suits they received is difficult to estimate.

The earlier account of 1351 also includes clothing of much the same kind for the two royal fools.

Micton's valet, Jehan le Mome, was issued with over a hundred pairs of slippers on his master's behalf and Jean le Fol's valet, Girardin, with four pairs of hose – 'de plusiers couleurs'. It is clear that apart from the suits for the special occasions, the normal fur which lined these suits was white lamb which, in an English account, would have established their position in the social scheme but this would take no account of ermine-lined hats, gold ear-rings and a velvet wedding suit. In fact the fool at court was certainly a unique person in a period when other members of society were divided into groups – even the highest nobles in the land. The French fools were given linen underwear, and several separate hoods, sometimes lined with gris or miniver. They always appear as *aumuces*. Kathelot, the royal hatter, was given pearls to decorate three of these hoods for fools in 1351, and this was one of at least two occasions on which hoods were issued not merely for Jean and Micton but also for two additional characters, Pierre Touset and Raymondit, who two years running were associated with Jean le Fol in receiving *aumuces*.[40] It seems that there must therefore have been two other fools of lesser standing who were, perhaps, called in for special events. They did not apparently receive anything but hoods from the argentierie, and they do not seem to appear anywhere else in the account of 1352, but, in the unpublished account of 1351, they can be found again in company with Jean le Fol and Micton.

It is worth noticing that in both these accounts, in the section which refers to furs, where one set of *aumuces* was lined with gris and one with miniver, Jean le Fol is named as 'maistre', whereas the other two fools have no similar titles, though they are mentioned as being given *aumuces* yearly. The *compte* reads: 'Pierre Touset Raymondit et ledit maistre Jean le fol pour fourrer a chascun d'eulx une aumuce qu'il soit accoustume de prendre au terme de Pasques.'[41]

Étienne's account of 1352 records the fact that one of the royal glovers, Hue Pourcel, was ordered to make a case for Jean le Fol's *gobelet*; it cost 20s. *parisis* and was delivered to Girardin. It was probably the same *gobelet* which introduced the first reference to Jean le Fol in the French king's *Journal* of expenditure during his captivity in England, which began in July 1359. Jean II had brought his fool with him, and on 8 July, scarcely more than a week after his arrival, a goldsmith, Hannequin, was paid for recasting – *refondre* – and regilding a chalice for the king and the *gobelet* of 'maistre Jean le fol'.[42] These two references to a gobelet belonging to the fool must surely not only mean that it was a favourite possession of his, but that he had been able to bring it with him through all the vicissitudes of the journey or, rather, journeys, for it must be presumed that the fool was with the king in his earlier captivity in Bordeaux as well as his later one in England.

Both the recasting of the goblet and the fact that the *Journal* records the making, a month or two later, of a special little table for the fool suggest that he may have taken his meals at the same time, if not at the same table, as the king, and there are other indications that he was treated in a very privileged way.

He had, for instance, his valet Girardin with him, who received three pairs of slippers on his behalf during that first July. Later, in November, and again in the following May, a certain Magister, who is also referred to as 'valet maistre Jean le fol', but who actually probably held some other post, received slippers on behalf of the fool. The theory that a fool who had a 'master' was a lunatic and not a sane man is difficult to apply in this case for Jean himself is referred to as 'maistre' on more than one occasion. His very high-quality clothing and proximity to the king over this isolated period would make it most unlikely that he was not sane.[43]

Thirteen pairs of slippers were, in fact, issued for the king's fool during the year covered by the *Journal* of expenses in England: a much smaller quantity than he had been given when they were both at liberty. This is typical in some respects, though not in others, where the clothing of the imprisoned king and his fool were concerned. Jean le Fol was given two suits, as had previously been the custom, but one consisted of three not four garments. He was given as well underclothing, hose, three cotes hardies and mantles and a pair of boots. We find that while in England he was given not lamb for the linings of his suits but gros vair and miniver – higher in grade – and that later he was given a rather large quantity of black lamb, probably either from Romania or Calabria, for lining a cote and a mantle.[44]

Jean le Fol's clothes thus seem rather more prestigious than they would have been in Paris eight years earlier, and, in so small a court circle as Jean II could maintain in England, which certainly did not include any other fool, his relationship with the king was probably even closer. All Jean le Fol's stuffs were handled by Tassin de Brueil, the king's valet and tailor, but as time went on and large sums of money were laid out for clothing in which the king would be entertained on his way back to France and must have been intended to be worn when he got there, we find Perrin the furrier cleaning and 'refreshing' some of the furs already worn by the king. No such process had been recorded in the inventories of the French court and, indeed, great emphasis seems to have been placed on new as against used furs. It may be remembered that some of Madame Ponce Clair's furs were not new, but then she was merely the wife of a lawyer.[45]

For the journey back to London from Somerton Castle to prepare for the king's departure to France, five coaches were ordered. The first coach conveyed the furnishings of the king's chamber, the second those of his chapel; the third coach carried the furnishings of Philippe's chamber, the fourth the equipment of the kitchen and the fifth Jean le Fol and Girardin, his valet.[46] The fool is not recorded as having been with the king during his last stay in London.

It may be that Jean le Fol would not have been particularly welcome at the royal parties in London and the south, for there is no evidence that any fool held a similar position in Edward's affections. A fool, Roberto le Fol, appears in queen Philippa's wardrobe account of 1333[47] as a minstrel, and whereas the

81

valets, under-clerks, pages and minstrels among whom his name is to be found were none of them issued with more than eight ells of cloth, a sheet of fur and a hood lining, Roberto received twelve ells of this striped cloth of Ypres, a sheet of budge, two sheets of lamb and his hood lining. Roberto's cobbler, Roger, was also given cloth, but much less of it and no fur. It is difficult to find any reference to a fool in Edward's great wardrobe accounts of the middle of the century, but in his account of 1363–4, a 'Rob' to ffosle' appears among the minstrels. This may well have been Roberto le Fol, because it was not at all unusual for the name of a member of the household to appear in these accounts over a long period of time and he may have been clothed, in the interim period, from the queen's wardrobe, since he appeared there in the first place. If it was he, however, who appeared in 1363, he was certainly given no special privilege as far as his clothing was concerned; if 'Rob' to ffosle' was the original master Roberto le Fol, his position at court was certainly not outstanding and he may have shrunk into insignificance because an intimate fool did not appeal to Edward III.

From the bare but revealing entries in the argenterie accounts, on the other hand, sometimes confined to a reference as brief as 'Maistre J. le fol, pour offrande le grant venredy, a la Croiz, 4d',[48] the sort of tender affection that must have existed between some French fools and their master at the court of France in the fourteenth century can be deduced. The fools at the French court seem, indeed, to be much nearer to some of Shakespeare's most sympathetic fools than to the multiplicity of court fools that appear to have surrounded Philippe le Bon and his contemporaries in the fifteenth century, or those of the English court in the sixteenth. Less openly, there may have been something of the same spirit in Italy between fools and their masters, for we come across a certain Valor de Florentia being referred to as 'ystrio familiaris et fidelis noster', and it is interesting here to see that Valor was called *ystrio* – actor.[49] It is clear, where the argenterie accounts were concerned, that they were nevertheless providing for the fool as confidante rather than as entertainer. For information as to what the fourteenth-century court fool looked like when he was wearing the distinctive costume belonging to his profession, there seems to be little if any documentary material, but there are hints in material that is pictorial, though it is to be found in somewhat unexpected and, it must be admitted, unsuitable contexts.

The first fool to appear in a work of art of the fourteenth century wearing a distinctive dress is probably to be found among the personifications of the Virtues and the Vices portrayed on the lower panels of the walls in the Arena Chapel in Padua, painted by Giotto round about 1305. The vice *Stultitia* is represented by a fool in unmistakably professional dress, but of an uncommon kind. From a band round his head, a wreath of tall feathers rises like a crown; his legs, feet and arms are bare, the skirt of his tunic is cut into deep scallops and descends into what is almost a train at the back. His sleeves are cut roughly short to above the elbow.

Round his waist is a twisted cord to which small round bells are attached at intervals; he carries a bauble. Giotto's fool is, of course, too early for the period covered by this study, and his dress would not be relevant but for the existence of an Italian drawing executed more than 150 years later which shows a fool in very different circumstances wearing an almost identical dress. The dress in these two works of art is particularly interesting in view of the strips into which the tunic and the sleeves are cut, for the device worn by a fool found its way very gradually into high fashion, where it remained as the serrated edges of courtly dress, and remained for a very long time – more than seventy years.

Giotto's representation of *Stultitia* which, being among the Vices, can perhaps be interpreted as 'light-mindedness', has some slight justification; a similar attitude must have inspired the artists responsible for a group of representations of fools that seem to be even more difficult to justify. Among the handsomely illustrated religious books of the Middle Ages many were psalters, in which the psalms of David are set out. Two of the most luxurious and famous produced in England just before the middle of the fourteenth century are the *Luttrell Psalter* and the *Gorleston Psalter*, but there were many more written and illustrated round about the same period, not only in England but all over Europe. The psalms are, of course, copied in Latin, and Psalm 53 in that language begins: 'Dixit insipiens in corde suo non est Deus.' At what moment in time the *insipiens* of Psalm 53 became not merely a professional fool but, in many instances, king David's own fool would involve some research; it is enough for the moment to understand that, by the middle of the fourteenth century, in a large number of illuminated psalters the initial D of *Dixit* encloses a dignified and usually enthroned king David reprimanding, with a pained but indulgent air, his fool, who has made a boob. Sometimes the king is replaced by the hand of the Almighty which emerges from a cloud to admonish an equally professional fool. Sometimes both the hand of the Almighty and king David are present. In most cases the fools themselves look a trifle surprised but seldom penitent.

The interesting thing about these court fools is that, far from following a uniform pattern, their dress (or sometimes almost total absence of it) is very varied. All these fools carry baubles, the mark of their profession above any other symbol, and there are certain characteristics which several have in common. If we are to rely on the evidence of these psalters, breviaries and bibles – and their artists seem, from the confidence with which they present them, to know what professional fools did look like – there appears to have been no national or regional character about their dress. In a breviary of Bohemian origin, now in the Prague university library, dated 1356, for instance, the fool in the initial letter to Psalm 53 is almost naked except for a breech-clout and a short shoulder-cape with an attached hood thrown back from the head. He wears a belt with a small hanging pouch, and almost certainly shoes, though the colour has faded here and it is difficult to be certain.

(a) King David, enthroned, admonishes his Fool.

(b) A Fool wearing a hood with three points, a houce and bare feet.

(c) Fool wearing only under-breeches, one with an open, one with a closed leg, and a hood.

(d) Barefooted Fool wearing a hood with two points ending in bells.

25 Fools enclosed in the letter D for 'Dixit insipiens . . .' Psalm 53.

Nakedness or, more probably, nakedness simulated by wearing long close-fitted hose with no over-tunic, is typical of some classes of fool. In a Scandinavian bible in Stockholm, a fool, drawn in a very elegant style, wears garments rather similar to those of the Bohemian fool, though he wears breeches of an extremely transparent kind, obviously meant to represent underwear, with, again, a shoulder-cape with its hood thrown back. This fool wears only one shoe, but a very fashionable one, cut into a trellis design. One leg of his thin breeches has an open end, the other fits tightly round the upper calf, an effect which will be discussed later. In the Bardolf-Vaux psalter in Lambeth Palace, the fool appears to be totally naked, though he, too, wears highly fashionable shoes. He carries a bauble and a ball or an apple (as do some other fools), and his nakedness may, like personages in religious dramas who were required to look naked, have been in reality, a flesh-coloured leather covering of the kind referred to in some inventories. Whereas some of these naked, or almost naked fools wear shoes, however, some of the clothed fools wear none. The fool in the *Luttrell Psalter* letter D, for example, wears a knee-length un-belted tunic with short cape-like sleeves, and on his head a hood with two 'horns', each terminating in a bell. The hood is turned back in front and seems to be lined with miniver; his feet are bare, as are those of a fool in a similar tunic (but with *three* points or horns to his hood, each with a bell on its end) in a mid-fourteenth-century psalter in the Bodleian. Another, however, includes a fully dressed fool who also wears an unbelted over-garment, boots and a hood with two ears and a central point.

Remembering the large number of slippers issued to French court fools, the bare feet of some of king David's fools may mean that this was not a part of their normal appearance but, rather, of their 'act'. The practice of wearing only one shoe might seem even stranger but for traces of something of the sort elsewhere. The famous Compagnie della Calza of Venice seem to have had their beginnings in the fourteenth century, and their distinguishing mark, which, in the sixteenth century, took the form of one plain and one embroidered stocking, appears to have originated in one stockinged and one bare leg – the stocking much torn about.[50] In a much earlier period still, there may have been some common source for this practice shared by companies of young men required to provide entertainments, and fools, but if this is true it has not apparently come to light.

The unbelted over-garment with cape-like sleeves worn by fools in several fourteenth-century manuscripts was not exclusive to them, but was worn by other people, not of the highest rank, as well. It can very probably, though not certainly, be identified as the *housse* or *houce* which was often issued to fools in France. The fools' hoods with two points or ears may always, as they were in the argenterie accounts, have been referred to as *aumuces*, for the very reason that this implied, as a rule, two points. During the Middle Ages and until well after the Renaissance canons in the Church of Rome wore shoulder-capes of fur to which were attached hoods with two points, one on each side of the head, called *aumuces*. In publishing a fourteenth-century inventory in the archives of Bruges, which includes a note of an *Amuctiam uni-corniam*, the editor noted that the *aumuce* may have been so named because it was usually equipped with *deux cornes*, like the mitres of bishops, called at that time *hoornen* or *stoyen*.[51] The bishop's mitre is derived from a very ancient cap of linen which did, indeed, have what appeared to be two small points. Originally they were worn one at each side but later the cap was turned round so that one point was at the front and the other at the back. That the change was not merely an eccentric spasm is proved by the fact that emperors, too, wore mitres. When Charles IV was crowned as emperor in 1355 the mitre was placed on his head, 'imponit mitram in captie', as tradition demanded, and over it the *imperatorium dyadema*. When an empress was crowned, however, an earlier tradition was followed and the mitre was first placed on her head with the horns to the right and to the left, 'cornua mitre sint a dextris et sinistris', and the coronet was then superimposed. The fact that the points were actually called horns is as interesting as the placing of them. It is also worth noting that the emperor's cap was called a *mitra clericalis*.[52] If any relationship had ever existed between the horned hoods of fools and the mitre of the bishop it may have originally emerged from the annual ecclesiastical feast of fools which, by the fourteenth century, was far removed from the fools in the royal courts. Only the word *aumuce* provides a possible link between them.

The tantalizing question of the category of hood named *aumuce* in the fourteenth century cannot quite be abandoned. Jean II's *Journal*, for instance, refers to *un aumucier de Londres* in connection with six *aumuces* ordered from him for the king on 26 June, when the last minute preparations for his departure from London were being made.[53] The existence of an *aumucier* trading in London proves, surely, that bicorne or unicorne, their structure was distinctive. In the case of these six, could they have been intended as the caps worn, of necessity, under the king's crown? Once back in France he would certainly have worn it on state occasions.

The situation is further complicated by a drawing of what must be regarded as a theatrical costume worn by an entertainer at the foot of folio 84r in the *Luttrell Psalter*. This man, who holds in the air a small hoop through which a little dog hurls itself, wears what may well be a mockery of the vestments of a bishop. He is dressed in a mantle, superficially rather like a cope made in stuff of a loud checker pattern of red and blue, with a mitre-like cap to match. Both the cap and the material of which it and the mantle are made would have been absolutely unacceptable as a part of normal dress in the early 1340s.

Like the dress of the dancing boys, also in the *Luttrell Psalter*, the dress of this entertainer is a rare example of what can genuinely be regarded as theatrical costume at this date. It seems probable, moreover, that most minstrels and court entertainers must as a rule have worn clothes that did approximate to the current fashion, because, in addition to

84

26 *Luttrell Psalter.* A professional entertainer, wearing theatrical dress, perhaps intended as a parody of the vestments of a bishop.

their official liveries, which are usually very much like those of the court valets, they were given so many presents of clothing. The poet Aliprando, for example (described by Muratori as unfortunate but truthful), says that, at the Gonzaga wedding in Mantua in 1360, 338 *robe* consisting of a *vestito,*

guarnaccia, guarnaccione, mantello and *cappuccio* were distributed to comedians and musicians – *buffoni* and *sonatori.*[54] Eight years later, at the wedding of Lionel of Antwerp to Violante Visconti, 'buffoni, zigoladri e sonatore' were given a great many suits by Galeazzo Visconti, money by Bernabo, the bride's uncle and lord of Milan and, in addition, by Lionel and his attendant nobles, 500 *robe.*[55] These clothes may, of course, have been purely theatrical, but if this had been the case would not the truthful poet have been tempted to say so?

As for the splendour of those gifts to minstrels, it may not even have been exceptional, for the translator of *William of Palern,* writing at the command of Humphrey de Bohun in about 1350, described the final coronation celebrations of the emperor and the empress in Rome and, after informing us that:

> *Fulle fiftene daies . that fest was holden*
>
> 5352

he says that:

> *no tong might telle . the twentithe parte*
> *of the mede to menstrales . that mene time was geve,*
> *of robes with riche pane . & other richesse grete,*
> *sterne stedes & strong . & other stoute giftes,*
> *so that eche man per-mide . might hold him a-paied.*
>
> 5356

All the same, as compared with the court fool, the individual minstrel hardly exists; he is merely a member of the court and grouped together with the valets. The fool, on the other hand has, at least, his *aumuce,* usually, if we are to believe contemporary drawings, not with two points but with two ears. But even here a teasing doubt as to its origin remains for Machaut, describing Apollo as angrily planting two asses' ears on the head of king Midas, in line 1697 of his *Fonteinne Amoureuse,* goes on to say that Midas successfully hid his two velvet ears with *aumusses vermeilles.*

X

National Traits and Deviations in the Dress of the Period

The existence of small but by no means unimportant national and regional differences in dress was mentioned at the beginning of this study. Many of them – differences in taste affecting combinations of colour, for instance – are no longer discernible, though they must certainly have been to those who were alive at the time; some other local variations are still very obvious. Tedious to describe, since they are often either small or subtle, it is important nevertheless to attempt to define at least some of them, because on them the understanding of the contemporary views of the clothing of foreigners depends, as well as the recognition of foreign dress in fourteenth-century works of art and even, occasionally, of the identification of the area in which works of art were done.

It is perhaps the remains of a tribal instinct that continued (and has continued) to make the presence of foreigners in any society so interesting and, in some cases, alarming. Jocelin of Brakelond, writing much earlier in 1183, in his chronicle of the abbey of St Edmund, related a remarkable incident concerning a retiring abbot who told his monks that he had journeyed to Rome in the days of the Schism when all clerks bearing letters of the pope Alexander were seized and sent back to him with noses and lips cut away. He, however, pretended to be a Scot, put on Scottish dress and adopted the behaviour of a Scot, and he often shook his staff as they shake that weapon they call a gaveloc – 'Scotti habitum induens, et gestum Scotti habens . . . baculum meum excussi ad modum teli quod vocatur gaveloc' – and so escaped persecution, which suggests remarkable discernment on the part of the Romans.[1]

In the middle of the fourteenth century, it would probably still have been possible to recognize a Scot in Rome, but what is certain is that, so far as dress was concerned, French influence was strong and French taste widely disseminated, in spite of the fact that, apart from the brief intervention of the duke of Athens in .Florence, the French, hard pressed at home, were not apparently to be found in large numbers outside the countries under their immedi-ate domination. Those countries were, all the same, important.

The royal court in Paris almost certainly influenced dress at the papal court at Avignon, especially during the papacy of Clement VI, a Frenchman. It was in his reign that French artists began to be employed to decorate the papal palace, whereas previously only Italians had been commissioned to work there.[2] French taste must have influenced John of Bohemia, who spent a great deal of his time at the French court, as did his son Charles who, from comparatively early childhood had been brought up in France; his tutor and life-long friend had been Pierre de Rosiéres, later to become pope Clement.[3] In 1348, when Charles had succeeded his father as king of Bohemia but not yet been elected emperor, he founded the university of Prague and based its statutes not only on those of Bologna but also on those of Paris.[4]

Circling round the French court were the kings of Navarre but equally close was the house of Anjou, whose members ruled both the kingdom of Naples and the kingdom of Hungary, and although contacts with Paris may not have been consistently close, it is only necessary to examine the miniatures which illustrate the statutes of the Order of the Saint Esprit of Naples and the Hungarian Illuminated Chronicle[5] to see that the general style of courtly fashions in both Naples and Visegrad was French, though perhaps not the purest French.

Already in the fourteenth century Italians were showing a taste for fashions in dress which exemplified the classicism that has been their characteristic ever since. By that time, in most Italian states, dress had lost almost completely the 'folk' quality, ultimately traceable to the late Roman empire, which Giotto had noticed and recorded in his Arena Chapel frescoes,[6] and Italian dress now followed (or led) the general European fashion while omitting its 'gothic' features. Sharp contrasts in colour and hard finicky ornamentation were absent in Italy and so, in consequence, were the rigid plaits and *cornettes* so popular among women in the north of Europe. Italian

27 Papal Palace, Avignon Frescoes in the *Tour de la Garderobe*, detail of a hawking scene, 1343–44. The young Frenchman wear fashions indistinguishable from those of their contemporary English counterparts.

sensitive of all. In the later nineteenth century, the abandonment by women of the bonnet in favour of the hat caused a stir which was not without its moral aspect, and more recently the actual arrangement of the hair on the heads of politicians has done something to affect their popular support. More fundamental are the ancient customs, sometimes embodied in religious doctrine, of concealing the hair completely, or of encircling the head with a cord or a band which sometimes developed in time to an expensively decorated structure.[7] It is natural, therefore, that it is in the treatment of the head and also, in the case of the sex which can grow hair on it at will, of the face, in which national or regional temperament and taste should have been most clearly revealed.

The dressing of the feminine head is always very noticeable, and, as we have seen, could, in the fourteenth century, arouse strong passions. More than any other feature of the dress of either sex, it marked the difference between the fashions of one advanced European country and another. The most striking head-dress worn by women in the middle of the century was not to be found in Italy or even in France, but was extremely popular in Bohemia, Hungary, Austria, the Netherlands and, strangely, England, as well as in Denmark.

This head-dress appears only once, if at all, in the great wardrobe accounts of the time, when, in the account of 1361–2, a certain Katharine of Grantham (Kat'ine G'nthm̃) charges 'xvjs' a piece for making five *couvrechiefs crispes*. Even this reference is not absolutely certainly identifiable as the popular and elaborately contrived veil of the moment, because a *couvrechief* could mean almost anything worn on or over the head by either sex, but it nevertheless, seems likely, in view of its high price, that this is what it was. As a rule, no doubt, the head-dress was made up in the chamber by maids and not by workers in the great wardrobe which would account for its almost total absence from the inventories. Worn by royal ladies as well as by those of the middle class, the head-dress consisted of a number of layers of veiling (almost certainly of fine linen) the edge or *selvedge* of each of which was woven in such a way as to produce a narrow quilling or frill. Surrounding the face, these frills, superimposed on each other, look thick and bulky but not, because of their fine texture, heavy. Elaborations or modifications of this particular fashion did exist and will be discussed later but on the whole they looked much the same wherever they were worn. The actual composition of this arrangement of veils can best be understood by studying the sculptured tomb effigies in which they can be found both in England and in other countries where they were popular.

The technique of introducing extra threads into the selvedge to produce a frill was not new. It can be found as an edging to garments worn by some figures on the Parthenon frieze[8] but it became immensely popular towards the end of the thirteenth century as an edging to single veils before the introduction of veils composed of several layers in the middle of the fourteenth century. Nor was the idea

women of mature age wore veils but they were thin and arranged in a simple style; young women plaited their hair loosely and wound it softly round their heads; young girls let their hair hang loose and uncurled.

From the earliest times, and even among the most primitive peoples, coverings and ornaments for the heads of both men and women have carried with them mystic significances. Just as the proximity to the person of all clothing stirs complex emotions, concealed, very often, by the crudest ribaldry, so that part of the dress which is nearest the face is the most soon abandoned, on the contrary, as a technique this type of frilling continued to be used throughout the fifteenth century even in Italy, as an edging to simple single veils while from the evidence of works of art it can be seen that veils in multiple layers continued to be worn in the north of Europe.[9] The northern fashion was naturally unacceptable to Italians and apparently, though with less reason, it would seem, to French taste too.

28 *Statue of St Anne*, detail, early fourteenth century. Veils, often of very thick linen, edged with a single frill, were very popular in the late thirteenth and early fourteenth centuries.

Another national, perhaps regional fashion which greatly affected the appearance of women in the later fourteenth century was a fancy, especially in Austria and Bohemia, for long blonde hair heavily waved. This preference is probably documented in poems and romances from those areas and it appears in such a wide variety of works of art that it would be difficult to ascribe its popularity to a single sculptor or painter or even to a single school. From glamorous young Madonnas painted for altarpieces to what are manifestly forward hussies portrayed within occasional initial letters in manuscripts, this thick luscious hair is constantly to be found; it does not appear in works of art of north Germany nor in those of France, England or the Netherlands. The centre of this particular fashion was probably Bohemia.

Far more pronounced was the local character of the fashions worn by women, and to some degree by men, in Catalonia and Aragon (so far as their dress can be seen from today to be narrowed to within one of those geographical limits). Unwelcome features in the new style of the early 1340s had been ascribed by some Italians to the presence of Catalan troops in Italy; their beards especially were disapproved of, and this disapproval continued to be voiced in the early 1350s, by which time beards were being worn by at least some men of fashion in most parts of Europe.

An altarpiece dedicated to the life of St John the Baptist, which, from those parts of the clothing depicted in it that correspond to the general European fashion, cannot be later than the middle 1350s and could be earlier, shows a donor, a man on the young side of the prime of life, a lutanist and king Herod, all wearing beards; those of the donor and the musician are forked, unlikely among fastidious men in Italy until later, but just beginning to appear elsewhere.[10]

The tunic of the kneeling donor would be typical of the beginning of the 1350s in its outline. Buttoned from neck to hem in front, its skirt is short and narrow and its belt set low. There is no indication of the padded belly, beginning to be found at about this time. In at least one or two details, however, it is unusual for its moment. In the first place, the sleeves are not set into the normal armhole, but are, rather, superimposed on the body of the tunic in a curved line, edged with trimming, a device which was to become very popular in the early fifteenth century in France when it would be known as *la grande assiette*,[11] but already present in the 'pourpoint of Charles de Blois'.[12] In the second place, the sleeves themselves, tight-fitting and buttoned from just above the elbow to the wrist, have, where the buttons begin, a horizontal slit through which the arm could be passed; if this were done, the lower part of the sleeve would hang down behind. This, too, was to become immensely popular, to continue to be worn as a part of high fashion well into the sixteenth century and to remain as a feature of some official dress until more or less today. Its appearance at this early date is remarkable, and it seems probable that it was Oriental in origin and introduced into Spain from the east. Hanging tubular sleeves can be found much earlier in, for instance, sculptured reliefs in Turkey from the seventh century; the much more ephemeral mid-fourteenth-century fashion for pendant strips, which had developed as a fashionable fancy in western Europe over a couple of decades, was quite independent of the much more hierarchical tubular sleeves from the east.[13] Nevertheless, these details in the dress of the donor would have looked interesting but not eccentric at an international meeting of gentlemen of the time, for, in other respects, his dress displays the contemporary elegance. His hair would, however, by its excessive length have caused comment, and so would his forked beard.

The clothes of the donatrix, of Herodias and of Salome, are interesting too. Both Herodias and the donatrix wear transparent, tightly fitted hoods on the head, with attached capes buttoned at intervals down the front over the throat. At first glance these seem no more than versions of the veils often referred to as *gorgets*, wound round the necks of mature women in the north of Europe, but those do not appear to have been hoods. The cape part of the thin tight hood of the donatrix lies over her shoulders, while, on her head, she wears an equally transparent cap over the hood, drawn up to a point in the centre of her forehead where her hair, if it showed, would be parted; over all she wears a floral coronet of the kind beloved by Machaut and Froissart. The outline

29 *Altarpiece of St John the Baptist*, Catalan, fourteenth century.
(a) Herodias and Herod at table, with Salome and a lutanist who wears a forked beard; his tunic, in any other part of Europe, would point to a date at the end of the 1340s.

29 *Altarpiece of St John the Baptist*, Catalan, fourteenth century.

(b) Donor, wearing a distinctive tunic which also follows the general line of the late 1340s (the altarpiece is re-garded as later); the setting of the sleeves, their hori-

zontal slits and the length and arrangement of his hair are local in character.

(c) Donatrix, wearing a veil almost exactly like that of Herodias and certainly local in style.

of the cap, however, was almost certainly restricted to Spain if not to Catalonia. In other respects, the dress of the donatrix is unremarkable, but both Herodias and Salome wear what must have been local variants of the north European sleeveless dress with deep open sides. Worn by Herodias, its back is very wide and forms not a tightly fitted over-tunic but something more like a mantle; the front, on the other hand, clings closely to the torso.

The line of the donatrix's cap is exactly reflected in the far richer head-dresses of saints represented in three Catalonian statues, also of the middle of the fourteenth century, two of them St Lucy and St

Ursula, the third unidentified.[14] All three wear strings of large beads of varying shapes and sizes which are passed round the back of the head, over the ears, and are drawn up to a point in front, again where the hair would be parted in the middle. With these each wears a crown or coronet, while another line of beads appears to join the complex head-dress further back. A very similar arrangement, though less elaborate, following precisely the same line, is worn by queen Joanna of Castile, wife of Henry II of Trastamara, as donatrix in what is probably a rather later altarpiece, perhaps of the time of Henry's accession in 1368.[15] A regional fashion of the kind represented solely by the *placing* of a cap or an orna- ment could well have remained static for a long time.

As for the dress of the sculptured saints, the main part which shows is, in each case, an enveloping mantle which displays no particular local character- istic, but St Lucy's dress is more visible and quite different from what can be seen of the other two. Gathered into a line at the base of the neck, it has a wide band of what is intended to represent embroid- ery round the neck itself and another round the hem, and in these respects it was probably closer to the ethnic style of the time, in spite of a girdle of richly encrusted simulated metal ornaments that could have been found anywhere in Europe. It may corres- pond to the embroideries which Giotto included as the dress of some carefully chosen characters in his Arena chapel frescoes which has a similar ethnic look and which, as has been pointed out, disappeared from dress in sophisticated Italian painting soon after his time.[16] Here and there, however, such embroid- ery lingered, as for instance, in the form of the patch of embroidery on the sleeve of the shirt of the Christ Child in the Henry II altarpiece just discussed. This particu- lar form of ornamentation, a legacy from Byzantine colonization, remained as an important part of 'folk' dress in many parts of Europe until recent times.[17]

Spanish fashions of a later period were certainly infiltrated by details borrowed from the orientals living in their midst, and this may have been the case in the fourteenth century too. Frontally buttoned coats existed in parts of the east long before they were adopted in the west in the fourteenth century, and so did those hanging sleeves from which our later official and academic sleeves were probably derived. Short coats, reaching to about the knee, buttoned down the front and with low-set belts were certainly associated in the western mind with certain of the peoples of the east: Turks, Tartars – Scythians. A group of men who appear in a mosaic on one of the arches of the western cupola of St Mark's basilica in Venice includes two who may well be the Scythians mentioned in the inscription.[18] They wear coats of the kind described above, and can be found in similar circumstances in other works of art elsewhere of about the same date or earlier. In the St Mark's mosaic, small differences between the dress of the various people in the group are carefully recorded.

This mosaic group gives some support to the authenticity of the head-wear shown of various heads carved round the capital of the column numbered 23 beneath the Ducal Palace in Venice. Above each head is engraved the name of the race to which it belonged: *Latini, Tartari, Turchi, Ungari, Greci, Goti, Egiziani, Persani.* Like most of the other capitals this is a replica of an earlier one, in this case carved in 1731, but the heads are probably reason- ably accurate representations of those on the original fourteenth-century capital. With its colonies all round the Mediterranean as well as on the Dalmatian coast, Venice was not in any sense a province of the Italian peninsula but a very distinctive sovereign state and a formidable trading power. The subjects carved on column 23 would be a natural expression of Venetian pride.

30 *Statue of St Lucy,* fourteenth century. Her headdress with its upward point resembles that of the Donatrix (fig 29c); the saint's dress is local in style and would have looked very strange in any other part of Europe.

Starting at the angle of the Ponte della Paglia, the capitals supporting the Ducal Palace were numbered in the authoritative guide to Venice by its author, Giulio Lorenzetti, who informed the reader that the replica, no. 23, was carved by Bartolommeo Scalfarotto. There is, however, a reference to the original capital by one who had actually seen it, Cesare Vecellïo, author of one of the first books on clothing and its history, *Habiti Antichi e Moderni*, published in Venice in 1589. Vecellio based his ideas on fashions of the past on earlier works of art and although he was wildly incorrect in the dates he ascribed to them, the very fact that he regarded them as sources of information is interesting. He referred to several of the capitals beneath the Ducal Palace and pointed out that the column numbered 23 by Lorenzetti had inscriptions identifying Turks, Moors, Saracens, Arabs, Tartars and Latins. It seems likely, therefore, that Scalfarotto copied the original as faithfully as he could.

Works of art reveal divergencies within much closer areas, many of which are no longer possible to identify. Nor can most of the references to foreign dress by the chroniclers be clearly understood today, and even the chroniclers themselves were very often at a loss for words in which to describe them. Neapolitan fashions, for instance, certainly differed in some respects from those worn at the court of France, in spite of the Angevin connection, for Matteo Villani says that when the distinguished Florentine, Nicolò Acciaiuoli, who had risen to the highest office in the state of Naples, visited his native city in 1354, he was accompanied by a great company of Neapolitan nobles and knights, young men dressed in strange and varied clothing with marvellous ornamentations which were, according to Matteo, of gold and silver and precious stones.[19] If these men had worn strictly French fashions, they would have been as instantly recognized as the dress of the duke of Athens and his followers had been twelve years earlier. Matteo was acute, too, when he remarked, in writing of the king of Majorca, that he had been brought up at the French court and that he did not resemble his compatriots, the Catalonians. He showed, he says, a good intelligence – 'molto scienzato e adorno di bei costumi' – and here it is not impossible that *costumi* actually meant civilized clothing rather than good manners.[20]

The strangeness of the followers of Acciaiuoli noticed by Matteo is supported by an entry in a Neapolitan inventory which refers to *un caprense* of woollen cloth of *accollea* colour[21] and two cotes hardies. The editor proposes that the term *caprense* indicates a garment in the Cyprus style.[22] Frescoes of the fourteenth century have survived in Cyprus in some churches; the clothing depicted in them has only a remote connection with current European fashions.[23]

Among other foreign nationalities, the Hungarian presence in Italy between 1333 and 1356 was intermittent but very important, and it, too, certainly made an impression which was eventually reflected in fashionable dress. Apart from sending out fairly frequent diplomatic missions to various Italian city-states, Louis of Hungary mounted two major military invasions: the first, to Apulia in 1348, was to avenge the murder of his younger brother Andrew and lasted until 1350; the second, as a result of a dispute with Venice over possessions on the Dalmatian coast, was to besiege Treviso, which, after a painful period, fell to its attackers.

Reporting this later Hungarian invasion of 1356, Matteo Villani described the troops as wearing, in general, *farsetti* (short padded jackets) of leather, which he calls *cordovano*. These, he says, they continue to wear until they are greasy, and then they add another and then another so that they are provided with good defensive clothing. He then goes on to describe the Hungarian practice of keeping cattle purely for the value of their fat and their hides, in which, he says, they do a great trade.[24] The appearance of Hungarian leather in the English great wardrobe accounts of the early 1360s supports Villani's statement as to its importance as merchandise.

In these military excursions, Hungarian troops were certainly mixed. Matteo Villani refers only to Hungarians and Germans, but among them must almost certainly have been Cumans, who had been invited to occupy certain depopulated areas of Hungary but who had very probably retained a distinctive dress; among the mercenaries, there may well have been Bulgars and Tartars too. That Tartars were regarded as uncouth can be judged by the comments of della Flamma on modern Italian youth, who, in 1340, he said, 'dress like Spaniards, wear their hair like the French, ride madly like Germans and speak like Tartars'.[25] Only an Italian could have thought of expressing himself in those terms at that moment.

In the illuminated Hungarian chronicle, *Chronica de Gestis Hungarorum*, Cumans are clearly identifiable when the miniatures are matched to the text, and some of the other carefully depicted dress, though more difficult at the present stage to understand, could certainly, after further research, be identified too.[26] When he was writing of the Hungarian siege of Treviso, Matteo, while he approved of their king Louis, an Angevin, described his troops as bestial and lacking in discipline.[27] He did not comment on the tall pointed hats which they almost certainly introduced into Italy, but the *Chronica* shows that in Hungary there must have been subtle differences between the tall conical hats worn by peoples either living in east Europe or invading it from time to time. The *Magyar Anjou Legendarium*,[28] with its far less sophisticated paintings, makes it plain that one single type was worn by ordinary members of the Hungarian populace, and some at least of these must have been worn by the various camp followers of the Hungarian armed forces in Italy. It has to be remembered that this was exactly the moment when elaborate hats begin to be found in argenterie and great wardrobe accounts, the actual form of which is never described, though the wealth of ornament is. It is at this time, too, that tall hats with high conical crowns, rounded at the apex, begin to be found in Italian works of art; in scenes of the *Journey* or the *Adoration*, for instance, they are often worn by one or two of the Magi.[29]

92

The Hungarian dress referred to by Matteo Villani and represented in the *Chronica* was not, of course, worn by the officials who surrounded king Louis, who, as the *Chronica* also shows, dressed like fashionable west Europeans of the time. In a report by the chronicler known as the *Anonimo Romano*, author of a life of Cola di Rienzo, Hungarian emissaries preparing the way for Louis' visit to Rome in 1347 are described as wearing rich clothing of green velvet lined with miniver and German mantles – 'con cappe allemana'.[30] Cola had himself been noticed as wearing a *cappa allemana* on at least one occasion, but there is no reason to think that this had any connection with the invading Hungarians, Cumanians, Germans and Tartars. Nor were the Italians necessarily more accurate in naming the mantle 'German' than we are today in calling toast made in the oven 'French', or than, most probably, were the Neapolitans in regarding their *caprensi* as Cypriot in origin.

In the text of the Hungarian chronicle, all German peoples, whether they came from specific places in the north or in the south of Germany, are called *alamanni*; they are given no distinctive dress in the illustrations, but, like the Angevins, wear clothing in the general European high fashion. In actual miniatures painted in south Germany at the time this is more or less borne out, though it is clear that, already by the middle of the fourteenth century, Germans were wearing the long hair which was to cause the Italians so much amusement a hundred years later.[31] One or two manuscripts decorated in the vicinity of Munich portray men, mainly household retainers, wearing livery, carrying out acts of violence on the saints condemned by their masters; their hair, usually fair, hangs to their shoulder-blades, but in other respects their dress corresponds to the elegant liveries worn in France and England.[32]

This seems to bear out the evidence in the Hungarian chronicle in which other invading races or supporters of the crown wear tall pointed hats or round quilted caps (familiar in Chinese painting): a few wear tall brimless fur caps. Where the illustrator wished to emphasize the violent aspect of the Tartars, he gave them tall conical hats, from the sharp points, of each of which a single feather rose. That this can reasonably be regarded as a genuine Tartar fashion is supported by a French illuminated manuscript called *L'Histoire des Rois d'Orient*[33] in which Tartars, mentioned in the text, are depicted in accompanying miniatures as wearing the same tall hats, from the apexes of which rise feathers. These, too, began to appear from about 1350 onwards in Italian paintings where people from the Orient were intended, after, that is to say, the first Hungarian invasion of Italy.

It may not therefore be too bold to suggest that the Hungarian and Tartar hats in Italy caught the public imagination and gave rise to the fashion for wearing something like them in the west. The bronze figure, cast in 1351, which stands on the clock tower in the cathedral square in Orvieto is known locally as *Maurizio*, though no explanation for this seems to be forthcoming. He is heavily bearded and wears a tall sharply pointed hat with a turned-up brim and an extremely fashionable tunic buttoned all the way up the front with close-set buttons and sleeves buttoned at the back from wrist to shoulder. The source of his design does not seem to have been discovered, but he looks uncannily like a character from the Hungarian chronicle.

More striking still is that description in the *Grandes Chroniques* of Jean II's triumphal entry into Paris after his coronation at Rheims in 1351, the year of the casting of *Maurizio*. When he rode through the streets, the whole city naturally turned out to see him, each Parisian *metier* wearing its own livery. Exactly what these were like we are not told, but what the Lombard bankers wore we are. They, too,

31 Tartars, from *L'Histoire des Rois d'Orient*, southern France, fourteenth century. Warriors wearing Tartar hats with up-standing feathers. Tartars are mentioned in the text on the page on which this drawing appears.

were dressed uniformly and in a mi-parti of two tartary silks – *deux tartares de soie* – which seems to mean a cloth of gold woven on a silk ground.[34] On their heads the Lombard bankers wore tall pointed hats – *chapeaux haulx agus* – also of mi-parti.[35]

The fact that the dress and particularly the hats of the bankers is described so carefully in the *Grandes Chroniques* suggests that, as well as being expensive, they were unfamiliar; and this excessively rich clothing, which must have competed with that of the royal party itself, becomes even more interesting when it is remembered that only four years previously, in 1347, the Lombards had been driven out of France by Philippe VI who had confiscated their goods and attached them to himself. The moment of the return of the bankers is not recorded in the *Chroniques*, but their reappearance at Jean's coronation is a sign, surely, that the £240,000 said to have been recovered from them had not proved their ruin and that they themselves were, by their very magnificence, determined to make this clear.[36]

The dress of the Lombards, with what may have been the latest thing in pointed hats, was obviously recorded by an eyewitness; most foreign and exotic dress of the fourteenth century appears only in works of art, whose creators must be judged for the authenticity of their reporting. Much of the clothing they depict was certainly taken from indirect sources – earlier works of art or travellers' sketch books – and great discretion must be used in determining what clothing the artist had actually seen and what he had not. Before leaving the *Chronica de Gestis Hungarorum* and the possible influence of Hungarians on contemporary high fashion, it is amusing to notice that, on the very last page, Bessarabian tribesmen, identified in the text, are in the act of attacking Caroberto and his army with stones. They wear long coats of sheepskin, with the fur on the outside and long hanging tubular sleeves, virtually identical to the coats worn by pilgrims on the road to Emaus in the Holkham bible of the earlier fourteenth century[37] and to the seventh-century reliefs at Mrèn.[38] Far from belonging to the current fashion, these coats could probably be traced back via Herodotus to the Scythians, but they could also have been seen in 1975 (and they may well survive today) as the clothing of Romanian shepherds – Romania being the modern name for the area that the fourteenth century knew as Bessarabia.

In contrast to the Hungarian chronicle, the illustrations to the well-known manuscript of the *Romance of Alexander* of 1344, which, since it deals, even if not with historical accuracy, with Alexander's Indian campaign, might have been expected to attempt some representation of Oriental dress, in fact includes almost none. Apart from a single miniature of four brown-skinned, bare-legged men with cloths knotted round their heads, all the other characters, including king Porus and his Oriental court, are fair-skinned and clothed in more or less European fashions, though they do often wear exceptionally long beards. The Bodleian Library's *Romance of Alexander* was produced in the Netherlands; it is a witness to the fact that, whereas Italy was constantly

pervaded by armed bands or actual armies of Spanish, Bohemian, Hungarian and English troops during the second half of the fourteenth century, the Netherlands were not. To citizens of the Low Countries, the only familiar foreigners, apart from the French and the English, would have been the Italian merchants and the German traders of the Hanse, who would not have differed greatly in their dress from the local inhabitants. It is perhaps significant that these very Germans were referred to in the Netherlands as 'Orientals'. Fruitful as a source of information on fashionable north European dress and to be discussed later, the *Romance of Alexander* hardly speculates as to what eastern aliens may have looked like.[39]

In quite a different category, but certainly to some degree regional, is the dress portrayed in the remarkable group of statues made for the façade of St Stephen's cathedral in Vienna. These represent members of the ruling family and their close relations: the archduke Rudolf IV, founder of the cathedral, his wife, Katharine of Bohemia, daughter of Charles IV, king of Bohemia and emperor; Charles's first wife, Blanche de Valois, Katharine's mother; Rudolf's father, Albrecht II – the 'old duke' – and his wife, Joanna von Pfirt; one of Rudolf's co-rulers, his brother, Albrecht III, and his wife.

There has been a good deal of discussion as to exactly when these statues were made and by whom, but it seems likely that they were conceived, if not executed, before 1365 when Rudolf died. Probably slightly earlier are the two tomb effigies of Rudolf and his wife Katharine, which may well have been done between 1358 and 1365, before, that is to say, his death – a not unusual practice.[40] Both on his tomb and in the standing figure of him designed for the façade, Rudolf is shown wearing a surcoat over armour, the ducal crown and a long mantle. The style of the surcoat, fitted closely to the waist and slightly inflated over the chest, would, for what was necessarily a functional garment, point to a date soon after 1360. Rudolf wears a short beard and, on his tomb, hair cut to cover his ears. On the standing figure the hair is rather longer, which suggests a very slightly later date.

Charles IV, king and emperor, is shown as a young man. His clothing is almost entirely hidden by a long mantle, but his tunic, covering the knee, can just be seen, and one arm in a sleeve tightly buttoned to the elbow. He wears the imperial crown.[41] If these statues were done round about 1360, Charles would still have been alive since he died in 1378. Although portrayed as a young man, however, Charles wears the long forked beard of the middle 1360s onwards, whereas in most of his other earlier portraits he wears a short round beard.[42]

It is, however, the dress of the women that is most interesting. Rudolf's wife, Katherine of Bohemia, wears, both on her tomb and on the standing façade figure, a frilled and layered veil of the type described earlier in this chapter. It has been considerably stylized by the sculptor, but is unmistakably with its extensions covering the shoulders, the version of this head-dress particularly worn in Bohemia and Hungary.[43] Her

(a)

(b)

32 Statues originally on the façade of the Stefans-
dom, Vienna.
(a) Blanche de Valois, first wife of the emperor
Charles IV, wearing her hair dressed in cornettes in the French style. She was a sister of
Phillippe VI de Valois.
(b) Joanna von Pfirt, wearing a layered frilled veil,
typically Austrian or Bohemian in its arrangement.
(c) Detail of Joanna's mantle, showing a remarkably clear rendering of the pleats with which it
is set into its yoke.

(c)

dress seems to have been the prototype for those of the other female figures, with a low-set belt and a band of simulated metal-work ornament which runs vertically down from her low-cut neckline to her belt in front. It may have had princely connotations, but this could not at the moment be proved. In complete contrast, Charles's wife, Blanche de Valois, sister of Philippe VI of France, wears pronounced *cornettes* which hang as double-back plaits on either side of her face – a manifestly French fashion. She, too, wears a low-set belt, but has *two* bands of simulated metal ornament running down the front of her bodice, which is very well observed in that small folds in its stuff indicate the effect of the heavy bands of decoration on the material of the dress beneath.[44] In her posthumous portrait in the triforium of St Vitus's cathedral in Prague, Blanche is the only one of Charles's four wives to wear *cornettes* and the only one who was a Frenchwoman.

Like Katharine of Bohemia, Joanna von Pfirt wears a layered frilled veil with shoulder extensions, one strip of decoration down the front of her bodice and a low set belt. Like the dress of Blanche de Valois hers, too, shows a remarkable understanding on the part of the sculptor of the structure of clothing and the behaviour of stuffs, both of which are rendered with considerable realism. Because the skirts of both Joanna and Blanche are more ample than their bodices, they must have been joined to them by a seam which the belt conceals. It is the treatment of the fulness of these two skirts which makes this group of statues so particularly important to the student of dress for, without actually including the stitches (which might, in the dress itself, have been just visible), the sculptor has explained the system by which, in a line of what would nowadays be called (for obvious reasons) 'cartridge pleats' the skirt is controlled just below the line where it must have joined the upper part of the dress. Other fourteenth-century works of art which reveal this technique may exist, but if so they are difficult to find.[45]

In addition to the pleated gathering of her skirt, the mantle worn by Joanna von Pfirt, which is cut very low round the shoulders, is joined to its yoke in the same sophisticated way. It is impossible to believe that the sculptor had not seen actual examples of this fashion. Joanna's crimped and layered veil, far more naturalistically interpreted than Katherine's, was evidently worn not only under the crown which she wore by right as an archduchess but also over a jewelled forehead-band.

If the statues of Joanna and Blanche were made after 1365 it seems unlikely that it was more than a year or two later and, to judge by their dress, both could have been made five years earlier. Katharine of Bohemia's dress does not reveal much character and her layered veil has been misunderstood which is perhaps significant. From the dress of Albrecht II, the 'old' duke, Joanna's husband features typical of the current fashion are completely absent and it has been suggested that the statue was carved in the fifteenth century; it will not be discussed here.

Apart from details of tailoring, the statues of the three royal ladies are important as records of the differences between French and German fashions in the manner of dressing the hair, differences of which the sculptor was clearly aware. In looking at the stiff plaits of Blanche de Valois it is easy to appreciate Gilles Li Muisis' abhorrence of *cornettes*, although to the modern eye they add a piquancy to her pretty face and they certainly seem to have a 'chic' which is not apparent in the frilled head-dresses of Joanna von Pfirt and Katherine of Bohemia.

Austrian and Bohemian panel paintings confirm the popularity of the crimped veils which could be found in Hungary too – three or four appear in the *Cronica*, worn by the queen. In English tomb sculpture they can be examined closely and some of them turn out to be even more elaborate than can be seen from paintings and, although there is a general similarity between them, their form was by no means always the same. Here and there French and German fashions seem to have been combined when a layered veil with frilled edges is worn over tightly plaited *cornettes* lying flat on the cheeks, which means that, when seen from the front, the veils themselves are rectangular and not semi-circular in outline. This squareness was formalized by the unknown mason who carved a corbel in St Mary's church in Bury St Edmunds, a sign of the current popularity of this type of head-dress. This is portrayed with real understanding of its structure by several sculptors of tomb effigies; it can be seen that

33 The head of a young woman which forms a corbel shows the popular contemporary veil worn in the English fashion but treated by the sculptor in a formalised way.

96

the complexity lay not only in the veils themselves but also in the under-caps or other devices needed to keep them in place. This is particularly true of the Despencer–Montacute tomb in Tewkesbury and an effigy in Pembridge church in Herefordshire. These tombs are not for the most part dated, and the practice of ordering tomb sculpture before death makes them impossible to date accurately from parish registers. From details of dress it can be assumed that they, and a great many more like them, must have been executed towards the end of the period with which the present study is concerned.

Elizabeth Montacute, lady Despencer, wears a long sleeveless over-dress open at the sides to the hips, with a stiff U-shaped plastron laid over the front ornamented with seven flat button-like roundels, which may or may not have been functional. A comparison between this dress and the over-dress with open sides worn by Herodias in the altarpiece on the life of St John the Baptist, by an unknown Catalan master, already discussed, is extremely interesting, for within the current European high fashion, national differences in taste are clearly revealed. The train of lady Despencer's dress appears to have been about ten inches long from the heel at the back, but where dresses had trains, their length seems to have varied considerably. Some lie not more than an inch or two on the ground at the back, others are long, and this seems to have been possible throughout the period.

Before leaving the discussion of crimped and layered veils, it is worth noticing that although they were not, apparently, worn in France, in the Netherlands they were. In a manuscript, not done before 1350 but probably soon after, and perhaps associated with Louis de Mâle,[46] the donatrix who kneels at the foot of the Cross of the crucified Christ wears a frilled veil which, though it belongs to the same category, is not exactly like those worn in Bohemia, Austria or England. Worn over *cornettes* which jut aggressively forward on either cheek, the layers of the veil with their frilled edges pass over the head and fall down to the shoulders on each side of the face. An elegant lady who sits reading a book at the foot of folio 11v in the same manuscript wears an exactly similar arrangement which seems to have been shared by at least a part of Scandinavia, as will be seen.

Most of the English gentlemen portrayed on their tombs at this period wear chain armour, and over it, as a rule, a surcote covering a cote. In the particularly splendid tomb of Sir Peter Grandison in Hereford, the shirt of the deceased is visible in what appear to be pleats *beneath* his coat of mail. Over it his cote has a scalloped edge, each scallop being outlined with embroidery, and, worn over it, his surcote, vertically striped in blue and white, reaches to about six inches above the knee in front but to half-way down his calf at the back, so that, when he was mounted, it would spread effectively over his horse's back. This fashion, though not unusual in England, was by no means exclusively English; standing knights in the S. Silvestro chapel frescoes in Sta Croce in Florence wear virtually the same dress. In other words, English knights would not have looked particularly foreign in Florence, nor Florentine knights in England; their wives, on the other hand, would.

34 Despencer – Montacute tomb, detail. The same type of veil, worn in England in a rectangular arrangement. This head, obviously carved from life, confirms the style shown in 33.

35 Missal of ? Louis de Mâle, c. 1350. The much simpler form of the fashionable veil, worn by the donatrix on the Crucifixion page of this missal, is typical of the south Netherlandish taste of the time.

Members of the public have always, it seems, been sensitive to the dress of foreigners, and generally disapproving, and no doubt some small differences in the clothing even of those armoured knights would soon have been spotted. It was not only in Florence, for instance, that the Frenchness of the dress of the relations and friends who came to share in the happiness and lordly standing of the duke of Athens was remarked on; for Agnolo di Tura, writing in Siena, said that those visitors from France were of both sexes, and that the men of Florence and the ladies too, took to wearing their styles of dress, which the authorities, much as they disapproved, could do nothing about.[47]

In spite, however, of an occasional gothic lapse, the character of Italian dress in the third quarter of the fourteenth century remained essentially classic. Its outlines were gentler and its decoration less insistent than its northern counterparts. The *cornettes* of France may have been worn by the Parisian visitors to Walter de Brienne, but it is doubtful that they were faithfully copied in Florence; if they were, they were quickly abandoned. The softly plaited hair which enlarged the Italian feminine head of the end of the 1330s, unveiled or veiled very lightly, was dressed more closely to the head as the 1340s passed into the 1350s. The head appeared smaller and, as a result, the whole figure taller, but at no moment was hair tortured into rigid shapes, nor were the heads of matrons concealed beneath layer over layer of eclipsing veils so that their true shapes and sizes were lost. When borders of parts of garments were deliberately cut into delicate leaf shapes in Italy (as did sometimes happen), it is not simply the painters' handling of such decoration that keeps it quietly subservient to the whole dress, but the absence of the reinforcing and decorative stitching in a contrasting colour which can be found, for instance, in the Frenchified clothing of the knights of the Order of the Saint Esprit at the Angevin court at Naples.[48]

Exhaustive research into local mutations in fashionable dress would be impossible in a study so general as the present one; an analysis of the clothing, very varied and a great deal of it foreign, in the frescoes by Andrea da Firenze in the Spanish chapel in Florence would, alone, be greatly rewarding, but this is not the place to do it. The shallow 'bowler' hats which seem to have been confined to France and perhaps the Netherlands in the late 1350s and after, and the rather coquettish knotting on one side of the head of the veils of older women in the same areas, are recorded in manuscripts that can be localized.[49] Nevertheless, one or two striking deviations from the roughly agreed European fashion should still be noticed, among them the clothing of king Christopher II of Denmark and his wife and daughter, recorded in their strange tomb sculpture in the church of Sorø. The bronze effigies were probably made in Lübeck, but the royal clothing is probably authentic. The queen wears a frilled layered veil of Netherlandish pattern, but the most striking feature of both her dress and that of her little daughter is the enormous three-dimensional bezants that decorate the mantles they both wear. Christopher died in 1332, but the tomb was certainly made later. Only a little later than the date of his death, we read that a Danish wife in 1334 was bequeathed *unum kylt*, presumably a corruption of the word *kirtle*, of green colour, while references to cloth of scarlet, cloth of Ghent and silk – *serico* – are frequent in Danish inventories of the 1340s and 1350s, all of which seem familiar until one comes across a lining not of menuvarius but of *sylfaar*;[50] sealskin does not seem to have been used at all further south. The garments of the Danes, and not necessarily royal Danes, bear on the whole the same names as those worn elsewhere: a deacon leaves his sister a *gartkors* in his will; the term sometimes appears as *wardaekors* or even *wartheknors*, all of which look strange to French and English eyes at first, but which are the equivalent, of course, of the French *gardecorps*, which can appear in Middle English as *wardecorse*. In most Danish inventories, however, the most usual entries are for a *tunica* or a *capucio*.[51]

Such terms were, as we have seen, current in Italy, France and England; their appearance in documents in countries which might be thought of as far from centres of fashion is an indication of the comparatively international nature of fourteenth-century

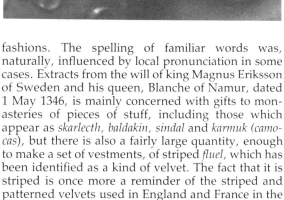

(b)

36 *Tomb of Christopher II of Denmark and of his wife and daughter.*
(a) Detail, head of the queen. This bronze tomb-sculpture demonstrates that the layered veils with crimped edges were as popular in Denmark as elsewhere.
(b) Both the Danish queen and her little daughter wear overdresses decorated with enormous bezants.

(a)

fashions. The spelling of familiar words was, naturally, influenced by local pronunciation in some cases. Extracts from the will of king Magnus Eriksson of Sweden and his queen, Blanche of Namur, dated 1 May 1346, is mainly concerned with gifts to monasteries of pieces of stuff, including those which appear as *skarlecth, baldakin, sindal* and *karmuk (camocas)*, but there is also a fairly large quantity, enough to make a set of vestments, of striped *fluel*, which has been identified as a kind of velvet. The fact that it is striped is once more a reminder of the striped and patterned velvets used in England and France in the early 1340s. There is also *laerift* – linen.[52]

The king of Sweden's will only includes stuffs which were to be used for vestments and church furnishings, but in some other surviving Swedish wills which were not royal, the usual garments that one would expect to find in the wardrobes of any European people of fashion appear quite clearly. In 1343, Larsi Borge left his sister Katherine his gown – 'veste . . . nigras mixtas'; Ulwid Bugesson in the same year left his wife *unam tunicam.* Elsewhere, seventeen ells of *panni bryggist,* which must mean cloth of Bruges, is mentioned; in 1346, Henrik, a canon, left his mother 'tabardum meum cum capucio', and to five poor scholars tunics of *burello.*[53] An interesting sumptuary regulation issued by king

Magnus restricted the gifts which a bridegroom might give to his bride: a horse, a saddle and bit, a short cape (*aema capo,* presumably long enough to cover the upper arms) and a hat. In other words, the equipment necessary for her to be able to transport herself to her new home; her actual trousseau must, as is customary, have been provided by her own family, in fact by her father.[54]

Few inventories of the court of the emperor Charles IV, king of Bohemia, have survived; those that have are concerned with his great collection of holy relics, most of them in the cathedral of St Vitus in Prague, some of whose other inventories do exist too. Textiles mentioned in the Charles documents, entries, for example, for 1354, include precious fabrics which once again bear the same names as those in general use all over Europe, and, as in the case of some of the rich materials in the collection of the king of Sweden, some of the silks themselves were probably actually made in the Orient: among them *axamita,* the *samitus* of the English and French accounts; *naseto* a version of the *nak* or *nagis* so frequently mentioned by Ibn Battuta and certainly an eastern silk – its name is derived from the Persian;[55] *tartarica* and *cendado;* and many others. Most of these silks had been made into altar-frontals or vestments; some must have been woven specially;

99

for a cope, for instance, which belonged to 'Master Stephen', was woven in gold with the letter S.[56] Many of these things, however, had been gifts from members of the royal family, and were almost certainly acquired abroad and not imported commercially. Charles's first wife, Blanche de Valois, for example, had given a dorsal curtain woven with a design of lilies and lions; Anne, two curtains woven with little eagles on a gold ground.[57] The gifts had been received, of course, at different times, but the inventories, sometimes drawn up yearly but not always at regular intervals, do not record the dates when they were actually given; it is the name of the donor which acts as a guide.

Charles's excursions outside Bohemia, even after he had settled there as king and emperor, were frequent; he visited Nuremberg fairly often, he went to Metz and repeatedly to Italy, but in no case did his personal clothing seem to have called for any special comment, so he is unlikely to have included any national deviations in his dress or to have looked foreign. Villani, as we have seen, described him several times as being dressed with extreme modesty and in dark colours – he was certainly no Cola di Rienzo or Walter de Brienne. Nor did his retainers arouse the sort of comment that was provoked by either the French who followed Walter or the Hungarians among the troops of Louis the Great, inventories of whose clothing have also disappeared. Further research would certainly uncover wills and wardrobe accounts in municipal and private libraries all over Europe, but, like those of Denmark, Sweden and Prague, they would almost certainly be found to include chiefly stuffs and garments already familiar in France, Italy and England. While Flanders cloth and Lucchese silks appear everywhere in Europe in the middle of the fourteenth century, it is clear that fashionable clothes worn by upper-class people varied only in detail as between one country and another; clothing worn by peasants (except in England, where they appear to have emulated middle-class dress in a simpler form) is another

37 *The Despot Olivier*, fourteenth century. A magnificent version of traditional local dress worn by an eastern ruler but slightly modified by the pressure of west European fashion, particularly in the sleeves and the low set of the belt.

matter, and one which could only be explored separately. There are also clear signs that in the less westernized countries such as Greece and Bulgaria, formal clothing tended to follow local tradition and to be far less susceptible to influences by centres of fashion in the west.

Evidence as to the sensitivity of local populations to the presence of foreigners is widespread. Petrarch was dismayed 'to see the lanes of Venice filled with a "filthy populace" of slaves which "infects with Scythian faces and hideous off scourings this most beautiful city"'.[58] That at least one Scythian face was recorded at about this time in Venice we have already seen, for among the heads of foreigners with which the sculptor decorated column 23 supporting the ducal palace is one who is designated a Scythian.

More dangerous still were foreigners in disguise. In England the king pardoned, but very reluctantly and only on the petitions of two cardinals, 'John de Florencia, John de Arecio, John de Urduno and Richard Felawe of Winchester', in that,

notwithstanding proclamations and inhibitions many times made that no alien or denizen on pain of forfeiture of life and limb and all else which he can forfeit bring within the realm bulls, letters or instruments prejudicial to the king or people unless he at once shew the same to the keeper of the port or the mayor and bailiffs of the town or place where he land, they brought in such while the king was without the realm engaged in war with France, and went from place to place in London clandestinely, sometimes in clothes lined with sendal as clerks, sometimes in clothes of divers colours as esquires, and sometimes in gowns [robae] and other cheap clothes as grooms and denizens, many times concealing the same bulls, letters, instruments and other things.[59]

This is not only interesting for the information it provides on the practices of foreign spies, but also as evidence of the recognition of the uniformity of the types of clothing worn by English people in their different stations in life.

XI

Fashion in Works of Art

The plan to ignore works of art and first to follow the course of high fashion through the account books of professionals and the responses of chroniclers and poets has been, of course, deliberate. In the preceding chapters, illustrations were interpolated only to explain forms and details of dress too tedious to read in words. But while modern historians are naturally made uneasy by evidence drawn from comments of chroniclers, based, sometimes, only on putative emotional jottings by their elders, so, conversely, art historians are naturally unwilling to believe that works of art, even when firmly dated, may legitimately be used as eyewitness records of the contemporary scene. Together, these two sources of information are more useful than they are apart.

It was no accident that the date chosen for the beginning of this survey was 1340, when, within two years of each other, Galvano della Flamma and Giovanni Villani were coming to very similar conclusions as to what was new in dress and when a group of works of art which manifestly set out to depict the social life of the time was being produced in various parts of Europe. If these can be seen to support the conclusions of della Flamma and Villani, it may then, on occasion, be permissible to examine one or two examples which record innovations in dress by implication rather than by open statement.

The illustrations to the Bodleian Library's *Romance of Alexander* were finished in 1344, for the artist recorded the fact.[1] The text, according to the scribe, was finished in 1338, so that the illustrations must have been painted between those years. To avoid damage to the miniature paintings, it was the usual practice for the scribe to complete his work first, leaving, as a rule, spaces into which decorated initials or actual pictures could be inserted.

It has been agreed that this copy of the Alexander story was made in Flanders, probably in Bruges. It is a lavish production which includes some whole pages of pictures as well as small illustrative scenes set into the text and a large number of lower borders, some of which have a tenuous connection with the story but most of which depict the lighter moments of life in northern Europe towards the middle of the four-

teenth century. The illustrations to the story, on the full pages or set into the text, also place almost all its episodes firmly in north Europe at the same period.

Most of the fully painted pages are divided into four compartments, each enclosing a separate scene. A good many of them are concerned with Alexander and his knights in battle or at least wearing armour; a popular theme, of course, at the beginning of the 1340s, especially with the English. It has been suggested that the book came to England fairly soon after it was done.[2]

As evidence of the fashions whose ingredients appear in the wardrobe accounts, the *Romance of Alexander* is exemplary. Alexander himself, invariably crowned, when he is not in armour almost always wears a loose over-tunic reaching to half-way down his calf in the *antiquo modo*, while his younger courtiers all wear over tunics to the knee in the *novo modo*. Some, but a minority, of masculine tunics, have buttons down the front but none below the waist – none, that is to say, *ad genua*. Most sleeves, on the other hand, are buttoned, some to the shoulder. Belts are set low and the skirts of the tunics *frounciate*. Class differences are fairly exact: peasants and children wear one single tunic with no over-tunic. When they are not in armour, almost all the knights – *chivaliers*[3] – attending on Alexander wear mi-parti, sometimes of a very exotic kind, and it seems quite certain that at this moment mi-parti was a part of high fashion and when used as a livery, as it was for the tunics of the Welsh archers, it was a sign of their attachment to a royal or noble house. The striped cloth of Ghent, which appears as one of the cheaper cloths in the great wardrobe and argenterie accounts, does not seem to be worn by the young aristocrats at Alexander's court; when they wear stripes as a section of their mi-parti they are diagonally woven, a much more exacting and therefore expensive process.

The hoods of the knights are always thrown back and the capes to which they are attached are conspicuously long, nearly reaching the elbow serrated round the edge in a simple scallop or otherwise ornamented with a modest line. In a good many instances, these upper-class men wear over-tunics with sleeves which reach the elbow only and then hang pendant to about mid-thigh – Villani's *manicottoli*, surely? Daggers hang from the centres or the sides of their belts, and so do small pockets; most tunics are open from the waist down, and, when worn by boys engaged in sport, they are tucked up into their belts at each side so that their *braccae* may show in front.

Several scenes of mourning, surrounding the death of Alexander, are depicted in the manuscript from folio 190 onwards. In every one the male mourners (there are no women) wear short mantles in two or three distinctive patterns, similar to those often to be found on the sides of English tombs of the period, worn by weepers.[4] One type is open down the right-hand side – a shortened version of much traditional official dress – one is tabard-shaped; all have hoods pulled down over the eyes. Although household servants – *valetti* – such as cooks appear in domestic circumstances along some of the lower borders, there are few peasants of a really tough type. There are huntsmen wearing boots buttoned up the front, and at least one herald, but, as might have been expected from the great wardrobe accounts, he is not distinctive in his dress.

The clothing of the men in these illuminations is consistent and limited in its variety, and this is true of the women's dress too. Almost all the women are young, and some, like their male counterparts, are adolescent. They almost all wear their hair dressed close to the head in an early version of the *cornettes*, disapproved of so greatly at a later stage. Over-dresses fit closely to about the waist, and then flare out a little; some are buttoned to the waist. Like the men they sometimes have pendant sleeves from the elbow, and many dresses have two little slits, cut vertically, one at each side, so that a pocket hanging from a belt worn round the under-tunic beneath can be reached. All the women wear dresses which terminate in a long straight line from shoulder to shoulder at the top, but the most interesting feature of their dress is the fact that quite a lot of it is patterned. The patterned stuffs have small, regular, all-over designs, recalling the embroidery on the *ghitas* of queen Philippa and her two daughters, entered in the great wardrobe account of 1342. Some of the girls in the *Romance* wear sleeveless over-tunics, others over-tunics which are not only sleeveless but open at the sides to the waist; and there the repertoire of feminine dress ends.

The *Romance of Alexander* is famous for its *bas-de-page* scenes of sports and pastimes, but these are not relevant here. There are several scenes showing young women active in the sports field, which, from the point of view of fashionable dress, provide an immediate sequel to the *Taymouth Hours* and the *Decretals of Gregory* already discussed. The *Romance* also furnishes considerable information on the wearing of clothes: some girls pin up their over-skirts all round to give themselves greater freedom of movement, others bundle theirs elegantly up over one arm. Apart from pilgrims and blind beggars, no one of either sex wears a hat.

The decorations on the pages of text in the *Romance of Alexander* appear to have been painted in a system-atic progression, starting from folio 1, because to-wards the end a very slight advance in the fashion is introduced – the cutting of the hems of masculine tunics into a simple line of scallops – whereas in the earlier part only the edges of their shoulder-capes were cut in this way.

The almost equally famous East Anglian manuscript, the *Luttrell Psalter*, was also, from internal evidence, illuminated round about 1340. Sir Geoffrey Luttrell, who commissioned it, died in 1345; his wife, who appears in at least one of the miniatures, in 1340; and there are other factors which support this date.[5] From the point of view of painterly style, the *Luttrell Psalter* is very different indeed from the *Romance of Alexander*; from the point of view of the information it provides on contemporary fashions, it is remarkably similar. Without entering into an inquiry as to how many artists may have been involved in painting its miniatures, two emerge very clearly, and it is interesting to observe that each had his preferred version of the current feminine manner of dressing the hair. He who may, as a temporary convenience, be named artist A, was responsible for the head of a lady enclosed in the initial D on folio 68, and, among others, for the Nativity scene on folio 86v. The lady within the letter D wears a veil set far back to show her centre parting, some of her hair on either side of it and what appears to be a jewelled metal band round her head covering the hair line. At each side her hair is dressed out with the aid of what can only have been fairly powerful and well-contrived springs, attached, perhaps, to the jewelled band. The young midwife in the Nativity scene wears an identical arrangement, but with no veil, so that she is intended, it seems, to be unmarried.[6] Several other women drawn by this hand wear precisely the same hair dressing.

Artist B, who created a quite distinct (and to varying degrees grotesque) facial type, painted all his upper-class women, including members of the Luttrell family, wearing a hair arrangement set very close to the head, which is a rather more complex version of the hairdressing used for women throughout the *Romance of Alexander*. It consists of a tiny fringe of hair which appears on each side of the face a little below the level of the ear, and, over it, either tight plaits, which were embrionic *cornettes*, or a little bunch of equally tight curls. The fringes of hair may, in fact, have been terminations of the plaits, which were then wound back over them, or uncurled ends of hair attached to the curls. This hairdressing is worn by four queens who ride in a covered coach on folio 33, and can be seen very clearly as worn by a female grotesque on folio 192v. The fact that this manner of dressing the hair is almost the only one to be found in the *Romance of Alexander* may suggest that it was a Netherlandish fashion worn in England by queen Philippa and adopted, perhaps, by members of the aristocracy and the leading courtiers.

In other respects, too, the two manuscripts agree as to the current fashion. There are pendant sleeves, but by no means everybody wears them; torsoes are tightly covered, belts set low and the skirts of male over-tunics are frounced and usually open in front below the belt. Most men of the medium class do not wear tunics buttoned down the front, but a few do – in no case do the buttons extend below the belt. A very few women wear dresses which are buttoned down the upper part.

The queens in the coach and the Luttrell ladies all wear over-tunics with sides open to the waist, but other ladies wear over-tunics with elbow-length sleeves and moderately long hanging pieces a good deal shorter than those worn by the men who do wear them.

There are virtually no serrated edges in the *Luttrell Psalter* (were the English behind the fashion in this respect?), nor, of course, were they mentioned in the great wardrobe accounts of the time, but this was to be expected because such information would not be relevant. There is, however, no shortage of men of the upper class wearing fashionable dress, one of the most sympathetic of whom is an extremely elegant gentleman, in, one would suppose, his early thirties, who reaches down for his tasselled purse for find coins to give to a crippled child. The skirt of his over-tunic is pulled aside to show a refined leg in well-fitted hose, and one must presume that he wears, therefore, a short pourpoint or aketon beneath his knee-length tunic and not an under-tunic, a glimpse of what was to be developed as a later fashion. Narrow pendant sleeves hang from the elbow, and the liripipe of his hood can be seen to reach almost to the level of his low set waist. No buttons show, so presumably this tunic had a neck opening wide enough to allow it, with difficulty, to be pulled off over the head. It should be compared with the tunic, simpler but not altogether dissimilar in cut, on folio 90.

A detailed comparison between the *Romance* and the *Psalter* discovers examples in both of them of a masculine tunic divided not vertically into two colours, as was more usual in mi-parti, but horizontally, at the line of the waist, a device frequently illustrated in the *Romance* but exceptionally in the *Psalter*, where, on folio 198, is a young man wearing a tunic with a tightly fitted torso and sleeves of pale stone colour but a pale violet skirt. Next to him a man struggles out of his over-tunic to show what was presumably the normal knee-length tunic beneath. This confirms the entries in the great wardrobe and argenterie accounts which list the garments that at this period composed the *roba*.

The fascinating range of characters and their activities in the *Luttrell Psalter* should be invaluable to the social historian, but here it is important to notice that the clothing they wear is very limited in its range. The difference between the youthful members of the upper classes who wear simple but well-cut clothing suitable for the games and sports in which they are involved and the equally simple dress of the peasants toiling in the fields is not great. On the whole, the peasants wear no hoods, but some carry them tucked into their belts at the back, and the liripipes of these hoods, though lengthened a little, are never long. This comparative uniformity again reflects the great wardrobe accounts, which, though they do not record any uniformity of cut, certainly show a strict uniformity of colour at any one moment in time. Where the women are concerned, the chief class differences

lie not in the style of their dress, which again is almost identical, but in the fact that all the working women have their heads muffled up in thick white cloths and wear aprons.

The chief artist of the *Luttrell Psalter*, artist B, certainly minimizes such class differences as there might have been in the actual cut of the clothing and the fact that some of it must have been tailored to fit while the rest must have been 'mass produced'. The sleeves of his peasants are far too tight to be functional, although some have turned them up at the wrist; their tunics, too, are tighter above the waist than would have been likely, but all this gives an amusing and probably deliberate homogeneity to the illustrations and, at the same time, provides a laughable piquancy in the contrast between the coarsely rough faces of the workers and the well-tailored simplicity of their dress. The countenances of the upper-class characters are not flattered either: most of them wear an expression of slightly anxious boredom which may have been no more than a careful suggestion of their rather advanced age.[7] Among the other people in the *Psalter* are several men belonging to an intermediate class – pilgrims, farmers – many of whom wear a garment that would not, perhaps, be too bold to identify as a *housse*.[8]

Most of the fourteenth-century frescoes that decorate the walls of the Papal Palace at Avignon are in a sadly damaged state, and not all of them are precisely dated. Among those which have survived is a set of hunting scenes in the *Tour de la Garderobe*, begun early in 1343 and finished in May 1344[9] for pope Clement VI and probably by a group of French painters who were working for him in the palace at the time. In the tower the *Chambre du Cerf* is painted with scenes of luxuriant vegetation, in one of which stand, in the foreground, two young men, one with a hawk on his gloved wrist; behind them are their two hounds. The dress of these two corresponds exactly to the fashion recorded in the *Romance* and the *Psalter*, though the paintings themselves have, of course, nothing common. From closely fitted torsoes their knee-length skirts are gently eased into a line covered by their low belts. From the mouths of their elbow-length sleeves hang narrow pendants, long enough to look very up-to-date for the period. One young man has removed his hood and slung it over his shoulder, the other wears his thrown back, his head covered by a semi-transparent white linen coif.

While both these men would have been totally unremarkable if, dressed as they are, they had been transported into the pages of the *Romance of Alexander*, it is the *Luttrell Psalter* which confirms the fact that thin linen coifs, a feature of high fashion in the later thirteenth century, had, by the middle of the fourteenth, moved out of the general masculine fashion to remain in a few special areas – one was the hunting field, another the law.[10] Seated on a horse and seen from the back on folio 159 of the *Psalter*, a young man wearing an exactly similar coif feeds a hawk perched on his gloved right hand. His tunic is cut in the style now familiar as belonging to the beginning of the 1340s, the moment to which the young hawker at Avignon belongs.[11]

Documented as having been executed between 1337 and 1339, the *Allegories of Good and Bad Government* in the Palazzo Communale in Siena should present a picture of Tuscan dress before it was submitted to the corruption of the example of the duke of Athens in 1342, and so, perhaps, it does. Most memorable are two or three separate groups of people in the fresco on the wall representing Good Government. The first group is composed of citizens, mature and well-placed men, wearing the long gowns appropriate to government officials, lawyers, academics and perhaps merchants; among them stands a man who is conspicuous because he wears a comparatively short tunic, though not nearly so short as the fashion of 1340 would demand; he is, perhaps, a knight in civilian dress. The gentlemen of the long gowns wear coifs under their hoods which are rolled up in the manner already widespread in Italy and in the process of becoming so in the north too. These are the men of the type Villani referred to as wearing the ancient and honourable dress of classical Rome, descended from the toga.

Another group, very different, also enjoys the benefits of good government; it is a band of young girls who dance in happy security in the city streets. Here are certainly no *cornettes*, no skin-tight dresses, though one girl does wear a mi-parti over-dress from whose elbow-length tight sleeves modestly extended hanging pieces represent the fashion of the end of the 1330s; the waist-line of her dress is set low enough to pass for 1340 and to have been included in the dress of the people of medium class in the *Luttrell Psalter*. Another girl wears the short sleeves of her over-dress cut into fluttering ribbons and a third a sleeve seamed up the back of her arm to her shoulder with large decorative stitches – these being local eccentricities.

It is, however, just outside the city that the normal adult fashions are to be found, worn by a little group which rides into the countryside on a hawking expedition, accompanied by a *valetto* on foot and two hounds. Both the *valetto*, who is hatless and wears a checkered tunic probably woven from the natural undyed wool of both black and white sheep,[12] and his master on horseback, who wears mi-parti, have low-set belts and tunics whose upper parts fit closely, but there are no hanging sleeves. The horseman from whose gloved hand flutters a hawk, wears a high-standing collar, a remnant of a somewhat earlier fashion when such collars had been twice as high, some of them retained in the official dress of the mature citizens. On the huntsman's head is a white coif, and over that a rolled hood. Before him rides a lady wearing a functional hat to protect her complexion from the sun and a style of hairdressing which does not conflict with the much tighter plaits of the north of Europe, but which is looser, softer and not only a slightly earlier but also an Italian version of the northern fashion, which was never to develop further in Italy. Her sleeveless over-tunic, from the armholes of which the dark sleeves of her under-tunic emerge, would be quite unremarkable in the north, where only the high collar of the huntsman would have looked conspicuous.

The dress in these elaborate allegorical paintings was carefully chosen. Of the enthroned figures who symbolize the virtues of good government – Justice, Prudence, Peace – only Peace wears a contemporary dress, in fact a summery undress whose small armholes and tight sleeves reflect the latest fashion. A glamorous figure in dishabille, she relaxes against a fresh linen cushion whose decorative embroidery would have taken many peaceful days at home to work, propped up against a cuirass of armour, useless in a country at peace. The other virtues wear earlier fashions which even to call conservative would probably be inadequate.

These frescoes reflect that period of transition between the softer, bulkier clothing so sympathetically drawn in the *Triumph of Death* frescoes in Pisa[13] and the frenchified styles that were to come. The dresses of the dancing girls vary between the two; the dress of the hunting party has already taken on a new sharpness.

There are, of course, other paintings which are dated sufficiently closely to 1340 to be consulted for the fashionable dress of the time, but Pietro Lorenzetti's triptych of 1342, all three of its panels devoted to the account of the *Birth of the Virgin*,[14] is not one. Here Pietro had chosen (or designed) clothing to set the scene back in time – not unacceptably far back, but to a point which would have prevented it from looking crudely modern. The devices he used to achieve this effect are fascinating but irrelevant here; his triptych has only been mentioned as a caution against the danger of accepting the dress in all dated paintings as overt evidence of the contemporary fashion; the expert eye may read the picture's date through the disguise, however.

Today the young people in the *Romance of Alexander*, the *Luttrell Psalter*, the Avignon and Siena frescoes look lively but in no way indecent. By the end of the decade, however, it becomes possible to see what it was that the chroniclers had feared when they condemned the current fashions. Just as the term *frounciata* had practically disappeared from the great wardrobe accounts, in which it had played so important a part at the beginning of the decade, so the gently gathered skirts worn by men in the early 1340s were replaced, in the early 1350s, by skirts which were straight, tight and, in consequence, looked shorter than they really were when the wearer moved.

The new masculine fashion of the beginning of the fifth decade of the century is perfectly illustrated in a pair of rather obscure frescoes in the Abbazia di Vezzolano painted by an unknown Franco-Italian artist, very probably between 1351 and 1354.[15] The frescoes, on the north side of the cloister, are indisputably by the same hand: one is an *Adoration of the Magi*, the other the *Encounter between the Three Living and the Three Dead*. The donor in the foreground on the right of the *Adoration* wears dark blue and white mi-parti, an over-tunic which has a hood so small that it cannot lie flat across his shoulders at the back. His belt is set very low and the straight tight skirt of his tunic ends well above the knee, so that were he not kneeling but standing, it would be considerably shorter than any in the *Romance* or the *Psalter*, all of which were frounced; nor does the donor's tunic appear to be open from the waist down in front, as those were. Although it is in no way decorated, his tunic is manifestly very stylish in cut. The tunics of the two younger Magi are both decorative and stylish. As was customary, the third Magus is represented as a very old man; here he wears a long white hooded gown lined with trimmed miniver.

It was usual, in medieval paintings, for each of the Magi to be differentiated in age – one very young, one in the prime of life and one old – and this happens here. The youngest, who kneels on the left, is very young indeed, a beardless adolescent; the second, near the centre, is very young, too, but he wears a minute forked beard, golden like his beautifully waved and rather long hair. Both wear up-to-date though not identical dress. It is clear that by this time the origins of what Villani had called *manicottoli* – pendant sleeves – had been completely forgotten, for the long narrow hanging strips of miniver, trimmed until hardly a trace of grey fur remains, worn by these young men bear no relation to the extended mouths of the elbow-length sleeves of the middle 1330s, from which their further extended descendants of the 1340s ultimately derived. The straight strips worn by the Magi, their long edges consistently parallel, emerge not from the sleeve itself but from horizontal bands, also of trimmed miniver, placed round it, half-way up the upper arm. It is just possible that these were the *poignets* of fur which occur in the argenterie accounts of exactly this date, which seem difficult to discover in works of art in the position in which, from their name, they should logically appear.

The Magus nearest the centre wears red and white mi-parti, very close-fitting and with a belt set extremely low and dipping across the front of his body. His thrown back hood, like that of his companion, is obviously very small. On the deep and also close-fitting cape to his hood he wears an ornamentation which is either a band of gold embroidery or a large chain composed of circular plates of gold. Unlike the youngest Magus, who is bare-headed, he wears a very striking hat, its brim pointed, lined with carefully trimmed miniver and held in place by a jewel; is this what the ermine-lined hats made by Kathelot the royal milliner had looked like?

The second fresco of this pair illustrates the allegorical scene, already long established as a subject for works of art, of three carefree huntsmen suddenly confronted by three cadavers, risen from the tomb. In this instance the legend is actually connected with the monastery itself.[16] The clothing of the three living riders completes the information provided by the *Adoration of the Magi*, for one horseman is seen from the back and reveals a hood with a cord-like liripipe which has reached the ultimate in thinness and could be attenuated no further. The drawing of this man is important, too, for the behaviour of the skirt of his tunic, which is so tight that, because he is seated in the saddle with his legs apart, is necessarily so stretched that it is pulled up to his thighs in folds. A second horseman wears a very similar hat to that of the Magus, but rather less grand, and he wears blue and white mi-parti with pink hose so that his dress is

virtually a replica of the donor's, though there is no facial resemblance.

There is a distinct difference in detail between the dress of the Magi, who wear 'full dress', and the much simpler hunting dress with no pendant sleeves worn by the horsemen, but there is no difference at all from the point of view of the current fashion. Indeed, both frescoes are veritable fashion-plates for the early years of the 1350s, in which not only are the sleeves of the Magi buttoned to the elbow with buttons set more closely than they would have been a decade earlier, but the brocaded sleeves of the angel who presents the donor to the Christ Child and his Mother are exactly similar. So stylish is this angel that it is almost impossible not to imagine a tight abbreviated skirt and elegant long hose beneath the pink drapery which covers his lower limbs.

Extracted from the pages of the *Romance of Alexander* and set into this scene of the *Adoration of the Magi*, any of the courtiers of the early 1340s would have looked strikingly old-fashioned in his dress. Just as the outlines of the stylish clothing of 1340 had a refinement which made the fashions of the middle 1330s appear clumsy and thick, so, in its turn, by the beginning of the 1350s, the dress of a decade earlier seems to have been composed of too much stuff and too many folds.

What those who commented on the fashions after the Black Death complained of, however, was too much ornamentation, too many jewels, and this is more difficult to discover in contemporary paintings, though their frames or the abstract patterns that surrounded them had become richer. But, though difficult, it is not impossible to discover a change in the decorations of the later dress. As has already been noticed, the knights of the Order of the Saint Esprit au Droit Désir did not, according to the statutes themselves as well as the paintings that illustrate them, as did the knights of the Orders of the Garter and the Étoile, wear a distinctive livery, though they did, on specific occasions, all wear white. The statutes state clearly that, apart from one or two similar regulations about colour and the placing and types of badges that could be worn, the knights could dress as they thought best.

In the full-page illumination to the copy of these statutes that survives from the middle of the fourteenth century, Louis of Taranto and Joanna of Naples kneel before a mandorla enclosing a representation of the Trinity. Louis in white wears the badge of the Order under his right arm; in other respects his dress is normal for the period, though exceedingly handsome. Not only are his pendant sleeves very long and narrow, but they are also deeply cut into an intricate leaf pattern down both of their long edges. The hem of his tunic is similarly cut, and so is the edge of the cape to his hood, which has a far longer liripipe than any that could have been found in the early 1340s. Moreover, above both these fancifully serrated edges is a wide band of blue and embroidery. Not in any respect ceremonial though very grand, Louis' dress would have looked outrageously theatrical a decade earlier.

Behind Louis kneels an attendant knight, also wearing the badge of the Order. The cape to which

38 Wall-paintings, 1352–1354
Top *Adoration of the Magi*, detail. The two younger Magi wear highly fashionable dress of the moment when the fresco was painted. Hats had only just come into fashion at the beginning of the 1350s.
Bottom *The Encounter between the Three Living and the Three Dead*, detail. The horsemen exhibit the serpentine line of the spine, induced by the shape of the tunics of the early 1350s and noticed by artists of the time. See also fig 8, above.

his hood is attached is no longer a simple semi-circle, but, cut away on the shoulders, it plunges to a long point in front and at the back; its edges are deeply cut into a leaf pattern. A modified version of this cape, edged not with a single but with a double row of dags, is worn by a knight who mourns at the death-bed of the emperor Henry II in a predella panel to Orcagna's altarpiece of *Christ in Glory*, dated 1358.[17] The skirt of the knight's tunic is very short and tight, and, like his cape, edged with a double line of dags at the hem. He stands in profile, and it is here that it is possible to see the very curious outline produced by the fashions of the middle 1350s, which must have been partly induced by the extremely low-set belt, lowered further across the front, and partly by what must in some if not all instances have been a thin layer of padding which smoothed out the natural formation of the masculine torso. Already hinted at in the fresco of the *Adoration of the Magi*, in an extreme form it appears repeatedly in the astonishing illuminations to a *Bible historiale* in French, to which the date 1355 is attached.[18] It would be easier to discount this as an eccentric oddity but for a *Roman de la Rose*, undated but manifestly of the same period, though not by the same hand. The suggestion that some sort of padding was worn by this time under the tunic might seem quite unwarranted, except that, at this date in the world of masculine fashion, under-tunics had evidently for the most part been replaced by padded doublets.

That this was indeed the case is supported by an *Ordonnance* issued in Paris in September 1358 in the form of *Lettres qui permettent aux Cousturiers de faire et de vendres des Doublez*. The letters, headed by the usual preamble: 'Charles, aisné Filz du Roy de France', continue by saying that, in consideration of the fact that most people make use of and dress themselves in doublets – 'plus de genz usent & se vestent de Doublez' – which *Cousturiers* knew quite as well as the *Doubletiers* how to make, 'because they understand sewing and cutting better than the doublet makers, and also because they employ more workers than the doublet makers and with more reason . . .'. In fact there had evidently been trouble, and the doublet makers had tried to declare a closed shop to prevent the couturiers from making doublets; but, the *Ordonnance* continues, 'now that doublets are more generally worn [plus en cours que autres vestemens] – and because they are more suitable to the present changed time . . .' and so the *Ordonnance*, in the name of Monsieur le Regent in Council, was issued.[19]

Like aketons and pourpoints, doublets were, as their name implies, made of two layers of stuff interlined with a padding, at this period evenly distributed, of cotton-wool or of layers of discarded cotton or thin wool stuff. Their effect was to produce a perfectly smooth surface, but they necessarily ended at the hips or a little below in order that the long hose could not only be attached to them by means of laces threaded through eyelet-holes, but could also be released when nature called. The termination of the doublet coincided therefore with the line of the very low-set belt, and this gave the effect of a belly that bulged slightly over it – the effect, in fact, that is represented in the *Bible historiale* and the Bodleian *Roman de la Rose*.

The same effect can be found elsewhere, for the fashion, though temporary, of course, was widespread. It is present in the Orcagna painting which has been discussed, but nowhere does it appear more strangely than in an altarpiece of 1358 by Lorenzo Veneziano, where not only is the little body of the Christ Child clothed in a tunic of the latest style, fastened by small buttons set close together above a belt placed very low, but an angel playing the organ in the foreground exhibits exactly the same smoothed surface above a belt which drops in a recondite line in front.[20]

Before leaving this strangely mannered period of the middle of the 1350s, it is worth noticing that, in the *Roman de la Rose*, other features point to this date. The lover, for instance, as he walks into the fields, wears a cape to his small hood cut into long and narrow leaf shapes that give a picturesque raggedness to his otherwise well-padded appearance, and, in the same manuscript, the lady on folio 150v wears a positively mannerist version of the open-sided overdress of the early 1340s, now developed to produce the appearance of a very narrow waist at the same time sharp and flattering.

Exactly how the curious fashion of the 1350s contrived to change into the rather more comprehensible style that succeeded it, and that can be seen to have emerged in a characteristic completeness by 1364, is difficult to determine; the transformation must, as usual, have been gradual and stealthy, and examples of its intermediate stages are hard to isolate. By 1364, however, the change had been achieved. The smoothness remained but with a totally new emphasis.

By a happy accident, an actual garment has survived which explains exactly what had taken place: the famous pourpoint of Charles de Blois, who died in 1364.[21] In what is in effect a padded doublet, its outer layer of splendid silk patterned with gold, the padding has been so disposed that it enlarges not the belly but the chest, and, by the closeness of its fit to below the hips, it must have maintained a corset-like grip round the body below the waist. Its sleeves are set on to the body part in the manner known as the *grande assiette*. It has been suggested that, in this case, the padding round the chest was a functional safety device to ward off attacks, but the new composition was, to judge from works of art, so widespread that this cannot have been the sole reason for its existence.

When they were actually worn, the effect of the garments made in the restrictive style of the de Blois pourpoint is well explained by the paintings which illustrate a manuscript account of the proceedings at the coronation of Charles V in 1364.[22] In these the king is shown in the sequence of gowns traditional for the monarch to wear on the occasion of his coronation, but the courtiers who attend him are dressed in the current and clearly latest fashion: the fashion of the pourpoint of Charles de Blois. Still further abbreviated than the skirts of the early 1350s, their tunics hug their hips, their belts no longer sag in front, their chests are very obviously padded.

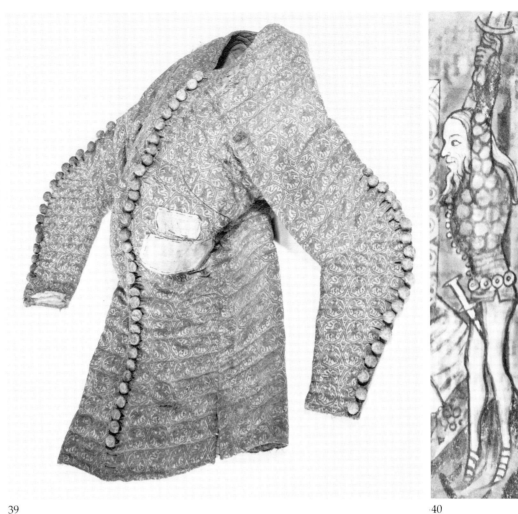

39 A new photograph which shows the true form of the pourpoint of Charles de Blois, who died in 1364. Because he had been regarded with veneration the pourpoint was preserved and it is likely, therefore, to have been worn by him at about the time of his death.

40 Weltchronik, Golden Legend detail, fol. 21ᵛ. Here the *grande assiette* construction, used in making the pourpoint of Charles de Blois, has been recorded by a contemporary artist.

39   40

A slightly later version of this style can be found in a variation of the *Golden Legend*, a German manuscript whose scribe finished his work in 1363,[23] and there are besides a considerable number of examples of this puffing out of the masculine chest recorded in works of art, many of them dated. Among them is a predella panel of Salome's dance in an altarpiece of 1364 by Orcagna,[24] in which the Italian version of it is worn by a musician and is, as would be expected, less extreme and less restricting than its French and German counterparts. It was, perhaps, the early stages of this particular fashion which inspired the current author of the *Eulogium* to attempt to describe a fashion worn in 1362 which, when seen from the back, could cause men to look like women. The passage is not clear enough to produce a mental image of the effect he was trying to record, but he may have been writing of the intermediate stage between the fashions of the middle 1350s and those of the middle 1360s.[25]

Looking back on the path followed by the changes in fashion between 1340 and 1365, it is interesting, as well as surprising perhaps, to discover that it is in the dress of men that the systematic progression took place, and it certainly seems true that, except for developments of comparatively small details, such as the lengthened and changed character of their pendant sleeves (which coincided with those of the men), women's dress continued on the whole not only to have consisted of the same three types of over-tunic that could be found in the early 1340s, but also that those three types had changed their design very little. There certainly are variations to be found in, for instance, the position of the waistline but this seems to have fluctuated throughout the period rather than to have followed a logical progression.

In its relative stability, the dress of women in this part of the fourteenth century reflected or, rather, forestalled the dress of women to be found in peasant communities all over Europe at a later date. In these village populations, because the men travelled, at least to some extent, into other areas, their local fashions changed rather more rapidly than those of the women who stayed at home and who maintained in their dress a kind of conservatism that underwent only very slow and minor mutations with the passing of time. Where the dress of women was concerned, therefore, the differences were geographical rather than chronological, and this, too, applied to women in the fourteenth century. As for the *corsettum*, the *ghita* and the *goune*, works of art are silent.

XII

Postscript

In considering the course of fashion over this specimen period of twenty-five years, at least one ingredient has necessarily been omitted: the check imposed on all forward movement by the status quo of tradition and taboo. Too familiar to be apparent to those who considered each novelty as it arrived, a thread of tradition nevertheless remained as a continuing link between the old and the new.

Man's was a bifurcated form, even at the most extreme moment of abbreviation and, whatever anybody may have declared, only from the middle of the thigh down. It was to be nearly 150 years before a man could appear in public revealing, through his covering of clothing, the form of his genitals or even of his buttocks. Hence, perhaps, the simulated nudity of some among court fools, single and unique personages in the hierarchy, to whom the normal rules of society need not apply. Women existed in a form which gave no hint of bifurcation at all; their dress remained a single unit below the waist, and hence, perhaps, the poets' lingering descriptions of shapely hips and thighs imagined or actually glimpsed in movement beneath the unit of their covering. No arm of either sex was ever left bare.

The heads of virgins were encircled by that single band which, though temporarily disguised in the fourteenth century as a garland of real or jewelled flowers, or as a bridal crown, had been worn by virtue of virginity in ancient Greece and far earlier. Matrons, those, that is to say, who were married, still necessarily covered their hair, even though, by 1340, the concealing veil was sometimes, though not always, not only transparent but often inadequately arranged as a covering. The later ritualistic nature of the masculine hat (if such was ever its true function)[1] had hardly yet emerged. The heads of both men and women in the north of Europe were, for most of the period, protected when out of doors, by hoods of more or less uniform design, until, with the arrival in European fashion of elaborate hats, also common to both sexes, the hoods of men shrank to a size so small that finally they were unable to pull them on to their heads and contented themselves, instead of wearing them as hoods, with rolling them up and clapping

them on to the tops of their heads as though they had themselves, indeed, become hats.

If such traditional scraps continued to survive within the unceasing stream of fashion, there existed in a far purer form, of course, those almost unchanging uniforms imposed on, or cherished by, members of some institutions – the Church and the university, for instance. Although, over long periods of time, the original functions of the separate parts of these static clothes were often so completely forgotten that, in their making, they became distorted as new tailors failed to understand their meaning, they retained their greatly respected positions as seemingly true reminders, if not survivals, of the 'good old days', and a rebuke to those who adopted ever newer ways of departing from them.

These dignified gowns had no influence on the current fashion, but because in their separate and distinctive forms they were worn by certain officials about the court, as, for instance, the *pallium* (*pallio*) of the royal treasurer of France, the *chlamys* of the English judge, the *toga* of the Venetian senator, some at least of them would be present in any royal ceremonial gathering, serving as a weighty reminder of the ephemerality of the fashion of the moment. At one equally fleeting moment in the past, however, each had, in its turn, been an expression of an equally ephemeral fashion. Moreover, as the years passed, some items of the current fashion itself were naturally in the process of becoming stabilized and were moving into the category of official dress. Even during the years covered by this brief study, it begins to be noticeable, especially in works of art, that once greatly fancied striped and checked fabrics, worn in the early 1340s in velvet by the royal princes of France, had been abandoned by fashion in the middle of the 1360s to remain fixed as the stuffs of household liveries and, later still, as the prerogative of barristers.[2] The white linen coifs, still ordered by the dozen by the captive king of France for the use of his young son, were already becoming associated with the law: the 'Order of the Coif' was already in sight.[3]

Such developments are clear, and, after further study of adjacent decades both before and after the span of this study, more examples of this congealing of certain details or of actual compositions could certainly be observed.

The springs and founts of changes of fashion would then, as now, be more difficult to discover. Some may well have been devised, in the first place, by some jaunty and popular man-about-court, not necessarily distinguished by birth but necessarily admitted to a fairly high position in the hierarchy; but so haphazard a method of producing innovations cannot have accounted for the relentless and regular movement of the stream. As for the interpreting of new ideas into practical terms, that, too can be no more than a matter of speculation. Was one of the members of the French court provided with a tailor who was particularly creative? Did members of the Italian Bardi or Peruzzi companies promote good Italian design in the north of Europe, suitably adapted to national taste, by introducing actual patterns of clothing with their other merchandise, patterns meant for the eyes of royal tailors alone and at a price? Where England was concerned, it seems clear that, if creative design existed here, it must have emanated from the privy wardrobe at the Tower rather than from the great wardrobe, for it was there that the painters and draughtsmen worked; in the great wardrobe, royal tailor followed royal tailor, and it is unlikely that each in turn would have proved to be a talented designer as well as a good craftsman and organizer, and the same, of course, must have applied in France.

The most substantial inventories and accounts to survive are naturally those of the royal wardrobes, though these, too, have mainly disappeared, except in England, France and, to some extent, Naples. The danger of relying solely on these as evidence of the current fashion is that, taken alone, they produce too simple a composite picture. Intermittent royal meetings in Westminster Hall or St Ouen were, no doubt, usually confined to those who had been issued with the season's liveries and were wearing them. Away from the royal courts, however, the nobles and higher clergy maintained their own households and regularly distributed their own liveries. On those occasions, therefore, when official gatherings included mixed assemblies, such as the farewell party given in honour of the departing king of France when minstrels from the households of the king, the prince of Wales and of the duke Lancaster all performed, an interesting counterpoint of colour, pattern and composition would have been produced. This intermingling of liveried groups must have been repeated further down the social scale, as well, of course, as on the battlefield, to which major landowners were required to send contingents of archers equipped by them and wearing their household liveries.

The Black Prince's *Register* gives several glimpses into this practice, but there are a considerable number of fragments of accounts and registers belonging to less exalted people which still survive. It would be quite wrong, therefore, to see the whole community of officials and aristocracy remaining for whole seasons in one approved uniform dress. When the delivery of the countess of Fife's officially bestowed garments was seriously in arrears, this must have been more wounding to her pride than to her wardrobe; there is no reason to believe that she was unable to provide herself with appropriate clothing.

111

Notes and References

I *1340: A New Fashion*

1. Makkai, L., '*Commerce et consommation . . .*', p. 650, relates that in the thirteenth century both the Flemish and the Italian merchants were referred to in Hungary as 'Latini' and that, as well as cloth from Ghent, cloth from Tournai (*pannus de dornic*) was imported for official dress.
2. *Roman de la Rose*, l. 91; the actor strolls into the fields in the early morning sewing up his sleeves:

    Lors tres une aguille d'argent
    D'un aguiller mignot e gent
    Si prins l'aguille a enfiler . . .
    Cousant mes manches . . .

3. Veblen, Thorstein, in *The Theory of the Leisure Class*, New York, 1905, regarded changes of fashion as a result of the desire to display conspicuous waste.
4. See, for example, the Slavonic MS. of the *Chronicle of Manasses*, in the Vatican Library, executed in 1345, in which Bulgarians are represented in clothing quite unlike anything worn in centres of high fashion at the time.
5. In the published translations of the Patent and the Close Rolls, the word *roba* is rendered, erroneously, as 'gown'.
6. It had become a 'vestige' in the way that buttons with no corresponding buttonholes still sometimes appear on the sleeves of formal jackets.
7. See the *Luttrell Psalter*, illustration 4 above.
8. A thirteenth-century mosaic in St Mark's, Venice, shows Scythians, identified by an inscription, wearing short tunics fastened all the way down the front to the waist. Demus, O., *Byzantine Mosaic Decoration*, plate 54, 'Scenes from the Acts of the Apostles'.
9. I have found only one example, the skirt of the Virgin as a little child, on the occasion of her presentation in the Temple, by Bernardo Daddi, 1339. Florence, Uffizi.

II *What They Said About It*

1. Bede Jarrett, OP, *Social Theories of the Middle Ages*, London, 1926, p. 49.

2. *Catholicon*. A copy by Guillaume de Dycka, dated in the text 1348. Liège University Library MS. 223e.
3. The Palazzo Vecchio was begun in 1298 by Arnolfo di Cambio, who also built the main part of the tower; the upper part was added in the fifteenth century.
4. *Cronica di Giovanni Villani*, Florence, 1823, vii, Lib. 12, p. 16.
5. Id., p. 23.
6. Gualvaneus de la Fiamma, RIS, xii. iv, pp. 37–176.
7. Id., vii, p. 177.
8. *In Historiam Ricobaldi Ferrariensis*, RIS, ix, col. 128.
9. Carlo Battisti and Giovanni Alessio, *Dizionario etimologico italiano*, Florence, 1957: 'Soccàpolo. v dial tosc, pis, cercine per portare sul capo qualcosa lucch. soccaporo, succaporo.'
10. Dante Alighieri, *Il Paradiso*, canto XV.
11. For the use of the term 'covered' in French and in English, see below, Chapter IV, p. 23.
12. *Historiae romanae fragmenta ab anno MCCCXXVII usque ad MCCCLIX*, RIS, iii, coll. 307–9.
13. *Chronique Latine de Guillaume de Nangis de . . . avec les continuations de cette chronique de 1300 à 1368*, H. Gerard, SHF, 1843, Introduction, p. xxv.
14. Id.
15. Id., p. xxxii.
16. Id., ii, p. 185: A.D. 1340.
17. *Chronicon Angliae ab anno domine 1328 usque ad annum 1388 . . .*, ed. E. M. Thompson, RS 64, 1874.
18. Id., p. 14.
19. *Cronica Johannis de Reading et Anonym. Cantuariensis 1346–1367*, ed. James Tait, Manchester, 1914, p. 88.
20. Id.
21. *The Brut*, EETS 36, vol. II, 1908.
22. Id., pp. 296–7.
23. *Grandes Chroniques de France*, ed. Jules Viard, Paris, 1937, SHF, ix, p. 285.
24. See Patent Rolls *passim*.
25. Pat. Rolls 1346, *Rotulus Normannie*, Calais, 2 October, mem. 21.

26. *C.M.H.*, vii, p. 342.
27. Blanche of Navarre was a sister of Charles the Bad and successfully espoused his dubious cause.
28. *C.M.H.*, vii, p. 347.
29. BL MS. Yates Thompson 13.
30. BL MS. Roy 10 E IV.
31. *Chronicon Henrici Knighton*, ed J. R. Lumby, RS, 1895, ii, p. 67.
32. *Chronicon Angliae*, op. cit., p. 26.
33. *Knighton*, loc. cit.
34. *Villani*, op. cit., pp. 280–81.
35. *Summa Theologica*, trans by the Fathers of the English Dominican Province, London, 1918, Pt II, second part: *Of Modesty in Outward Apparel*, clxix, pp. 304ff.
36. Id., loc. cit.
37. Richard Trexler, *Synodal Law in Florence and Fiesole, 1306–1518*, Vatican Library, 1971, p. 116.
38. *Summa Theologica*, Pars II. ii, quaestiones cxlv–clxx.
39. Id.
40. *Chronicon Estense*, RIS xv. iii, p. 118.

III *The Great Wardrobe and the Round Table*

1. Society of Antiquaries of London, MS. 541 (1330): '6 lb candles of Paris [candeƚ p'is] price 12d . . . for an aketon [ad j Aketoner]'. Also Philobiblon Society, London 1855/6, *Compts de Denis de Collors*: '. . . pour cire de bougie à ciré le dit pourpoint, 11d'.
2. Stuffs remaining from the time of William de Kirkeby are listed on fol. 174 of a great wardrobe account of Queen Philippa (1333). See BL MS. Cotton Galba E III. That stuffs were often transferred later to the great wardrobe, having been purchased several years earlier, is clear from PRO E361/3 *passim*.
3. Pat. Rolls 1346, 12 March, mem. 2: 'notification that the king has given back to William de la Pole his houses in Lumbardstrete, London, which had been taken into the king's hands, to hold as he held them before. Mandate to John Coke, keeper of the great wardrobe, which is now in the said houses, to be carried to the Tower of London and put back there again, and the houses to be delivered up to the said William.'
4. An entry in the Pat. Rolls headed Dec. 4 1339, Antwerp, mem. 6, directs that robes shall be made for one of the king's serjeants-at-arms.
5. T. F. Tout, *Chapters in the Administrative History of Medieval England*, vol. IV, p. 374.
6. e.g. PRO E101/390/5.
7. Tout, op. cit., vol IV, p. 397. It can also be noted that, in a great wardrobe account of liveries issued in 1361, a suit was issued to only one assistant clerk. See PRO E101/393/15.
8. For a discussion on the changing situations of the various ranks at courts, see N. Denholm-Young, *Country Gentry in the Fourteenth Century*, pp. 25ff.
9. Pat. Rolls 1349, 21 June, mem. 26: 'grant . . . of keeping of the lands and heirs of Adam de Yeddyng to hold during the nonage of such heirs with their marriage . . .'
10. An account of William de la Zouche, clerk of the great wardrobe in 1330, shows that activities at the Tower include work on banners and armour while, at the same time, embroiderers were employed on work on a velvet suit for the queen. See Society of Antiquaries of London, MS. 541.
11. PRO E101/390/5.
12. Made very clear in the description of the liveries issued in 1333 recorded in BL MS. Cotton Galba E III *passim*.
13. Society of Antiquaries of London, MS. 541.
14. The riding coat of the eighteenth century became, later, the full-dress tail coat. Corduroy trousers, adopted by intellectuals in the 1920s, had originally been worn exclusively by road-menders and farm labourers.
15. PRO E101/388/8.
16. Imitation jewels called *doubletta* were made of a piece of coloured metal foil sandwiched between two pieces of glass, as see, for instance, the Crouchback tomb in Westminster Abbey, and the tomb of Christopher II of Denmark and his wife and daughter in the church at Sorø. For a discussion on the 'courtpiece', see below, p. 00.
17. PRO E101/389/14.
18. For her connection with Lionel's future title as duke of Clarence, see Denholm-Young, op. cit., p. 107.
19. The word *fururata* or *furrurata* which, in French accounts, usually means simply 'lined', in English accounts definitely means 'lined-with-fur'.
20. See above, Chapter III, p. 14.
21. Later known as the Black Prince. These accounts often include, apart from seasonal liveries, gifts between members of the court circle.
22. Close Rolls 1344, 4 October, Waltham, mem. 15. Here John Charnels is referred to as clerk of the great wardrobe.
23. *Archaeologia*, xxxi, p. 5.
24. Tout, op. cit., vol. IV, pp. 382–3.
25. 'Pairs of robes' are often referred to in French *argenterie* accounts, where they simply mean several sets of garments.
26. Mem. 36 of E361/3: John Marreys, submitting his expenses states that the present fashion demands more work: '. . . respectum qᵈ suptunice & cloche Reg' stdm talliatur modo usūtam demandant plures custus circa opato'os eardem rerum f'tis.'
27. PRO E101/389/14, mem. 1.
28. L. Fumi, *La Moda de' vestire in Lucca dal sec xiv al xix*, p. 38.
29. PRO E361/3, mems. 39 and 40.
30. Id., mem. 35.
31. Id., mem. 36.
32. Pat. Rolls 1345, 18 January, Westminster, mem. 6.
33. Tout, op. cit., vol. IV, p. 382.
34. Id., p. 381.
35. Pat. Rolls 1345, 8 July, Reading, mem. 30.
36. Pat. Rolls 1345, 20 December, Westminster, mem. 14.
37. Pat. Rolls 1340, Westminster, 8 March, mem. 22: '[Customs] . . . 40d on every scarlet cloth dyed in grain, 2/-s on every cloth wherein the grain is mixed, 18d on every cloth without grain . . .'.
38. *Archaeologia*, xxxi, p. 6. It is made fairly plain in

the corresponding passage in E361/3 that the velvet was, in fact, already in stock and was transferred from an earlier year (mem. 40).

39. *Chronica Monasterii de Melsa*, ed. E. A. Bond, RS, 1868, iii, p. 52.
40. Pat. Rolls 1343, 27 May, Westminster, mem. 24. The duke of Gueldres was Edward's brother-in-law; he had married his sister Eleanor.
41. Pat. Rolls 1343, 9 July, Westminster, mem. 9.
42. Pat. Rolls 1344, 20 December, Hoxne, mem. 7.
43. Pat. Rolls 1344, 16 January, Ditton, mem. 1.
44. *Chronicon Angliae*, p. 17: '. . . Eodem tempore, Philippus de Valoys rex Franciae, hoc facto provocatus regis Angliae, coepit et ipse rotundam aedificare tabulam in terra sua; ut sic attraheret militiam Alemanniae et Italiae, ne ad regis Angliae tabulum properarent . . .'
45. Murimuth, *Continuatio Chronicarum . . .*, ed. E. M. Thompson, RS 1889, p. 155: '. . . die videlicet Januariae xix . . .'
46. Rymer, V, 400.
47. See note 43 above.
48. Murimuth, op. cit., pp. 155 and 231–2.
49. Murimuth is himself mentioned in E361/3, mem. 36, in connection with wax he was committed to supply as an executor of a late bishop of London.
50. *Chronica Monasterii de Melsa*, iii, p. 52.
51. *Archaeologia*, xxxi, p. 8.
52. Id.
53. Pat. Rolls 1344, 10 March, Westminster, mem. 32.
54. Close Rolls 1344, 1 February, Westminster, mem. 29d.
55. E101/390/9, mem. 2. About fifteen cloths were bought from him by the great wardrobe.
56. Close Rolls 1344, 10 October, Westminster, mem. 10.
57. The term 'Almain' covered a very wide area and included Reval (where houses occupied by the Hanse still survive) as well as the north Netherlands.
58. CMH, vii, p. 16.

IV *English and French Royal Clothing in the Early 1340s*

1. Masson, Frédéric, *Le Sacre et le Couronnement de Napoléon*, Paris, 1908, p. 298.
2. PRO E101/385/12. On this, see S. M. Newton, *Queen Philippa's Squirrel Dress*, in Festschrift für Sigrid Müller-Christensen. Bayerische Nationalmuseum, Munich 1980.
3. This is another of the garments that cannot, at the moment, be identified.
4. PRO E101/389/14, mem. 2.
5. Society of Antiquaries, London, MS. 541.
6. There seems to be some doubt as to whether they were actually married on this occasion or only betrothed. See N. Denholm-Young, *Country Gentry in the Fourteenth Century*, p. 107.
7. PRO E101/389/14, mem. 1: '. . . uniū robe longe p dno Rege faciend furur' & p'filiand de pann' s'ca de iiij, garniament' cont' solempnitateo nupiciarj dm̄ lionelli fit sm̄ . . .'
8. PRO E101/390/1: 'Empcion draperie mercerie pellure speciare naperie tele lin canab et al rer offic

magne garderobe Regis tangent fact p Thome de Crosse cli . . .'
9. *Nouveau Recueil de comptes de l'Argenterie*, ed. Douët D'Arcq (subsequently referred to as *Nouveau Recueil*), p. 20ff.: 'compte particulier de draps d'or et de soie rendu par Edouart Tadelin de Lucques Mercier du roi Philippe de Valois en 1342' (Paris, BN MS. fr. 20638).
10. *Comptes de l'Argenterie des Rois de France*, ed. Douët D'Arcq (subsequently referred to as *Comptes*), p. 3.
11. Id., p. vi.
12. In the Public Record Office, membrane 1 is sometimes the first, sometimes the last.
13. This *argentier* is identified by among others, Douët d'Arcq, as Guillaume de Montreuil; but he appears in the accounts variously as Monsteriolo, Mousterevl, Musterolie etc.
14. The word *parisis* or simply par or the letter p is always appended to show that the currency of Tournai is not intended. Douët D'Arcq, *Comptes*, p. 338, note: '. . . Il faut se rappeler que . . . les prix sont ici en monnaie parisis, qui est d'un quart plus forte que la monnaie tournois.'
15. *Journal du Trésor de Philippe VI de Valois*, ed. Viard, p. 71, pièce 272.
16. The clerks of the great wardrobe, in common with other royal servants, were issued with liveries which appear in the accounts. In France, their liveries appear in the *Journal du Trésor*.
17. e.g. *Journal*, 1350, p. 845, pièce 5032.
18. Id., July 1348, pièce 1526: 'Guillemus de Musterolie nuper argentarius Regis, pro denariis, solutis Johanni de Rodemaque tailliatori domine ducesse Normannie . . .' On 20 June 1349, 'Stephanus de Fonte' appears as *argentarius Regis*.
19. See Appendix IV, s.v. *grain*.
20. This practice seems to have been dropped, for in the argenterie account KK8 (Paris, Archives) *cendal* is measured by the *aune*, e.g. fol. 24v. KK8 is an account of 1351.
21. *Nouveau Recueil*, p. 24. But the term is also used in this account for covering cushions.
22. See John Nevinson, 'Buttons and Buttonholes in the Fourteenth Century', *Journal of the Costume Society*, 1977, p. 38.
23. *Comptes*, pp. xl, xli, xliii.
24. *Nouveau Recueil*, Tadelin, p. 36: 'Item. L'Argentier le doit pour xxij pièces de toilles de Reims que l'Argentier ot de li pour la livrée madame la Royne . . . Et cousterent à l'aune de Reims, c'est assavoir vj pièces countenans a l'aune de Reims iiijᶜ xviij aunes, vjs l'aune à ladicte aune de Reims, valent vjˣˣ xij£ xviijs.'
25. T. I. Léonard, *Histoire de Jeanne I*, e.g. p. 165: '. . . Ad opus ducis Calabrie rotundellus unus, surcottus unus . . .'
26. See Appendix IV s.v. *samite*.
27. *Nouveau Recueil*, Tadelin, p. 25.
28. *Encl. Tech.*: 'Les quenouilles pour les filasses diffèrent de celle qui servent pour les laines ou pour les soies, en ce que ces dernières sont terminées par un croissant de métal ou de bois auquel on attache ce que l'on veut filer . . .'

29. *Nouveau Recueil*, Tadelin, loc. cit.
30. There has been much speculation (in print) as to the nature of the corset, but the varied character of corsets referred to in great wardrobe and *argenterie* accounts at this period cannot be accommodated happily within any of the suggestions so far put forward.
31. *Sarge noir d'Irlande*: Irish serge occurs fairly often in French but not in English accounts at this period.
32. BL MS. Cotton Galba E III, fol. 189^v.
33. *Histoire de Jeanne I*, p. 165 (1338). Both Jeanne and Marie had several corsets. Each, for instance, had 'corsettus unus ad perfilum panni di seta coloris viridis'. Fifteen years later, in 1353, Jeanne had, 'Plusieurs corsets de lane de Bruxelles, l'un brun clair, orné d'une boutonnière a entrelacs ouvragée d'or, de soie et de perles; un autre de couleur paille ecarlate garni de 224 vairs et de 41 hermines . . .' (Id., t. iii, pp. 24–5).
34. *Nouveau Recueil*, Tadelin, p. 30.
35. E 361/3, mem. 43.
36. The word *bezant* is derived from a coin of Byzantium, and it seems very probable that these were themselves used as ornaments on clothing, as, indeed, coins were in the Near and Middle East until very recently.
37. See Héjj-Détán, *Hungarian Jewellery of the Past*, pp. 15–18. These 'spangles' were also an important part of the booty captured at the battle of Visby in 1360 – many are in the Historical Muscum in Copenhagen.
38. *Comptes*, 'Mots techniques', pp. 364–5: Corset: 'Il est bien difficilt de preciser ce que c'etait . . .' Douët D'Arcq here lists corsets and their particulars at some length as they appear in the accounts in this volume.
39. *Comptes*, de la Fontaine, p. 177: 'Ledit Robert, pour les fourreures d'un corset ront d'escarlate pour madicte dame une fourreure de menuvair de 160 ventres; pour manches 24, et pour un chaperon à enfourmer, 90 ventres . . . Pour 12 ermines et 18 létices a pourfiller le corset et le chaperon dessus diz . . .'
40. *Histoire de Jeanne I*, I, p. 165.
41. See below, page 29.
42. See H. Laurent, *Draperie des Pays Bas en France*, Chs. III and IV, pp. 83–150, for the markets used by the French and Netherlanders.
43. Id., Ch. VI, pp. 156–8.
44. e.g. PRO E101/390/5: '. . . Unius suptunice estival p equitat'a p Rege' (*Archaeologia*, xxxi, p. 7); and *Comptes*, de la Fontaine, p. 87: 'seurcos a chevaucher . . .'
45. *Recueil d'Anciens Inventaires*, ed. M. Brun-Durand, I. p. 390ff.
46. Id., p. 402, pièce 77.
47. Id., p. 403, pièces 88 and 89. Camelin was a woollen cloth thought by some to have been named after the colour of the coat of a camel.
48. This term, usually abbreviated to *pers*, is common in both French and English accounts, and, according to Douët D'Arcq, signifies dark blue colours. The extended form *persico* is very uncommon; in some documents it appears earlier as *persam*. See *Recueil d'Anciens Inventaires*, p. 402, pièce 82. See also Appendix IV, s.v. pers.
49. Popellus, the early summer fur of the squirrel. See Veale, pp. 226, 228.
50. *Poésies de Gilles li Muisis*, ed. Kervyn de Lettenhove, p. 44: '. . . Meskines sont les dames; li varlet sont li sire . . .'; p. 154.
   Pluseurs portoient bien jadis vièses viestures,
   Et en faisoient bien varlet siervant parures
   Et se passoit-on bien de ches simples coustures
   Se faisoit-on moult bien rappariller fourures.
51. Chrétien de Troyes, *Ywain, the Knight of the Lion*, trans. Ackerman and Locke, p. 32: '. . . The damsel pretended to send out someone to seek my lord Ywain. Moreover, she provided him with a robe of fine red material lined with fur with the chalk still on it. . .'; p. 40: '. . . The lady likewise came forward arrayed in imperial dress, consisting of a costume of new ermine with a diadem . . .'

V *Court Dress after Crécy*

1. *Chronique et Annales de Gilles le Muisit*, ed. Henri Lemaitre, Paris 1906.
2. op. cit., p. 246: 'Habitus eorum erat quod super vestimenta seu consueta habebant unum colobrium, quod vulgariter *clocke* nuncupantus; super quod colobio ante habebant unum crucem rubram et retro in dorso similiter, et erat ab una parte scissum . . . et habebant sua capucia super capita eorum et desuper unum capellum, in quo erat una crux rubea consuta ante et retro . . .'
3. *Poésies de Gilles li Muisis*, ed. Kervin de Lettenhove, II, p. 29.
4. *Chronique et Annales*, p. 229; *Poésies*, II, pp. 32, 288, etc.
5. *Poésies*, II, p. 230: 'Loenge à Dieu . . . de chou que li veue li est recouvrée, qui avoit estet aveules trois ans et plus . . . se fu aidiés par un maistre nommet Jehan de Meence [Mayence] qui ouvra en ses yeuls d'un instrument d'argent a manière d'aiguille, sans peler, a pau d'angousce et tost passée. Et fu faite cheste cure, et vey des deus yeuls selonc son eage souffiscamment, l'an de grace MCCCLI, environ le fiest saint Remi . . .' For Li Muisis' apology for his use of the Walloon language, see id., p. xxviii.
6. See illustrations 8 and 38.
7. Anonimo Romano, *Vita di Cola de Rienzo*, p. 78.
8. Id., p. 42: '. . . cappa alamanna'; p. 98: '. . . con cappe alemanne'; this last refers to the murderers of prince Andrew in Naples in 1347.
9. Id., p. 86 '. . . si vestio la dalmatica già stata d'imperatori; quella dalmatica vestono l'imperatori quando s'incoronano; tutta é di minute perle lavorata, ricco é quel vestimento.' The emperors referred to were probably the Holy Roman emperors, who did wear dalmatics at their coronations.
10. Id., p. 76: 'vestuto era de bianche vestmenta de seta forrate de zannaro infresate de auro filato . . .'
11. Id., p. 80: ' ". . . per te, Tribuno, forer piu con-

venevole che portassi vestimenta onesta e da bizoco, che queste pompose" e cio dicendo, li mostró la punta della quarnaccia . . .'

12. F. Gregorovius, *A History of Rome in the Middle Ages*, vol. VI, trans. Hamilton, 3rd edn, p. 358.

13. *Chronique de Guillaume de Nangis*, ed. H. Gérard, p. 237: '. . . quod perlae et lapides magno pretio vendebatur, et vix Parisius poterant talia reperiri . . .'

14. Paris, Archives Nationales KK8, fol. 26.

15. Id., fol. 26v.

16. See below, Chapter VI, p. 47 and *passim*.

17. *Comptes*.

18. Id., p. 287ff.

19. Blanche's father, Peter I de Bourbon, married Isabella, sister of Philippe VI de Valois.

20. PRO E101/391/15 in *Archaeologia*, xxxi, p. 9ff.

21. Chapter III, p. 15 above.

22. Tout, op. cit., vol. IV, p. 131.

23. Pat. Rolls 1347, 8 October, Calais, mem. 3, pp. 563–8.

24. See below, Chapter VI, p. 41 and *passim*.

25. *Cronaca*, di Matteo Villani, ed. Dragomanni, II, Lib. 9, cap. ciii, p. 293.

26. *Ordonnances des rois de France*, II, pp. 371–2.

27. *Comptes*, Jean II, p. 234: '. . . une robe 3 garnemens pour le roi, cote, seurcote, housse, chaperon . . .'

28. *Comptes*, de la Fontaine, p. 87. These may, perhaps, have been the small 'tabs' that often appear at the neckline in front.

29. e.g. etymology of the word: the French word *farce* can mean a stuffing, but also a buffoonery which is 'stuffed out', from the original 'farcing' in repeating the words or syllables in the liturgy at the Feast of Fools.

30. *Decameron*, II, 2.

31. Id., II, 5.

32. *The Poems of Lawrence Minot*, ed. Hall, p. 34.

33. This must have been the name used only for a very short time both in England and in France; similar garments, called *camicie*, are not found either earlier or later.

34. *Comptes*, de la Fontaine, p. 97.

35. See note V 8 above.

36. Nicholas, *Archaeologia*, xxxi. This is on the whole a faithful transcription of the MS. now numbered E101/391/15, but some of the dates have been misread and the word *soudatum* appears throughout as *sondatum*, which is meaningless. See Latham *s.v. solidus* 1) related to soldering or welding.

37. PRO E101/391/15, mem. 14, in *Archaeologia*, xxxi, p. 54.

38. 'rakematiz' is sometimes thought of as being related to the Italian word *ricamata* = embroidery, but this is by no means certain.

39. The word is connected with the idea of weaving with a double threat: see Appendix, p. 138.

40. PRO E101/391/15, mem. 19.

41. PRO E101/391/15, mem. 6: '. . . j roba ij garn̄ de pano ad auñ poudr̄ cū stelt t crescentib3 de auro / j pann̄ a'd aur̄ cigaston'.

42. Id.: 'paño ad aurū cui' campedo erat yndi coloris poudr̄ cū volucrib3 t losenges textis de auro / iij pann̄ de auro cigastoṅ . . .'

43. PRO E101/391/15, mem. 19.

44. Léonard, *Histoire de Jeanne I*, t. I, p. 347, Reg. Anj. 357, fol. 188v: '. . . trigintanovem buttoni de naccara muniti auro et lapidibus preciosis . . .'

45. PRO E101/391/15, mem. 13.

46. Id., mem. 13.

47. Id., mem. 12, in *Archaeologia*, xxxi, p. 47. It is impossible to judge to what extent English clerks were exact in their naming of stuffs. *Camoca* is a corruption (very widespread in Europe) of the Iranian *kamkhā*, in modern India kincob, a cloth of gold. The term comes from the Chinese *km* = 'gold'. See *Travels of Ibn Battuta*, ed. Gibb, ii, p. 446.

48. *Comptes*, de la Fontaine, p. 135. *Paonasse*, in Italian *pavonazzo* or *paonazzo*, literally peacock colour. It was certainly a subdued dark colour worn by the elderly, lesser academics and the clergy as well as for mourning. Perhaps because *bruno* signified mourning in Italy, *pavonazzo* is sometimes thought of as being some tint of brown; it was probably a dark blueish purple, but this is not certain.

49. *A parer*: literally to adorn, etc., but also to set out, to make a show.

50. *Vita*, p. 42: '. . . et cappuccio alle gote de fino panno bianco; in capo havea uno cappelletto bianco nella rota dello cappelletto stavano corone de auro infra le quelli ne stava una denanti le quale era partuta per' mieso. Dalla parte de sopra dello cappelletto sceneva una spade de ariento nuda e la sua ponta feria in quella corona, e si la partiva mieso.'

51. Id., p. 116.

52. *Oeuvres*, v, p. 250.

53. *Comptes*, p. 298.

54. See below, Chapter IX, p. 80.

55. PRO E101/391/15, mem. 20, in *Archaeologia*, xxxi, p. 60.

56. Paris Archives nationales KK8, fols. 15 and 24.

57. *Ordonnances des rois de France*, iii, p. 10ff., August 1355. Issued from La Noble Maison de St Ouen.

58. Id., p. 11: 'Item, nul Orfevre ne peut ouvrer a l'Or a Paris qu'il ne soit à la touche de Paris, ou meilleur . . .' Note: *touche* = 'titre'.

59. There is a particularly good collection in the National Historical Museum in Copenhagen, many from the battle of Visby, fought in 1360.

60. 'Cyprus' thread was the normal thread used in England and France for important embroideries in metal. According to Douët D'Arcq, it was made by winding narrow strips of gold or silver-gilt round a core of silk thread. See *Comptes*, 'Mots techniques', p. 393.

61. *Chronique de Guillaume de Nangis*, ed. H. Gerard, t. ii, p. xxxj: '. . . Le faste et la dissolution augmentent parmi les chevaliers et les nobles. Ils ornent de perles et de pierres précieuses leur capuchons et leurs ceintures, se qui fait croitre considerablement le prix des perles. Commencement de l'usage d'orner les chapeaux de plumes. Les nobles ne songent qu'au jeu et au plaisir . . .'

62. *Ordonnances des rois de France*, ii, pp. 371–2, 194: *Des Cousturiers*.

63. *Comptes*, 'Inventaire de l'argenterie dressé en 1353', p. 324: '. . . pour j chapiau de bievre fourré d'ermines semé de perles d'Orient . . . et y faut 8 roses de perles, contenant chascune rose 21 perles et 14 autres perles, lesquelles ledit Etienne doit rendre pour ce qu'il les a ostées . . .'

64. *Decameron*, x, p. 6.

65. Id., loc. cit: '. . . bionde come filo d'oro e co' capelli tutti in anellati e sopr' essi sciolti una leggiera ghirlandetta di provincia, e nelli lor visi piú tosto agnoli parevan che altra cosa . . .'

66. Id.: '. . . dalla cintura in su era strettissimo e da indi giú largo a guisa d'un padiglione . . .'

67. Guillaume de Machaut, *Poésies lyriques*, ed. Chichmaref, p. 90, lxxxii (2), 'Rondel'.

68. Guillaume de Machaut, *La Louange des Dames*, ed. N. Wilkins, p. 52, 'Ballades', 8 (c. 1356).

69. *Oeuvres de Guillaume de Machaut*, ed. Hoepffner, *Le Jugement dou Roy de Behaingne*, p. 70, l. 336ff.: '. . . mignotement chaucies'.

70. Chichmaref (ed.), op. cit., p. xiii: '. . . entered the service of John of Luxemburg king of Bohemia in about 1323'.

71. *Romance of William of Palerne* (translated from the French at the command of Sir Humphrey de Bohun, c. 1350), ed. Skeat.

72. Id., p. 182, l. 178ff.

73. *Piers Plowman*, Passus II, l. 9, 10.

74. *Sir Launcefal*, ed. Bliss, l. 943ff.

75. *Ipomedon*, l. 2384ff.

76. Id., l. 367ff.

77. *The Romaunt of the Rose and Le Roman de la Rose*, a parallel-text edition, ed. Ronald Sutherland.

VI *Tournaments and Orders of Chivalry*

1. George Hill, *A History of Cyprus*, v. ii, p. 319ff.

2. N. H. Nicholas, *Archaeologia*, xxxi, p. 104ff.

3. Elias Ashmole, *The Institution, Laws and Ceremonies of the Most Noble Order of the Garter*, London, 1672.

4. Denholm-Young, *The Country Gentry in the Fourteenth Century*, p. 44: 'The king took part [in jousts] as a simple knight, i.e. a knight bachelor.'

5. Id., p. 144.

6. M. McKisack, *The Fourteenth Century*, p. 273: 'it was widely believed that the revenues which the pope and other foreigners derived from English churches went to sustain the king's enemies overseas'. The author quotes Murimuth, pp. 173–5, and, in stating that, in 1343, 'Edward III voiced the resentment of his people in a strong letter', refers to *Foedera*, ii, 1233–4.

7. PRO E101/389/14, mem. 1.

8. B. C. Hardy, *Philippa of Hainault and her Times*, p. 76.

9. Denholm-Young, *The Country Gentry in the Fourteenth Century*, p. 145.

10. PRO E101/389/14, mem. 1.

11. Id., mem. 4.

12. C. Jamison, *History of the Royal Hospital of St Katharine by the Tower of London*, p. 13.

13. Id., p. 27.

14. *Foedera*, V, p. 363. Also Tout, op. cit., vol. III, pp. 161–2, and Jamison, op. cit., p. 27.

15. PRO E101/393/15 (1361), mem. 9.

16. Beltz, *Memorials . . .*, p. li. He follows Ashmole in this opinion.

17. A fugitive dye based on woad was used for cheap cloths which do not often appear in inventories. See, for instance, the will of Francesco Caracciolo, detto Greco, of 3 January 1362, which directs that he shall be buried in *panno di lana grossa, di colore turchino* and that the same cloth should cover his bier and be provided for tunics and hoods for the eight poor men who should carry it, in *Archivio per le province Napoletane*, ann. xxi, facs. 1, Naples.

18. e.g. Froissart and Machaut.

19. Beltz, *Memorials . . .*, p. xlvi, discusses this theory and dismisses it.

20. R. Barber, *Edward, Prince of Wales and Aquitaine*, p. 87.

21. *Archaeologia*, xxxi, pp. 34–5; PRO E101/390/5, mems. 8 and 9.

22. Id., p. 10: mem. 11.

23. Id., p. 25: mem. 6.

24. PRO E101/390/9, mem. 4.

25. PRO E101/391/14.

26. Id., mem. 8.

27. *Archaeologia*, xxxi, p. 36.

28. PRO E101/394/12. This account starts with coloured longcloth, which means that the cloth in grain has disappeared with any other of the more expensive cloths of Brussels.

29. PRO E101/394/16.

30. Id., membrane 17 (the pencil numbering has numbered the *last* membrane as 1, and so on).

31. To name the recipients of ceremonial clothing seems to have been an innovation in court ritual that appeared first at about this time.

32. Elizabeth de Burgh, countess of Ulster, died in November 1360, Henry of Lancaster in 1361. William de Bohun also died in the year covered by this account.

33. Froissart, *Poésies*, ed. A. Scheler, v. iii, p. 426.

34. Id., v. I, p. 348.

35. Guillaume de Machaut, *Poésies Lyriques*, ed. Chichmaref, V, 'Ballade', cclxxii, p. 235.

36. *Winner and Waster*, ed. I. Gollancz, pages unnumbered; l. 59–62, 92–4, 95–6. In 1354, richly embroidered belts were the height of fashion.

37. *La Prise d'Alexandrie*, ed. M. L. de Mas Latrie, *passim*.

38. Peter I ascended the throne of Cyprus in 1359; his attack on Alexandria was made in 1365. See Hill, *A History of Cyprus*, p. 333.

39. *La Prise . . .*, ll. 58–65.

40. The original colour of the habit of the hospital Order of the Saint Esprit, for instance, was blue.

41. *La Prise . . .*, l. 401ff.

42. Id., l. 420ff.

43. Id., p. 277.

44. Hill, *A History of Cyprus*, v. ii, p. 308, fig. 6.

45. Papiers et notes diverses d'Etienne Lauréault de Foncemagne (c. 1779), BN MS. Fr. nouv. acq. 3294 (ii), fol. 63.

46. M. Dacier, 'Recherches historiques sur l'établis-

sement et l'extinction de l'ordre de l'Étoile', in *Memoires de Litterature tirés des registres de l'Academie royale des Inscriptions et Belles Lettres*, 1777, xxxix, p. 662.

47. *Recueil des ordonnances de nos Rois*, pub. by Dom Luc d'Achery, t. III, p. 730 (Dacier, op. cit., p. 665), Institution de l'ordre de l'Étoile.

48. Dacier, op. cit., p. 663.

49. Id.

50. *Chronique de Jehan le Bel*, ii, p. 174: '. . . l'an de grace Mil CCCLII le roy Jehan de France ordonna une belle compagnie grande et noble sur la Table Ronde . . .'

51. Foncemagne, op. cit., 67.

52. Froissart, v, pp. 308–9.

53. Beltz, *Memorials* . . ., cxiix.

54. Froissart, v, pp. 308–9.

55. *Ordonnances des rois de France*, II, 465–6.

56. The feast of the Assumption of the Blessed Virgin Mary is on 15 August.

57. Paris, BN. MS. 6465. See *Grandes chroniques de France enluminées par Jean Foucquet*, Paris, n.d.

58. Paris, Archives nationales MS. KK8.

59. For a discussion on the term *camocas*, see above V, note 47.

60. St Maurice.

61. Paris, Archives nationales MS. KK8, ff.7 & 8v.

62. Id., fol. 9.

63. Id., fol. 18v.

64. Id., fol. 1v.

65. Opinions vary as to the date of this manuscript, but it is usually regarded as having been done the middle or later 1370s, whereas the fashions seems to suggest a date not later than the end of the 1360s.

66. See Foncemagne, 72v (19, 20).

67. BN MS. Fr. 4274: 'Manuscrit de l'Ordre du Saint Esprit par le Roy, Loys de Sicile et de Hierusalem lan mil trois cent cinquante deux'. When de Viel-Castel prepared his 'facsimile', the manuscript was in the Louvre.

68. In his notes, Salviac de Viel Castel related the story that Henri II was presented with the MS. when he passed through on his way from Poland to ascend the throne of France. Henri, said to have been inspired by the MS., founded his own Order of the Saint Ésprit and then ordered the original to be burnt 'Par une fausse delicatesse; his Chancellor, Chiverni, refrained from doing so and secreted it. No other plausible explanation of its arrival in France has so far been put forward. Salviac de Viel Castel, *Statuts de l'Order*, p. 27.

69. E. G. Léonard, *Histoire de Jeanne 1*, iii, p. 18, explains that throughout the Middle Ages the 'merveilles opérées par le Mage Virgile' were a part of the local folklore.

70. Id.

71. Matteo Villani, i, iii, Lib. 83, p. 274: '. . . e fatto il giuramento, si vestirono d'una cottardita e d'un assisa e d'un colore . . .'

72. There seems no doubt that the first meeting took place in 1353 and not on the occasion of the coronation in 1352; it is hardly likely that the illustrations to the statutes would have been done before the Order had actually come into being.

73. Léonard, loc. cit.

74. Österreichische Nationalbibliothek, MS. 1921, called 'c 1350'.

75. This procession, which the public is permitted to witness on obtaining a ticket in advance, takes place in late May or early June.

76. *Inventaire des meubles de monsieur le duc de Normandie dauphin de Viennois, fait en l'anee 1363*, Paris BN MS. Fr. 21447. Cf. KK8, fol. 6v, where there is an entry for 108 large pearls to put on the 'aumuce soustern la couronne du Roy a la feste de l'estoile'.

77. *Comptes*, p. 209: '. . . pour 2 anniaux d'or achetez . . . pour le Roy, és quiex a 2 pierres taillees en chascune des quelles a une estoile . . .'

78. *Ordonnances des rois de France*, iii, p. 397: 'Mandement pour faire fabriquer des gros Deniers blancs a l'estoile dans les monnoys de Paris, de Rouen et de Troyes' (fév. 1359). There is a specimen in the collection of the Musée de la Légion d'Honneur, Paris.

VII *Fashion after Poitiers*

1. 'Estienne Marcel, Jacques Marcel, Imbert de Lions, Pierre Bourdon, Jehan Marcel, drapier, touz bourgois de Paris', are mentioned in 1339. See *Documents Parisiens du regne de Philippe de Valois*, ed. Viard, i, p. 67. The Marcels were evidently a family of merchant drapers.

2. *Grandes Chroniques de France*, ed. Delachenal, ii, p. 84ff: '. . . aucuns menesterieux jugleurs ne joueroient de leur mestier . . .'

3. Id., p. 89.

4. *Comptes*, p. 211. Jean's *Journal* includes a list of his attendants to which Rymer's list corresponds fairly closely. In both lists the name of his fool is omitted, but his tailor, Tassin de Brueil, is named. Froissart, vi, p. 452; 'Le roi Jean avait avec lui un fou nommé maître Jean et aussi un roy des ménestereulx.'

5. Rymer, *Foedera*, 1708, vi, p. 135: 'Johannes Peterii, secretarius Johannis de Francia Adversarii Regis, habet Literas Regis de Salvo Conducto veniendo in Regnum Angliae cum Financia, Robis, ac aliis Necessariis ipsius Johannis de Francia, per Tres Hebdomadas . . .'

6. *Comptes*, p. 233. Regnault, Philippe of Burgundy's tailor, was given material 'pour refaire pourpoins, mantiaux et autres choses pour monseigneur' (Philippe was in captivity with his father); and id., p. 252, Perrin, the king's furrier, is paid *pour rafrechir* fur of his *cote hardie à chevaucher*.

7. Three million crowns, CMH, vii, p. 446. Tout, op. cit., vol. III, p. 243. Two French crowns equalled one English noble. 'That sum was therefore no less than £500,000 sterling, an unheard of amount for such a purpose up to that date.'

8. *Chronica Johannis de Reading et Anonymi Cantuariensis*, ed. Tait, p. 167.

9. Id.: '. . . in super Paltoks aliis vestibus curtis-

simus lanis et aliis tenuis obturatis ac consutis per totum . . .'

10. Id.: 'caligis etiam tibiis longioribus ad curta vestimenta colligulatis ligulis quas harlotes, gadelinges et lorels vocabant . . .' – all names for worthless people.

11. *Eulogium Historiarum sirc Temporis*, ed. E. S. Haydon, RS 1863, iii pp. 230, 231.

12. Id., p. 230: '. . . et lingua materna vocatur "Goun", et bene, quia "Goun" dicitur a "Gounyg" quod proprie sonare dicitur "Wounyg" quasi "aperta derisio" '.

13. Shoes with long points were also called *poulaines*, but this consistent association with Poland has never been satisfactorily explained. Shoes with long *turned-up* points have always, however, been worn by peoples living in areas where long damp grass or heavy snow were usual, e.g. Lapland and the uplands of Turkey.

14. *Eulogium*, loc. cit.

15. *Chronique Guillaume de Nangis*, ed. Gerard, t. II, p. 367.

16. Id., p. 368.

17. PRO E101/393/15, mem. 13: 'Eidem ad unū paltok de panno nigr dat' dno Reg p Johān Chaundos liniand et stuffanʒ p man' pda Willi Hervy.' Tout Chps III, p. 225 'John Chandos, the vice-chamberlain . . .'

18. See Appendix IV s.v. aketon.

19. PRO E101/393/15, mem. 12: 'ad unum goune p Regina Scotie de panno mixt in gño faciendʒ et furrurandʒ de dono dno Regis p mān p'to Hervy'.

20. PRO E101/393/15.

21. *Eulogium*, p. 231: 'Habent etiam caligas bipartitas et stragulatas quas cum corrigiis ligant as sous "paltokkos" . . .'

22. PRO E101/394/16.

23. Id., mem. 16 (new numbering): 'Eidem as unū gonne long' frounciat' p dno Rē'.

24. Id., mem. 15:

Eidem garnistura unus goune long' plicat' per totum p dna Regina necnon p eodem gonne infra terra extendit	x uln p iiij qrt Tele flandra iij uln iij qrt . . . canabe' dj lb fili

25. For a discussion of the term 'baldekyn', see Appendix V, p. 137

26. It will have been noted that William Hervey delivered suits to the king of England as well as to the king of France.

27. *De Nangis*, op. cit., p. 236–7: '. . . Incoeperunt etiam tunc gestare plumas avium in pileis . . .' A fashion inspired, perhaps, by the presence of Hungarian and Tartar troops at the siege of Treviso in 1356, or their earlier appearance in Italy at the beginning of the 1350s. See S. M. Newton, in *Journal of the Warburg and Courtauld Institutes*, forthcoming.

28. PRO E101/394/16, mem. 14: 'Eidem as uni' Jakʒ de tela de Reÿns liniad cum sindon de trp & tela pis p Re fac & stuffandʒ cū sic' opto & coton stuff.'

29. CMH, vii, p. 354: 'They were known as the Jacques, from the garment of that name worn by peasants' in reference to the year 1357. Froissart, in referring to Jaque Bonhomme (VI, p. 449), 'et sa grande compagnie', seems, perhaps, to suggest a different origin for the name.

30. Froissart, v, p, 260: 'Si tenoit li rois d'Engleterre ou chief de sa nef, vestis d'un noir jak de velviel, qui moult bien le séoit.'

31. Froissart, vi, p. 98 and note.

32. *Chronica*, p. 167.

33. PRO E101/393/15, mem. 9: 'Eidem p duas garnament' dni' Regis broudat & aliis diu's rotalibʒ ipsiū dm Reg' . . .'

34. PRO E101/394/16, mem. 12: 'Eidem p elargacoē uniu' zone p Rege de velvett rub ħnes cum ceris de auro & ✝ris de pers / 1 qrt uniu' uln velvett'.

35. PRO E101/393/15, mem. 9: '. . . unius cloc' long' p Rē de panno virid öroud cum Ramis & foliis de aur' et s'ico . . .'; 'unius cloc' long' eodem dno Rege de panno blankett broudat cum wrethe & cum Ramis & foliis de aur' et s'co . . .'

36. In July 1360.

37. *Comptes*, 'Des mots techniques' p. 383: '*Hopelande* . . . Je crois pouvoir affirmer que ce n'est guére qu'a partir du régne du roi Jean que le nom de ce vêtement apparait dans les textes.'

38. Froissart, vi, p. 28: '. . . il s'arma bien et faiticement, et puis vesti une houpelande par dessus, et pris son mantiel encore par-dessus.'

39. The word begins to appear in England after the middle of the century, but not as representing a garment in common use. In France it was mentioned as being made for Philippe le Long in 1316. See *Comptes*, p. 12.

40. *Comptes*, p. 229.

41. Id., p. 233: '. . . pour 5 aunes de rousset et 7 quartiers, pour fairs 8 paire de chauces pour monseigneur Philippe.'

42. Id., p. 250.

43. Pat. Rolls 1360, 26 April, mem. 20.

44. *Comptes*, p. 264: 'Maistre Girart d'Orliens, pour refaire, de charpenterie et repaindre de nouvel la chaière du Roy, par Gale de Melin (Melun) et Copin le paintre . . .'

45. Pat. Rolls 1361, p. 512.

46. *Comptes*, p. 274: 'Un homme de Douvre, appellé le *rampeur*, qui rampa devant le Roy contremont la roche, devant l'ermitage de Douvre . . .'

47. Id., p. 277.

48. Id., p. 251: 'Lunday xxvᵉ de May. Un batelier de Londres qui mena le Roy et aucun de ses gens d'emprés le pont de Londres jusques à Westmoutier dvers le royne d'Angleterre . . . et y souppa.'

49. Id., p. 125: 'Pour faire et forger le tuyau du pié de la couppe de St Louys, et le reburnir tout de nouvel . . .'

50. Id., note by editor: 'Du Cange . . . cite un inventaire des meubles de Louis le Hutin: "C'est l'inventaire de l'eschanconnerie etc. Item, la coupe d'or de Loys, ou on ne boit point".'

51. Id., p. 274: '. . . Un escurier du Roy d'Angleterre qui apporta au Roy le propre gobelet à quoi ledit roy d'Angleterre buvoit que il li envoioit en don, et le Roy li envoia en don le propre henap à quoy

il buvoit qui fu monseigneur St Loys . . .'

52. *Chronique Normande*, ed. Molinier, p. 153 (1360).
53. *Grandes Chroniques de France*, ii, pp. 327–31; Froissart, vi, p. 291; *Chronique des quatre premiers Valois*, p. 121: '. . . et avoit à Paris, quant le roy Jehan y entra fontaines qui rendoient vins de plusieurs manières.'
54. PRO E101/393/15, mem. 13:
    xi uln pann mixt larg' de – Brycell de dono
                                         Regis Ffranc
    iij qr̄t uln pan sanguine –.in gno de
                                          empt' . . .
    and a considerable quantity of trimmed miniver 'de dono Reg' ffnc', but:
    de empt xxvj best' Ermyns
                iiij uln j qtr Rubant' aur' siric de empt'.
55. Tout, op. cit., vol. VI, p. 48.
56. See p. 44 above.
57. PRO E101/393/15, mem. 13. Described as a robe of three garments 'de sect militum de Garteris'; the previous entry included 'ad mittend' dno Regis ffranc'.
58. PRO E101/393/15, mem. 13.
59. Id., mem. 10: 'Eidem ad unam rob' ꝑ eadem dña ꝑ sponsalibȝ.
60. CMH, vii, p. 360: '. . . September 1364 . . . a few months later John de Montfort was recognized as duke of Brittany.
61. PRO E101/393/15, but see also Rymer, (1708), p. 156 (1360): 'Rex, dilecto Clerico suo, Johanni de Neubury; custodi Magnae Garderobe suae, salutem. Mandamus vobis quod, dilectae nobis, sorori dilecti & fidelis Johannis Ducis Brittanniae, Robae competentes pro tribus Domicellis & uno Armigero suis unam Robam pro valletto camrtse suae liberetis habendas de Dono nostro . . .' So it is clear that Joanna had a household of her own.
62. Eleanor de Bohun, who had married James Butler, second earl of Ormonde.
63. PRO E101/393/15.
64. *pyncons*: Latham: *pincernia*, slippers.
65. Matteo Villani, *Cronica*, I, Lib. v, cap. xxxvi, explains that the Hungarians bred an immense number of cattle, but for their leather and their fat. Hungarian leather and leatherwork became famous.
66. S. Runciman, *A History of the Crusades*, vol. 3, p. 442.
67. *Chronicon Angliae*, p. 53 (1363): '. . . Eisdem diebus tres reges, scilicet Franciae, Cipriae et Scocie, visere et alloqui dominum regem Angliae . . .' Knighton, ii, p. 118, talks of four kings assembled in London, but says that Jean arrived after the feast of the Purification.
68. Carswell, the king's tailor, seems to appear in PRO E101/394/16 as W . . . (rest of the name difficult to read) de Kareswell, but as Rico' de Careswell in E101/394/9. Most authorities regard Richard as being correct.
69. PRO E101/394/16, mem. 17.
70. *Grandes Chroniques*, ii, p. 341.
71. PRO E101/394/16, mem. 5.
72. Runciman, *Crusades*, iii, p. 442; Froissart, vi, p. 381.
73. *Chronique des quatre premiers Valois*, p. 143: '. . . Et fut ce corps du dit roy Jehan appareillé comme il est acoustumé en tel cas à si tres hault, si noble et si puissant prince . . .'
74. *Grandes Chroniques*, ii, pp. 342–4.
75. *Chronique anon. de Valenciennes*: 'Et quant tous les seigneurs qui conduisoient le corps du roy, furent pres de Paris, on prépara et aorna le corps du roy Jehan ainsy qu'on debvoit faire, et le coucha-on dedens ung lit tout ainsy comme s'il dormist, et luy mist-on la couronne aux flourons d'or dessus le chief, et le couvry-on de draps d'or . . .'
76. Froissart, vi, p. 409: '. . . a grant proucession et a plus de mil torsses.'
77. See Appendix V.
78. *Munimenta Academica*, p. 382. From a manuscript of about 1350 is a list of garments which conform to the statutes of the university of Oxford; it includes *tabardum furratum* at *quatuor denarii* and *tabardum sine furrura* at *tres denarii*.
79. *Piers Plowman*, Text A, Passus V:
    107 Thenne com Couetyse . . .
    109 He was bitel-brouwed . . .
    111 In a toren Tabart . . .

VIII *Livery and the Dress of the Poor*

1. Paris, Archives nationales, MS. KK8. Douët D'Arcq says that all the French *argenterie* accounts began with the best woollen cloths, and this was so in England too.
2. Id., fol. 15.
3. PRO E101/393/15, mem. 13 (modern numbering).
4. Id., mem. 11.
5. Id., loc. cit. The earl of Richmond was John of Gaunt.
6. Id., mem. 9.
7. Id., mem. 3.
8. *Popellus*: the summer fur of the squirrel. See Veale, pp. 226, 228.
9. PRO Pat. Rolls 1361, 26 October, Westminster, mem. 18.
10. Veale, loc. cit.
11. Paris, Archives nationales MS. KK8, fol. 20v: '. . . mon dit seigneur le dauphin donna a Bartram du Cloz son tresorier iij fourreur' de grosse porpres x£ la piece pour les elles de la houce vij.' Id., fol. 19v: '. . . pour les iij Damoiselles de ma Dame la dauphine cissavoir Dameton Climence du pailloer et Jouhanne pour chascune ij fourr' lune de menu porpres. . .'
12. PRO E101/393/15, mem. 4: 'Thome Stanes . . . malemann dm̄ Rⁱˢ . . .' Latham: 'malemannus etc., rent-paying tenant.'
13. Id., mem. 5.
14. See Chapter VII above, p. 58, for Jean II's clothing at this time.
15. Pat. Rolls 1347, 6 November, Westminster, mem. 24: '. . . customs on all cloths of wool made in England . . . a moiety of such custom on every other cloth of half grain or in which the grain has been mixed . . .'
16. Close Rolls 1361, 2 March, Westminster, mem. 39d.

17. Pat. Rolls 1358, 20 February, Westminster, mem. 31.
18. PRO E101/393/15, unnumbered membrane which follows membrane 4. The first use of the term 'fox terrier' in the OED is Byron's.
19. Pat. Rolls 1360, 14 August, Westminster, mem. 3d.
20. PRO E101/394/16, mem. 13. By this time John of Gaunt had become duke of Lancaster.
21. Close Rolls 1349, 3 October, Westminster, mem. 14: 'Order to pay to John de Pasterheye what is in arrear to him of his wages of 2d a day and 10/-s yearly for his robe . . . because he was maimed in the king's service . . . such wages and robes to be received for life . . .' In 1346 a John Helmeswell was described as having given: 'long service and because he was maimed in the king's services so that he cannot now labour with him. . .'; and he, too was given a pension and suits of clothing for life. See Pat. Rolls, 6 June, Porchester, mem. 1.
22. Pat. Rolls 1352, 2 June, Windsor, mem. 18.
23. Pat. Rolls 1344, 12 June, Westminster, mem. 48.
24. Pat. Rolls 1352, 6 May, Windsor, mem. 7.
25. Pat. Rolls 1341, 26 January, Westminster, mem. 48–9.
26. Pat. Rolls 1344, 17 October, Westminster, mem. 28.
27. Pat. Rolls 1350, 23 June, Westminster, mem. 18.
28. Pat. Rolls 1352, 8 July, Westminster, mem. 19.
29. Pat. Rolls 1358, 1 October, Westminster, mem. 28. The king's surgeon, Richard de Wy, was granted, for 'long service, of his accustomed wages, to wit 12d a day and 8 marks a year for his robes to be taken for life at the hands of the keeper of the king's wardrobe as well when absent from the household as when present'.
30. Rymer, *Foedera*, ii, ii, p. 73.
31. Close Rolls 1341, 24 May, Westminster, mem. 2.
32. Close Rolls 1352, 18 July, Westminster, mem. 18.
33. Close Rolls 1355, 20 November, Westminster, mem. 15. In 1364, a long order was issued stating that because people who had not undergone the usual apprenticeship were selling cloth, the price had risen steeply and this practice was not to continue. See Pat. Rolls 1364, 15 July, Westminster, mem. 45.
34. Pat. Rolls 1353, 21 November, Westminster, mem. 8.
35. Pat. Rolls 1348, 14 November, Sandwich, mem. 22.
36. *Register of Edward the Black Prince*, iv (1351–65), p. 213: 25 July 1357, London, Bishop of Ely's Inn.
37. Id., Pt I (1346–8), p. 14: 14 September 1346, Westminster. When these orders were repeated in later years, it was almost always stipulated that the green should be on the right.
38. BL MS. Roy 6 E VII.
39. *Cronica*, Lib. 4, Cap. xliv, p. 347 and *passim*.
40. *Oeuvres de Guillaume Machaut*, ed. Hoepffner, v. iii.
41. The houpeland had come into fashion at just about this time and was therefore still unsuitable as the livery of a servant.
42. The meaning of this word has not, it seems, been discovered.
43. See current references to these by the chroniclers, Chapter VII, p. 54 above. It seems to be generally agreed that the word means in the 'Polish style'. Elsewhere in the poem (l.2954) Machaut writes:

    S'il avoit une cote grise
    De drap de Pouleinne ou de Frise

    which means cheap stuff from Poland or Friseland.
44. Machaut, *Confort d'Ami*, l. 3731ff.
45. For a discussion on this term, see Appendix, p. 133.
46. Paris, Archives nationales MS. KK8, fol. 15v. But the dauphin and his brothers also wore cotes hardies and unlined houces for hunting. See *Comptes*, p. 89.
47. Clothing for this marriage appears in Étienne de la Fontaine's account for 1352. See *Comptes*, p. 175ff., and in KK8.
48. *Ordonnances des rois de France*, ii, p. 352 (1349).
49. Id., p. 468: 'Personne ne travaillera du mestier pendant les quatres festes de la Vierge, le jour des Dimanches, ni aux Festes des Apostres . . .' In Flanders the same ruling obtained; for instance no shearer, valet or apprentice might work by candlelight nor on 'jour de feste sollempneuse'. *See Recueil des documents rélatifs à l'histoire de l'industrie drapière en Flandre*, première partie, i, p. 16.
50. *Les Journaux du Trèsor de Philippe VI de Valois*, December 1349, p. 571.
51. G. de Valons, *Le patriciat Lyonnais . . .*, p. 188.
52. Archiv . . . de la Ville de Rheims, t. II, p. 1125.
53. RIS, xiii, ii, p. 58 ii.
54. Id., p. 70. *Pannus romanolo* seems to have been the general term for a cheap locally made cloth.
55. Close Rolls 1359, 12 February, Westminster, mem. 34.
56. *Grandes chroniques de France* ii, p. 110.
57. *Chronica*, i, Lib. 4, cap. xliv, p. 346; cap xcii, p. 392.
58. Id., ii, Lib. 11, cap. lxvii, pp. 467–8.
59. *Grandes Chroniques*, ix, p. 27.
60. *Chronique des Quatre premiers Valois*, p. 149. For Charles's entry into Paris after his coronation, the burghers were wearing a livery of green and white to wipe out, no doubt, the memory of earlier troubles. See id., p. 148.
61. Froissart, vi, p. 37; *Chronique de Berne*, p. 265 *Grandes Chroniques*, I, pp. 146–50.
62. *Inventaire des archives de la Ville de Bruges*, p. 99.
63. Pat. Rolls 1340, 9 May and 21 June, Westminster, mems. 2 and 10.
64. *Inventaire . . . Ville de Bruges*, p. 121.
65. *Annales de Flandre*, ii, p. 488.
66. CMH, vii, p. 362.
67. *Ordonnances des rois de France*, iii, pp. 467, 603, 641. In England, a similar order was passed in 1361, ordering Jews and prostitutes to wear distinguishing badges on their outer garments. See Meaux, p. 155.
68. *Poésies*, iii, p. 216, l. 12:
    Venin qu'il n'est si fort pourpoint
    Qui en peust le cop retenir . . .

69. Id., t. I, *L'Espinette Amoureuse*, p. 182, l. 3216.
70. *Poésies*, ii, p. 306: *Pastourelles*, I. See Appendix for this poem, p. 128.
71. *Piers Plowman*, A text, Passus V, l. 45ff.
72. See Appendix, p. 132.
73. *Oeuvres*, iv, p. 424. *Piers Plowman*, Prologue, l. 84ff., refers to lawyers in hoods of silk.
74. *Piers Plowman*, Passus VII, l. 256ff.
75. Id., Passus III, l. 276ff.:
    Schal no seriaunt for that seruise . were a selk houue,
    Ne no Ray Robe . with Riche pelure.
76. CMH VII, p. 739.
77. *Poésies*, ii, p. 192, '*Ch'est li complainte des dames . . .*', a dialogue between abbots and women.
78. Id., p. 44, *Deus judex, justus, fortis et patiens.*
79. Id., p. 154, *Ch'est des séculers.*

IX *Actors, Minstrels and Fools*

1. *The Register of John Grandisson, Bishop of Exeter*, ed. Hungeston-Randolf, i. iii, p. 1120.
2. Id., '. . . sub pena Excommunicacionis Majoris . . .'
3. *Grandes Chroniques de France*, ii, p. 86: '. . . que aucuns menesterieux, jugleurs ne joueront de leur mestier'; 'wilful begging of stalwort / or able-bodied / men is forbidden to every Christian man . . .' See *An Apology for Lollard Doctrines attributed to Wicliffe*, Camden Soc., p. lv.
4. G. C. Pola Falletti Villafalleto, *Associazioni Giovanili . . .*, i, p. 416.
5. *Comptes*, p. 265: 'un menestral qui joua d'un chien et d'un singe devant le Roy qui aloit aus champs ce jour, 1 escu vault 3s 4d.'
6. *Comptes*, p. 228: 'Le roy des menestereulx, sur la facon de l'auloge qu'il fait pour le Roy, 17 nobles, valent 113s 4d.'
7. Pola, op. cit., i, p. 153.
8. A. Wagner, *Heralds and Heraldry in the Middle Ages*, p. 26: Throughout their history the heralds and the minstrels are closely linked as colleagues or as rivals . . .'
9. PRO E101/394/16, mem. 4.
10. *Comptes*, p. 265.
11. Murimuth, *Continuatio Chronicarum . . .*, p. 231.
12. *Comptes*, p. 263.
13. PRO E101/390/5, mem. 7, in *Archaeologia*, xxxi, p. 30.
14. Froissart, ii, p. 49.
15. E101/390/5, mem. 10; p. 38: '. . . ad faciend̄ unā robam p R͛ . . . broudata cū pennis phesanoz.' But, as well, actual pheasants' feathers, with 'pipes' to hold them, were issued for the Bury joust. See mem. 9; p. 36.
16. Id., mem. 10; p. 38. In the account 1347, but actually held, perhaps, in 1348.
17. Id., mem. 11; p. 43.
18. E101/394/16, mem. 11. Carde seems to have been an inexpensive heavy imported cotton material.
19. A. Ancona, *Origini del Teatro italiano . . .*, i, p. 77, note 3: '. . . veniat Salvator indutus dalmatica . . . Adam ĩndutus tunica rubea, Eva vero mulierbri vestimento albo, peplo serico albo . . .'
20. Id., p. 207.
21. RIS xii, iv, Gualvaneus della Flamma xxviii/153, p. 22, who says that in front of the church of St Laurence 'erat Herodes effigiatus cum scribis et sapientibus . . .', which may mean that they were a sculptured group.
22. Now a musical society, the Coro Polifonico Romano, which operates in the Auditorio de Gonfalone, via del Gonfalone 34a.
23. Della Flamma, loc. cit., p. 51. '. . . et fuerunt de genere de confarioneriis xii omnes vestiti et calziati similiter . . .'
24. Ancona, op. cit., I., p. 164.
25. BL MS. Add 47682.
26. G. Cohen, *Le Théâtre en France au moyen age*, i, p. 52. Hedroit also comes into the miniature painting representing the Road to Calvary in the *Heures d'Étienne Chevalier*, illuminated by Fouquet.
27. Paris, BN MS., Fr. 146.
28. *Vita di Cola di Rienzo*, Anonimo Romano, p. 116: '. . . uno vestuto de cuoro de vove (bove); le corna in capo havea, vove pareva, iocao et saltao . . .'
29. *Luttrell Psalter*, BL MS. Add. 42130, fol. 164v.
30. Summa Pars II. ii, Question clxviii, Article iii, Objection i.
31. Id., ii, 16; viii, 63.
32. *Chronicon Angliae*, ed. Thompson, p. 11.
33. *Comptes*, p. 150: 'Des draps vermeux achatez pour les encourtinemens fais en la Noble Maison, a la feste de l'Etoille, pour 7 aunes et demie de drap vermeil, delivrees en ce terme pour faire couvertoueir a lit pour ledit fol.'
34. Id., p. 161.
35. Id., p. 149: 'Ledit Jehan Perceval pour 3 aunes d'un drap ouvré à chaennes délivré audit fol, pour faire un corset sengle pour la saison d'esté, 32s p l'aune, 41 16s p.' In the same account, chaennes of silver are entered as being forged.
36. Paris, Archives nationales MS. KK8, fol. 110.
37. Id., fol. 24.
38. A. Prudhomme, 'De l'origine et du sens des mots dauphin et dauphiné', *Bibliothèque de l'Ecole des Chartes*, liv, 1893.
39. KK8, fol. 24. Jean de Garlande's thirteenth-century *Dictionarius* refers to 'capellarii faciunt cappella de filtro et de pennis pavonis . . .' (p. 20). This suggests that they were already a part of accepted official wear in France.
40. Id., fol. 18: '. . . pour lv doz de gris a fourr' iij aumuces l'une pour maistre Jehan l'aut' pour pierre touser et la tierce pour Raymondin'.
41. *Comptes*, p. 160.
42. Id., p. 207.
43. For the theory that fools who were provided with 'masters' or governors were lunatics, see A. Renel, *Réchaches Historiques sur les Fous*, pp. 24ff.
44. *Comptes*, p. 210.
45. See above, p. 27.
46. *Comptes*, p. 241: '. . . louage de 5 voictures . . . une pour maistre Jehan le fol'.
47. BL MS. Cotton Galba E III.
48. *Comptes*, p. 242.
49. G. Yver, *Le Commerce et les Marchands . . .*, p. 37.

50. The *Compagnie della Calza* were probably originally based on the Florentine *Compagnia della Gazza* which had as its original livery a poor dress, one leg covered by a worn old stocking, the other uncovered – *veccia divisa della calzia atacciata e delle gambe scalze*. S. Morpurgo, *La Compagnia della Gazza*, in *Misc. fiorentina di Erudizione e Storia*, t. II, 1897.

51. *Inventaire des Chartres*, sect. prem., ed. Gilliods van Severan, t. ii, p. 220.

52. Iohannes Porta, *Liber de Coronatione Karoli IV imperatoris*, ed. R. Salomon, in *Scrip. Re. German*, 1913. B. Jarret, in his book on Charles IV, says that at the coronation of Henry VII both emperor and empress wore their mitres with the points at the sides (p. 152).

53. *Comptes*, p. 265.

54. Muratori, *De spectaculis et Ludis Publicis*, Cap. 36, col. 840:

> Tutte le Robe sopra nominate
> Furon' in tutto trent'otto e trecento
> A' buffoni e sonatori donate

55. Id., col 841:

> Messer lionel colla sua compagnia
> D'altri Baroni, per farsesi onore
> Robe cinquecento ai Buffon dasia
> Bernabò lor fe' dar danari ancora

X *National Traits and Deviations in the Dress of the Period*

1. *Chronica Jocelini de Brakelonda de rebus gestis Samsonis Abbatis Monasterii Sancti Edmundi*, ed. Rokewode, p. 35.

2. Although Matteo di Giovanetti seems to have remained in charge, names such as Dominique de Boulbonne, Robin de Romans and Bernard Escot begin to appear on the pay-roll during Clement's papacy. See Labarde, *Le Palais des Papes* . . .

3. In 1323, John, king of Bohemia, moved his seven-year-old son from Prague to Paris, where he was educated. Baptized Wenceslas, on his confirmation in France he was renamed Charles. See CMH, vii, p. 160.

4. After its sanction by Papal Bull in 1347. See Walsh, *The Emperor Charles IV*.

5. *Chronica de Gestis Hungarorum*, Budapest, National Szechenyi Library MS. Clmae 404.

6. Giotto made a distinct difference between the dress worn on 'fashionable' occasions, e.g. the marriage of the Virgin, and those of everyday life, e.g. the Annunciation to her as a simple girl in her home. In the former, she wears an elegant and untrimmed dress with a train, in the latter, a thick dress edged with embroidery and braid.

7. For a discussion on the forms of some fourteenth-century crowns, see A. H. Benna, 'Erzherzogshut und Kaiserkrone' in *Mitteilungen des Österreichischen Staatsarchivs*, 25, Vienna, 1972.

8. British Museum, Elgin Marbles, slabs xxxix–xlii; figures 112–120.

9. As worn, for instance, by Arnolfini's wife: Jan van Eyck, London, National Gallery, no. 186.

10. Barcelona, Museu d'Art Catalunya. This fashion appears repeatedly in Catalan art of the moment, e.g. the Jaime Serra altarpiece in the same museum.

11. For later developments of this fashion, see A. Harmand, *Jeanne d'Arc: ses costumes, son armure*, Paris, 1929.

12. See illustration, p. 109.

13. e.g. sculptured relief figures on the Cathedral of Mrén in Turkey, dated in the seventh century by Michel and Nicola Thierry in *Cahiers Archeologique*, xxxi, 1971, p. 43ff. As late as the seventeenth century, European ambassadors were compelled to kiss the sleeves not the hand of the Grand Vizir. See Boppe, *Revue de Paris*, Aout 1903, p. 600.

14. Museu d'Art Catalunya.

15. Collection D. Roman Vicente, Saragossa.

16. Giotto was not alone in recording this kind of dress; see, e.g. the fourteenth-century statue of St Catherine in the Museo Castello, Verona.

17. In the simplest type of peasant shirt, the line where the sleeve joins the body-piece is frequently marked by a patch or a line of embroidery, the patterns on which have been given symbolic names such as 'river'.

18. In an arch of the western cupola, a scene of the Apostles' *Martyria*, with the inscription *Mars ruit, anguis abit, surgunt, gens Scythica credit*; thirteenth century. See O. Demus, *Byzantine Mosaic Decoration*, p. 70.

19. *Cronica*, I, Lib. 4, cap. xci, p. 391.

20. Id., I, Lib. 1, cap. xxvii, p. 34.

21. Here *acolé* is definitely referred to as a colour. See Appendix, p. 133

22. *Archivio storico per le provincie napoletane*, t. xxi, 1896, pp. 481–2.

23. e.g. in the church at Asinoli, late fourteenth century, but Europeans occur in other such frescoes too.

24. *Cronica*, I, Lib. 5, cap. 1, p. 508.

25. RIS xii. iv, Gualvaneus della Flamma, p. 37, *176.

26. But see I. Zichy in *Petrovics Elek Emlékkönyv* on clothes in the MS. The article has a summary in German.

27. *Cronica*, I, Lib. 6, cap. lv, p. 511; and cap. lxvii, p. 521.

28. Published in 1973 by Magyar Helikon, Budapest. The pages of this MS. are now dispersed among several libraries.

29. See Chapter XI below, and illustration.

30. Anonimo Romano, *Vita di Cola de Rienzo*, ed. Frugoni, p. 98.

31. Frederick's III's nobles were mocked for their long blond hair when they accompanied him to his coronation in Rome in 1452. See S. M. Newton, *Commentari*, Rome, vii pt. iv, 1957, p. 245.

32. Munich, Staatsbibliothek, Cod. Ger. 5 and Cod. Ger. 6, with date 1363 on f. ccix.

33. Vienna, Österreichisches Nationalbibliothek, MS. 2623, *Histoire des Rois d'Orient*, f. 21r, etc.

34. A *tartare* was sometimes a garment, but not, I think, at this early date; see Appendix, pp. 137, 138.

35. *Grandes Chroniques*, i, p. 27.

36. Id., ix, p. 313.
37. Holkham Bible: BL MS. Add. 47682 f. 36r.
38. See note 13 above.
39. Oxford Bodleian Library MS. 264.
40. It is very usual to find that orders for tombs were placed a considerable time before the death of the person involved which means that, though in some respects the effigies are excellent, as evidence of the fashions of the period they cannot be regarded as absolutely precise.
41. A jewelled coronet surrounding a mitre-shaped cap. See Benna, op. cit.
42. As in the frescoes at Karlsteyn and the sandstone figure made for the Charles Bridge, now in the National Museum, Prague.
43. e.g. in Prague, Klementinum MS. xxii A 6, in the Czech language, dated 1376, and *Chron. de Gest. Hung.*, ff. 57 and 70v.
44. The inclusion of details which show the behaviour of textiles is a sign that the artist was familiar with the garment he is portraying; copies of earlier works of art invariably fail to be convincing in this respect.
45. For an example of similar pleats in the later fifteenth century, see E. Birbari, *Dress in Italian Painting*, fig. 70.
46. Brussels, Bibliothèque Royale MS. 9217, *Missal, c.* 1350, ff. 11v and 115v. Louis de Mâle's coat of arms seems to have existed on the MS. but to have been obliterated later.
47. RIS xv. iv, ii, *Cronache Senese di Agnolo di Tura del Grasso*, An. 1342, p. 535: '. . . omini e donne presero quella portatura del vestire. Unde per li savi di Firenze fa biasimata e non vi potere reparare.'
48. Paris, BN MS. Fr. 1489 *passim*.
49. Brussels, Bibliothèque royale, *Chronique universelle*, MS. 9104–5, ff. 93 and 337v, for instance.
50. *Testamenter fra Danmarks Middelalder indtil 1450*, ed. Ersler, p. 70; 1334 Will of Archbishop Karl, Dipl. Svecanum, iv, 373, Rep. 1687: 'Item . . . uxori ipsi s unum kylt coloris.' Id., p. 100: 'Maj 13 Biskop Jokob, Roskilde: Item cuilibet servientium in navi nostra tunicam et caputium de sylfaar.'
51. Id., p. 78, 1338?: 'Tucho . . . Diacu, Kannikilund: Item Luice sorori mee unum gartkors . . .' p. 110, 1352: 'Petrus Helghonis, Kaldet Kanuti, Kannikilund: Item domino Esgero cappam cum wardaekors et capucio viridis coloris . . .' p. 85, 1342: 'Maj Magister Henrik Provot i Roskilde: . . . domicelle Ingeburgi ibidem blaveum meum Warthekors cum suffuratura de variis pellibus.'
52. *Svenskt diplomatarium*, ed. B. E. Hildebrand, v, 1341–7.
53. Id., pp. 152 and *passim*.
54. Id., p. 475.
55. *The Travels of Ibn Battuta . . . Ad 1325–1354*, ed. H. A. R. Gibb, ii, 445: 'The governor of this city [the city of Ayā Sulūg] is Khidr Bak . . . He sent me nothing but a single robe of silk woven with gold thread [of the kind] that they call nakh . . .' *Le Livre de Marco Polo* (French text, 1298), ed. A. J. H. Charignon, i: '. . . A Bagdad sont travaillées de nombreuses sortes de draps de soie et d'or; ce sont le "Nasich" le "Nac" le "cramoisi" et maints autres draps d'une trés belle facon.'
56. *Chramovy poklad u Sv Vita Praze*, ed. Podlaha and Sittler, p. xxvi, Za. c 282.
57. Id., Za. c 359 and Za. c 413.
58. B. Z. Kedar, *Merchants in Crisis: Genoese and Venetian Men of Affairs and the Fourteenth Century Depression*, p. 127.
59. Pat. Rolls 1347, 16 February, Reading, mem. 32, p. 249.

XI *The Fashions in Works of Art*

1. Oxford, MS. Bodley 264, illuminator Jehan de Grise.
2. 'Belonged probably to Thomas, duke of Gloucester, d. 1397.' See Pächt and Alexander, *Illuminated Manuscripts in the Bodleian Library Oxford*.
3. Identified as such in the text.
4. e.g. Reepham, Norfolk. Tomb of Sir Roger de Kerdiston, + 1337. Church of St Mary.
5. BL MS. Add. 42130.
6. Throughout the Middle Ages and later, it was obligatory for all married women to wear their heads veiled.
7. On f. 158v, Sir Geoffrey, his wife and his sister-in-law are all represented as elderly; the family assembled at table on f. 208 are not represented as old, but wear the air of boredom often associated in works of fiction with the English aristocracy.
8. On f. 147v, for instance, and worn by a fool on f. 167.
9. See L. H. Labaude, *Le Palais des Papes et les monuments d'Avignon au XIVᵉ siècle*, p. 14.
10. For the history of the wearing of the coif by serjeants-at-law, see A. Pulling, *Order of the Coif*.
11. See illustration 27, p. 87.
12. After a pattern of stripes, a checker pattern is the simplest to achieve on the loom and wool from sheep of different colours the cheapest way of producing varied colour. Tartan patterns almost certainly originated in the interweaving of natural wools of different shades.
13. See L. Bellosi, *Buffalmacco e il Trionfo della Morte*.
14. Siena, Museo dell' Opera del Duomo.
15. Marziano Bernadri, *Tre Abbazie de Piemonte*, Turin 1962, pp. 50–85.
16. Id.
17. Florence S. M. Novella; the date is either 1357 or 1358.
18. Brussels, Bibiothèque royale, MS. 9634–5.
19. *Ordonnances*, iii, p. 262.
20. Venice, Accademia.
21. Lyon, Musée des Tissus.
22. BL MS. Cotton Tiberius B VIII.
23. Munich, Staatsbibliothek, Cod. Ger. 6.
24. Also thought to be by Giovanni del Biondo. Weltchronik, Florence, Accademia.
25. *Eulogium historiarum*, iii, p. 230.

XII *Postscript*

1. A theory held, perhaps with justification, by the

late James Laver. See James Laver, *Clothes*, London, 1952, pp. 172–4.

2. In the fifteenth and sixteenth centuries, English barristers wore a mi-parti dress of plain and striped material. This was abolished at the time of the Commonwealth and never restored.

3. The whole question of the covering of the head but not by a hat, is discussed in a curious and interesting account of the *Order of the Coif* by Alexander Pulling, Serjeant-at-Law, published in London, 1884.

On barristers' dress, see W. N. Hargreaves-Mawdsley, *A History of Legal Dress in Europe until the end of the Eighteenth Century*, Oxford, 1963.

Appendix I

A Pastourelle by Froissart

The three volumes devoted to poetry (numbers 26, 27 and 28) in the Corpus of Froissart's *Oeuvres*, published in Brussels between 1867 and 1877, were edited not, as were the rest, by Baron Kervyn de Lettenhove, but by Auguste Scheler; these, the *Poésies*, are rather confusingly numbered within the *Oeuvres*, tomes I, II and III. Froissart's *Pastourelles* are included in the second volume of these three. They are untitled, and for the most part undated, but the pastourelle which appears first and concerns a *houpelande* is, Scheler pointed out in his introduction, to be found on the verso of folio 54 in MS. 831 and on the verso of folio 139 in the MS. 830, the only two manuscripts in which they are included. They were published again by Rob Roy MacGregor in *The Lyric Poems of Jehan Froissart* in 1975. Mr MacGregor designates MS. 831 as A and 830 as B in his edition, and points out that both the manuscripts are listed in the *fonds français* in the Bibliothèque Nationale in Paris. He also says that Scheler would have preferred to use A but was prevented from doing so by the current Franco–Prussian War, though he did have a brief opportunity to compare the two versions. In fact there are only few and minor differences between them where this particular poem is concerned. For a discussion on the dating of the *Pastourelles*, MacGregor refers the reader to an earlier study by E. Hoepffner, *La Chronologie des Pastourelles de Froissart*, published in honour of Émil Picot in 1913.

Hoepffner quotes the line (26), 'C'est pour la nouvelle maniere', as evidence that the *houpelande* was a newly arrived fashion and supposes that, because the two places mentioned by Froissart in the first line of the poem are in Flanders, it is likely to have been written when he was there rather than in Paris or in England, which might mean that it was written before 1360. Scheler's statement that, in both the manuscripts, the pastourelle in which a shepherd calls the attention of his companions to knights riding by wearing a newly fashionable garment, called a *houpelande*, the poem appears on the verso of a pastourelle that can be dated with some confidence in the year 1364, and early in that year, moreover, that seems to provide convincing evidence as to the date. The Pastourelle on the recto (numbered II by Scheler) begins: *Entre Eltem et Wesmoustier* and ends each verse with the words: *Cils qui porte les flours de lys*, which must mean that the poem refers to the return of Jean de France to voluntary captivity in England, early in 1364 (for a discussion on this date see page 000 above). The procession to Westminster of 'those who wear the fleurs de lys' is again observed by a group of Froissart's sophisticated shepherds, one of whom wears a *grand loudier* and another a *sousquanie*, but it is the hankering after a houpelande in Pastourelle I that signals, surely, a positive craze for the new garment.

XIV

Pastourelles

I

Entre Aubrecicourt et Mauni
Près dou chemin, sus la gasquière,
L'autre jour maint bregier oï,
Ensi qu'à heure de prangiere.
5 Là disoit Levrins Cope-osiere:
"Seignour, veïstes vous point hier
Chevauceurs par ci chevauchier
Ne houpelandes deviser?
J'en vi cascun une porter,
10 Mès j'en oc joie si très grande
Qu'onques puis ne fis que viser
A vestir une houpelande."
– "Houpelande, vrès Diex, hé mi!"
Ce li dist Willames Louviere,
15 "Et que poet estre, or le me di;
Bien cognois une panetiere,
Un jupel ou une aloiere
Unes wages, un aguillier,
Un lievre, un coler, un levrier,
20 Et se sçai bien moutons garder.
Sainnier et le pousset oster;
Mès je ne sçai, si te demande,
Qui te poet mouvoir de penser
A vestir une houpelande."

25 – "Je le te dirai, entent ci:
C'est pour la nouvelle maniere,
Car l'autrier porter une en vi,
Mance devant, mance derriere;
Ne sçai se la vesture est chiere,
30 Mès durement fait à prisier;
Bonnes sont esté et yvier,
On se poet ens enveloper,
On y poet ce qu'on voet bouter;

On y reponroit une mande,
35 Et c'est ce qui me fait penser
A vestir une houpelande."

– "Par ma foi", dist Anseaus d'Aubri,
"Je sçai bien qu'au temps çà arriere
Bregiers les portoient ensi,
40 Mès c'estoit de toile legiere,
Car encor ai je la premiere
Qui fu à mon taion Ogier."
Dont dist Adins, li fils Renier:
"Ansel, pour le corps Saint Omer,
45 Veuilliés le demain aporter,
Se metterons sus no viande,
Car aussi puis je desirer
A vestir une houpelande."

– "Seignour", dist Aloris d'Aubri.
50 "Et foi que je doi â saint Pierre.
G'irai à Douai samedi,
S'acheterai une aune entiere
De drap, se ferai la plus fiere
Qu'on vit ains porter sus bergier,
55 En aurai je assés d'un quartier
De drap pour faire ent une ouvrer?"
– "Nennil; il t'en faut pour doubler
Noef aunes d'un grant drap d'Irlande."
– "Haro! trop me poroit couster
60 A vestir une houpelande."

Princes, là les vi aviser
Et dire entre euls et deviser:
C'est bon qu'à tous bregiers on mande
Que cescuns se voeille accorder
65 A vestir une houpelande.

Appendix II

Gilles li Muisis on the Current Fashions

Gilles li Muisis, abbot of the monastery of St Martin at Tournai, dictating the bulk of his later poetry in about 1350, mused at length on the good old times – *anchienement* – in *Li Estas de tous gens séculers*. Then, he insisted, money was stable, justice was maintained and everywhere people wore well-ordered and decent clothing. Women followed the right path without vaunting pride and extravagances, dressing their heads and their bodies according to their position in society. Princesses and queens followed the appropriate rules, the wives of barons dressed their hair into only the very smallest of horns, while the wives of citizens wore clothing that was different again and suitable to their standing, wearing no other ornaments round their heads than their own beautiful plaits of hair. 'I used to see white gorgets and kerchiefs, gowns that were long and wide. For high feast days women wore their very finest suits, for Sundays and ordinary feast days their medium finery and for everyday their ordinary dress, because for every woman three suits of clothing sufficed.'

The abbot returned to the theme in poem after poem, one of them in the form of a dialogue between abbots and women. A rather shorter poem takes the form of a dialogue between abbots and men, but the most substantial and the one which expresses most of his views on the subject of dress is *Li Estas de tous gens séculers*, a poem divided by several sub-headings. A selection of verses relevant to the subject of contemporary dress is printed below. It will be noticed that Gilles li Muisis looks back to what he regarded as the good old days when buttoned sleeves were worn only by women of ill-repute and that others sewed up their sleeves, a practice also recorded in the *Roman de la Rose*. Li Muisis also refers to *cotes* themselves, fastened not with buttons but with strips of material which he calls *lopins*.

His most recurring theme, though, was the fashion for wearing tight plaits of hair which he called *cornes* and head-dresses known as *hauchettes*.

In his introduction to the *Poésies*, the baron Kervyn de Lettenhove pointed out that Gilles li Muisis 's'excuse des incorrections locales de son langage de son *Walesc* selon son expression'.

Li Estas de tous gens séculers

. . . De che temps me souvient, je vic le revenue;
Adont estoit justice partout bien maintenue,
Et li boine monnoie d'argent bien soustenue;
De florins couroit pau selonc me retenue.

On portoit les abis ordenés et honniestes;
On alast tout partout, c'estoit toutes fiestes;
On ne savoit nouvielles de wières, de tempiestes
Je vic k'on s'entr'amoit plus que biestes demiestes.

Comment orghieus et envie règnent ès femmes

. . . Anchiènement les fames chelle voie tenoient;
Toutes humles habis et honniestes portoient;
Sans orghuel, sans quintises, les kiés*, les corps ornoient
Et selonc leur estas avoir leur souffissoient.

Selonc les maladies fait-on les médechines.
C'est voirs que moult de fames sont gentieus par orines*,
Si kon chevalereuses princesses et roynes;
Chelles ont par coustume de leurs adours doctrines.

Moulliers sont à signeurs, si les convient orner;
Jadis les veoit-on moult petit encorner,
De leur cheviaus sans plus, si que nuls suborner
Ne les pooit nul mal en l'oraille corner.

Bourgeoises, autres fames, autres abis portoient,
Et selonc leur estas leur abis maintenoient,
Les cheviaus d'autres fame nullement ne portoient,[1]
Mais des leurs bielles traices entour les kiés faisoient . . .

Je vi les moulekins* les anchiènes porter,
Depuis blans warcolles*, blans quariaus* resorter
C'estoit trop bielle cose d'elles vir cohorter,
En honneurs se savoient bien et biel enhorter.

A ches manches pendans surcos adont portoient,
D'abis larges et lons trèstoutes se viestoient,
Et souvent par vinages ensanle s'assanoient;
Tout chil qui leur maintiens veoient, les prisoient . . .

Pour nueches, pour haus jours, boines reubes avoient;
En fiestes, en dimenches leur moyennes portoient,
Et par les honmes jours des menres se passoient,
Car troy paire de dras as femmes souffisçoient.

On portoit caperons u de drap u de saye;
Li fouret de cendal leur sanloit* cose gaye;
Leur mère resanler volloient et leur taye:
Par droit li boine vois le boine canchon paie.

Estrois sorlées à las et manches boutenées
Che portoient adont les femmes diffamées.
Pour boutons dorelos portoient les senées,
Et de manches cousues estoient bien parées.

Par des sous les mamelles haut et biel se chindoient;
Lors joyaus as chintures portoient et pendoient,
Et de petits lopins* lor cotes lopinoient;
Et trèstout leur abis, honniestes se monstroient.

Or estoient aucunes u rèses u tonsées
Et les autres estoient et bien et biel huées;
Traiches de kevelures de senais assanlées.
Et tout entour leur kiés portoient ordenées.

D'apariaus de hauchaites n'estoit nulle nouvielle;
En leur simple abis veoit-on tost le bielle;
En sages et en humles nuls orghieus ne revielle,
Devant humilitet tost oste se vielle.

On ne pourtast pour riens cheviaus d'estragnes femmes,
Ne de mortes aussi, che fust trop grant diffames,
Ne meskines*, ne filles, ne trèstoutes les dames
Pourquoi? S'on le tenist, che fust hontes et blames.

Mais en tele manière leurs corps, leur chief ornoient
Et en humilitet leur abis ordenoient,
Que chil qui leur maintiens et leur pors rewardoient,
Et marit et tout homme les femmes hounouroient . . .

Deus judex, justus, fortis, et patiens

Orghieus se tapisçoit, or pert tieste levée;
Orghieus voelt que li femme soit quointement parée
Dou chief, de tout le corps noblement achainmée:
Orghieus fait toutes femmes jeuer à simagrée.

Tout chou que femmes voellent, marcheant tantost vendent;
Robes, caperons, pliche pour monstre faire pendent;
Li baron, li parent de riens ne les reprendent;
A leur filles les mères les quointises aprendent . . .

On me dist de leur kiés comment elles les pèrent,
Comment cornes, haucettes et chil cheviel appèrent,
Et le plentet d'espingles leur warcollet compèrent,
Comment al adouber meskines se despèrent . . .

Elles monstrent hatriaus, gargates et poitrines.
Helas! che ne sont mie les anchienes doctrines;
Anchiènement amascent mieuls gésir en espines
K'elles usascent tant d'espingles, ne de pines . . .

Glossary

(*from Kervyn de Lettenhove edition*)
moulekins = Vêtement en usage au commencement
du XIVe siècle
orines = origines
warcoles = collarettes
quariaus = étoffe
sanloit = souliers
lopins = petits morceaux d'étoffes
meskines = servante
hatriaus = la gorge
gargate = la gorge

130

Appendix III

Extracts from Some Sumptuary Regulations, 1340–65

At intervals during the fourteenth century, the heads of state in most European countries issued regulations governing personal expenditure: how much could be spent on weddings and sometimes on funerals; what food the comparatively poor were allowed to eat – usually meat or fowl not more than once a day, and for other meals either milk or cheese. No such beneficial rules were imposed on the rich. Clothing came under special scrutiny almost everywhere, and here, again, the population was divided into precise categories, according to some extent to rank but mainly to income.

The Church also issued its own regulations, aimed less at special income groups but directed, rather, towards the general control of ostentatious luxury and devices meant to deceive. In Florence in the early years of the fourteenth century, very detailed rules were issued by the Church, and many of them, like all sumptuary regulations, became irrelevant as fashions changed, though the prohibitions governing the wearing of false hair were probably applicable throughout the century, or at least until the fashion for short hair and compact hair dressings came into fashion.

In 1310, Antonio d'Orso Biliotti, bishop of Florence and Fiesole, gave orders that nobody of any class or standing whatsoever was to indulge in fraud by wearing on the head, with intent to deceive, any fluffed-out false hair – *zazzerris* – long falling hairpieces – *casciettis* – strands of hair or curls, although any woman whose own hair was manifestly inadequate might wear plaits of flax, wool, cotton or silk attached to her own hair, thus avoiding undue ornamentation while appearing natural. The original of the passage is quoted by Richard Trexler in his *Synodal Law in Florence and Fiesole*.

Nearer to the period covered by the present study were the regulations laid down in the city of Lucca at the end of the 1330s and reissued in later years. The *Bandi Lucchese del secolo decimoquarto*, published under the editorship of Salvatore Bongi in 1863, were typical of the attitude to personal expenditure all over Europe. The *Bandisce* of 11 April 1337, like almost all the Lucchese regulations concerned with clothes, apply only to women's dress and to those artisans who wove the stuff of which it was made. They begin by stating that no lady or woman – *donna o femma* – must presume to wear pearls on the head or any head-dress or garland that cost more than a stated sum; equally strict rules prohibited the making or wearing of gold or jewelled belts or other ornaments. No gold fringe or cloth of gold was allowed unless it had been bought at an earlier period; the top price that might be paid for any stuff worn by either married or unmarried women was stated. Silk cloths with interwoven patterns and velvets were forbidden, only plain silks were allowed. The number of garments that could be worn was regulated, and so was the length of the train. Nobody, either in the city or outside it, was to break any of these rules by cutting or sewing forbidden stuff. The only fur allowed was *vair*, and no stockings – *calsoraio o calsiuolo* – to be made for any female over the age of seven.

A sumptuary regulation of 5 January 1346 was concerned with the weaving and dyeing of stuffs, especially silk materials. In this category there appears what may seem a strange prohibition: that of forbidding the weaving of any stuff from the hair of asses, horses, bulls or buffalo, but this may indeed have been a temptation of the time, for English regulations as applied to the wool trade forbade the intermingling of such types of hair with English wool.

In Spain, as in Italy, each independent state issued its own rules. In Castile, in 1348, Alfonso XI was as much concerned with the clothing of men as of women and stated quite simply that no man might wear ornaments of gold braid, lace, ermine, rubies or other precious stones, buttons of gold, silver or enamel; nor must his clothing be embroidered with gold thread, silver or silk, nor sewn with jewels nor trimmed with fringes; there appear to have been some exceptions, but belted knights, although they were allowed any belts they preferred, still might not wear belts made of gold thread nor even embellished with it or sewn with precious stones.

Alfonso further directed that only the heir to the throne – *Infante* – was permitted to wear cloth of silk or gold, though his sons could wear brocaded or silk garments so long as they were not ornamented with gold or jewels; other men were permitted sendal, taffetas and *tomasol* (apparently a shiny material) for linings. There were, however, exceptions made for weddings and knightly assemblies, where men of wealth were allowed to wear cloth of gold or of silk. As for women, those who should know better, the regulations state, wear trains at court, in the palaces and in the cities; these are costly and financially damaging to their husbands. Except when they are riding pillion on horseback, when trains were permitted, they should wear gowns which reached the ground only, or, perhaps, with trains no more than the length of two fingers on the ground.

Further regulations applied to the wives of citizens or merchants who owned horses and their relations, who were allowed to wear white fur and sendal with some gold braid; and this applied also in Seville, which drew up regulations too. Again the test seemed to be the ownership of a horse: those who did own one might permit their wives to wear sendal and white fur with some gold ornaments; those who did not, could not allow their wives to wear white fur, sendal or any ornaments of gold.

Artisans of Seville were not to give wedding gifts of clothing except of a dark colour or white, and sendal was to be restricted to a very small amount, used as a little trimming only.

As well as strict rulings regarding the making of stuffs and the prices that could be charged for the making of specific garments, Pedro the Cruel, in 1351, attempted to control the clothes worn by women 'companions' of the clergy by reissuing earlier instructions that their clothes were to be confined to striped cloth of Ypres, striped *tiritani* or striped Valenciana – an indication of the esteem in which striped woollen cloths were held by this time. Over their heads, their white veils were to be encircled by a bright red band, three fingers wide, to distinguish them from other women.

Repeatedly reissued, these, and many other injunctions from various parts of Spain, were published in 1788 by Juan Sempere y Guarinos, as a *Historia del Luxo y de Leyes suntuarias de España*.

Venice began its sumptuary regulations of 1360 with statements as to how much money could be given as a wedding present and continued immediately with the limitation imposed on the value of gold, silver and precious stones that might be worn by girls over the age of eight. These are followed by orders as to the maximum value of jewelled buckles, belts, purses, chains and little knives that were permitted to women in any station of life. No married or unmarried woman was to have or to wear stuff embellished with gold, silver or pearls except for a brooch. Restrictions were laid on silks and velvet worn on the head, but cendal was excepted. No Venetian boy over twelve years of age was to wear gold, silver or pearls above the weight of 12 ounces, no vair or gris or velvet, no fastenings on belts to exceed the value of 12 ducats; no male between the ages of twelve and twenty-five was to wear on his *clamide*, *capa*, *risalio* or other mantle fur of gris or vair; linings of suits were not to cost more than 10 ducats. These and other Venetian sumptuary laws of the year 1360 were published by Romolo Broglio d'Ajano, *Die venetianische Seidenindustrie und ihr Organisation bis zum Ausgang des Mittelalters*, Stuttgart 1893.

In England, in 1363, sumptuary regulations were inscribed in the *Rotuli Parliamentorum*, published as the *Statutes of the Realm* in 1810, in the original French with a parallel text in the English of the period. It is stated that because of the 'Outrageous and Excessive Apparel of divers people', servants, grooms and artisans are not to wear gold, silver or enamel. The cloth of their suits, including their hose, is not to exceed 2 marks the piece. They are to wear no budge but only lamb, cony, cat and fox. Master craftsmen are not to wear cloth costing more than 40s. the piece, and no gold, silver and so on. Wives were not to exceed the cost of their husbands' clothing for their own; their veils were not to cost more than 12d. each. The regulations are long and detailed and cover a wide field. Walsingham recorded them in a shortened form and was quoted by Camden, also briefly. He also made the comment that the laws had no effect – 'Sed haec omnia nulli effectum capiebant.'

To the student of dress, sumptuary laws, even though ignored, are important as guides to the temptations of their periods. It is noticeable that, in the middle of the fourteenth century, as well as prohibitions on the wearing of gold, silver, jewels and enamel, fine furs were forbidden to several categories of people, thus confirming the strictly limited categories of people to whom they were issued by the official wardrobes. Richly ornamented belts, too, must have been coveted by everyone everywhere at the time.

Appendix IV
Garments, Stuffs and Colours

It will be seen immediately that the brief list of items of clothing, stuffs and colours included in this appendix is not intended to be in any way comprehensive. It is no more than an attempt to provide some examples of some of the differing opinions and explanations published by earlier students of the subject, and, in the light of the present study, to view them critically. A great deal has certainly been overlooked by the present author; few final conclusions have been reached, a good deal of material by earlier authors has been rejected on the grounds that support for their views has seemed inadequate. The survey of opinions on the term 'pers' has been included as an example of this.

Although garments, materials and colours were subject to extremely rapid changes of fashion, the general terminology was often retained over a long period, with the result that the same name may, over the years, have been given to things of very widely different character, as happens now and has happened in the recent past: a crinoline need no longer be constructed of *crin* – horsehair was abandoned very quickly. Some of the original character does, however, usually survive, and later references may often provide a clue as to the nature or identity of some puzzling garments, fabrics or colours. In using early dictionaries and glossaries, it also has to be remembered that their authors often relied to some degree, and often very greatly, on earlier works. John Balbi's famous *Catholicon*, so frequently copied after its first compilation in 1286 and later published, was indebted to some extent to two earlier works, encyclopedias compiled in about 1053 and 1212.

The excellent introduction and notes by Albert Way to his edition of the English–Latin dictionary, the *Promptorium Parvulorum*, compiled in about 1440 by 'Brother Geoffrey', discuss the debt to the *Catholicon* and include references to later works as well, of which John Palsgrave's French dictionary of 1530 can prove unexpectedly useful. In the *Promptorium Parvulorum*, there appear terms which had manifestly changed their meaning since the middle of the fourteenth century, and this, in itself, is an interesting comment on the nature of fashion.

In the end only strictly contemporary sources can be regarded as absolutely reliable (though even here the clerks and tailors were, as has been pointed out, under no obligation to be accurate). Nevertheless, authors or clerks who were personally familiar with the object themselves, though they may have used a private language, were, on the whole, consistent in the terms they used for specific things. Later scholars, even those as scrupulous as Du Cange, were, for obvious reasons, not really acquainted with the things they were identifying.

In publishing his *Comptes de l'argenterie des rois de France*, in 1851, Louis Douët D'Arcq added a glossary of technical words which occur in the *comptes* in that particular collection. On the evidence he drew from them, Douët D'Arcq based his carefully reasoned explanations of the nature of the garments, fabrics and colours he had extracted from them. This glossary is still to be greatly recommended; in only a very few cases has the study of other contemporary inventories and accounts shown his reasoning to be at fault.

The abbreviations used in the list below are as follows:

Dizionario etimologico italiano:	*Diz. et. it.*
Douët D'Arcq:	D. D.
Du Cange:	Du C.
Godefroy:	Gode.
Grande Larousse:	*Gr. Lar.*
Greek:	Gr.
Latham:	La.
Latin:	Lat.
Francisque Michel:	Mi.
Oxford English Dictionary:	OED
Pegolotti:	Peg.
Promptorium Parvulorum:	*Pr. Par.*

Names in italic are those of authors to be found in the bibliography.

Acolé/accolé/accolie: Two separate theories have been

put forward concerning the meaning of this word. *Laurent* follows *Espinas*. *Laurent*: 'Les "accolées" etaient evidement des draps ou les rayures étaient accollea' (Espinas, ii, p. 156). D. D.: 'c'etait vraisembl-ablement des drap à raies doubles et rapprochées'. But it has also been thought of as meaning 'without colour': *Dic. tech. polyglo.*: 'Span. acoluria, falta de pigmentos biliares na urina; Fr *acoluria.*' It seems, however, that the term is certainly botanical: *Gr. La.*: '*acolée* Genre de plantes hepatiques v. gymnomitrum [wild columbine]', and therefore a dull purplish colour. *Archivio storico per le provincie Napoletane* 1896, p. 481: '. . . un caprenso di panno di lana di color accollea'. Paris, Archives nationales, MS. KK8: '. . . un fin marbre violet de graine . . . vj autres acolez violez deliv' aus phisiciens'. Acolé appears sometimes in a list of striped cloths (v. App. V), but from these it is clear that it is used in the sense of a colour.

Aketon, doublet, pourpoint, etc.

Aketon: It is doubtful whether at any one time the exact differences between an aketon, a pourpoint, a doublet, a courtpiece and a jupon were absolutely defined. In France, the cotehardie comes into this category, and in England, from the early 1360s, the paltok. PRO E101/391/11 consists of: 'Particulars of an account of John Goldbetere for making a doublet' in 1347, but the heading on the account itself reads not as above, but as the making of a 'p' point cū vam-braces'. John Goldbetere's doublet/pourpoint was covered with *cammelace* and tied with gold ribbons. *Heyd*, II: *aketon* from cotton, Arabic *kotn*. Planché quotes the Chron. Bert du Guesclin, 'Le hacuton fut de bonquerant', but probably misread *bouquerant* as 'bonquerant'. Mi. ii: '. . . je crois que le mot auketon désigne un pourpoint piqué que l'on mettait sous le haubert et qui était ordinairement de coton blanc'. PRO E101/392/14 (1359–60) has doublets covered with linen and fustian and aketons covered with cloth of various colours. But see Appendix V for an *aketon* for the king covered with camocas.
    Doublet: *Catholicon*: diplois, duplex vestis et est vestis militaris.
    Paltok: *Pr. Par.*: *Baltheus*. E101/394/16 (1363–4), by which time paltoks were in general use at the English court.
    Jupon: *Winner and Waster*: 115, 'With a jupown full juste, joynede by the sydes', is a clear indication that, in the view of the author of that poem at least, the *jupon* did not have a front fastening in some cases.

Atour: General term for head-dress of a woman, used rarely at this period in inventories and accounts, but see D. D., where both *atours* and *tourez* occur: *Comptes*, p. 293. Li Muisis: '. . . leurs cornes, traices, adours ostoient . . .' Occurs very frequently in French in the fifteenth and sixteenth centuries especially in accounts of René d'Anjou.

Couvrechief: Sometimes refers to a stuff, sometimes to an object. Ordonnances des rois de France: 'de Toilles appellées couvrechiefs . . .' D. D.: 'Et furent de cueuvrechefs blans, broudées et orfroisiées par dessus' (given by the queen to the young princes of Navarre, 1342). PRO E101/394/9 (1361–62) lists five varieties: crispes, cambrey, relusant, cipré, boillez'; all were issued by the piece and may have been veils. E101/390/5 (1343–4): 'ij cou'chiefs curt p̄ Rege faciend consuta t' radiat' de albo s'ico.' These appear in the same section as 'v volupiorȝ pro capite Regis', which were also elaborately worked; La. identification of volupior as 'wool-wrapper' could, in view of the above, appear misleading.

Glaucus: Lat. from Gr. Used as a rule to denote a quiet colour round about grey, e.g. greenish grey and bluish grey, but could at some periods mean bright or, shining, and hence, no doubt, *Pr. Par.*: 'ȝelhwe (yellow) = *glaucus*.' La.: . . . "yellow" post 1394. *Glaucus* appears in some English great wardrobe accounts. PRO E101/393/15 (1360–61): 'pann mixt glaus' issued to knights, squires and valets.
    See also the entry for *Pers* in the present list.

Grain/graine: Name given to a dye made from insects known as *kermes* which infested certain trees in parts of southern Europe and which, when dried, were mistaken for grains or seeds. The word *kermes* existed in many variants and gave rise to such words as *crimson*. The dye produced from these insects was the strongest and most satisfactory form of red and, because in some areas the insects were known as *vermiculi* (or variants), the word vermilion could be used for the dye they produced. Mixed with other dyes, *grain* could produce purple and violet: Paris, Archives nationales MS. KK8: 'un fin marbre violet de graine'. Not to be confused with cochineal, which produced an inferior red dye.

Moison: Measurement. Used especially in French argenterie accounts with reference to cloth of Brussels. Peg. gives a table of comparative measure-ments of stuffs made in Venice, Antwerp, Brussels, Nîmes and Montpellier. D. D., *Comptes*: 'marbré brun de la grant moison de Broixells'; 'merbré cendré de courte moison'.

Paddebury: Apparently not to be found in any diction-ary or glossary and used, it seems, in only one instance in this period: PRO E101/389/14 (1342–3): 'ad un' paddebury fac & furr' 2/-s'. This was a comparatively low cost for making a garment for the king. May have been used in connection with his crossing to Brittany.

Pallium: Used especially in France to denote official dress. *Ordonnances des Rois de France*, 1349: 'Magister Petrus de Lingonis consiliarus Regis . . . pro pallio suo . . .'

Pers/persico/Persam: D. D. (1352): '. . . un fin pers asuré, des loncs de Broixelles . . .' La. '1) *persic/um*, peach . . . *pers/icum* . . . 'perse', dark blue cloth . . .' *Gr. La.*: '*Pers, Perse* adj. (pér, pér-se) La nuance quē l'on désignait jadis soūs le nom de *pers* doit sans doute son origine a quelque substance colorante que l'on tirait de la Perse. Toute fois Du

Cange, suivi par. Littré, le fait venir du Latin per-sicum, pêche, pretendant qu'il y a de l'analogie entre la couleur perse et celle de la peche, ce qui nous parait peu fondé. Ménage a recours au grec *prasos*, poireau; mais ici le passage de *prasos* à *pers* semble difficile). Se dit d'une nuance de bleu particulière: *Des yeux pers. Chaperon de couleur perse* (Acad). *Minerve aux yeux pers, La déesse aux yeux pers.* Expressions par lesquelles les poétes ont traduit l'expression homerique Glaukopis Athêne. *Tout le reste entourait la déesse aux yeux pers.* La Fontaine. – s.m. Drap bleu pers: Un manteau de PERS.'

This *Larousse* entry leads into the question as to the tint of the colour referred to in fourteenth-century great wardrobe accounts and other inventories as *glaucus*, which is certainly *not* blue in a Swedish inventory (*Svensk-Diplomatarum*, 1341–7), where the entry 3845 is a list made of the possessions of Ingeborgs of Sweden after the death of her husband: 'unum antependium de veluro blaueo et glauco . . .'.

It seems certain that *pers* was used to mean some sort of blue in the fourteenth century, but whether pale or dark is so far impossible to discover.

Samite/samitellus: See *Muratori*, ii, diss. xxiv: '. . . sive serici ut Examiti . . .'. Lat. *Examitus*; Gr. *Hexamitos* = six threads. D. D. has a long entry for *samit*: 'Etoffe de soie, se rapprochant beaucoup du satin', but there seems no evidence for the resemblance. Used extensively in France and England for furnishings as well as clothing. For her anointing at her coronation, queen Philippa wore a 'tunic '& mantel' doubl'' of *samitellus*.

Sindon: Sometimes confused with *cendal*, which can appear as *sendal* (*Pr. Par.*), but whereas *cendal* is certainly silk, sindon is probably either cotton or hempen stuff. 'Sindon of Lombardy' mentioned in E101/388/8. Often qualified as 'strengthened' afforc'. E101/394/12 'sindon de trip'' (Tripoli?), 'per ell 3/-s, per piece 26/-s'; 'sindon afforc'' 14d the ell, 20/-s the piece', and in most accounts prices are round about the same. Also came from Cologne, apparently, Antiquaries MS. 541 (1330): 'sindon de colon' p̄ stuffur' (an aketon). Du C. considered *sindon* to have been the *byssus* of the Bible. OED 1) a fine thin fabric of linen; a kind of cambric or muslin. But the earliest reference to it there is of 1450, by which time it may have changed its character. *PR. Par.*: 'Sendel = sindon (Catholicon).'

Tull/Tuly: *Winner and Waster*, 82: 'Tasselde of tuly silke, tuttynge out fayre'; in reference to the arms of England. *Pr. Par.*: 'Tuly, coloure – puniceus vel penicus CF in urina [puniceus = red, purple: cruor; rosa; crocus].' *Diz. et. it Tulle* (mod. *tulle*).' Mi.: suggests (II, 248) that *Tuly* is a stuff, probably in the fourteenth-century cotton.

Appendix V

Some extracts from the English Great Wardrobe Accounts Relevant to the Making of Special Garments and the Costs and Lengths of Stuffs in General Use

E101/390/5 (1343–4): *Doublet and aketon compared*

Two doublets for the king, materials used:

Two doublets		*One doublet*	
sindon	2 ells	sindon	1 ell
green longcloth	2½ ells	green longcloth	2½ ells
linen of Rheims	12 ells	linen of Rheims	6 ells
linen of Paris	12 ells	linen of Paris	6 ells
silk ribbon	3 pieces	silk ribbon	3 pieces
silk thread	¼ lb	silk thread	⅛ lb
cotton wool	3 lbs	cotton wool	1½ lbs

Nine aketons; covered with striped fustian, each enclosed a coat of mail or plate:

Nine aketons		*Rough estimate for each*	
fustian	23 ells	fustian	2½ ells
bolt cloth	29 pieces	bolt cloth	3.2 pieces
short linen of Rheims	8 ells	short linen of Rheims	1 ell
short linen of Paris	58 ells	short linen of Paris	6.4 ells
sindon afforcat'	1 piece + 2 ells	sindon afforcat'	0.11 pieces
silk thread	¾ lbs	silk thread	.08 lbs
cotton wool	21 lbs	cotton wool	2.3 lbs
linen thread	4 lbs	linen thread	½ lb
deer skin	1	deerskin	½
wide gold ribbon	1 piece	wide gold ribbon	0.11 pieces
aiguilettes	216	aiguilettes	24

One aketon for the king:

camocas	4 ells
linen of Rheims	4½ ells
linen of Paris	4½ ells
cotton wool	3 lbs
silk thread	¼ lb
sindon	1 ell

[Taking into consideration the varying widths of the materials, it is still clear that there is very little difference between the amounts used for the king's doublet and for his aketon.]

Clothes and stuffs for making them for the memorial service at St Paul's following the death in England of Jean Iİ of France on 8 April 1364. Included in E101/394/16, mem. 15.

Eidem (William Kareswell, Edward's tailor) ad unam cotam & unam cloc' long cum capuc' de pann̄ nigr̄ long in g'no (in grain) p̄ fun'alibȝ dm̄ Regis ffranc' faciend' & furrurand'

vij ul̄n dj̄ pann̄ nigr	In g'no
j furr de ccxlj ventr'	m'n pur'
j cloc' de Dclvij ventr'	m'n pur'
j capuc' de lxxviij ventr'	m'n pur'

Eidem ad facturam c cot' cum tot capuc de pann blankett curt p̄ portoribȝ torch̄ ('torch-bearers) p̄ eisdem funal' R̄ⁱˢ ffranc in e'llia sci Pauli.

iiijᶜ ul̄n dj̄ pann	Blanket curt
vj ul̄n p̄ iiij qrt	Tele Henaudz [Hainault linen]

Eidem (Roger Sutton, tailor to Edmund of Langley) ad unan cot' & una' cloc' long' cum capuc' de pann' nigr in g'no p̄ eodem dn̄o p̄ fun'alibȝ R̄ⁱˢ ffranc fac' p̄ mil r̄p̄r xv die apl (April 15).

vij ul̄n pann̄ nigr' long' In g'no

800E101/392/3 (1350–1)
Furs in order of value:

Ermine
Trimmed miniver (menuvarius puratus)
Semi trimmed miniver
Coarse miniver (menuvarius grossus)

Bishe
Popellus
Stranling
Budge
Lamb

E101/392/3 (1350–1)
Precious stuffs; in order:

Velvett'
Camac'
Baldekyn'
Rakematȝ

Nak
Cigaston
Pann̄ arg'
Zatan̄
Samitell'
Nasskyki

E101/394/9 (Heading missing, but 1361–2)
Precious stuffs; in order:

Velvett
Satyn
Pann̄ adaur' de Luk   (Lucca)
Pann̄ adaur' Baldekyn
Pann̄ adaur' doutrem'   (d'Outremer)
Racamatȝ arg'
Sigaston adaurum
Pann̄ s'ic Baldekyns   (pannus serico)
Camaka dupl'
Camaka sengl'
Tartarin

Comparative lengths of pieces of stuffs of various types

Cotton MS. Galba E III (1333)

Cloth of Louvain:	long cloth 27 ells
	short cloth 23 ells

These measurements for woollen cloths seem to have remained more or less constant.

E101/390/1 (1343)

Brussels long cloth, scarlet and in grain	28 ells
Short cloth and blanket	23 ells
Striped cloths	24 ells
Cloth of Candlewickstrete	38 ells
Velvett'	8 ells
Samitellus	7½ ells
Fustian	16 ells

E101/391/4 (1342–3)

Blanket col', curt', russet curt'	23 ells
Radiat'	24 ells
Candlewickstrete	24 ells

E101/394/12 (Probably 1361–2) (Isabel's marriage clothes are included in this)

Baldekyn	6½ ells
Sarznett'	11 ells
Satyn	8 ells
Velvett'	8 ells

137

Prices of stuffs: woollen cloths are listed as by the 'cloth' (pannus), silks by the 'piece' (pecia).

SILKS
E101/390/1 (1343)

Velvet		*price per piece*
Velvet striped gold,	bought in Bruges	£7. 0. 0.
Coloured, 'various',	bought in London	3. 13. 4.
Coloured, 'various',	bought in London	5. 0. 0.
Coloured, 'various',	bought in London	4. 10. 0.
Striped	bought in London	4. 0. 0.
Length of piece 8 ells		

Camocas		
–	bought in Bruges	1. 0. 0.
Various colours	bought in Bruges	1. 1. 0.
Powdered with gold	bought in London	3/-s per ell
Red and Ynde	bought in London	3/-s per ell
'Double' camocas	bought in London	16¾ ells for £5. 13 .4.

Length of piece not stated but likely to be between 7 and 8 ells.

Ciclaton		
Cloth of gold	bought in London	4. 0. 0.
Cigaston		
Cloth of gold	bought in London	3. 6. 8.

Length of piece not stated.

Diaspinus		
Gold	bought in London	1. 10. 0.

Length not stated.

Tartarin		
–	bought in London	1. 2. 0.

Length not stated

Disapinettus		
	bought in London	15. 0.

Length not stated

Samitellus		
	bought in London	1. 4. 0.

Length of piece 7½ ells

Prices of stuffs

WOOLLENS
1343 E101/390/1

In grain, per cloth	
Violet	£8. 0. 0.
Mixed, brown?/red	8. 13. 4.
Murray	9. 0. 0.
Murray	7. 13. 4.

Length of each cloth 28 ells

Brussels longcloth	
Mixed red/brown	4. 0. 0.
Mixed acol	4. 0. 0.
Mixed red/brown	6. 13. 4.
Acol	6. 13. 4.
Marbryn/keynet	6. 13. 4.
White	5. 0. 0.

'Various' colours	5. 6. 8.	
Russet	6. 10. 0.	
Green	6. 10. 0.	
Garnet	8. 0. 0.	
Length of each cloth 28 ells		

Coloured short cloths		
White	2. 6. 8.	
kernet (garnet)	1. 1. 0.	
Length of each cloth 23 ells		

Striped cloths		
'Divers' colours	2. 6. 8.	
Brown stripe, camelyn ground	2. 0. 0.	
White ground	2. 3. 4.	
Red, brown, white	2. 0. 4.	
Glaucus stripe, murray ground	2. 0. 0.	
'Ash' colour, white stripes	2. 0. 0.	
White stripes, acol ground + pattern	2. 6. 8.	
Glaucus stripes, mixed ground	2. 1. 0.	
Length of each cloth 24 ells		

Blanket		
per cloth	3. 2.	
Length of cloth 23 ells		

Candlewickstrete		
per cloth	1. 15. 0.	
Length of cloth 38 ells		

Bibliography

Ancona, Alessandro d', *Origini del Teatro italiano*, i, Florence, 1877; reprinted, Rome, 1966.

Anonimo, Romano, *Vita di Cola di Rienzo*, ed. A. Frugoni, Florence, 1957.

Anstey, H., *Munimenta Academica, or Documents illustrative of academical life and studies at Oxford*, ii, RS, 1868.

Achery, Dom Luc d', *Recueil des Ordonnances des Rois de France*, ed. Delaurière, ii, iii, Paris, 1729.

Ashmole, Elias, *The Institution, Laws and Ceremonies of the Most Noble Order of the Garter*, London, 1672. Reprinted in facsimile edition by Muller, London, 1971.

Azarii, Petri, *Liber gestorum in Lombardia*, ed. F. Cognasso, RIS, xvi. iv.

Balducci: Pegolotti, Francesco, *La Practica della Mercatura*, ed. A. Evans, Cambridge, Massachusetts, 1936.

Barber, Richard, *Edward, Prince of Wales and Aquitaine. A Biography of the Black Prince*, London, 1978.

Barberino, Francesco da, *Reggimento e Costumi di Donna*, ed. G. E. Sansone, Turin, 1957.

Baudot, Jules, *Les Princesses Yolande et les ducs de Bar, de la famille des Valois*, Pt I, Paris, 1900.

Bellosi, Luciano, *Buffalmacco e il Trionfo della Morte*, Turin, 1974.

Beltz, G. F., *Memorials of the Most Noble Order of the Garter*, London, 1841.

Birbari, Elizabeth, *Dress in Italian Painting, 1460–1500*, London, 1975.

Bishop, Morris (translator and editor), *Letters from Petrarch, Selected and Translated*, Indiana University Press, 1966.

Boase, Roger, *The Troubadour Revival*, London, 1978.

Boccaccio, Giovanni, *Decamerone*, I Classici popolari, Milan, 1966.

Brayley, E. W., *Westminster Abbey*, London, 1818.

Bruges: Inventaire des Archives de la Ville de Bruges: i.i., Inventaire des Chartes par L. Gilliods van Severen, première serie, treizième au seizième siécle, ii, Bruges, 1871–85.

Brun, Durand (ed.), *Recueil d'Anciens Inventaires*, i: Inventaire des Biens, Mobiliers et Immobiliers d'un Jurisconsulte de Valence 1348, Paris, 1896.

Calendar of the Close Rolls, H.M. Stationery Office.

Calendar of the Patent Rolls, H.M. Stationery Office.

Calendar of State Papers, Venetian, H.M. Stationery Office.

Cambridge Medieval History, vii: *Decline of Empire and Papacy*, Cambridge, 1932.

Canel, A. *Récherches historiques sur les fous des rois de France et Assessoirement sur l'emploi du Fou en général*, Paris, 1873.

Capasso, Bartolommeo, *Le Fonti della storia delle provincie napolitane dal 568 al 1500,* ed. F. O. Mastrojanni, Naples, 1902.

Catholicon, The, Dictionary of John Balbi of 1286, ed. S. I. H. Herrtage, EETS, 75, London, 1881.

Chadwick, Henry, *Pelican History of the Church*, vi: *The Early Church*, London, 1968.

Chandos Herald, *The Black Prince, an historical poem written in French with translation and notes by the revd. Henry Octavius Coxe MA*, London, 1842. [Printed for the Roxburghe Club.]

Chestre, Thomas, *Sir Launfal*, ed. A. J. Bliss, London, 1960.

Choisy, F. T. de, *Histoires de Philippe de Valois et du roi Jean*, Paris, 1688.

Colvin, H. M., *The History of the King's Works*, 2 vols., H.M. Stationery Office, 1963.

Comptes de l'Argenterie . . ., see Douët D'Arcq, L.

Deanesly, Margaret, *A History of the Medieval Church, 590–1500*, London, 1969.

Delepierre, Octave, *Analyse des Travaux de la Societé des Philobiblon de Londres*, i, ii, v, London, 1854–62. *Notes et documents relatifs à Jean, Roi de France et sa captivité en Angleterre*, par S. A. R. le Duc d'Aumale, London, 1854–62.

Demus, Otto, *Byzantine Mosaic Decoration*, London, 1947 (reprinted 1957).

Denholme-Young, N., *The Country Gentry in the Fourteenth Century, with Special Reference to the Heraldic Rolls of Arms*, Oxford, 1969.

Depping, G. B., *Règlements sur les arts et métiers de Paris*, Paris, 1837–85.

—, *Histoire du Commerce entre le Levant et l'Europe depuis les Croisades . . .*, 2 vols., Paris, 1830.

Dinaux, Arthur, *Trouvères, jongleurs et ménestrels du*

nord de la France et du midi de la Belgique, Paris, 1837–63.

Douët D'Arcq, Louis, *Comptes de l'argenterie des Rois de France*, Paris, 1851.

—, *Nouveau Recueil de comptes de l'Argenterie des Rois de France*, Paris, 1874.

Dozy, R., *Dictionnaire détaillé des noms des Vêtements chez les Arabes*, Amsterdam, 1845.

Erslev, Kr., *Testamenter fra Danmarks middelalder indtil 1450*, Copenhagen, 1901.

Espinas, Georges, and Pirenne, Henri, *Recueil de documents relatifs a l'histoire de l'industrie drapière en Flandre*, Brussels, 1906.

Evans, Joan, *Art in Mediaeval France 987–1498*, Oxford, 1948.

—, *Dress in Medieval France*, Oxford, 1952.

Fouquet, Jean, *Heures de maistre Estienne Chevalier*, ed. L'Abbé Delaunay, [n.d., n.p.]

Froissart, *Oeuvres de Froissart*, ed. Kervyn de Lettenhove, t. 3–6 Chroniques; *Poésies*, ed. Auguste Scheler, Brussels, 1867–70.

Fumi, L., *La Moda de vestire in Lucca dal sec. XIV al XIX*, Perugia, 1902.

Garlande, Jean de, *Dictionarius Esercizi su i primi elementi della Grammatica Latini*, Rome, 1839. In the BL copy, bound in with the above are: *Lexicographie de xii*[e] *et du xiii*[e] *siècle; Trois traités de Jean de Garlande, Alexandre Neckam et Adam du Petit-Pont*, ed. Auguste Scheler, Leipzig, 1867.

Gay, Victor, *Glossaire*.

Gibb, H. A. R. (ed.), *The Travels of Ibn Battuta AD 1325–1354*, 3 vols. Hakluyt Society, ser. 2, nos. 110, 117, CUP, 1958–72.

Gilliodts van Severen, Louis, *Cartulaire de l'ancienne estaple de Bruges*, Bruges, 1904.

Gollancz, Sir Israel, *A Good Short Debate between Winner and Waster: An Alliterative Poem on Social and Economic Problems in England in the year 1352, with modern English Rendering*, OUP, 1930.

Grandisson: *The Register of John Grandisson, Bishop of Exeter*, ed. F. L. Hingeston-Randolf. Diocese of Exeter Episc. Registers, London, 1899.

Green, Louis, *Chronicle into History: an Essay on the Interpretation of History in Florentine Fourteenth-century Chronicles*, CUP, 1972.

Gregorovius, Ferdinand, *History of the City of Rome in the Middle Ages*, iv, trans. A. Hamilton, London, 1894–1902.

Gross, C., *The Gild Merchant, a Contribution to British Municipal History*, 2 vols., Oxford, 1890.

Guillemain, Bernard, *La Cour pontificale d'Avignon 1309–1376, é ude d'une société*, Paris, 1962.

Gualvaneus de la Fiamma, *Opusc. de rebus gestis 1328–1342*, RIS, xii, iv, xii, 4, 1900ff.

Hald, Margrethe, *Primitive Shoes*, National Museum of Denmark, Copenhagen, 1972.

Hallam, Henry, *View of the State of Europe during the Middle Ages*, 10th edn, London, 1853.

Hardy, B. C., *Philippa of Hainault and Her Times*, London, 1910.

Harmand, Adrien, *Jeanne d'Arc: ses costumes, son armure. Essai de reconstitution*, Paris, 1929.

Hecart, G. A. J., *Serventois et Sottes Chansons etc.* [pamphlet] Valenciennes, 1833.

Héjj-Détári, Angéla, *Hungarian Jewellery of the Past*, trans. Lili Halápy, and S. M. Newton, Budapest, 1976.

Heyd, W., *Histoire du commerce du Levant au moyen âge.* traduction francaise de Raynaud, Paris 1885, 2 vols.

Hill, Sir George, *A History of Cyprus*, ii, CUP, 1948.

Hodgett, Gerald A. J., *A Social and Economic History of Medieval England*, London, 1972.

Hughes, Dorothy, *A Study of Social and Constitutional Tendencies in the early years of Edward III*, London University Press, 1915.

Iorga, N., *Histoire des Roumans et de la Romanité orientale*, iii, Bucharest and Paris, 1937.

Ireland: *Historic and Municipal Documents of Ireland 1172–1320, From the Archives of the City of Dublin*, ed. J. T. Gilbert, RS, 1870.

Jamison, Catherine, *History of the Royal Hospital of St Katharine by the Tower of London*, OUP, 1952.

Jarrett, Bede, *Social Theories of the Middle Ages. 1200–1500*, London, 1926; new imp., London, 1968.

—, *The Emperor Charles IV*, London, 1935.

Joseph of Arimathie, otherwise called the Romance of the Seint Graal or Holy Grail, ed. W. Skeat, EETS, 44, London, 1871.

Journaux du Trésor de Philippe VI de Valois, Les, ed. Jules Viard, Paris, 1899.

Jubinal, Achille, *Jongleurs et Trouvères, ou choix de Saluts, Epitres Rêveries . . . des xiii et xiv siècles*, Paris, 1835.

Kaiser Karl IV: *Führer durch die Ausstellung des Bayerischen National museums München auf der Kaiserburg Nürnberg*, Munich, 1978.

Kedar, Benjamin J., *Merchants in Crisis; Genoese and Venetian Men of Affairs and the Fourteenth Century Depression*, Yale University Press, 1976.

Kervyn de Lettenhove, J. M. B. C., *Froissart. Étude Litteraire sur le XIV siècle*, Paris, 1857.

—, (ed.), *Poésies de Gilles Li Muisis*, Louvain, 1882.

Knowles, Dom David, *The Religious Orders in England*, i, Cambridge University Press, 1950.

Kumaner Bildercodex, facsimile of Osterreichischer National bibliothek MS 370, 2 vols., Graz, 1967.

Labande, L.-H., *Le Palais des papes et des monuments d'Avignon au XIV siècle*, Marseilles, 1925.

Langland, William, *Piers Plowman: The A version. Will's visions of Plowman and Do-Well*, ed. George Kane, London, 1960.

Piers Plowman, edited from the 'Vernon' MS. by Walter W. Skeat, new edn, EETS, Oxford University Press, 1968.

Langlois, Charles-Victor, *La vie en France au Moyen Age du xii au milieu du xiv siècle*, 4 vols., Paris, 1924–8.

Laurent, Henri, *La Draperie des Pays Bas en France et dans les pays Mediterraneens (XII–XV siècle)*, Paris, 1935.

Léonard, Émil G., *Les Angevins de Naples*, 3 vols., Paris, 1954.

141

—, *Histoire de Jeanne I reine de Naples, comtesse de Provence (1353–82)*, Monaco, 1936.

Lethaby, W. R., *Westminster Abbey and the Antiquities of the Coronation*, London, 1911.

Li Muwit, Gilles Levi, Eugenia, *Lyrica italiana antica . . . dei secoli xiii, xiiij, xv*, Florence, 1905.

London: *Liber Albus* ed. H. T. Riley, iii: Translation of the Anglo-Norman passages with glossaries, appendices and index, RS 1862.

McFarlane, K. B., *The Nobility of Later Medieval England*, Oxford, 1973.

McKisack, May, *The Fourteenth Century 1307–1399*, Oxford, 1959.

MacGregor, R. R., *The Lyric Poems of Jehan Froissart, a critical edition*, University of North Carolina, 1975.

Machaut (Machault), Guillaume de: *Oeuvres de Guillaume Machaut*, ed. Ernest Hoepffner, Paris, 1908.

—, *Guillaume de Machaut Poésies Lyriques*, ed. Vladimir Chichmarev, 2 vols., Paris, 1909.

—, *La Prise d'Alexandre*, ed. M. L. de Mas Latrie, Geneva, 1877.

—, *La Louange de Dames*, ed. Nigel Wilkins, Scottish Academic Press, 1922.

Magyar Anjou Legendarium, ed. Ferenc Levárdy, Magyar Helikon, 1973.

Masson, Frédéric, *Le Sacre et le Couronnement de Napoleon*, Paris, 1908.

Mélanges Offerts à Emile Picot, Paris, 1913.

Merkel, Carlo, Come vestivano gli uomini del "Decameron". In *Rendi conti della Reale Accademia dei Lincei*, ser. 5, vol. 6.

Michel, Francisque, *Recherches sur le commerce, la fabrication et l'usage des étoffes de soie . . .* , 2 vols., Paris, 1852.

Minot, Lawrence, *The Poems of Lawrence Minot*, ed. Joseph Hall, Oxford University Press, 1897.

—, *Poems written anno MCCCLII by Laurence Minot*, ed. Joseph Riston, London, 1825.

Molinier, Émile, 'Inventaire du tresor de l'Eglise du Saint-Sepulchre de Paris, 1379', in *Mémoires de la Société de l'hist de Paris*, t. 9, 1882.

Monaci, Ernesto, *Appunti per la Storia del Teatro italiano. I Uffizi Drammatici dei Disciplinati dell'Umbria*, Imola, 1874.

Muratori, L. A. De, 'Spectaculis et Ludis Publicis mediiaevi.' Dissertatio 29a from *Antiquitates italicae medii aevi 2*, Milan, 1739.

Myers, A. R., *The Household of Edward IV. The Black Book and the Ordinance of 1478*, Manchester University Press, 1959.

Niccolini: Ginevra Niccolini di Camugliano, *The Chronicles of a Florentine Family 1200–1470*, London, 1933.

Ordonnances des rois de France, see Achery.

Pächt, Otto, and Alexander, J. J. G., *Illuminated Manuscripts in the Bodleian Library Oxford*, 3 vols., Oxford, 1966–73.

Palmerii, Mattheir, *Vita Nicolai Acciaiouli*, ed. Gino Scaramella, RIS, xiii. ii.

Pastor, Ludwig, *The History of the Popes*, i, ed. F. I. Antrobus, Kraus reprint, 1969.

Pegolotti *see* Balducci.

Petrarca, Francesco, *Le rime spares e I Trionfi*, ed. E. Chiorboli, Bari, 1930.

Francisci Petrarcae Epistolae de Rebus Familiaribus et Varie, i, iii, iv, ed. Josephi Fracassetti, Florence, 1859–63.

Picot, A. E., *see* Langfors, A.

Piponnier, Françoise, *Costume et vie sociale. La cour d'Anjou xiv–xv*, Paris, 1970.

Pistoia: *Storie Pistoresi*, ed. S. A. Barbi, RIS xi. v.

Planché, J. R., *A Cyclopaedia of Costume*, 2 vols. London, 1876–9.

Poerck, Guy de, *La Drapérie mediévale en Flandre et en Artois*, Bruges, 1951.

Pola, Guis. Falletti-Villafalletto, *Associazioni giovanili e Feste antiche loro origini*, 4 vols., Milan, 1939.

Polo, Marco, *Le Livre de Marco Polo*, i, ed. A. I. H. Charignon, Pekin, 1924.

—, *The Book of Ser Marco Polo*, ed. Sir Henry Yule, 2 vols., London, 1903.

Ponting, K. G., *A History of the West of England Cloth Industry*, London, 1957.

Porta de Annoniaco, Iohannis, *Liber de Coronatione Karoli IV imperatoris*, ed. Ricardus Salomon, Scriptores Rerum Germanicarum, 1913.

Power, Eileen, *The Wool Trade in English Medieval History, Being the Ford Lectures*, Oxford, 1941.

Promptorium Parvulorum sive Clericorum Dictionarius Anglo Latinus Princeps, ed. Albert Way, 3 vols, Camden Society, 1843–65.

Pulling, Alexander, *The Order of the Coif*, London, 1884.

Raine, E. J., *Historical Papers and Letters from the Northern Registers*, RS, 1873.

Réau, Louis, *Iconographie de l'art chrétien, t. 2: Iconographie des saints*, Paris, 1959.

Rheims: *Archives Administratives de la Ville de Rheims*, ii, Paris, 1848.

Rienzo, Cola di, *La Vita di Cola di Rienzo*, ed. Zefirino Re, Florence, 1854. See also *Anonimo Romano*.

Ritson, Joseph (ed.), *Ancient English Metrical Romances*, London, 1802.

The Romance of William of Palerne (translated from the French at the command of Sir Humphrey de Bohun c.1350), ed. W. Skeat, EETS, 1, London, 1867.

Romanin, S., *Storia Documentata di Venezia*, iii, Venice, 1912.

The Romaunt of the Rose and Le Roman de la Rose, see Sutherland, R.

Rosenthal, Joel T., *The Purchase of Paradise. Gift giving and the Aristocracy, 1307–1485*, London/Toronto, 1972.

Runciman, Steven, *A History of the Crusades*, iii: *The Kingdom of Acre and the Later Crusades*, Harmondsworth, 1965.

Rymer, Thomas, *Feodera*, t. v and vi, London, 1708.

Salviac de Viel Castel, Horace de, *Statuts de l'Ordre du Saint Esprit au droit désir*, Paris 1853.

Sapori, Armando, *La Crisi delle Compagnie mercantili dei Bardi e dei Peruzzi*, Florence, 1926.

Savel, Jean, *Le livre-journal de Jean Savel, 1340–41*.

142

Sayous, Édouard, *Histoire Général des Hongrois*, i, Paris, 1876.

Scheler, August, see Froissart; Li Muisi

Sinor, Denis, *History of Hungary*, London, 1959.

Sir Gawaine and the Green Knight and Pearl, ed. A. C. Cawley, London, 1962; reprint, 1976.

Southern, R. W., *Western Society and the Church in the Middle Ages*, Harmondsworth, 1970.

Stanley, Arthur Penrhyn, *Historical Memorials of Canterbury (1855)*, London, 1906.

Steenackers, F. F., *Histoire des Ordres de Chevalerie et des Distinctions Honorifiques en France*, Paris, 1867.

Sumptuary regulations, see separate section below.

Sutherland, Ronald, *The Romaunt of the Rose and Le Roman de la Rose, A Parallel-Text Edition*, London, 1967.

Svenskt Diplomatarium 1341–1347, ed. Bror Emil Hildebrand, Stockholm, 1858–65.

Szentpétery, E. (ed.), *Scriptores Rerum Hungarorum*, v. II, pt ii, Budapest, 1938.

Thomas Aquinas, St: *The Summa Theologica of St Thomas Aquinas. Literally translated by Fathers of the English Dominican Province*, Part II, 2nd part, London, 1918.

Tout, T. F., *Chapters in the Administrative History of Medieval England*, vols. III and VI, Manchester, 1928.

Traill, H. D., *Social England*, vol. II, London, 1893 (with J. S. Mann, 1901).

Tre Abbazie del Piemonte, ed. Marziano Bernardi, Istituto Bancario San Paolo di Torino, Turin, 1962.

Trexler, Richard C., *Synodal Law in Florence and Fiesole 1306–1518* (Studi e Testi 268), Vatican, 1971.

Troyes, Chrétien de, *Ywain, The Knight of the Lion*, trans. R. Ackerman, and F. W. Locke, New York, 1957.

Ugglas, Carl R., *Gotländska silverskatter från Valdemarstågets tid*, Historical Museum, Stockholm, 1936.

Ugolini, F. A., *La Prosa degli "Historiae Romance Fragmenta" e della cosidetta "Vita di Cola di Rienzo"*, Rome, 1935.

Valons, Guy de, *Le Patriciat Lyonnais aux XIIIᵉ et XIVᵉ siècles*, Paris, 1973.

Veale, E. M., *The English Fur Trade in the Later Middle Ages*, Oxford, 1966.

Venice: *Storia Documentata*, see Romanin, S.

Viard, Jules, *Journaux du Tresor de Philippe VI de Valois suivis l'Ordinarium Thesauri de 1338–1339*, Paris, 1899.

—, *Documents parisiens du regne de Philippe VI de Valois 1328–1350, Extraits des Registres de la chancellerie de France*, t. II: *1339–1350*, Paris, 1899–1900.

Victoria History of the Counties of England, various volumes, London, 1900 onwards.

Viel Castel, Horace de Salviac de, *see* Salviac.

Wagner, A., *Heralds and Heraldry in the Middle Ages*, London, 1956.

Walsh, G. G., *The Emperor Charles IV 1316–1378. A Study in Holy Roman Imperialism*, Oxford, 1924.

Wells, J. E., *A Manual of the Writings in Middle English*, London, 1916.

Wyclif: *An Apology for Lollard Doctrines, attributed to Wicliffe*, ed. J. H. Dodd, Camden Soc., 20, London, 1842.

Wright, Thomas (ed.), *Political Poems and Songs Relating to English History Composed during the Period from the Accession of Edward III to that of Richard III*, 2 vols, RS, 1859.

Yule, Sir Henry, *Cathay and the Way Thither*, vol. 3, Hakluyt Soc., 1914.

Yver, Georges, *Le Commerce et les marchands dans l'Italie meridionale au XIII at au XIV siècle*, Paris, 1903.

Zichy, Graf Stephan, *Petrovics Elek emlekkönyv (Hommage à Alexis Petrovics)*, Budapest, 1934.

Ziegler, Philip, *The Black Death*, London, 1969.

Articles

Benna, A. H., 'Erzherzogshut und Kaiserkrone', *Mitteilungen des Osterreichischen Staatsarchivs*, 25, Vienna, 1972.

Bevere, Riccardo, 'Suffragi, espiasioni postume, riti e cerimonie funebri dei secoli XII, XIII e XIV', *Archivio storio per le Provincie Napoletane*, anno xxi, fasc i, Naples, 1896.

—, 'Vestimenti e Gioielli in uso nelle province napolitane dal XII al XIV secolo', *Archivio per le Provincie Napoletane*, anno xxii, fasc i, Naples, 1897.

Boppe, A., 'Jean-Baptiste van Mour. Peintre Ordinaire du Roi en Levant 1671–1737', *Revue de Paris*, Aout 1903.

Casati, C. (ed.), 'L'Ospidale di S Nazzaro in Brolo volagarmente detto dei Paci', *Archivio Storico Lombardo*, I, ser. i, 1874.

Dacier, M., 'Recherches historiques sur l'etablissement et l'extinction de l'Ordre de l'Etoile', *Memoires de Litterature tirés des registres de l'Academie royale des Inscriptions et Belles Lettres*, xxxix, Paris, 1777.

Hoepffner, E., 'La Chronologie des Pastourelles de Froissart', in *Mélanges offeres à Emile Picot* (q.v.).

Kosegarten, Antje, 'Parlerische Bildwerke . . . aus der zeit Rudolf des Stifters', *Zeitschrift für Kunstwissenschaft*, 20–21, 1966–7, Vienna.

Långfors, H., 'Deux Temoignages inedits sur le costume des Elegants au XIV siècle, in *Mélanges offeres à Emile Picot*, q.v.

Lejskova, Milada, 'Droji sat Kraloven z Hrobky Ceskych Kralu v chrame sv. Vi a v Praze', *Pamatky archeologicke*, vol. I, 1931.

Makkai, László, 'Commerce et consommation de draps de laine en Hongrie aux XIIᵉ–XVIIᵉ siècles', *Estratto dal volume Produzione. commercio et consume dei Panni di Lana*, Instituto internazionale di Storia Economica F. Datini, Prato, Florence, 1976.

Nevinson, John, 'Buttons and Buttonholes in the Fourteenth Century', *Journal of the Costume Society*, 1977.

Portal, C., 'Le Livre-Journal de Jean Saval, marchand-drapier de Carcasonne 1340–1341, *Bulletin historique et philologique du cormoé des travaux historiques et Scientifiques*, 1901.

Salter, Elizabeth, 'The Timeliness of Wynners and Wastour, *Medium Aevum*, xlvii, 1978.

Scheler, Auguste, 'Étude lexicologique sur les Poésies

143

de Gillon le Muisit', *Mémoires couronnes et autres mémoires publiés par l'Académie royal des sciences, des lettres et des beaux arts de Belgique*, Brussels, Janvier 1886.

Staniland, Kay, 'Clothing and Textiles at the Court of Edward III 1342–1352', *Studies Presented to Ralph Morrifield*, LAMAS, Collectanea Londiniensia, 1978.

Szekely, György, 'A nemetalföldi ésaaz angol posztó rajtáinak elterjadése a XIII–XVII századi Közép-Európában', *Külonlényomat a Századok*, 1968, Evi 1–2 számából.

Thierry, Michel et Nicole, 'La Cathédrale de Mren et sa Décoration', *Cahiers Archeologiques*, Paris, 1971.

Thordeman, Bengt, 'Armour from the Battle of Visby', *Vitterhets Akademien*, Stockholm, 1940.

Walcott, M. E. C., 'Inventories of the Abbey at Dissolution', *Transactions of Middlesex Archaeological Society*, 1873.

Chronicles

Chronicon **Angliae** *1328–1388*, ed E. M. Thompson, RS, 1874.

Chronicon Galfridi le **Baker** *de Swynebroke*, ed. E. M. Thompson, Oxford, 1889.

Chronique de Jehan le **Bel**, ed. J. Viard and E. Déprez, SHF, Paris, 1904–5

Corpus Chronicorum **Bononiensum**, ed. Albano Sorbelli, RIS xviii.i, I.

Chronica Jocelini de **Brakelonda**, *de rebus gestis Samsonis Abbatis Monasterii sancti Edmundi*, ed. J. G. Rokewode, Camden Society, 13, 1840.

Brut, *The, or Chronicles of England*, ed. from MS. Rawl. B171 Bodleian and others by F. W. D. Brie, EETS, 136, London, 1908.

Chronographia *regum Francorum*, 3 vols., ed. H. Moranvillé, Soc. de l'hist. de France, 1897.

Chronicon **Estense**, ed. Giulio Bertoni, and Emilio Paolo Vicini, RR II SS, Xv, 3.

Eulogium *Historiarum sive Temporis*, ed. F. S. Haydon, RS 1868.

The New Chronicle of England and France in two parts by Robert **Fabyan**, ed. Henry Ellis, Paris, 1811.

Annales de **Flandre** *de P. d'Ondegherst*, ed. Lesbroussart, t. II, Ghent, 1879.

Recueil des Chroniques de **Flandre**, ed. J. J. de Smet, Brussels, 1884.

Les **Grandes Chroniques** *de France*, i. *Chronique des regnes de Jean II et de Charles V*, ed. R. Delachenal, SHF, Paris, 1910; ix (Charles IV le Bel – Philippe VI Valois) ed. J. Viard, SHF, Paris, 1937.

Chronica de **Gestis Hungarorum**: *The Hungarian Illuminated Chronicle*, trans. Alick West, Budapest, 1969.

Chronicon Henrici **Knighton**, ed. J. R. Lumby, RS 1895.

Die **Limburger Chronik** *des Tilemann Elten van Wolfhagen*, ed. Arthur Wyss, Monumenta Germaniae Historica, 1883.

Chronique et Annales de Gilles **le Muisit**, ed. Henri Lemaitre, Paris, 1906.

Chronica Aegionii **li Muisis**, *Abbatis xvii sancti Martini Tornacensis ex autographis*, ed. J. J. de Smet, Brussels, 1841 (from *Recueil de Chroniques de Flandre*).

Chroniques de **London** *depuis l'an 44 Hen III jusqu'a l'an 17 Edw III*, ed. G. J. Aungier, Camden Society, 1844.

Chronica Monasterii de Melsa **(Meaux)**, ed. E. A. Bond, RS 1868.

Continuatio Chronicarum Robertus de Avesbury: Adae **Muimuth**. *De gestis mirabilis regis Edwardi tertii*, ed. E. M. Thompson, RS 1889.

Chronique Latine de Guillaume de **Nangis** *de 1113 à 1300 avec les continuations de cette chronique de 1300 à 1368*, ed. H. Gérard, SHF, Paris, 1843.

Chronique Normande du XIVᵉ siècle, ed. A. and E. Molinier, SHF, Paris, 1872.

*Cronica d'***Orvieto** *dal 1342 al 1363*, ed. Gamurrini, RIS, Milan, 1845.

Chronicon **Parmense**, ed. Giuliano Borazzi, RIS, ix. ix.

Cronica **Raphayni de Caresinis**, RIS xii. ii.

Chronica Johannis de **Reading** *et Anonymi Cantuariensis 1346–1367*, ed. J. Tait, Manchester, 1914.

Scriptores Rerum Hungaricarum . . . *partim primum ex tenebris eruti*, ed. Schandtneri, Joannis Georgi Tyrnov (?).

Cronache **Senese** *di Andrea Dei, continuata da Agnolo di Tura dall Anno 1186 fino a 1352*, RIS xv. vi.

Chronique des Quatre Premiers **Valois** *(1327–1393)*, ed. Siméon Luce, SHF, Paris, 1862.

La Chronique de Gerard de **Vigneulles**, ed. C. Bruneau, Metz, 1927.

Cronica di **Giovanni Villani**, v, vi, vii, ed. F. G. Dragomanni, Florence, 1845.

Cronica di Matteo Villani, ed. F. G. Dragomanni, Florence, 1846.

Westminster *Chronicle* (which forms Appendix A to the introduction to the *Chronica Johannis de Reading*), ed. J. Tait, Manchester, 1914.

Unpublished

English great wardrobe accounts, PRO category E101 1330 to 1362/3.

Great wardrobe accounts consulted in the Public Record Office, 1337–62: E101 388/8; 389/14; 390/1; 390/5; 390/9; 390/10; 391/6; 391/11; 391/14; 392/3; 392/14; 393/15; 394/9; 394/12; 394/16. Enrolled accounts, wardrobe and household: E361/3.

Liber Viaticus of Jan Streda, MS. xiii A 12 (c.1360), National Museum, Prague.

Manuscrit de l'Ordre du Saint Esprit par le Roy Loys de Sicile et de Hierusalem, MS. fr. 4274, Bibliothèque nationale, Paris.

Inventaire des meubles de monsieur le duc de Normandie, dauphin de Viennois fait en l'année 1363. xviiᵉ siècle, Papier 109, feuillets, 350 sur 235 millimétre. Rel veau Rac (Montemart 74), MS. fr 21447. Bibliothèque nationale Paris.

Papiers de Foncemagne Recherches historique sur l'Etablissment et l'Extinction de l'Ordre de l'Étoile (Papiers et notes diverses d'Etienne Laureault de Foncemagne obit. 1779), MS. fr. nou. acq. 3,294, II, fol. 63, Bibliothèque nationale, Paris.

Argenterie account, bound in folio containing several

accounts listed by Douët D'Arcq, beginning with K223. Cote KK8, Archives Nationales, Paris.
Catholicon, commissioned by Jean de Mierle, prévôt of Saint Trond, Benedictine monastery; copyist Guillaume de Dycka who includes the date of completion, 1348, 15 December. Bibliothèque université 223E, Liège.

Index

149